Hindsight:

Coming of age on the streets of Hollywood

Sheryl Recinos, MD

Cover art: Roxana Recinos
Cover photo: Michelle Mansker
Cover model: Carmen Recinos
Editor: Kate Padilla

To Byron, Roxy, Isaac, & Carmen, thank you for every single moment of every day.

Byron, haha, I love you MORE (It's literally in a book, so I win!)!

For my children, thank you for showing me what it means to grow up "normal" and for being such amazing, goofy kids. Love you more than words.

reflections

on a life
that was almost lost
a life
that was saved
for some greater purpose
i can only hope
that all of the pain
all of the loss
the emptiness that once consumed me
will always remain
in small doses
as a reminder
of how far i've come
and how much farther
i have yet to travel
welcome
to the story
of how i became me
no apologies
no regrets
only gratitude
for second, third, and one thousandth chances
to live a life
that almost wasn't

Hindsight:

Coming of age on the streets of Hollywood

Sheryl Recinos, MD

FOREWORD

"What's she here for?" I asked the nurse as she placed a new chart in the rack. It was the only chart, and I needed to see one more patient before my lunch break. There were too many pages of paper notes on the top; this patient had obviously already been seen. Yet, she was back in the rack for new visits.

"She's a mess," the nurse told me. "Came in as a rape victim but refused the forensics exam. Twice."

I reached for the chart and began studying the notes. "Why?"

"She's really out of it. Probably on drugs, but we can't get a tox screen until after the exam."

I nodded. "Okay, I'll see her."

After reviewing the chart, I walked down the long corridor of the emergency room to the gurney where my new patient was waiting. She was lying on the bed, eyes closed. I studied her for a moment; my medical studies had taught me that almost half of the physical exam comes from observation. She was unkempt; her hair was messy and she had last night's makeup on a tearstained face. Her body was thin. She wore her street clothes underneath a white sheet; she was awaiting a rape kit and they would be taken into evidence when she was ready. Her feet were bare; dirt lined the bottoms of her feet. I scanned the room for shoes and saw an aged pair of stilettos. Her breathing was regular; I watched her chest rise and fall a few times to be sure of it.

"Ms. Garcia," I began, hoping that she would awaken easily.

My patient groaned a quiet but clear, "Go away."

"Ms. Garcia, I'm Dr. Recinos," I said, stepping closer to the bed. "Can you open your eyes for a moment?" I maintained a safe distance; everything was still evidence yet to be collected.

Heavy eyelids lifted upwards, just enough for a catlike slit of light to pass into her brown eyes. "Leave me alone," she mumbled.

"The forensics team needs to see you," I said. "Are you okay with an exam?"

Her head moved faintly. A tiny nod.

"Alright. I'll have them take you back upstairs soon," I told her.

I walked back out to the nurse's station, bewildered. When the nurse turned around, I asked her, "What happened upstairs?"

The nurse sighed heavily. "She was too altered for an exam."

"Interesting," I said. "Okay, she seems like she might try again. I'll come back and chat with her after my lunch break." I gave the nurse my handset number and hurried back to the doctor's cubicle, where I added the chart to my growing stack.

"Be back in thirty," I told one of my coworkers before heading off to the break room upstairs.

As I sat down to eat, I heard a familiar code being announced overhead. Code Grey. The code that represented a combative patient. Code Greys were called almost as commonly as Code Blues at my hospital; Code Blues referred to a failing heart and the need for urgent CPR. The microwave beeped, and I reached for my

1

lunch just as my handset rang.

"Dr. Recinos, that patient is flipping out," the nurse said rapidly.

I pulled the ramen noodles out of the microwave as I spoke, "What happened?"

"Well, I went to draw labs, and she scratched my arm and tried to punch me."

I sucked in a deep breath. "Alright, I'm on my way," I said, leaving my noodles abandoned on the table. I hurried down the single flight of stairs and across the hospital to the emergency room, where my patient was now awake and screaming. Even before I slid my badge to open the double doors back onto the unit, I could hear her terrified scream.

"Get the fuck off me!" she yelled. I rushed towards the gurney where I'd left her just a short while ago. Now, she was awake, halfway between sitting and lying down, with her eyes still slit-like and her mouth spewing out profanities.

"She had a seizure, and then she started fighting everyone. We need to restrain her," the nurse told me.

I shook my head. "No. She was just raped. Of course she fought back," I said, moving closer, through a crowd of techs and nurses, past the security guard. "Everyone out, I need to talk to my patient," I announced, and the numerous staff members trickled out of the room.

Once the room had emptied, I placed the rolling doctor's chair close to her gurney and sat down. "I'm Dr. Recinos. I came to chat with you earlier, but you were sleepy."

"Don't touch me!" she screamed.

"I won't," I told her. She turned to look at me, her eyes focusing on my face as they widened slightly. Her eyes were pretty, brown, and held unshed tears.

"That bitch grabbed my arm," she said.

I nodded. "I know. She was trying to help, but I'm guessing you didn't want to be touched?" I asked, my words intentionally soft spoken.

The girl moved into a seated position, her wild hair falling around her face in untamed curls. She shoved a thick strand behind her ear and studied me.

"Where are you from?" I asked.

She bit into her lip, considering the question. "Denver," she finally answered. Her tone had changed from screaming to frightened in the time that it took her to answer my question.

"That's pretty far," I told her. "How did you get here?"

Her gaze slipped down to the floor. I watched as her hands fidgeted around the edge of a broken purse I hadn't noticed earlier. "Two guys grabbed me and brought me here," she told me quietly.

"When was that?" I asked.

"Last week," she told me. "And I didn't have my medicine, so I had a seizure after they raped me last night," she told me.

I nodded. "What do you normally take?"

She reached into the purse and handed me an empty medicine bottle. I made a note of the name and dosage after quickly reading where she filled it, the date, and her name. I handed it back to her.

The empty bottle slid into her bag. I caught a quick glimpse. No cell phone, no wallet. Just a hairbrush, mirror, and some business cards.

"Do you have someone you'd like me to call?" I asked.

"I don't know the number," she said. She slowly pulled the stack of business cards out of her purse and tapped on a taxi service card a few times. I took another hard look at her. Seated, I could see that she was in a very thin tank top and skirt.

"Alright. I'll get you started on some seizure medicines and we'll try to help sort this out for you."

She nodded, her eyes still holding onto their reservoir of tears. "Thank you," she told me.

I hurried back to the social worker's office at the back of the ER and told the worker on duty my suspicion. "I have a trafficking victim."

He sat up straight in his chair and listened to my evidence. When I finished, he nodded slowly. "I'll call the hotline," he told me. There had suddenly been a nationwide push to identify and protect trafficking victims, and our county had its own hotline. "I'm glad that you were the one to see her," he added. I nodded slowly, uncertain.

I called the medicine team for an admission and begged them to keep her overnight. The doctor on the phone relented, only because of my patient's seizure. "We can't release her, they could be waiting outside for her. She'll die out here," I pleaded.

"*If* she's a trafficking victim," the doctor on the other end of the phone said, irritation edging into her words. "Fine, I'll take her," she finally agreed.

I hurried through the rest of my shift, grateful that I'd been heard. By the time that I finished work that day, I realized why no one else saw the clues that I'd seen. Clothing inappropriate for weather. No personal effects. Stilettos and taxi business cards. This patient was a puzzle for me; a puzzle that I slowly pieced together and understood as I engaged her in a real conversation. I was not surprised the following day when the admitting physician called me to let me know that the Department of Missing Persons had called them asking about my patient. I was not shocked that her family drove overnight to come pick her up several days later. I knew her story because I'd seen so many like it.

I've had numerous patients like this one that have shown me why my journey into medicine was so important. Patients whose lives depending on me being able to piece together the struggles that they had endured to help them move towards healing. Honestly, I didn't understand it at first, when I was a bright-eyed, eager medical student. However, as my training continued, and the number of patients that I was able to connect with and fight for grew, I realized that my past was not only relevant, but life-saving.

This is my story about who I was in my teen years, and I firmly believe that who I was shaped who I am today. Every dark moment, every painful encounter has led to a deeper understanding of humanity. Thank you for your willingness to learn about my journey.

1
BEFORE WE FELL APART

With a shaky hand, I unlocked the door. Twisted the door handle. Stepped outside.

It was night; the brilliant dark sky glistened with light from far away stars. It wasn't quite silent; I could hear the gentle chirping of crickets and the ominous sound of something else. I wasn't sure what that something else might be. Cars? People? A monster?

I slowly closed the door behind me, careful not to make noise.

Careful footsteps, avoiding the brick on the walkway that tended to crunch when it was stepped on. I felt a sense of impending doom. I had to hurry.

Across the side yard, over our gravel and dirt driveway. Almost to the fence.

I heard the door open. Something was coming.

A flashlight shone brightly, its beam aiming for me.

"Who's out there?" I heard my father's voice beckoning. My dog awoke in the backyard and howled loudly.

I glanced back, just as the light landed on my small, five-year-old frame. Caught.

"What are you doing?" my dad yelled, when he realized who had made the noise.

He rushed towards me, and I quickly realized my oldest brother stood beside him. David carried a baseball bat, to stop whoever was intruding on their land.

I cowered under my father, afraid. "I was going to the store," I lied. "I wanted a pack of gum."

My father stared at me. Through me.

"Go inside," he commanded. His voice was thick with anger, booming. "We'll talk about this in the morning."

I paused, glancing back towards the beckoning light of the nearby shopping center. I was so close. I would've asked anyone. I instinctively knew what I so desperately sought; I was going on a quest to find new parents.

I walked back inside, went to the room I shared with my brother, Nick, and threw my backpack next to my bed.

We were going to *talk* about what I'd done. I cried myself to sleep, not for the first time.

But the morning came and went, and we never spoke about the time I tried to run away.

We had been a family of seven. To the outside world, we appeared to be a normal family. Two parents, a handful of kids. A dog, a cat. A large enough house, a backyard to play in, in a nice neighborhood. Zoned for a decent school. A transplanted family; my mom was born in upstate New York, and my dad was from New Jersey. They'd lived in the Northeast for most of their lives and had eventually settled down in a small town near Allentown, Pennsylvania. Right around the time Billy Joel crooned about how the town was falling to pieces, my dad lost his job as a chemist for a local zinc company. He needed work, so we moved to North Carolina, to relocate near a lithium plant. I was three.

We lived on the school bus route, and I began riding the bus with my brother Nick once I started school. Sometimes, if I was lucky, my oldest brother David would drive me to school instead. We would watch Inspector Gadget together and eat an extra bowl of cereal. I fondly remember the times that we would arrive late, guilty expression on his face, because hanging out was more fun. And probably because working nights as a pizza delivery guy was exhausting for him. When we finally left for school, he drove with the sunroof down and his car sped past all the other slower drivers in our town. He raced to get me to school, so I could become smart like him.

But it was my sister, Melinda, who I idolized. She was the smartest, funniest almost-grown-up that I knew. She was a cool teenager, and I was her pesky, annoying little sister who misbehaved. She hated watching me and Nick; we tormented her, and she couldn't yell at us or spank us. If we told on her, she would get punished, even though she was watching us for free.

I generally enjoyed school, and I was eager to learn so I could be "as smart as Melinda," or wise enough to figure out David's numerous tricks.

After school Nick and I would race to David's room, begging to play with his "junk box," a little cigar box full of screws and nails and magnets. Broken toy cars, paper clips, buttons, dice. Empty lighters, damaged Lego pieces. I would do anything to play with that box.

Sometimes, he would close his door and we knew we couldn't play with the box. But other days, he would surprise us with a list of tasks to do. "I'll let you play with the junk box for twenty minutes if you wash the dishes," David would tell me. I would race downstairs and wash every dish until it was spotless for those precious minutes. And when my twenty minutes was up, I would reluctantly hand back the box. I didn't want to, but I would do whatever he told me to. I couldn't risk losing my chance to play with the junk box.

Other times, if he was really in a good mood, or if he had a date with his girlfriend, Denise, he would ask me to wash his car. Usually by saying something like, "I'll let you wash the knives if you wash my car." The knives! The sharpest of sharp knives. David was wise beyond his years; he rarely had to do any chores because Nick and I competed to finish his work.

On days when David didn't want to deal with an annoying kindergartner asking him questions, he would simply close his door. Other days, he would sit with me and Nick in the living room and teach us how to play Pong on his new Commodore 64. He was building video games in school, and soon after, he bought an Atari with his pizza delivery money.

Kevin left first. I wouldn't learn the reasons until I was an adult, but what I knew at five years old was that one of my brothers was gone. He was a mystery to me. A brother I couldn't remember; a big brother who had liked me enough but who was suddenly gone. The house had a stillness to it as it enveloped the absence of my brother. I was five years old, and he was thirteen. He'd been taken away, and he never came back.

I didn't want my parents to send me away. I tried as hard as I could to behave, so that I wouldn't share the same fate.

Our last vacation as a family was when everything began to unravel. A slow pulling away of the curtains, not complete, but opening just enough for me to catch a glimpse that change was coming.

I couldn't have been more than seven years old. We were traveling back to Pennsylvania and New Jersey to visit friends and family, since we'd spent the past several years in our new home in North Carolina. It was a long road trip with a shrinking family; Kevin was gone; he'd been sent away to a place called "foster care;" a place in which children didn't return from. He'd been quickly replaced by a foreign exchange student from Germany, but that didn't last either. David left soon after, on his way to college. He was studying computer science at Western Carolina University in Cullowhee, up in the mountains. Denise had gone with him.

We had just spent the morning at a friend's farm, and we'd enjoyed fresh green beans and seasonal fruit. It could have been one of the happiest summers of my childhood. We had already dined on Tastykakes and A-Treat soda, both of which couldn't be found in North Carolina. The rest of the trip would be spent visiting my dad's old friends.

We had made all the stops; we'd even visited my dad's favorite hobby train store. My dad was a big S gauge train collector. He kept an entire room full of his trains when I was growing up, and he would lock himself in there for hours to build and design the perfect world. We rarely were given a chance to see these trains in action; they spent most of their time being painted and displayed. Inside of the store, my dad introduced us to the owner. We were able to look at, but never touch, the trains lining the walls and shelves. Everything was so shiny, so fresh. So impressively detailed with perfect mathematical scale. An entire shop made for little old men who collected model trains.

I remember feeling so special to be included. My dad let me go with him! I was so happy to stroll through the store, imagining what these trains would look like in my dad's collection.

Would he get a new engine? Would he need little trees and little people to line the tracks? My mind was painting a world full of little people living along a trainline, with everything perfectly sized to S gauge. I wanted to build trains when I grew up.

We went from store to store, my dad saying hello to his friends. We'd been living down in North Carolina for a few years by this point. I could tell my dad had not wanted to leave, and he enjoyed the small town feel of my birthplace.

Our trip ended, and we began our southward descent back to our home in exile. A few hours into our drive, we stopped to get gas. My dad was pumping the gas, and for some reason I wandered outside of the car. Those were different times, and it wasn't unusual for a little kid to wander around the parking lot seeking their own entertainment.

I had a habit of always staring down at the ground, and an uncanny ability to find things. I often found quarters, nickels, and dimes. Sometimes a whole dollar.

But on that day, I was elated when I saw them. Two tiny cars. Micro cars, really. Probably from the micro machines craze that had the fast-talking announcer on commercials. They had been abandoned, probably by some other wandering kid.

Two toy cars! I scooped them up in my hands, and I wanted to celebrate my new discovery. It was like Christmas, in the middle of a hot summer, during a long road trip. I was the youngest of five kids; or was it four kids, now that Kevin had been taken away into foster care? Most of my toys were of the secondhand variety. But these cars, they looked new. One red, one yellow. Shiny. Ready to take an adventure with us.

I climbed back into the car and shared my discovery with Nick. We were both enjoying them, riding them around the backseat. They travelled imaginary roadways and sometimes crashed into each other.

We were lost in our playtime, driving down the road. And then my dad saw the cars.

"Where did you get those?" he demanded, eyes glaring directly at me. I held one car, my brother held the other at this point. My dad had pulled over the car and was staring at me.

"I found them," I told him.

His face contorted into rage. "You stole them. How could you steal from my friend?"

"What?" I asked, incredulous. They had been alone, abandoned. On the asphalt. Needing a kid to love them.

"You stole them from my friend's train shop. Why would you do this?"

"But I didn't!" I protested.

He snatched them from both of us. By now, hot tears were pouring down my cheeks. I didn't steal them. I really didn't. Why would he think I'd stolen these toys? I'd never stolen anything before that day.

He threatened to march me back to his friend's train shop and make me apologize, but we were already beginning our return trip towards North Carolina. Instead, he tucked them away in his shirt pocket and kept driving. Every several miles, he recalled his anger and yelled at me again.

I stared out the window, tears falling from my cheeks. What had happened? I didn't understand why he was so mad at me. I just wanted to play, and if I hadn't rescued the cars, they probably would've been run over by somebody anyway.

My mother said nothing. She sat still in her chair, unmoved by the argument unfolding around her.

We continued our journey south. We had planned an excursion in Washington, D.C., and I saved my meager allowance all year to buy something nice at one of the museums. I had been so excited about this trip.

My dad announced to everyone that I wasn't allowed to buy anything. And that he was watching me to make sure I didn't steal anything else.

My face turned beet red and I shoved my hands into my pockets. I wasn't a thief! I had just wanted to play.

Nick stepped a little farther away from me, just out of our dad's line of sight. I was his target now. Kevin was gone. He was finally seeing me.

We wandered through the great museums, and I watched my siblings search for souvenirs. My father kept me at his side in all the gift shops, just to make sure I didn't steal anything. I remember staring longingly at the stuffed animals and little trinkets, wishing I could spend my six dollars on just one thing.

I don't remember the museums. I don't remember any of the beautiful exhibits or the history every building told through its architectural design. But I remember the pain of knowing that I was somehow different. Excluded.

The rest of the car ride home, everyone talked about how much fun they'd had. I sulked quietly in my corner, and throughout the drive my dad recanted my "theft" to me or to everyone else. My mom stayed quiet for most of the ride. She didn't, or couldn't, come to my defense. Nick had a gentle look of apology in his eyes, but he also carefully distanced himself from me.

Weeks after we'd returned home, after my dad had mailed the cars back to his friend at the hobby shop, he received a letter. The letter told him the truth; his friend didn't sell those cars in his shop. He sent them back to my dad.

My dad read the letter, and then threw the cars in the trash. "Well. At least you didn't steal them from my friend," he said. "Where did you steal them from?" he asked. The anger had dissipated, but there were still unpredictable moments of rage.

I sighed. I would not win this battle. "I found them."

"You should have left them wherever they were."

I looked at my father, but quickly glanced away. I was unable to face him head on at such a young age. All that misery; a ruined trip. And he still presumed that I was a thief. "I found them," I repeated, as I ran off in another huff of angry tears.

2
BROKEN HOME

My mom's big, blue car was humming gently as we climbed into it. My brother and I were strangely surprised that our mother had parked her car in front of our house. As we stepped off the school bus, she corralled us quickly into the car. "We're leaving your father," she told us when we were both seated.

What? Why? I chewed down hard on my lip. This was all my fault. I had been watching one of those sitcom dramas the previous week, and the character on the show had divorced parents. He was bragging about how he got to have two Christmases.

I didn't want two Christmases.

"Do we get to stay in our school?" I asked.

"Why are we leaving?" Nick asked.

I held my backpack on my lap, suddenly full of meaningless stuff. Homework, science fair announcements. Who cares about the science fair when your life is falling apart?

My mom wasn't really answering us, and she was talking a bit fast about a lot of things. "I found a new place in the mountains. I already moved all of our stuff up there while you were in school."

"But I don't want to go," I whined. "What about my cat? And my dog?"

The car propelled forward, ignoring my childlike pleading. Nick glared at me. He didn't want me to keep complaining. I stuck out my tongue at him and shrugged.

We drove to the outskirts of our small city in North Carolina, and then up towards the mountains. We were heading somewhere that I had never been before. But this didn't feel like an adventure.

Why were we leaving? "Are you getting a divorce?" I blurted out.

My mom said, "Maybe."

We arrived in front of a small trailer park, surrounded by the forest. I could see six or seven other mobile homes. And there were other kids, playing outside. My mom parked in front of the first one, at the bottom of the hill. It was white and rectangular and didn't look like home. There was tall grass on the side of our new home; someone had left it untamed.

We followed her from the car to our new place. She unlocked the door and we caught our first glimpse of our new lives. The room was littered with trash bags full of our belongings. There were second-hand sofas and a dining room table. I wanted to cry, but I held it together because Nick was still glaring at me.

"Does Dad know where we are?" Nick asked. I looked up at our mom. Nick was so smart, and he always asked the best questions. We were close in age; just fourteen months apart. We were in that awkward two-month gap that happened each year, when he could pretend that he was two whole years older than me, until my birthday would come and settle the score.

Mom shook her head. "Go outside and play," she told us.

I didn't want to play. I didn't want to be a trailer park kid of a divorced mom.

My parents had never even fought in front of me. Sure, they were always quiet. I couldn't remember them even speaking to each other. But I hadn't heard them fight. Don't you have to fight to get a divorce?

I walked up the hill towards a group of kids playing next to a trampoline. I shrugged and decided that I should at least have fun. Then, when our dad came to pick us up, I would be able to tell him about the trampoline and the trailer park kids.

Nick followed me, but he was abnormally quiet. I wondered what he was thinking. We usually spent our afternoons goofing off, playing video games, or playing with our pets. Sometimes we played a bit rough with Sneakers the cat, but she didn't seem to mind.

"What's your name?" one of the kids, the boy, had seen us.

"Sheri," I said. "And this is Nick." He waved at them.

"I'm Joey. And that's Sara," he said. They smiled hesitantly at us.

I glanced at the trampoline. I'd always wanted to jump on one of those. Would I feel free, would I soar? "We just moved in to that first trailer," I told them. "Do you want to play?"

Joey noticed my fixation with the trampoline. "Sure," he said, pulling off his shoes and climbing over the rail. "Let's play."

We followed him onto the trampoline and began jumping around.

Sara asked me, "Are you going to go to our school?"

"No," I told her. "My mom says she'll drive us all the way to our old school."

Sara looked a little sad about that. I shrugged. "We're only here temporarily." I kept jumping. "Until our dad comes to get us."

Nick climbed up and jumped too, but he remained quiet. Pensive. I caught his facial expression between jumps. He wasn't enjoying this. He was jumping because I was jumping.

When their mothers called them to come home, we also got off the trampoline and scrambled to put our shoes back on. "I don't want to go back in there," I told my brother, pointing to our shabby little trailer at the bottom of the hill. "I want to go home."

Nick agreed. "I wonder if Dad knows how to find us."

We played outside for several hours; exploring the grassy area near the edge of the forest. There were all sorts of bugs crawling near the rocks, and I even found a bunch of rollie pollies. They reminded me of the critters behind our tree in the backyard. Where our dog lived. "Will Dad remember to feed Tansy?" I asked.

"Of course," Nick said.

When it started to get dark, we went inside. Dinner was waiting, but my mom had never been a great cook. We sat down at a large table that was meant for a bigger family. "Does Melinda know that we've moved?" I asked. She was away at an in-state boarding school for smart kids. Lucky. Actually, we were the last two of five siblings. Did any of them know where we were?

Was this why Melinda had gone away? She sat down with Nick and me before she left and asked us to tell her what we thought about her choices. She had been accepted to a summer camp at the beach, where she would speak in German the whole summer and become fluent. She was excited. But she'd also been accepted to the North Carolina School of Science and Mathematics. My dad liked to call it

10

"Nerd School." When she excitedly told our parents about both acceptances, their responses weren't as happy. They didn't share her enthusiasm as she pleaded to go, and I could recall yelling and something else. Finally, they told her that she had to choose. A summer away studying German, or two years away in a state sponsored school studying science. Both were marvelous, both were freedom. She wanted both, and she wanted neither. She wanted to stay to protect us, but she wanted to get away, to protect herself. She started crying when she discussed her options with us, and she was asking for something we were afraid to agree to. We wanted her to stay, but we told her to go. And she left.

We began that new life in a quiet way. We were always a family that didn't confront the hard topics. We had never really discussed why my brother Kevin had been kicked out at thirteen. Or why he was temporarily replaced with that foreign exchange student. He didn't want a pesky little girl sitting in his room, asking him questions. All he wanted to do was call some girl and ask her if she was coming to America too. I hated him for taking my brother's place so quickly. But that didn't last, and he was sent away too. Besides, we never really talked about my mom's frequent trips to New York, either. She kept going away to visit her aunt.

I tried to dissect the family moments that I had tried so hard to ignore. Quiet dinners, during which my parents never spoke. Times when my mom ate beside me, making faces out of her noodles and tomato sauce. When I tried to play with my food, I was scolded. But she wasn't. The awkward car trip back from Pennsylvania the previous summer, when my dad accused me of being a thief and a liar. The times since then, when I'd felt like I was walking on eggshells. The way my dad roared at us like an angry lion when we misbehaved. Was that normal? I couldn't decide. What I did know was our family was broken. For some reason, the illusion of my parents getting back together never surfaced. We left, and I knew that they were done. Yet, I'd never seen them in an argument.

We spent the next week driving back and forth to our old school, but my mom looked nervous when she picked us up each day. I kept expecting to see my dad, but he never came to find us. She finally sat us down one afternoon and told us she was moving our school. The drive was too hard, and she was legally separated from our father now. Moms always got custody. That was just how things were.

I begrudgingly showed up to our new school the following morning. New kid, trailer park, new free lunch passes. I didn't like having to use a free lunch pass. Everyone would know we were divorced kids. It was like we'd been branded.

Nick was shuffled off to his own class, and I was introduced to my fellow third graders. The teacher told me I would be Sheri number three. I had never been in a class with anyone who had my name before. And now I was number three. I hated my new school already.

The classes were different. I wasn't in the academically gifted group anymore. At my old school, we used to get a few hours per week in the computer lab to play Oregon Trail or other enriching games. But my new school didn't have an academically gifted group. I was bored and frustrated. A school library book was always kept in my hands. Might as well read. I'd already learned everything else they were teaching.

We finished our first week at that school. Then the second week. We had been gone from our family home for almost three weeks when our heater broke. My mother was trying to figure out how to keep us warm at night, as we were on the final stretch of winter and it was chilly at night. Our neighbor came down the hill to offer us a warm place to stay. He didn't ask about the plastic bags full of our belongings in the living room that had never been unpacked, or the two anxious kids shivering in layers of clothing on the sofa.

I followed my mother up the hill, close enough to hold her hand. Yet I can't remember ever being so close to her to actually hold her hand. We walked in parallel; a concerned mother flanked by two sleepy, shivering children.

We entered a mobile home I'd never been in before, and a woman directed us to a small bedroom. The home was at least fifteen degrees warmer and I could feel the relief of my body starting to return to normal. My mom told Nick and me to lay down, and we did. I wrapped myself up in a thick blanket and dozed off in the strange new bed.

Hours must have passed before I heard her screams. "I won't do it!" I heard a woman yelling. I squeezed my eyes shut at first, trying to tell myself that it wasn't happening. It can't be real. It had to be a nightmare.

Suddenly, my mother was standing over me. "Wake up," I heard her say to me. I opened my eyes, but all I saw was darkness. I balled my little hands into fists and rubbed against my eyes, trying to force them to see in the absence of light.

"We have to leave," she told me. I sat upright. Her voice had taken on an eerie quality, like in the scary television shows I wasn't supposed to watch. My eyes began to adjust, as I saw lights flickering into my darkness from an adjacent room.

That was when I saw Nick. He was standing against the wall, coat already zipped up. Something on his face startled me awake. I stood and followed them. As we rushed out of the trailer, I could hear our neighbors yelling at my mother. A string of expletives escaped his mouth as he hovered in the doorway; some that I recognized and many that I didn't. "Crazy bitch!" he yelled finally, as we rushed down the hill, too fast.

I watched in horror as my mom fumbled with the keys, trying to get us back inside the safety of our cold trailer. I kept looking back, expecting to see someone running towards us. Would our neighbor come to our mobile home and hurt us? Were we safe?

When we went inside, I reached back to close the door behind us, but she stopped me. Her words came fast, her gaze faraway. "No," she told me, rushing around the small trailer home. She started turning on all the lights. She opened all the doors, wide open. Our trailer became a beacon of light on a dark night.

Lights, cold mountain air. I sucked in a deep breath and felt the chill growing deep within my lungs. I was shivering, but I wasn't sure if it was from the wintry air or from a growing sense of dread. My mom raced towards me, handing me a white trash can. She scurried away again, leaving Nick and me in a shocked silence. What was happening?

She rushed back to the dining room and began frantically setting the table. Dishes clanged against the table as she haphazardly set a plate at every seat. She threw all our money onto the plates, then went back to the kitchen. No, I wanted to scream. We need that!

When she returned, she emptied several packages of dried spaghetti noodles into my wastebasket. I started to cry. Something very bad was happening.

Next, she brought raisins. She was always a fan of raisins and bought them in big boxes. I watched in terror as she dumped a large package of raisins on top of the pasta.

She glanced into the wastebasket and appeared satisfied with her creation. She set down the empty box on the floor, alongside the discarded spaghetti containers. When she whisked away again, I glanced over at my older brother. His face had gone pale and he looked the same as I felt. Horrified.

She returned with a pile of blankets and passed them to Nick. "Why?" I whispered, my one brave word hollow and floating across the room. To this day, I'm not sure if I actually said the word or she just knew I needed an answer.

"I saw this in a movie once," she told us. She quickly rushed to the doorway, and when we hadn't moved, a look of sheer frustration passed over her features. "Let's go," she ordered.

We obediently followed behind her, our eyes darting around like wild animals. Would the neighbors find us? Where were we going? She wouldn't let us close the door.

She walked us down the hill, past our car. Towards the main road. I glanced back at the mobile home, the rays of light from the open doors and windows propelling into the cold, dark night. Nick clutched his blankets firmly, and I wrapped my shivering arms around the wastebasket. The mountainous air blew across our faces as we followed our mother. The only noise was the sound of our feet crunching against frosty grass and our mom's feet tapping against the pavement of the road as we rushed away.

I kept glancing back, until I could no longer see the light of our house. Where were we going?

Finally, after what felt like hours, our mom stopped walking. She turned around to look at us, and tidied Nick's pile of blankets before setting her hand on his shoulder for a moment. "You'll be safe here," she told us.

I looked around. Here? We were beside a mountain road, standing over a small ditch. Everything around us was nearly pitch black, and even the moon and stars above us were separated from us by clouds.

"Sit down," she said.

Nick spread out a blanket on the ground beneath us, and we sat. We each took a blanket from the pile and wrapped it around ourselves. In my arms, underneath my blanket, was that damned white trash can.

"I'll be back," my mother said after we'd finished covering ourselves.

My jaw dropped open as I watched her walk away, back in the direction we'd just traveled from. Tears began to fall again as I watched her silhouette fade away into the night.

A long time passed before either of us spoke. Our mother was gone. Something had happened to her, and she wasn't acting like our mother. We were sitting on a thin blanket in a ditch, along a cold mountain road in North Carolina.

A dog barked in the distance.

I stared straight ahead, hoping she would return. Afraid she would return.

"I'm scared," I whispered.

"Me too," Nick said.

Eventually, he told me to lay down and sleep. "I'll keep watch," said.

I was exhausted and frozen. I laid down under my blanket and reached into the trash can. The long, dry noodles and squishy raisins made my stomach churn. Were we supposed to eat this? Out of a trash can?

I pushed the trash can away and fitfully forced myself to sleep.

I awoke shortly after, to see Nick staring out into the night. The dog was still barking, and it wouldn't stop. "Where is it?" I asked him quietly. "Are we safe?"

"I'm not sure," he told me. "It's okay, go back to sleep."

"But I have to go to the bathroom," I told him.

"Wait," he said. The telltale headlights of a car coming up the mountain had begun to flash from far away. We both covered ourselves with the blankets and waited in silence for the car to pass. After it was gone, he told me to wait still.

Many minutes passed before he told me I could go to the bathroom. I nodded and stood up, walking further down the ditch. "Don't look!" I hissed over at him.

After I went to the bathroom, I hurried back to the blankets and wrapped myself up again. "She hasn't come back?" I asked.

"No," he said. I couldn't see much of his face in the dark, but I could see his eyes sparkling from beside me as we both faced the road where we'd last seen our mother.

We sat together for a long time, before he told me to go back to sleep. I didn't want to, but he was older than me. For once, I didn't feel like arguing. I nodded and curled back under the blanket, still shaking from the relentless cold air.

The next time I awoke, there was a man's voice standing somewhere over us.

"Oh, my," I heard him say. I pulled the cover back just enough so I could see the flashing blue lights. My brother was standing up beside him, his small frame overshadowed by the tall man in a dark uniform.

"Did you find our mom?" Nick asked.

My eyes locked onto the officer's face. Had he found her? Was that why he was here?

The man took off his hat and pushed a trail of sweat off his forehead. He glanced from Nick's expectant eyes to my own. He looked startled for a moment, as if he hadn't realized there were two of us. He shook his head sadly. "The neighbor called us, their dog wouldn't stop barking and they thought there was a prowler."

I turned back, towards the sound of the howling dog somewhere behind us. It hadn't stopped; its rhythmic barks had blended with the midnight cool air and the hushed darkness of our little hiding place. "But our mom," I began, stopping myself.

"Get in the car, kids," the officer said, gesturing to the back seat of his patrol car. Nick was closer to the car. He reached back to grab his blanket. I stood slowly, stretching my frozen legs before moving forward. My world was spinning. The blanket that had been wrapped around me fell to the floor, and I bent to pick it up.

The officer reached for my blanket, so I grabbed the white trash can instead. He glanced inside and let out a low whistle. I grimaced, then followed Nick into the backseat of the car. The officer haphazardly folded the remaining blankets and handed them to us before climbing into the front seat.

"But she might come looking for us," I said suddenly, once he turned the key in the ignition. The car roared to life, and the officer strapped on his seat belt.

I clutched my trash can tightly in my arms, hugging it against my chest. The dried spaghetti shifted slightly, making a rattling noise against the side of the can. The raisins meshed between the long thin noodles, creating a rough leftover soup. My mom had always made the worst leftover soups; everything from the week, poured into a pan of water, boiled down into a tasteless, watery mess of leftovers. I stared inside of my container, trying not to cry again. I needed to be big, like Nick. He was not crying. His face was serious.

We wove down the mountainous roads, retracing the path we'd walked with our mother the previous night. The earliest strands of daylight were beginning to filter through the night sky, marking the change in time. A new day was coming. Other kids would awaken soon; yet our lives had irrevocably changed while they were sleeping.

"It's there," Nick said, pointing to a brightly lit trailer to our left. The officer pulled over for a moment, pondering the mobile home that was pouring out light into the mostly dark morning. The tiny place we'd called home for the past several weeks announced our absence to the world. Doors stood open, filling the world with synthetic light.

The officer nodded, then merged back onto the empty mountain road. He continued the descent back into town.

Our mom was still missing.

He pulled into a small police station and escorted us inside. The moment our feet crossed the threshold into the station, everything went silent. People who had been working on their cases or answering phones stopped talking and stared at us. Two small kids; abandoned in the mountains. Carrying blankets and a trash can.

The officer directed us to a small waiting room with plastic chairs and a desk. I sat down in one of the chairs against the wall and set the trash can next to me, in an empty chair. I pulled my knees against my body and hugged myself, trying to stave off the cold feeling that had seeped into my skin.

The officer came back to check on us, and shyly handed us a warm paper bag from Hardee's. "In case you're hungry," he said, offering the bag to us. Nick accepted it and thanked him.

The man stepped away, out of sight. I could hear him in the hallway talking with another officer. Another officer teased, "You never buy anything for anybody."

Our officer sighed heavily. "It's just so sad," I heard him say before his voice disappeared down the hall.

So sad. My eyes watched the inner workings of the police department, trying to figure out who knew where my mom was. I crept over to the doorway and stared at the movement around the station. Finally, I heard someone say her name. I needed to know the details. Where was she? What had happened to her?

"She was hiding in a farmer's yard, so he shot at her," one of the officers was saying.

My eyes widened in horror. The other officer asked how she was, and if she'd been shot.

"Luckily, no. She'll be evaluated at the hospital."

I swallowed hard. Not shot. Evaluated. Whatever that meant.

And then I saw the lady in the suit. She had entered the building, dressed fancily and wearing too much perfume. She asked the officers where the children were, and then all eyes were suddenly pointed in my direction.

I should have combed through my hair. I should have worn cleaner clothes. They would think I had a bad mother, I thought to myself. The woman came over to us and started to talk sweetly to both my brother and me. "I'm a social worker," she told us. "I need to talk to each of you to figure out where you should live."

She talked to Nick first, and then to me. I just stared at her, eyes wide and mouth silent. I let out an occasional "yes" or "no." Did our parents hit us? I thought about that one. Not so much anymore. They stopped hitting us mostly after Kevin went to foster care.

I stared at her, really seeing her for the first time. Perfectly styled hair, makeup. Pant suit. Fake pearls. She was here to put us into foster care. When Kevin went to foster care, we never saw him again. Foster care was a place where kids left to, and they didn't return. It had already been almost four years, and he wasn't part of the family anymore. I didn't want to go to foster care. But I didn't want to go back with my father, either. Mom had said bad things about him. I just wanted to see him. I just wanted my life to go back to normal.

I didn't know what I wanted.

"No," I said. It was a half-truth. I hadn't been hit for a while, but that didn't mean it had never happened. I just didn't want to talk anymore.

The woman seemed pleased enough with my answers, and the interview ended. I was dropped off back in the same conference room where my brother was waiting. I sat on the vinyl chair and traced the outline of the white wastebasket with my fingers.

"Why do you think she wanted me to carry spaghetti?" I asked my brother.

He shrugged. Our mom was really smart, so I was sure she had a reason. But I couldn't figure it out, and I guess he couldn't either.

A long time passed before our father arrived. He looked worried, and he spoke to the police officers quickly before he was corralled into the room where we were nervously awaiting news.

"Let's go home," he said. Nick stood up.

I hesitated. "What about Mom?"

Our father looked angry, or maybe sad. I couldn't figure out the emotion on his face at that moment. "Let's go," he repeated.

I reached for the trash can filled with dry spaghetti and raisins. He shook his head. "Leave it," he told me.

I glanced at the items that my mom felt we needed. They were our emergency supplies, and my dad wanted us to leave them behind. I bit down on my lip and followed my dad and brother out of the room.

My dad shook hands with one of the officers before we left. I didn't feel like talking anymore. I didn't want to thank someone for having my mom "evaluated." I wanted my life to be normal again. I wanted to be the goofy kid who came home from school and fought with my brother. In a home with two parents, a dog, a cat, and older siblings who were away in school and (gulp) foster care. I wanted my life back.

Instead, we returned home, to a place that did not have two parents. We were in uncharted territory. My dad was granted temporary custody of us. *Dads don't get custody of their kids*, I thought to myself repeatedly. And I was not going to see my mom for a while, "because she is in the hospital," my dad kept explaining.

Yes. Everything had changed.

3
DADS DON'T GET CUSTODY

We returned to our former elementary school, where I was just Sheri and I could buy school lunches because my dad worked. He tried to return to life as usual, but even he couldn't pretend away the absence of our mother.

We were alone in the afternoons until he arrived home at five thirty every day. We ate structured meals; hamburger helper, tuna helper, spaghetti, soup, and whatever else he could cook quickly.

Our dad started to drop us off at school in the mornings, and then we could still walk or take the school bus home. It was weird to be from a broken home. In the late 1980s, divorce was uncommon, and when it happened, the kids rarely stayed with their dads. So, we were anomalies. Weird little kids who had been abandoned by our mother in the mountains.

On the surface, we returned to our regular lives. My science fair project was selected for third prize, which was joyful and sad. I had worked on the poster with my mom before everything had happened. I missed my championship basketball game, and our team lost anyway. Melinda continued to do well at school, where she was studying classes at a college level even though she was only in 11th grade. She even had a class called fractals and chaos. I had no idea what fractals were, but I sure did know chaos. David was away at college, and he was apparently doing well also. Everyone was moving forward.

But then, the court date came. My mom and my dad, in front of a judge. Apparently, my mom had been "healed" and was out of the hospital again. She had left my father, but now, with no recent job history and no money until the divorce was finalized, she was left with nowhere to go. My mom had been living in a hotel for a few weeks, and her money had run out. Dads don't get custody. It was the late 1980s, after all.

Therefore, the judge picked an unusual solution. My mom would return to our house, and stay in my room with me, until the divorce was finalized. I was excited at first, because that meant my mom was coming home. I didn't understand what this really meant. All I knew was my mom would be home for my ninth birthday.

That arrangement didn't turn out as I had expected. I slept on the floor of my room, while my mom took over my bed. My bedroom became her place of respite. I inherited the task of passing messages between my mom and dad, most of which were angry and demanding action. My brother retreated into becoming an obedient child who never got into trouble. I, on the other hand, thrived on any sort of attention.

"Tell your mom she needs to clean her dishes," I heard my dad saying. I didn't want to be a part of yet another fight. When no one was looking, I snuck into the kitchen and washed my mom's dishes that evening.

When I got back to my bedroom that evening, mom was talking about distant travels and pen pals in South Korea and other places. She'd always been a wealth of information. Because of my mom, I had pen pals in Canada, New Zealand, and various parts around the United States. I dreamed of that glamorous life, when we could travel to meet these people in real life. Anywhere but here.

My mom wrote a few letters that evening, and then turned out the lights for us to sleep. In the morning, she was back to being angry with my father again. "Tell your dad he owes me money," she told me.

I shrugged it off and rushed to the awaiting car. Dad was still driving us to school, even though Mom was home. He still had full custody, in their strange arrangement.

We continued in that back-and-forth manner for several months, until the divorce finalized. I was relieved when my mom had her settlement money and was able to put down money on a house. Being the go-between was breaking me, with every argument, and every unkind word they said about each other.

My mom bought a house, a small two-bedroom house with a little yard. It was perfect. Even if it was on the wrong side of town. At least she had her own place.

The night she moved out, my dad baked a cake. He wanted to throw a "party" to celebrate our mom was gone. He gathered all of us into the dining room; Nick, me, Melinda, who was home visiting from school. I heard his praise that my mom had left, and I walked out of the room. I hid in my bedroom, suddenly empty. I curled into a corner on my part of the floor, leaving my mom's bed vacant. That was her bed now. Tears fell heavily. I remember my sister coming to my room later that evening to check on me, and I cried to her about how hard it had been. She agreed, lamenting about the fact that she'd been so far away when everything had happened. She loved us, but she still had to leave the following day to return to school.

I became a divorced kid. I would go to my mom's house after school on some days, and then always return home to my dad's house. My mom would show up with her big blue car and I knew it was her day. I went to her house happily. Cheerfully. It was different to visit; it was nothing like those scary three weeks in the mountains. I could pretend everything was perfect there, and I was able to ignore all the things that were bothering me at my dad's house.

A year after the incident, life started to become routine again. I finished fourth grade. Summer came and went. I spent most of my days alternating between riding bikes around my dad's neighborhood with Nick or hanging out at my mom's house. I was learning to bake and had been making cakes and cookies with my mom on her days off. She was working at a truck stop diner then. When she came home, she usually was very tired. My cakes would cheer her up. We would sit and talk about her customers while I served her hot tea and cake.

The summer transitioned into fall, and it was time for me to begin fifth grade. School days meant that I couldn't spend lazy days at my mom's anymore. She was working more now, and I wanted to see her more often. I started demanding to live at her house. My dad ignored me, although he occasionally reminded me that he had full custody.

Nick didn't come with me every time that I visited. He was almost twelve, and he was starting to go to our mom's house less. We didn't talk much about it, but I sensed that he felt differently than I did about our mom.

And then, it happened. Nick wrote a story in school about a hurricane that passed through our town and it caused mass destruction. It was called Hurricane

Hugo.

And soon after, a Hurricane warning was announced. Hurricane Hugo was aiming towards our inland town, and school was cancelled for the storm. My brother had predicted mayhem. At first, we were excited to have a day out of school. It was raining heavily outside, but then there was a brief period of calm. We didn't know it yet, but we were in the Eye of the Storm.

The power went out. The phones went out. We were caught by our father, towel drying our dog in the rain. He yelled at us to go back inside, and then left to go back to work.

Trees fell, communication stopped. The world was cut off from us.

When the storm finally passed, there was mass destruction. Trees littered the ground, and power lines were draped around broken trees and severed branches.

We began the clean-up process. I climbed a fallen tree but lost my footing. I slipped until I landed knee down, a branch stabbing me on the side of my knee. I was a child without an accessible mom, and my dad was busy cleaning. I pulled out the branch and attempted to clean the wound. A scar would later form, reminding me of that first time I had to repair myself.

As soon as enough trees had been removed from our yard and our block, I demanded to go to my mom's house. "I have to see her," I pleaded with my dad. "I have to know that she's okay."

We drove slowly, avoiding power lines and tree branches that littered the roadway. A ten-minute drive stretched out into forty minutes. When we turned onto her block, I saw it. Her car was gone. Her house was destroyed.

As soon as my father parked the car, I jumped out and raced up to the front door. Busted windows, but the glass was shattered inward. The door was unlocked. "Mom!" I called. No answer.

I rushed inside, my father trying to catch me. What would I find? "MOM!!!!" I yelled, commanding her to appear.

Nothing.

I searched all five rooms; both bedrooms, the bathroom, the living room, the kitchen. My mother was gone. She was gone, and something had happened here.

"She's missing," I said finally. "We have to find her."

My dad agreed. Something bad had happened. We went to talk to the neighbors, and they told us that she had given them her car. My dad questioned them further, demanding to know how much she had sold it for, when she had sold it, when they had last seen her.

She was gone. We called the police and filed a missing person's report.

And then, we returned to sort out the mess she'd left behind. The living room, with glass all over the floor. Broken from the inside. Ketchup and mustard sprayed across the white walls, in some sort of writing that I couldn't decipher. The kitchen, with dishes cracked and broken to pieces on the floor. But the cabinets were closed. Her bedroom, a hole punched in the floor. But the windows in that room had not been broken. The guest bedroom, windows broken, glass everywhere. Papers, soaked from the rain that had assaulted the house at the height of the hurricane, littered over the floor of every room. Photographs rumpled and bleeding their images away.

"We have to clean this, for when they find her," I begged my father. There was no consoling me. I started picking up the pictures and placing them on top of towels. They had to be saved. This was her history. Her beautiful photos. Our photos. Us.

I cleaned every paper, every piece of glass. My dad helped me place all her things in boxes. My hands were painted with lacerations from the glass by the time we finished. Everything would be saved. We would save her.

We finished the task after two days. Everything salvageable was packaged and removed. We set up a section of boxes in the basement of my dad's house. I stared at the photographs of her youth, wondering who she had been, and who she was now.

My mom's stuff, for when we found her.

The clean-up continued, and soon after, the power was restored. We still didn't have water, and my dad took me to meet a friend of his in the next town over. She had water. Her name was Terri, and apparently, my dad really liked her.

We went and showered at her house. She lived with her parents, and they had a nice home. Her dad was older, funny. He seemed friendly. I hung out with him after I'd showered, and he told great stories.

I stared at the pictures on the walls. Terri, her sister, her mother, her father. No grandkids. Apparently, Terri had been married before, and then divorced. She had also apparently been dating my father. He hadn't told us.

In fact, he'd promised me a few months ago that he wouldn't marry again. Right before he started dating. There had been a few first and only dates. Nothing special. I hadn't paid enough attention, and I hadn't realized he'd found a girlfriend.

We left, but the sense of unease that had started with my mom's broken house continued to build.

The kitchen telephone rang. My father answered it. They'd found my mother.

David, Melinda, Nick, and I drove together to see her. The drive took several hours, and I wondered how she'd gotten so far from home. She was in a hospital in the mountains, and she'd been there since the hurricane passed through our town.

When we arrived, we passed through security and they took us to a private meeting room. There was a sofa and several chairs. We sat down and waited for her to come in to see us.

When she walked in, she didn't look sick. She looked mostly like herself. Perhaps a little tired, but not sick. "Hi, Mom," I called. I was excited to see her.

She looked up at us then, her eyes the same brilliant light blue color that I'd always known. But she didn't seem like herself.

"What did he do to you?" she shouted. She pointed a long, thin finger at me.

"What?" I asked.

"Your father! He beat me and stole everything!"

David shielded me and Nick, taking us outside. "What's wrong with her?" I whispered. I wanted to cry, but even more, I wanted answers. What hadn't they been telling me? I knew my dad hadn't beaten her. We hadn't seen her since before the storm. I'd cleaned her house. Nothing was stolen. This didn't make sense.

The story started to unravel. She'd been diagnosed with bipolar disorder when she was twenty-seven years old. She'd had her first breakdown when they lived up north, and she'd thrown an air conditioner out of the second story window.

When I was born, she had grabbed me and ran from the hospital. I was a newborn, and she raced to get away from my father. She called him a terrorist. I was rescued at the edge of the parking lot and rushed back to the safety of the hospital, away from my mother.

When the Vietnam War had happened, she grabbed my three oldest siblings, and driven them far away, hiding them. The war was coming to America, and she had to get away.

She'd been hospitalized frequently. I hadn't known. All those times she'd been "visiting her aunt" had been cover-ups. She'd been in the mental hospital.

And again, she was in the mental hospital now. "What can we do?"

David sighed. "We wait until she gets better."

The car was found a week after my mom turned up. My dad was driving through a neighborhood when he saw my mom's car. He called the police, and they came to investigate. The family with the car produced the pink slip. The officer chuckled. "Idiots," he reportedly said.

My father told us the story as we sat down at dinner. The pink slip was signed in the wrong place. My mom had apparently signed the car over to herself. It was now parked in our driveway, waiting for my mom to get better.

Dinner was our usual hamburger helper. Fortunately, it was much better than when my mom had cooked for us. Boiled hot dogs, badly cooked pasta. And the infamous leftover soup. My dad had bought our dog to eat leftovers, since my mom kept serving the soup. But no more, everything was replaced now that we had a single dad.

I pushed the coils of pasta around on my plate. "Thanks, Dad," I told him. He'd rescued my mom's car.

I was so relieved. Things were coming back together. We'd been able to finish cleaning the house, and it was ready to be sold again. At any price. My mom would need the money when she got out of the hospital.

And then my dad dropped his bombshell. "Terri and I are getting married," he told us.

I dropped my fork. "No," I said.

Nick and I locked eyes. No.

Terri had been coming over more often, inviting herself into our lives. I wasn't ready for another big change. "No, you promised!" I wailed.

My dad shook his head. "You can't expect me to stay single. She's good for me."

"No!" I shouted. By this point, I was standing, shoving my chair forward. I left my plate on the table and retreated to my room.

4
MARRIED AGAIN

The wedding was quickly planned. My dad wasn't wasting any time. The day before the wedding, my soon to be stepmother and I quarreled. "You're not my mom!" I shouted at her. To my father, "I won't go to the wedding."

Melinda was visiting, as she would be watching us while they honeymooned. "If Sheri doesn't go, I won't go either," she said firmly.

I was winning. We could stop this.

My father looked at us both, disappointment heavy in his eyes. "What would people think?" he asked.

"I don't care," I told him.

We argued for the rest of the day. I didn't want this woman moving into our house. Something about her was unkind, cruel. I sensed her disdain towards me.

The day of the wedding came. My dad pleaded. I relented, but only because he looked sad. I still didn't agree. This was wrong. We couldn't accept this woman into our family.

The ceremony moved forward, and I suddenly had a stepmother. They left, and I sulked in the house with my siblings. I baked for the whole week. I found my sister's Betty Crocker cookbook and thumbed through the recipes. Cookies, cakes, pies. I needed an outlet for my anger. The only thing I refused to make was Italian wedding fingers.

Terri took over the kitchen. That was my last week that I was allowed to cook in our kitchen. She was the boss, and she would prepare Southern meals for us every evening.

Slowly, she started rearranging the house. Doilies. Fake flowers. Sofa cushions. Photos removed from the wall. My mom's presence was erased.

Dinners became country fried steak, dumplings, chicken casserole. Thick Southern sauces and gravies over everything. The chicken was never fully cooked, and we were expected to eat it.

"She has depression," my dad told me. "She gets sad if you don't eat her food."

I didn't care. My stomach hurt when I ate the pink chicken. The bloody beef. The strange Southern dishes we'd never eaten before, since we were from the North. Everything had a different flavor, one that reminded me that my whole world had shifted, again.

Summer came, and Terri was hospitalized for her depression. I soon learned she was in the same unit where my mom had usually gone. I also learned she didn't like children, but she'd chosen to marry a man with five children. Four, if you subtracted Kevin.

I was so grateful for summer vacation. It had been a harsh year. My mother's house, my dad's new marriage, my mom's new life at an apartment a few blocks away. I was exhausted, and even the many days of school that I'd skipped due to fake illnesses didn't take away the feeling of dragging through each day.

I'd been so excited Terri was in the hospital. Summer break and freedom from "the Terror," as David and I had secretly nicknamed her.

5

HOSPITAL

One day, a week into my summer break, my dad commanded us to wake up early. I groggily sat upright in bed. Why? We were on break.

He took us to a family meeting with Terri, at the hospital. I didn't want to go. It was my vacation, and I wanted to sleep in. I'd stayed up late the night before, reading and playing video games. Nick and I had bought the Legend of Zelda, and we were racing across the fantasy world every day. We had to collect all the keys and other items, and it was a painstaking journey. One that would probably last all summer, and I was looking forward to continuing the journey.

We followed our dad into a small conference room. Terri was there, and she looked annoyed. Great, she didn't even want us there. I glared at her psychiatrist. "We don't need a family meeting. She isn't our mother," I pointed out.

The doctor looked at me, inspecting me in a way that made me nervous. Then he turned to my father, a man whom he'd known for many years. He'd cared for both his wives by now, and he knew my father's version of events. "We have space on the other side for her."

My eyes widened. My dad was nodding along as the psychiatrist spoke. I didn't understand. Why was my dad agreeing with the psychiatrist?

"We have a place for you to rest on our adolescent unit," he continued. Nick zipped his mouth shut. Something was happening. Something bad.

I stood up. "No, I'd like to go home now. I'm tired and I want to go back to bed."

"We'll let you rest on the other side."

A group of men came to the doorway, to corral me to the other side. What was happening? Where were they taking me? Why wasn't my dad stopping them?

I fought against them. Why were they grabbing my arms? They overpowered me with their sheer strength and size. I was eleven by then, tall but not strong. They carried me to the other side and shoved me into a locked room.

What had I done? What had I said wrong? I didn't consider Terri family. A family meeting was a farce when there wasn't a family to begin with.

A tall man entered the room. I tried to escape. "Let me out!" I screamed. Tears were flowing. What was happening?

Another man came in, and he injected me with something in my thigh. My strength failed, but my inner fight continued. I wailed at the top of my lungs. Let me go! I didn't do anything.

I screamed until my throat was raw. I screamed until they were exhausted with my sheer determination, and they tied me to a bed with restraints. I stayed there, in that isolation room, drugged, for the better part of my first day in the adolescent psychiatric ward.

"Are you calm now?" someone was asking. I opened my eyes and stared at a tall man, standing over me. At some point, they'd stripped me of my clothes and exchanged them for a hospital gown. I was still harnessed to the bed; big thick brown leather bracelets were wrapped around my hands and feet. There was no escape. I shook my head. I had to get off this bed.

A nurse joined him, and yet another person stood at the doorway. Apparently, it had taken six people to restrain me. I was stronger than I looked; stronger than even I knew, and angrier. They untied me, watching me closely the whole time. I immediately began massaging my wrists, trying to relieve the throbbing pain from being tied down too tightly.

They escorted me to a room. My new room. I was left alone in that room, to think about what I'd done. But what had I done? I couldn't figure it out.

I stood up, staring out the window. I was on the dreaded Seventh Floor. The place where they locked my mom away whenever she lost it. When she tore out windows and painted the walls with ketchup and mustard. When she marched her kids into the mountains and left them. Where my stepmom went, when she was so depressed that her naughty step-kids wouldn't eat her nasty bloody chicken.

The window was reinforced, and there were strategically placed screws and nails in the framework. Even if I managed to open it, I would have to travel seven floors down. My bed only had two sheets. I wouldn't make it.

My bathroom had tiles. Grout between the tiles. Drilling a hole through the wall would only take me to the room next door. The ceiling was a regular cement ceiling. No escape there, either.

I sat down on my bed and cried. I hated them all. They'd left me here, and I couldn't understand it. Sure, I'd skipped some school earlier that year. But I'd stopped, after my teacher pointed out that all my "absences" were on Wednesdays and had threatened to send the truancy officer. I'd stopped altogether when I suddenly had a stay-at-home stepmother. No point taking a day off and staring at her. My attendance had improved, and I'd finished out the year with good grades. I'd actually been behaving. Or at least, trying to.

My nurse came to get me. "It's breakfast time," she told me. I nodded, still feeling the haziness from the antipsychotic medication they'd forced into me. I wasn't hungry, but at least the mention of breakfast informed me that a full day had passed.

My throat hurt. I followed her to the dining room, where several other kids were seated. The dining room would become one of the two rooms where I would spend my summer. There were tables, chairs, and a door. A door! The door led to the outside world. I watched it from the corner of my eye. Maybe.

I sat down at the table and watched how each kid maneuvered around the room. A tall boy with good hair sat next to me. He was eating cereal from a plastic bowl. The kind they gave us in hotel rooms. I surveyed the room. There were more cereal bowls on the counter, milk in cartons seated beside them.

I stood and chose a pack of cereal. I wasn't hungry, just mad. I needed to figure out what I'd done and find a way home. I must've really pissed off my dad.

Fine, I would stop being mean to my stepmom. I'd just ignore her instead.

I sat back down and opened my cereal and milk. I artfully poured the milk over each flake, making sure it was fully drenched. Something soothing, to help the time pass until someone could explain to me what I needed to do.

I watched as the flakes turned soggy. I stirred them around, letting them disintegrate. The boy next to me whispered, "You should eat that."

I looked up at him. He was older than me. In fact, everyone was older than me. I would soon learn that I was the youngest kid on the ward. Eleven-year-olds don't usually get admitted to the adolescent psych unit. Adolescent was a big new word for me, but it meant twelve and older. I carefully surveyed the room, noticing the nurse watching me closely. I nodded and obediently ate the soggy flakes.

Group time came soon after breakfast. Keith, I learned, was fifteen. He was waiting for placement at a nearby group home, and he had anger issues. He looked like a football player. I remembered his kind warning over breakfast. Sophie was a fourteen-year-old who had been caught running away from home and sleeping with boys. Renee was a sixteen-year-old who was very pregnant and had also left home. I started to hear their words. Everyone here had run away before.

Maybe I should, I wondered. They all ended up here anyway.

No one knew about that time when I was five.

The counselor looked at me. "Sheri why are you here?"

I swallowed hard. I did not know. And now I was supposed to tell everyone? Crap. "My stepmom is on the other side. I told them I didn't like her, so they brought me over here." The other kids all stared at me. Keith gently shook his head to the side, letting me know I'd given the wrong answer.

But what was the right answer?

Afterwards, it was medicine time. I sat back down, waiting for the other kids to get their meds. A nurse came up to me, her hand on her hip. Exasperated, she told me, "You need to get your meds."

"What?" I asked. What meds? I didn't take meds. My crazy mom and my crazy stepmom both took meds.

I followed her to the medicine line. When it was my turn, they handed me a tiny paper cup with two pills in it. "What are these?" I asked.

"Lithium and Depakote," the nurse said. She was heavyset, with short curly hair and too much makeup. I hated her already.

"But why?" I questioned.

"The doctor ordered them," she replied, her voice harried.

"What doctor? I haven't seen the doctor."

"Take your meds, or go back into isolation," she said.

I glanced down the hallway, seeing the nearby room with the glass window on the door. "Fine," I said, and I let her take me back to isolation.

"None of that screaming today, or we'll restrain you again," she warned.

"Whatever," I muttered. I wasn't taking meds. I didn't need meds. I needed new parents.

She took me to the room, where she told me to enter and closed the door behind me. I heard the lock twist shut. I sat down on the floor of the room, staring at the white walls. I could out-wait them. I was patient. I traced pictures on the walls with my finger; pictures of wildlife and flowers. Trees. A wilderness full of freedom from everything. Everyone. I traced myself into the picture. I wanted to be free.

I moved around the room slowly, examining every speck on the white walls. Had someone left that mark? Was that a place where another trapped kid had touched?

Hours passed. Time was ticking by slowly. Every few hours, someone would look in, and ask me if I was ready to take my meds.

Lunch came. I didn't eat.

Dinner came. I stared at the tray of unsuitable food. Nope, not for me.

I waited. They waited.

I fell asleep on the cold, linoleum floor. I heard people passing by, talking just loud enough to hear, but not enough to distinguish their words. Isolation was freeing. I didn't have to pretend I had a reason for being here. I didn't have to talk to anyone. I was alone.

Morning came. I'd spent my second full day in isolation. When I awoke, I finally felt hungry. I'd cried all my tears and my throat was raw. I really wanted to pee.

A nurse opened the door and came in. Someone else stood at the doorway, waiting for me to erupt. I didn't. She took my vitals. "Time for your medicine," she commanded.

I stared at the teens passing by, on their way to breakfast. "Fine," I mumbled. They won. I stood up and followed her to the medicine line. I swallowed the two treacherous pills and hoped I'd done enough to go home now.

I sat in the group, trying to say something therapeutic. "I've learned I have anger issues," I lied. "I need to be nicer to my stepmom."

The counselor looked at me and called me on my bullshit. "What changed?"

I didn't answer. Nothing had changed except my answers. I felt angrier. More defeated. More alienated from my former life.

A month had passed. I'd spent several more days in isolation, and even more staring around the room in a psych-med induced stupor. I hated this place. I wanted to go home. Why was I still here?

I'd quizzed the older kids on foster care, group homes, running away. I was learning about alcohol, marijuana, and harder drugs. I didn't want to try drugs, but alcohol sounded like it might be a nice change from feeling trapped. I wanted to feel free. They had moved me into a shared room with the pregnant girl, I guess because they thought she'd have maternal instincts and I'd behave with her, because you don't mistreat a mom.

Throughout the group, my eyes strayed to that secret door. For me, it represented a possible escape route. No one ever came in through that door. It was always locked. I sighed. There was no escape. I was stuck there until they decided I could leave.

I'd started my period in the psych ward. No one explained anything to me. Nobody told me what it meant. I finally begged for answers from Renee, my pregnant roommate, who explained what girls' bodies did and what it meant to have a period. And to not have one.

Keith left. He was sent away to a boys' group home a few hours away. For boys with anger issues. I'd never seen him angry. He probably had a fake diagnosis, too. After all, we were in the land of TV commercials showing how you could "fix" your difficult teens by shipping them off to a hospital.

My psychiatrist had showed me a set or Rorschach ink blots. At the same time, I'd been sketching more, since there were no books to read. I frequently drew animals and imagined freedom. When he showed me the ink blots, I pointed out animals. Birth, death, life. I saw so many vivid animals. I remembered the long summers I'd spent flipping through the encyclopedias we kept in the sunroom. Reading about animals, life, farms. He thought I was a sociopath. Apparently, my IQ test revealed that I was much smarter than they'd realized. And I was eleven. That really pissed him off.

I wanted to go home. I missed my dog Tansy and my cat Sneakers. I missed Nick and lazy bike rides, goofing off with him and his friends. I sometimes missed my dad, but I was mostly angry with him. I didn't miss my stepmom. They hadn't let my mom visit me.

A second month passed. I recall sitting in the hallway, in a chair. I'd been placed on punishment for mouthing off to the nurse, but the isolation room was occupied. An actual crazy kid was in there. I could hear him screaming and thrashing in the bed. He would definitely get a shot of thorazine. The nurse finally came and sat down next to me, ready for a heart to heart.

"I used to work on the adult side," she confided. "I remember seeing you visit when your mom was over there."

I looked at her quizzically. I didn't remember ever visiting my mom. She'd been in New York, visiting her aunt. Why couldn't I remember?

When my time out ended, I followed the group to the television room. There was breaking news. Kuwait had been invaded. The U.S. was sending troops.

The group leader switched off the television. Depressed, defiant, screwed up kids didn't need to know about current events. A tape player was brought in instead, and handouts were distributed. Michael Jackson's "Man in the Mirror" began to play, on repeat. I read the words on my piece of paper.

We listened for a few times before the counselor addressed us. "Who is your man in the mirror? What ways does he need to change?"

I mumbled something about behaving and following directions. Whatever it took. I wanted out. The meds made me feel numb, and my stomach always hurt. I didn't like the food. And school was starting soon.

A few days later, my dad came to pick me up. Nothing had changed. I wasn't "cured," and I wasn't any more willing to tolerate him or my stepmom after my two months and ten days in the adolescent psych ward. I was still the same me, but different in the hidden parts. I would leave someday. I now knew I had options. The kids had taught me how to leave, and I knew then that someday I would go and never come back. I vowed then that my dad would never lock me up again.

6
LIKE IT NEVER HAPPENED

School started. Sixth grade; the first year I would go to school without Nick. He'd moved on to junior high school, and I was in the highest grade on campus. It was lonely. I'd spent the whole summer in the hospital, and everyone was talking about their summer vacations.

I wouldn't tell anyone. I couldn't.

I stood in the lunch line, waiting for my turn to buy food I didn't want. A girl next to me teased, "You're a dirty blonde." I looked at her, shocked. What did she know? I wasn't dirty. I wasn't. Did she know about the psych ward?

I walked home after school that day, stopping at the drugstore. I walked up and down the hair color aisle. I would not be a dirty blonde. I needed to feel clean; safe. I finally selected a bottle of platinum blonde hair dye and presented it to the cashier. She raised an eyebrow but accepted my payment of wadded up dollar bills. She handed me the bag, and I nervously accepted it. The rest of the walk home, I felt nervous with the weight of the purchase in my hand.

The instructions were simple enough. Mix, spread dye on hair, wait, then rinse. The smell was overpowering, but as I painted my hair into a lighter, less dirty color, I felt a sense of peace. It seemed the streaks of darkness from my summer in the mental hospital were being cleansed. I was purging the cheap industrial shampoo from my shoulder length hair.

When I washed out the dye and towel dried my hair, I glanced anxiously into the mirror. Would I look different? I did. My hair was golden blonde, suddenly not carrying the undertones of darkness that my classmate had commented on. I liked the result, and I was ready for whatever punishment I would face from my dad and stepmom for dying my hair. Maybe they'd throw me back into the hospital again. By then, I didn't care. I had taken my first step towards recovery after a long summer of pain.

No such punishment came. In fact, they didn't notice my hair. My stepmom had apparently been released from the hospital a few weeks before me, and they'd let her "settle in" before letting me go home. Because her place in my home was more important than my own. Settling in seemed like a metaphor for ignoring me.

I had started cheeking the meds. I didn't like how they made me feel. I would only take a few the day before blood draws, just in case they would be able to tell that I wasn't taking them. I had a small container full of unwanted lithium and Depakote in my bedroom.

"Did you dye your hair?" my stepmom asked during dinner, a week later. Yes, I proclaimed. I stared across the table at her, awaiting the assault of angry words. But no one argued with me. They just ignored me, which felt safer.

My stepmom had started dieting, so all the food was lean and still bloody. I learned safe words for turning down her meals. "I'm dieting," I would respond back to her. I didn't have to eat it if I was watching my weight.

School continued. I started planning my escape. I found a brown lunch bag and decided I would fake school lunch. I pocketed the dollar and ten cents my dad sent me with each day for lunch. As long as I had a brown paper bag, I could make it look like it had food and I didn't have to spend the money. I read through each of Stephen King's books at lunch, to pass the time. *The Stand*, *It*. Huge, thick books that sixth graders usually didn't read.

Sometimes I would even bring peanut butter and jelly sandwiches, so my teacher wouldn't get mad at me. She'd started to notice I wasn't eating. And that I was reading horror novels.

Whatever, I had a high IQ. And I was not a sociopath, I told myself.

One afternoon, I sat down in my bedroom and plotted my escape. I would run away to the beach the following summer. I would need as many dollars as I could collect from not eating lunch, and beach clothes so that I could blend in.

Meanwhile, I kept visiting my mom a few times per week. She'd moved into an apartment a few blocks away; across the main road dividing our town. She lived across that road, behind the grocery store, in the row of white apartments. There was a forest of bamboo and kudzu alongside her apartment, competing for space to grow. Someone had imported the bamboo, and it had spread like wildfire.

I had my own key, because she worked long hours. She had worked at a variety of places since the divorce; first at Target, then at a factory, then a restaurant, then a truck stop diner. It was hard to keep up. When she came home, she usually looked exhausted and fragile. She'd settled for a life so distant from her life with my dad. But she was glad to be divorced from him, even if it meant not having custody of us.

Her apartment was sparsely furnished. She'd rehung the pictures I'd salvaged from the house she destroyed a few years ago. Mismatched furniture filled the rooms, all the pieces having a secondhand life with my mother.

She liked to sit in her living room and watch the small color TV she'd won at the mall a few months earlier. She'd entered one of those contests where you fill in your name and phone number and laughed that she never won anything. And then she won. I still remembered her excitement when she brought it home, and I rushed over to see her prize.

Since Terri had married my father, I'd been banned from cooking at my house. The kitchen was her place. I wasn't allowed to bake anymore, because she always needed to have the kitchen ready for her bloody creations. At my mom's apartment, though, I could cook whenever I wanted. I would often arrive after school and prepare her a cake or cookies. Baking for my mother always gave me comfort; I was able to do something that made my mom's day better. I enjoyed watching the slow rise of the cakes and breads in the oven as they changed from recipe to dessert.

Sometimes I would wait for her to get home, but on other days, when she was working late, I would leave her a note next to a warm chocolate cake or a stack of oatmeal raisin cookies. Other times, I would prepare her favorite dish, a pineapple upside down cake with little maraschino cherries in between each pineapple hole.

The place where I felt the happiest was with my mother. But whenever I asked her if I could move in with her, she would recite that my dad had custody. I was beginning to understand what it meant to have a bipolar mom, and I wasn't mad at her. Her face wore a mask of sadness. I wasn't sure if she wanted me back and he wouldn't allow it, or if she'd decided that this new life was better without the responsibility of raising a broken child. My anger turned inward, when it wasn't focused at my father and his new wife.

One weekend, my dad piled Nick and me into the van. He loaded up with chips and sodas. It would be a "road trip." At first, I didn't want to go. But then he told me Terri was staying home. Not going would mean hanging out with her, while going without her would mean my dad might be nice again.

Nick sat in the front, and I took my seat in the middle row. Dad and Nick chatted easily about school. Nick was in seventh grade and had been having a hard time in his math class because he was "smarter than his math teacher," as my dad often bragged. I enjoyed their easy banter, and I helped myself to a handful of potato chips from my dad's Tupperware while I listened to them chat. There was something familiar about how they talked to each other. I missed it. It felt a little like how he had sometimes talked to me, before Terri. Before my mom left. Before everything had happened.

He hadn't told us where we were going. An hour passed, and then another fifteen minutes. He pulled off the interstate and started to wind the van down a country road. Nick was talking about gym class, and how he was trying out for the soccer team in the spring.

My dad turned on his signal, and then turned the van to the left. He pulled over in front of a long brick building. "Get out," he said, suddenly looking at me.

What? I frantically took of my seat belt and got out of the van. Where were we?

Nick and my dad got out too. My dad called me over to where he was standing, in front of a sign. "Boys and Girls Home." I re-read the sign. This wasn't good.

"This is where we sent Kevin," my dad said.

Nick took a step back. I stood as tall as I could. What was happening? We'd been having a decent morning, and I hadn't fought with my dad for days.

"Do you see the grass?" he asked. I nodded. The building sat within a field of well-cut grass. "The kids cut that."

He paused dramatically, letting me take in all of what he was telling me before he added, "If you don't start behaving, I'll send you here too."

I stared back at him. I had argued with my stepmother frequently, especially after the hospitalization. But I hadn't even done anything yet. They didn't know I was planning to run away. All they knew was I'd been battling with my depressed stepmother who hated kids. "Fine," I muttered. Might as well.

We got back into the van, but the mood was somber. Nick tried to continue the conversation, tried to be the good kid. He kept steering my dad away from me. He was an expert in deflection by this point, and I was an expert in resistance. We would've made a great team, except I was getting closer and closer to imploding.

32

Fine, I thought to myself. They were planning to send me away.

I started noticing the little clues, the things I had ignored. When I was permitted into my dad's room – which was protected by a heavy lock on the door – I saw brochures for residential treatment centers. Places to send bad kids.

My dad grounded me the next day, after I refused to wear socks to school. I argued with him, telling him I didn't like them. I didn't understand why it mattered, anyway. I hated socks, not because I disliked wearing them, but because the one day I'd forgotten to wear them, my dad had decided to pick a fight with me. Ever since then, I'd stopped wearing them.

I sketched dark drawings of a girl, running away from home. I began to fill a notebook with dreams, hopes, and lists. I tucked that notebook away where no one would find it. What would I need to get away? I made a list and started collecting the items that I thought I needed.

On the way home from school each day, I started to visit the nearby Target and Kmart stores. It was surprisingly easy to quickly fold a shirt or shorts or bathing suit into my pockets. I tried it first and realized that no one was paying attention to a quiet elementary school girl. I was still too young to be an adolescent. Eleven-year-olds aren't supposed to be so broken.

I started a secret stash; everything I would need for my escape. I would make my way to the beach, where I figured I could move into one of the RV trailer camps. Surely no one would notice me. Anything and anywhere would be better than wherever my dad planned to send me this time.

Melinda was the one who stumbled upon my secret stash of summer clothes. Growing up as the youngest of five, my wardrobe primarily consisted of hand-me-downs. I didn't have a lot of new, trendy outfits, and she would have recognized most of my clothes as stuff she had worn at my age. She must've been looking for something in my drawer when she found the dozens of articles of clothing I'd collected.

"Where did you get this?" my father yelled at me. Yes, this time I had stolen it. I glared at him, the self-fulfilling prophecy of my life taking shape.

Then, I stared at my feet. "Kmart," I whispered. Well, Kmart and Target. But he was already filling it into a plastic bag.

"You're taking it all back," he told me. I watched his fast movements, the bag overflowing.

I nodded, fear in my eyes as I followed him to the car. He was carrying the whole bag of my supplies. How could I escape, if I couldn't prepare?

I trembled the whole way into the Kmart. He requested to speak to the manager, who took me to the back room and had me sit down by his desk. The security officer came in and took my picture with a polaroid camera.

"You are not allowed back in our store," the security officer said, waving the square of film in front of me as my picture began to form. "If you come back, you will be arrested for everything here," he pointed to all of the clothing on the desk, "and for trespassing."

The manager sat across from me, rage on his features. "What were you going to do with all this stuff?" he asked.

I couldn't maintain eye contact. I glanced down at my hands, which were still shaking. "I don't know, Sir," I croaked out, my words slippery with fear. I was going to run away. Could they have figured it out, from the collection of clothing and bathing suits? Did they know I was leaving? Would they realize I'd decided to flee to the ocean?

My father thanked him, and we left. He yelled at me all the way home, and then sent me to my room.

After the shoplifting incident, I began to isolate myself even more. I sat down on the grass during recess, watching the other kids play without me. After school had restarted in the fall, I'd only had one friend that I could talk to, but we'd drifted apart. I shoved a platinum blonde strand of hair behind my ear and let the tears fall. I needed to leave, but my supplies were suddenly gone. And I had no way to retrieve new ones.

I heard the bell to go to class. I quickly swatted away the tears and rushed to the bathroom to clean my face. I stared at myself in the mirror. My cheeks were flushed, and my hair was messy. I combed my fingers through my hair, hoping to hide my distress. The last thing I needed was for my dad to realize how upset I was. He already threatened to take me back to the hospital every time I didn't obey him. *Clean your room, or you're going back to the hospital! Get better grades, or you're going back to the hospital!* This wasn't something the psychiatrist could fix. I didn't know what to do, and I had no one left to talk to.

A few weeks passed. I ate lunch alone; or, at least I pretended to eat. I walked home alone. I was not sure I'd make it all the way until summer. Maybe I should just leave early, I pondered. Nick and I were growing apart; he was pulling more into himself and finding ways to meet all my dad's expectations. I was the angry child, hating the moments when my dad changed his reference to his "four kids" and said he had three instead. First, he had subtracted Kevin out of our lives, and then, he started to exclude me.

Life was spiraling out of control. I argued with my dad every night, often screaming "I hate you!" and running off to my room. There were stashes of unswallowed pills in every corner of my room. I was not bipolar; I knew it. But I couldn't figure out what it was that was making me so unsettled.

I didn't know where I would go, or how I would get there. My eleven-year-old brain couldn't wrap itself around the situation. How could I get away, before they sent me away again? No one knew that I would often wake up in a cold sweat, afraid I was locked in a little white room with no escape. With brown leathered restraints and thorazine coming for me. My dad wanted to control me, but I couldn't even control myself. I sat up in my dark room, hyperventilating, trying not to let anyone else hear me when the fear crept back in. I wouldn't go back. I couldn't survive another two months and ten days in the psych ward.

I'd gone weeks without having a real conversation with another kid. I was barely eating, because I was trying to save every dollar for an escape. I didn't know what to do, or who to talk to.

One night, two police officers were waiting for me when I arrived home from the library after school. I'd been reading a book as I'd walked slowly through the back road to my neighborhood, engrossed in another survival story. When I got to the house, I saw a police car in the driveway.

Weird.

Had something happened to my mother?

I closed the book and ran inside. "What happened?" I asked breathlessly.

My dad was standing in the living room with my stepmom, Nick, and both officers. "Where were you?" one of the officers immediately asked me.

I looked around the room, trying to figure out what was going on. "At the library. Same place I go every day," I told them.

"No, you weren't," my dad told me.

I raised my arm with the book in it. "Yes, I was."

The officer interjected. "It's okay. We've got some beds at the detention center, if you do this again," he told me.

Do what? Followed by, Oh my God, it's happening again.

I lowered the book and clasped it against my side. "I went to the library," I repeated softly.

The officer stared at me for a long moment. "Let us know if you'd like to go to the detention center."

I shook my head. No thanks.

"Call us if she gives you any more trouble," the officer told my dad.

As soon as they left, I ran to my room. I picked up the phone, ready to call anyone to tell them how miserable I was. But there was no one to call.

7
DONNIE

That was when the new girl arrived. Melissa. She had dark brown crimped hair, and she wore tight jeans and t-shirts with band names on them. Her hair and clothes reeked of tobacco. Her family had moved from somewhere up north. Near Virginia.

She exuded anger, and the other girls stayed away. I was drawn to her.

"Do you smoke?" she asked. I shook my head. We were eleven, what an odd question.

She invited me to her house after school. When I went to her house, I realized she lived in the apartment complex a few blocks behind our elementary school. I'd spent half of the year walking to the library, devouring books I wouldn't check out, and then walking slowly home. But now, there was a new girl. A new friend.

She had an older brother, Clint. He and his friend Donnie were sitting in the living room, smoking cigarettes and playing video games. They were both fifteen; older and wiser. Clint had dark hair like his sister, and Donnie had dirty blonde hair that fell into his face. I sat down next to Donnie. Melissa sat on the floor.

"Do you want to try one?" Melissa offered me a cigarette she pulled from the pack of Marlboro reds on the coffee table. I shook my head.

She shrugged and placed the cigarette to her lips. She expertly struck a match and lit her cigarette, inhaling deeply. A long pause passed before she blew out a trail of smoke. I watched as she continued working her way through the cigarette, and the boys fought their way through space on their video game.

Afterwards, I walked home at just the right time. My dad didn't notice the slight pep in my step, or the way that I suddenly felt more whole again. If I stayed quiet, he didn't notice me at all.

I usually stayed to the library until five o'clock, so I started going to Melissa's for a few hours in the afternoons instead. We quickly became a group of four friends, spending time watching MTV and playing video games. The three of them smoked, and none of them judged me for not wanting to try a cigarette.

When winter came, we had an uncharacteristic snow storm. Usually, snow didn't reach as far south as North Carolina, and if it did, it usually didn't stick. On that day, we had just arrived when the principal decided he would close the school. There was too much ice was on the roads, so school buses couldn't pass.

I'd already been dropped off. I didn't want to walk home and deal with my stepmom for a whole day, so I chose instead to walk with Melissa to her house. I was eager to finally have a full day to hang out with my new friends, instead of just a few stolen hours before I had to return home.

I felt a small snowball land on my face. Clint and Donnie were waiting for us. A mischievous glint danced in Donnie's eyes. I bent down and quickly formed a snowball of my own, launching it back at him. We played for a few minutes before starting to walk. We laughed all the way to Donnie's apartment, on the other side of the complex.

Donnie's place was smaller and messier. There were ashtrays on the counter, table, and coffee table, all overflowing with cigarette butts. Clothing and beer cans were displayed around the room. He moved some of the clothes aside on the sofa, giving me a place to sit. Melissa knew I liked him, so she excused herself and her brother, so I could hang out with Donnie.

"Hi," I said nervously, after our friends had left.

"Hi," he answered back, pushing his hair behind his ear. He sat down next to me, but closer than he usually did.

I felt his hand enclose around my hand and I smiled up at him. I couldn't believe an older boy was interested in me! The closest I'd been to having an older guy pay attention to me was when Keith had warned me to behave at the hospital the previous summer.

We chatted about music, mostly bands I hadn't heard of but would try to learn. My mom mostly played Billy Joel music at home, and my dad loved the Oldies, so I was limited in my musical knowledge. He wanted to know if I liked Guns N Roses, Aerosmith, and Billy Idol. He was asking about music that had come out the previous summer.

But I hadn't had a summer. I didn't know about anything that had been released during that time. When most kids were enjoying themselves, I was swallowing pills and forcing my way through group therapy. Or staring at the walls of the isolation room, hating how easily I was punished.

My face must have changed when he asked about summer. "Let me cheer you up," he offered. I stared at him expectantly. He stood up and paced to the kitchen. When he returned, he had two beer bottles in his hand. He expertly opened them and handed me one.

I accepted the bottle, bringing it close to my lips. It smelled like a field of wheat, but also had a tangy odor I couldn't identify. Remembering the stories from the hospital, I realized that I'd been wondering what it would be like to forget.

I took my first swig, and let it set on my tongue for a moment. I didn't like it, but I didn't hate it either. It was sour and felt thicker than I had expected. I glanced over at him, his face watching me. He was an older boy, and he liked me. I swallowed my first sip, then took another. And another.

When I set the bottle down onto the coffee table in front of me, I noticed he hadn't finished his. He was smiling still. "You're pretty," he offered.

No one had ever told me that. I smiled back.

The moment his lips touched mine, I knew this boy could teach me to forget. He was soft, warm, and tasted like a strange mixture of cigarettes and alcohol. Afterwards, he walked me back to Melissa's house. The day had passed us by, and I had to get home.

"Give her some breath mints," Donnie commanded. Right. We had to cover the scent of beer. Melissa winked at me and handed me a few tic-tacs.

And then she walked me back to the edge of her apartment complex, begging for details. Had we kissed? And only kissed?

I laughed. Of course, that was all we did. I was eleven!

As I walked home, I noticed all the snow had melted. I was heading into a war zone, but at least things were looking up. I'd kissed a boy, I'd found out I liked the way beer made me feel. For once, I didn't feel numb.

When I got home, the battle began. "Where were you all day?" my dad wanted to know.

I shrugged. "I went to Melissa's house," I told him. "I'm home on time."

Terri was in one of her moods. She'd cooked something incompletely again, and she wanted us to sit together as a family. She'd recently started dieting again, and the meals she offered us now had less flour, less gravy, but still the same amount of undercooked meat.

I sat down at the table and stared at the chicken breasts in front of me. My stomach rolled at the sight of the light red puddle of juice at the bottom of the glass casserole dish. I couldn't do this tonight. I didn't want to throw up my beer, but I also didn't want to deal with another fight.

I served myself the smallest portion, not really sure how I would get out of this one. I'd spent so much of my childhood avoiding my own mom's bad cooking. Shoving pieces of food into napkins and flushing it down the toilet when no one was watching. But they'd learned my tricks, and after all, Terri was depressed.

Before we had a dog to eat the leftovers, before we had a microwave to reheat them, there were two boiled hot dogs. My eyes closed, and I remembered the night that my mom made hot dogs for me. I had just turned seven, and my sister told me our taste buds change every seven years. She was right. I hated hot dogs. They tasted sour and stale. And my mom always boiled them in water before serving them. That night, she served me two hot dogs. My dad yelled at me for not eating them. The side dish was canned pork and beans, which I also hated. I refused the beans, so I was offered a plate with two hot dogs instead of one. I wouldn't eat them. My dad yelled at me, and then put them in the refrigerator. The next morning, they offered them again. "You won't get anything else until you eat them!" he yelled at me. Lunchtime came. I finally ate them, and then ran to the bathroom to throw up.

When I reopened my eyes, I saw the bloody chicken and knew this wouldn't end well. "Can I be excused?" I asked, hopeful for an easy resolution.

My stepmom's face went blank. Her medicine had a way of masking her features into an emotionless expression. I stared at her. Short brown curly hair, thick glasses, small frame. Wearing clothing two sizes too large. She hated me, but she never said it directly to me. It was okay, I hated her too.

"Terri worked hard on this meal," my dad said. He put down his fork and stared at me.

"It's not even cooked!" I countered, cutting into the meat and exposing pink flesh.

Nick watched me from across the table. I felt his foot kick my leg. Hard. He didn't know I'd had my first beer, and he couldn't know that my stomach was already on fire. But he clearly didn't want to see another fight.

"Eat your dinner," my dad said.

I shook my head. No. "No!" I told him, standing. I pushed my chair in dramatically. "I won't eat bloody chicken!" I shouted, fleeing from the room and racing up the stairs.

As my feet hit the ground, my dad stood up. "Come back here!" he shouted.

I swung open my door and entered my room. I could skip another meal. I didn't need Terri's uncooked meals. I slammed the door shut and secured the lock. I hated this place, and I hated that everything had changed so fast in such a short time.

I sat down at my desk and stared at the Book for the hundredth time. There had to be somewhere else that I could go. Anywhere else. I flipped open the Book. I had seen an advertisement in my teen magazine for a book with all the addresses, descriptions, and application info for boarding schools, and I'd immediately called for my copy. Here it was, in my possession. I'd flipped through it, circled pages, frantic to find one that would take me on a scholarship. Anywhere but here. I had begged my dad to send me to any of them, but he'd said it costed too much. I didn't want to stay here, in a place where I was always under the threat of "going back to the hospital." And then there was the new threat; the group home where I would cut the grass all by myself. I flipped through the pages again, wondering how much it cost to send a kid to the hospital or the group home.

8
THE FIRST ESCAPE

A few weeks later, we had another fight. Terri was offended by something I'd said to her. I didn't really care. She wasn't my mom and she should've never married my dad. She hated kids, and she chose to marry a man with five kids. Not my problem.

That was when I decided to leave. I packed my backpack and waited for the sound of my dad closing himself into his room. He always made sure to set his lock firmly in place. The lock had been installed shortly after Terri had arrived, because she wanted privacy. I supposed she felt like she needed a place to lock herself away from the kids she'd inherited.

When the house grew dark and everything was quiet, I expertly crept down the stairs and left through the back door. It was late, perhaps after ten o'clock. My feet silently took me down the driveway; I'd learned years ago not to even bother with the side yard. I walked around the corner and down the road, away. Past the bank. Past the Taco Bell that endlessly called out, "May I take your order?" through our windows at night. Past the myriad of other small businesses, through the shopping center. Between the Target and the Winn-Dixie. Up the road, past my brother's junior high.

When I got to Nick's school, I paused. Where would I go? I hadn't really planned a destination. I just wanted to get away. I needed to feel the cool spring air in my lungs and feel the freedom of being outside. I couldn't handle the constant arguing with my dad. I was tired of the quiet complaints from my stepmom.

Did they know I was gone? I doubted it. I strolled into the parking lot of the junior high and passed behind the school. Everything was closed, quiet. I could see a few lights left on inside, which helped me navigate the darkness of the grassy field behind it.

I wandered to the open property of the museum next door; we had our very own nature museum in my small town. There were long paths around a pond, and a replica of a Native American camp and a colonial village. Everything was closed and locked. I checked each of the log cabins in the colonial village, deciding none of them could offer me a place to sleep that night.

I wandered to the nature trail. There was an old water wheel, endlessly spinning a slow trickle of water into the river. I sat down on a park bench near the wheel, letting myself relax against the thick stone chair.

Quiet. It was so quiet, so very calm. I had not been anywhere this still in a long time. I closed my eyes and leaned into the bench. I wondered what it must have felt like for the earliest settlers. Had they found serene places like this, devoid from the noise of angry parents and rebellious pre-adolescents?

Behind me, I heard a wise owl calling out. "Hoo, hoo," it cheered. I thought I knew the answer, but I didn't want to complete my thought. I would be in a group home soon enough, or perhaps, back in the hospital. Or even detention, I thought, remembering the cops.

I shivered from the cold. Perhaps sitting down on a chilly stone bench wasn't the best idea. I stood up and continued walking down the dark paths. The only light in this area came from the moon above the small forest that filled the museum's land. I wandered around the pond, lazily watching the small bubbles form from movement of fish and turtles. I figured there might be snakes in there, but I'd never seen one.

After a few hours of lazy wandering, I realized that I needed a plan. Where would I sleep?

I walked back to the main road. No cars were passing by. I hadn't seen any police cars. No one was looking for me.

I darted across the road. I was in front of my beloved library, but its warm books were protected from the cool spring night. I sighed heavily and walked on. I could see my brother's school on the left, and there was a church ahead of me on the right. I glanced between the two buildings, trying to decide where to go next. As I continued to walk, the playground behind the church came into sight. I smiled, in spite of my predicament. Of course!

I wandered over to the playground and set my backpack in the metal tunnel underneath a jungle gym. I glanced inside of it, making sure there was enough space for me. There was, and it was slightly insulated from the nighttime breeze. Shivering but feeling safer in the enclosed space, I let myself drift off to sleep.

Every few hours, I awoke and peered out into the world around me. No blue flashing lights, no loud voices calling my name. No one was searching for me.

When daylight came, I stood up and stretched. I felt hungry. I hadn't packed any food. Just my notebook, my jacket, and a change of clothes. I really needed to plan better.

I sat down on a swing in the playground, and let the swing carry me up into the air. Back and forth, with and against the breeze. I felt strong, sure of myself.

Through the trees, I heard the morning bell from my elementary school behind me. The elementary school was one block further from the middle school, and there was a shortcut through yet another thicket of trees between the church and my school. I wondered what they were having for breakfast. My stomach growled. I realized how hungry I was. My last food had been a smooshed peanut butter and jelly sandwich in lieu of bloody chicken.

I jumped off the swing and stood up straight. I'd survived a night on my own. I didn't have to consider this as a failure, but more as a practice session. I could survive as a runaway.

I shrugged, then picked up my backpack. Time for school.

My dad yelled at me that evening, but I didn't care. It was an ordinary evening for me. Where did I go? What was I thinking?

Questions that I wasn't planning to answer.

He threatened to send me away. I shrugged. I didn't care. I was tired of his empty threats. I'd started to think he wasn't going to do anything. He kept talking about sending me someplace else, but he also kept complaining about his endless bills from the hospital. Apparently, he was receiving numerous large bills from my two months, ten days he'd left me at the hospital the previous summer.

Good. I didn't believe he would do it. He needed every spare dollar for Terri's frequent hospitalizations. When she got re-hospitalized that week, I was relieved. We would have peace for a while. And there was no way in hell I would set foot in that hospital for any family meetings, ever again.

Whenever she was gone, our meals reverted to hamburger helper, tuna helper, and any other "helper" my dad could find at the grocery store. I didn't like it, but my stomach didn't turn when I ate those meals. I was grateful for a short reprieve from the chaos in my home.

My mom's big blue car was waiting for me after school a few days after I'd run away for the first time. I figured my mom would want to talk to me about my escape, so I mentally prepared myself for a confrontation. Instead, my mom had brought a bag of old bread sitting beside her on the front car seat. "Let's go to the duck pond," she told me softly through the open window of her car. Her eyes looked faraway, sad.

It wouldn't have been too unusual to go to the duck pond with my mom. We'd gone there together before; sometimes we would find hungry mallards and swans. She told me there were geese that had flown all the way from Canada. I slid into the chair next to her, ready for a casual afternoon.

But something was different this time. When we arrived, she parked further away from the pond, near the tombstones. The graveyard encircled the tiny pond; it was almost as if the cemetery owners had created the pond as an afterthought. A place to mourn without staring at all the decaying graves.

She turned to face me, and her blue eyes held my gaze. They were like pools to another world; a distant place she would sometimes let me travel to. "I need to show you something," she told me.

We hadn't been to this part of the cemetery before. I followed her out of the car to a long stretch of grass, interspersed with flat gravestones. She started walking more stiffly, her eyes searching for something. I was starting to feel dizzy; I was alternating between looking at her and looking at the ground. Trying not to lose my footing as we stepped past the dead.

When she stopped several yards later, I paused. What had she found? What secret was I about to learn?

I moved wordlessly from behind her, taking my place at her side. We were standing too close; we were a family that never touched. She shifted away just enough to remind me that I was in her space. I looked up at her face, trying to figure out what emotion was crossing over her features. I couldn't.

Instead, I glanced down. And then I saw it.

Three little words.

The Brown children. My non-existent siblings.

My mouth gaped open for a moment. I'd always known my mom had lost a few babies to stillbirths. Her history had been told to us over the years, perhaps in monotone. I heard it replaying in my mind. "We couldn't have kids," my dad's voice echoed. "So, we adopted David, and then Kevin." And then Melinda came, after they'd barely signed the paperwork. A third child, too soon. Nick and I came years later.

I waited for her to say something.

There were no flowers. No names, no dates. These children who weren't children at all, and this reminder of them. Were they my older brothers or sisters? The other gravesites held small bouquets of flowers. Some had elaborate decorations. After all, a holiday had passed recently. People were remembering the ones they'd lost.

"Mom," I said softly, reminding her I was standing beside her.

"Oh," she said quietly. "He wouldn't let me see them." I looked at her, our eyes meeting. "Your father. He didn't let me hold them. I wanted to say goodbye. I needed to say goodbye."

My mother, who never held me. She'd never held those babies either. Was that the beginning of her madness?

"I needed a place to go, to mourn them," she told me, her eyes turning back to the tiny tombstone on the ground. I knew she'd had three stillbirths, and that after her last stillbirth she'd had Nick and me.

Three living kids, born of her womb. Cesareans, because she'd had a horrible accident as a child and the scars ran across her abdomen. We'd been born wrong; vertical incisions in a place meant for horizontal cuts. Three cesareans.

If even one of those stillborn babies had survived, there would be no me.

I had always understood the significance. Every time my father joked that he only wanted four kids, I cringed. I was the fifth. Joke or not, that last one was always me.

Her voice cracked just a little. "I couldn't bury them," she said, her words heavy on the light breeze. "He didn't let me talk about them."

I nodded slowly. My father never wanted to talk about the things that broke us. We didn't talk about my summer at the hospital. Years later, I would still grieve not being able to be heard. Not able to express my own secret losses.

We were a family that didn't talk. Didn't touch. We existed around each other.

My mom continued staring absently across the rows of gravesites. Graves holding bodies, decaying in boxes. Our gravesite, for my siblings that never were, was empty. There was no box with a body. Their bodies had been discarded somewhere. Medical waste.

The weight of her words, the complexity of her pain; I could see the hollow parts of her begging for sunlight.

"It's beautiful," I said, hoping those were the right words.

My mom's thin lips formed a tight smile. One that wasn't happy but was willing to soldier on. "Let's go feed the ducks," she said.

I nodded, and we walked slowly back to the car to get the old bread.

9
RUNNING AGAIN

A few months passed before I dared to run away again. I was torn between my fierce loyalty to my mom and the growing chasm between me and the rest of my family. School had become my only refuge; I was constantly on edge at home. Between my dad's attempts to medicate me and my stepmother's desire for total control, I was falling apart.

One afternoon, I curled up on Melissa's sofa and told Donnie that I wanted to leave again. Melissa had told me my family was pretty messed up but hadn't offered much advice. I needed an exit strategy.

I took a slow sip of beer from a can that Donnie had handed to me. "There's an empty apartment in my complex," he said. "I know how to break in."

I turned to him, intrigued. "They won't find me there?"

"Not at night," he told me.

I didn't think to ask what would happen during the day. We agreed I would run away the next day, after school. I went home and packed my backpack, adding a few bags of chips and an extra peanut butter and jelly sandwich. The hunger from my first escape had been my downfall. As long as I had an extra meal, I'd be alright, I told myself.

The following day, I sat impatiently through my classes. When the school day was over, I hurried to walk home with Melissa. Donnie came over when he finished school. We went to his house and played video games and shared a few beers. He smoked, and I watched him take long, slow drags on his cigarettes. I had never been interested in smoking, but something about the way that the ash collected at the end of the burning cigarette fascinated me.

"When do we go?" I asked. My overly full backpack sat on the carpet beside me.

"Soon," he said, alternating between killing space invaders and flicking ash off his cigarette into an awaiting glass ashtray beside him.

I nodded, remembering he was older than me. I'd barely had my twelfth birthday, and he was already fifteen. Of course he had a plan.

We waited until nightfall and then he told me it was time. We crept across the apartment complex and he told me to wait near a row of trees while he got inside. I tried to look nonchalant but really, my nerves were growing.

"I'm in," I heard him whisper loudly, calling from the doorway. He'd gotten in through an open window, apparently a trick he'd employed previously.

I hurried across the short distance, then crossed through the open door. He quickly closed it behind me and secured the lock.

"Oh," I said, realizing that we were suddenly alone. Together.

The apartment was empty; no furniture, no evidence of other people. There was a living room, kitchen, bedroom, and bathroom. "The electricity is on," he told me, "but we can't turn on the lights."

"Why not?" I asked curiously, following him through the apartment into the bedroom. He opened the closet door.

"The lights," he said. "If they see lights on, they'll know we're here." The carpet was beige, and the walls were bright white. Everything about the apartment screamed newness. New opportunities.

"How long can I stay here?" I asked.

He shrugged, opening the closet door. He walked into the large closet, and I followed behind him. He closed the door. We were suddenly shrouded in darkness.

"I can't see," I said.

He laughed quietly. "Wait," he said, reaching his arms around me and kissing me suddenly. "Did you run away to be with me?" he asked.

I pulled back from him. "No," I said. "I need to get away from my family."

The distance between us grew. He stepped further away, then began fumbling with something in his pocket. He pulled out a small flashlight and pointed it towards the back of the closet before turning it on.

"Let's sit down," he said, his eyes serious. I nodded, watching the light dance across his face. I'd been so eager to have a boyfriend and a place to go I hadn't planned my escape very well. Donnie didn't really think I wanted to get away, I realized.

I sat down next to him, and we leaned against the wall. "So, you've never done it?" he asked.

I shook my head. No. This was not why I'd run away.

"Donnie, I need to get away. I can't go back there," I told him.

He nodded, as if he was finally seeing me. "You didn't come here to have sex with me?" he asked me, more directly this time.

"No," I told him. We were leaning side by side against a bright white closet wall in an unrented apartment. My backpack sat to my right, my boyfriend to my left. I stared at the circle of light against the back wall. "I told you about my stepmom," I said.

He sighed. "You have to get out of here in the morning," he told me.

I nodded. "Will you stay here with me?" I asked, suddenly afraid of being alone in this place.

"For a little while," he said. "But then you need to get out of here. I don't want to go to juvie," he confided.

"Me either," I agreed.

Silence filled our secret hiding space. A long time passed, and I had not been paying attention to the expression on his face. "We can't go out anymore," he finally told me several hours later.

I nodded slowly. Right. I wasn't giving my virginity to him. "You can go," I said softly. He didn't need to stay here with me out of pity. We'd shared enough firsts; first beer, first kiss, first breaking and entering.

"You'll be okay?" he asked but didn't wait for an answer. He stood and smoothed out his pants. "Keep the flashlight," he told me right before he snuck out of the closet.

After he was gone, I opened my backpack and went through the contents. One sandwich, two bags of chips, a plastic baggy with some Oreos, and two cans of soda. Again, I hadn't planned well. I didn't have enough food for forever away from my family. I sighed and opened the bag containing the peanut butter and jelly sandwich. It was mushed by then, but I didn't care. It was way past dinner time, and I'd just been dumped.

The next morning, I awoke to the sound of someone crawling through the window. I sat upright, my body aching from its unnatural position on the floor of an empty apartment. I shivered in my small closet, afraid of whoever had just entered the apartment.

The closet door burst open suddenly, and my now ex-boyfriend was hovering over me. "You have to get out of here," Donnie said. "Your dad called Melissa's parents. What if the police come?"

I stared at him, his face covered in shadows. He'd left the door open this time, and I could see daylight trickling in through the bedroom windows.

"But where do I go?" I asked.

He shrugged. "School. Home. You're too young to run away," he told me.

"Okay, fine," I answered, accepting that I'd failed at running away again.

10
AS FAR AWAY AS POSSIBLE

It was just another warm September night. There was nothing special about that night, and yet, everything changed in an instant. I remember sitting in front of the television, trying to ignore the chatter in the other room. My dad and my stepmother were upset with me, and I was probably at fault. It had been a hard week for me, and I'd been secretly wrestling with an idea about second chances.

I don't remember what they said, or what I said back to them. We argued. I was thirteen, angry, and overly emotional. But I was also miserable, lonely, and suicidal. I'd spent the better part of an evening the previous week staring at a bottle of pills. I'd considered ending it all. I'd had angry thoughts about telling my family how it really felt to be me. But I also knew none of that really mattered. At some point in my suicidal planning, I flipped through an atlas. I was bored, lost. And somehow the page opened to a map of the United States.

My eyes wandered across the two pages, creating an invisible line between my home state of North Carolina, and the other side of the country. California. Los Angeles. That looked far enough away. Maybe I could just leave, start over. Find a new family. Maybe I could just disappear.

Hands trembling, I opened another book; a telephone book. I dialed the number for our local Greyhound station.

"How much is a ticket to Los Angeles?" I heard myself asking.

"One hundred and twenty dollars," the voice on the other end of the phone said. I thanked him and hung up.

If I could find one hundred and twenty dollars, I could live. I could make it through another night, I told myself.

I shoved the bottle of pills back into my desk and opened a blank notebook instead. It was time to plan.

And plan, I did. I packed an emergency backpack full of my favorite clothes, a few notebooks so I could write America's greatest novel, and a stash of pens. I would find my new life in California.

I somehow made it through the next day, and the next day. I did not kill myself. I did not open the drawer with the pills again. I watched. I waited.

And then we had an argument. I cannot remember why we argued, or what triggered it. But my dad stormed out of the house. He locked his bedroom door before leaving, as always. He always made such a big show of locking his bedroom door.

I sat in complete silence, waiting for him to leave. *Full House* played in front of me on our family television. I waited until my dad and my stepmother drove away, with my obedient older brother in the back seat, and I wondered. Would he have one hundred and twenty dollars in his room?

I turned off the television and thought about the lock. I could try to get in through his bedroom window, I told myself. I rushed outside, placed a ladder against his bedroom wall, and peered in. No such luck, he had every window locked.

But I saw the envelope on the dresser.

My dad liked to divide his paycheck into distinct, marked envelopes and budget his life each month into the food envelope, the gas envelope, and miscellaneous stuff. I knew he had just been paid, so there was a chance that I would find one hundred and twenty dollars.

But his door was locked. At first, I tried to open it a few times like they do in those spy movies. Plastic cards, hair pins. Nothing would work.

Finally, I got desperate. What if he came home? What if I could never leave? What if I needed to just end it all?

I turned around and glanced around the room. The house I lived in when I was growing up had been reconstructed over time. The room leading to his bedroom was called our "sunroom." It was full of windows and was originally designed as a porch, and this master bedroom tomb, my father and stepmother's reclusive hiding space, was the newest section of the house. The sunroom held books, plants, and there was a small box of tools in the corner.

My eyes fixated on the toolbox. Maybe, I thought. Maybe I could find a way to get in, to get one hundred and twenty dollars.

I rummaged through the box, realizing screwdrivers would not work. And then I saw the hammer.

The clock beside me warned me that they would be home in another hour or so. Could I break the lock and leave fast enough?

I held the hammer in my hands, feeling its full weight. If I did this, there would be no turning back. If I broke that lock, no matter how much was in that envelope, I would have to leave. I had two ways to leave; the permanent one or the escape plan.

Tears streaming down my cheeks, I carried the hammer to his door and began to hit the lock. My first hit was weak, scared. I was timid and shaking. I hit the lock again, and again, until a new strength overcame me. I had to leave. I had to get out. I wanted to have a chance to live. I hated myself, I hated my family. I hated everything about my life. I was a miserable, frightened, lonely thirteen-year-old: I had nobody to talk to, I was always punished for something, and I knew that my only peace had been when I was walking to and from my junior high. I didn't fit in, and the new school year was breaking me again. I was tired of getting in trouble for stupid things like walking to the library after school or not wanting to wear socks. I was tired of always being wrong, of always being told I wasn't good enough. I was tired of my dad trying to control everything about my life, and tired of my stepmother treating me badly. She never wanted kids, why the hell had she married my father, who had five kids and two small grandchildren? I was tired of being punished for the many things I kept doing wrong, like when my sister found out I had shoplifted a bunch of clothes. Didn't they know I was packing to leave? That everything I had done in the past few years was a slow exit strategy, and that I'd almost given up completely a week ago?

The heavy sound of the hammer as it crashed into metal filled the room, until the lock gave way. It fell; backwards onto the floor of the forbidden room. I took a deep breath and tried the doorknob.

The door opened. I tossed the hammer aside and ran into the room. I knew the clock was working against me. I had to leave fast.

I raced to the dresser and opened the envelope. I counted the money fast; two hundred and fifty dollars! I had enough! I breathed a sigh of relief; the inward battle between dying and leaving had been settled.

I ran upstairs and grabbed my backpack. I flung it over my shoulder and hurried back down to the kitchen. Quickly, I filled my bag with any small snacks that could fit. Once it was full, I rushed outside and breathed in the autumn air. It was time.

I walked faster than ever down the road, away from my house. Away from the place full of terrible memories. I passed the bus station and kept walking. The next bus was scheduled to leave in the morning. I needed to hide for the night.

Several miles later, I realized I wasn't shaking anymore. I was terrified, but something small inside of me felt free. I was going to have a chance to live.

I found an old building that looked like it had seen better days and decided to camp out for the night. I watched as the sky changed to complete darkness and wondered if my father was looking for me. I knew he had not looked for me when I had runaway twice before, but I'd never escaped my hometown. But this time, I'd taken my dad's money. I decided he was probably looking for me.

By morning, I knew I had to get as far away as I could. What if the police were looking for me? I'd broken into my dad's room with a hammer. I quickly ate a breakfast of crackers and backtracked my steps. I arrived at the bus station sometime after nine in the morning.

With a silent prayer that they would sell me a ticket, I approached the counter. The old man at the register looked at me closely for a moment and then asked me where I wanted to go. His eyes crinkled around the edges as he spoke.

"Los Angeles," I told him. I counted out the handful of crisp bills.

He sold me a ticket.

I thanked him and took a seat in the corner, where I could watch all the cars that entered the parking lot. I was so afraid my father would show up; he had to have figured out my plan.

He was too smart and methodical; he would know I was leaving for good this time.

Nobody came.

The bus arrived, and without any hoopla or questions or scrutiny, I presented my ticket to the driver and was invited onto my awaiting ride.

I found an empty seat towards the back, next to a window. I dug my fingernails into my thighs, trying to contain my fear. What if the police stopped the bus? What if they found me?

The bus pulled out of the station. It started its routine course down familiar streets. I saw a light blue car pass by in the other direction. A sinking feeling filled the pit of my stomach as I watched my mother drive by, looking for me.

My mother.

I bit my lip, fighting off tears. My mother was the one reason I had never left this town before. My only reason not to swallow an entire bottle of pills and drift off into an eternal sleep.

I traced an outline of her car on the window as the bus continued its journey.

I stared out the window as we made our way down that same road I had walked the previous day, when I escaped.

When the bus merged onto the interstate, I was finally able to close my eyes and begin to forget. I needed to forget this town. I needed to forget this place that had brought me nothing but pain.

I needed to forget the look on my mom's face as she frantically searched for me.

And I needed to never find out that my mom baked a plate of cookies and left them on the table, window open, so that I might smell them and come inside.

11
CALIFORNIA

Three days to reach the other side of the country.

There was something both freeing and deeply disturbing about the ease with which I traveled alone, across the country, at thirteen years old. I traced our route on a small map that I kept in my backpack, and I waited patiently each time I deboarded and stood in line for my connecting bus. I washed myself in bathrooms, ate dry packs of crackers and sparingly spent change to buy a drink every twelve hours or so. I watched in awe and fear as immigration officers entered the bus in Texas and spoke to everyone; removing only those who did not speak English for a further interrogation. I was so afraid they would find me, but nobody paid much attention to the not-quite-old-enough girl in the back of the bus.

Somewhere between the New Mexico-Arizona desert, he noticed me. He was an older gentleman, self-described as a recently released convict from Florida. I shared a seat with this man who told me he knew that I was a runaway and whispered that he could turn me in. I obediently followed him off the bus when we arrived in Los Angeles. He made me follow him to a dark alley a few blocks away, where he raped me.

I stood in the alley way for a long time afterwards, not sure who I was anymore. Was this better than home? I wasn't sure. A new pain, one I'd never known, screamed at me from every nerve ending in my body. I adjusted my outfit and placed my backpack back onto my shoulders, retracing the short walk back to the bus station. I found a place to sit down, but soon found that I was in excruciating pain. Ugly tears began to fall.

An older African American woman walked up to me, perhaps seeing me in a way that no one else had ever truly seen me. She asked me a few deliberate questions, and then told me which buses to take to get to a program in Hollywood that could help teens like me. Some place called LAYN. She'd recognized me for who I was, in just a matter of moments.

I didn't have anywhere else to go, so I followed her directions and boarded my first city bus. I watched as the large, expansive city rolled past me. I waited until I arrived at the end of the first bus line, then connected to the next bus. I clutched my backpack tightly; I only had about eighty dollars left before I would never have food again. What had I done? I stared down at my hands, clenching the backpack so tightly until my fingers turned ghostly white.

Maybe my father was looking for me.

Probably not.

I watched as the city unfolded before my eyes. I had never been in a big city before, and I was suddenly very small.

I liked it.

It's easier to hide in plain sight when no one knows who you are or how badly you hurt.

I didn't know Hollywood was even in Los Angeles before that morning. And suddenly, I could see a sign on a hill that said Hollywood, in great big white letters.

The bus driver called out the name of my street. Cahuenga.

I stood up and exited, ready for my life to change again. Each step that I took up Cahuenga Boulevard made me feel more nervous, and the pain from what had happened never went away. But there was something hopeful about this place full of stars on sidewalks, street vendors washing their little plots of concrete for the morning's sales, and the bright neon colors hanging on clothes racks at several stores that I passed. I walked up the winding road, which is on a mild incline towards the mountains. My body hurt, and I was afraid everyone could tell by looking at me that I was suddenly *not a virgin.*

I read the numbers on the buildings. The one I was supposed to go to looked so plain, but it seemed to be buzzing with activity. Music blared from a boombox, and several teens hung out in front. I noticed several of them were smoking cigarettes, chatting about something.

"Hi," I stammered.

One of them turned and looked at me. She was tall, thin, with long red hair and permanent distrust on her face.

"Is this LAYN?" I asked.

She nodded and pointed me towards the doorway. I thanked her and slowly walked up those steps. Each step hurt. Everything hurt.

Before I could knock, the door suddenly opened. Someone was leaving, and they'd almost smacked me with the door. It was a tallish young man in a trench coat. He apologized.

I nodded sheepishly and walked inside.

A youth counselor seated at a desk noticed me first. "First time?" he asked.

I nodded.

He asked me for a few details; my name, date of birth, and age. He then toured me around the downstairs area.

There was a dining area, replete with plastic containers filled with a variety of cereal types and milk strewn around a table. I realized I was starving.

There was a play room, with a foosball table. There was also a tv room, with an old black and white TV that looked like a grey snow storm.

I went back to the dining area and helped myself to a bowl of cereal. The milk was a little warm, but the cereal tasted amazing. I ate two bowls. Maybe if I was full, I wouldn't hurt so much.

After I ate, one of the counselors pulled me into a room for something called an "Intake."

I gave brief, curt answers to her questions.

At the end, she offered me a bed in their shelter. But there were strings attached.

"We have to call your parents for permission within 72 hours," she was telling me. I shook my head. I did not want my father to find me. I'd been through too much to get to where I was.

I reluctantly agreed to go there for the night, but only if they didn't call yet.

I sat down in the dayroom, wondering what to do. I wasn't used to not going to school. I was supposed to be in the seventh grade, learning about plays or science or something. But here I was, watching my new life unfold in front of me.

The redhead sat down next to me. "How old are you?" she asked.

"Thirteen."

She probably heard a touch of that Southern accent on my one word. I barely had one, compared to everyone else I knew back home, since my family was originally from up North.

"Go home, kid," she said, and then she stood up and walked away.

I bit down hard on my lip. No, I felt myself screaming inside. But I said nothing.

No was a word I did not know how to say very well, I thought sadly. Because no, I did not want to go back, even if it meant that people might hurt me like that guy from the bus.

I watched and waited, and when the afternoon van arrived to take the "shelter kids" back to the overnight program, I got on. I watched everything in silence, only speaking when spoken to.

I walked into the shelter, not quite sure what to expect. It was another nondescript building, with a tall fence around the back of the building. There was a large dayroom, where I opted to sit on one of the large, black sofas.

My eyes caught on some of the photos along the walls. Celebrity baseball games, fundraisers for this program. People who cared about kids like me.

I made it through the motions, and then graciously went upstairs when they opened the dormitories. I found myself in a large room filled with over a dozen beds. The dorm room for girls. They told me that the boys had one too, but I did not care. I just wanted to shower and be safe.

I took the longest shower of my life and felt the tears being rinsed from my cheeks.

"Hurry up," I heard one of the girls saying. I finally turned off the water and wrapped myself with a towel before exiting the shower. I had tried to scrub away the dirtiness, but had only succeeded in making my skin appear blotchy red.

"Sorry," I said meekly and rushed into a bathroom stall to change.

As I laid down in my bed in the girls' ward, waiting for the lights to go out, I wondered if I would be brave enough to let them call my dad.

The next morning, we were given the choice to walk back to the day program or to take a ride. One of the older girls introduced herself to me and asked me to walk with her. I admired her trendy outfit and her self-confidence.

I put all my belongings back into my backpack and began the mile or so walk back to the drop-in shelter.

"Why did you come here?" she asked. Her eyes sparkled when she spoke, and she had a cheerful smile pasted on her face. She was beautiful; her cocoa skin and jet-black hair shined flawlessly. Her clothes were new and stylish. Her bright red lipstick accentuated her features perfectly.

"Because it was far away," I admitted.

She continued to interrogate me, then dismissively told me the same as the other girl. "Go home, girl."

I sighed. I was not going to go home.

I was grateful to arrive at the drop-in program. I ate my bowl of cereal with not-quite-cold-enough milk and watched the city through the windows of the dayroom.

Someone sat down next to me. It was the guy from the previous day, the tall one.

"Hi," he said. "I'm Scarecrow."

I chuckled. "Scarecrow? Why would your parents name you that?"

He laughed too. "You're new here, aren't you?" he asked.

I nodded. We chatted for a while, and he told me his real name. Apparently, runaways and other people who did not want to be found used made up names instead of their real names. It was supposed to be safer. After he explained a few more things to me, he asked me if I liked the shelter.

I shrugged. "Not really," I told him. "I don't want them to call my dad. They said they can't call my mom, because she isn't my guardian."

He nodded, a kind smile on his face. "You could squat with me," he offered.

"Squat?" I asked naively. There were so many new words here. I hadn't figured out this new dialect just yet.

"You know, stay in an abandoned building. I have a safe spot."

I looked at him closely. He had sadness in his eyes, like me. "I've done that before," I said, thinking about the night when I first left. When was that, five whole days ago? I was already a completely different person. I could feel myself changing.

"Maybe," I told him.

The day passed by slowly. One of the counselors approached me and offered to call my dad with me. I glanced over at Scarecrow, who had been hanging out with me throughout the day.

"No, I'm okay. I'm going to go hang out with Scarecrow," I said.

The counselor said something else to me, but already, I wasn't listening. I shrugged and walked over to Scarecrow.

"Let's go," I told him. He smiled and stood up, and quickly left the building with me.

We wandered around Hollywood for a few hours, with him showing me some of the sights. He showed me a popular hangout spot of his, Tomy's. "They make breakfast all hours of the day," he told me. I read the signs on the windows. Pancake special, one dollar and ninety nine cents.

"Let's get pancakes," I said.

His eyes widened. "You have money?" he asked.

I nodded. "Just a little," I lied.

We sat down at a corner table with a view of the Boulevard and he ordered pancakes with scrambled eggs. I counted out a few dollars for our shared meal, keeping the rest tucked neatly in my pocket.

In between bites, Scarecrow told me the history of Hollywood. Or Hollywoodland, as it had previously been named. Our tentative connection frightened me, but every fiber in my being screamed that I was unsafe alone. Besides, his eyes drew me in. He was so attentive, and he listened to every word I said.

I didn't want to think about the man from the bus.

The afternoon was passing us by, and I needed to figure out where I'd spend the night. My one night on the streets had broken me, and I was terrified. At the same time, I sensed a connection with this older boy. "Can I stay with you tonight?" I asked.

He nodded, stretching a long arm and placing it loosely on the back of the chair behind me. I leaned closer, just enough to feel the warmth from his closeness, but just out of reach.

As darkness arrived, we slipped away from our corner in the dimly lit restaurant and stepped back outside. I followed behind him as we walked up a long road, towards an abandoned building. His squat.

"A lot of buildings got damaged during the riots," he explained. I nodded slowly, recalling the news stories about the Los Angeles Riots several months earlier. I watched him scale over a small fence, and then I followed. We snuck around a large, empty apartment complex, until we reached the parking garage. He opened one of the storage closets on the wall and told me to climb in.

"Up there?" I asked. It was such a small space, and I was afraid. But I'd already given up my spot at the shelter, and I had no other good options. I crawled upwards into the cabinet and laid down obediently against the wall.

He climbed up next, and then closed the door. "We have to be quiet," he said. Apparently, he explained, police raided squats regularly, and we had to hide as best as we could.

The space was small, and I leaned against him. He felt warm and his heartbeat was dancing against my ear.

"Do you like me?" he asked.

"Maybe," I answered. I was in uncharted territory and sinking fast.

He tried to kiss me, but I started to cry.

So instead, he held me in his arms, and asked me what had happened. He somehow knew.

I told him about the man from the bus, and he let me unleash all my sadness and ugly tears. Afterwards, I fell asleep against him, wondering if this could be my new life.

The next day, we went to the shelter for breakfast. One of the case managers tried to pull me aside to talk to me, but I didn't want to talk. She told me that she was worried about me, but I refused to go back to the shelter.

The redhead from the previous two days said nothing to me. I made eye contact, daring her to tell me to go home again. She didn't. I left with Scarecrow.

"Let's go see Mann's Chinese," he told me. I had no idea what he was talking about, but I walked with him anyway. We held hands, and I read all the names on the stars as we strolled down Hollywood Boulevard. I read some of them aloud if I recognized the actor or singer. He carried my backpack for me when I was tired, and he listened to me when I talked.

Mann's Chinese Theater was apparently a famous movie theater. We laughed and walked around, looking at the handprints and footprints etched forever into the cement. He told me stories of Hollywood history only the insiders new. "Did you know famous people used to walk up and down these streets?" he told me. He continued his history lesson, and we stopped in several souvenir shops to glance at relics of the past. I was fascinated by Hollywood, and I was still surprised I'd accidentally come here. I hadn't even realized that Hollywood was in Los Angeles.

When we started a slow stroll back towards the squat, he noticed a ticket booth on the corner. We stopped in front of the booth and I watched as he chatted with one of the workers, whose sign offered free tickets to TV show tapings.

"Want to see a new talk show?" he offered to me after he'd heard which shows were taping that day. I nodded. It sounded cool. And I didn't have anything better to do.

We were both issued tickets and directed towards a waiting bus. We boarded the bus together and sat down next to each other. There were couples and vacationing families. And then there were the two of us; an almost couple of broken street kids.

I rested my head against his shoulder, suddenly grateful I wasn't alone anymore. I felt safe, even though it was a weird sense of safety. How could this kid understand me better than anyone else?

But he wasn't a kid, actually. He was nineteen. I smiled. I suddenly had a boyfriend; an older, sweet boyfriend, and we were going somewhere fun together.

That's how I ended up on the first real date of my life. The bus drove us across town to a television studio, where we watched an unknown talk show called Vicki. We were coached on when to laugh and clap, and I marveled at the behind the scenes aspects of TV tapings I'd never been aware of. I smiled throughout the commercial breaks when the studio audience won prizes and shared where they were from.

When one couple stood up and announced that they were from North Carolina, I started tapping my legs nervously, trying to hold in my fear. Scarecrow patted my leg. "Don't worry," he told me, in that way that a guy tells a girl that everything will be alright. My dad wasn't going to find me.

When the bus brought us back to Hollywood, it was already dark. We made our way back to the squat, and we curled up next to each other. Caught up in the moment and wanting to wash myself clean from what had happened the other night; wanting to choose for myself who I would sleep with, I let him remove my clothes and take our relationship further than I should have. We were two lost souls, and we each had our own set of motives. I wanted to wash away my feeling of brokenness. I wanted to feel safe. And in that brief moment, I felt safe.

He held me that entire night, and the next day, we were laughing and holding hands again.

12
601

We went to LAYN for breakfast, but the counselor told Scarecrow that they would call the police if he didn't stop hanging around me. Apparently, they did not like our age difference.

I dug in my heels. This was my life, my decision. My freedom was hard-won, and it was mine. It had cost me so much.

We left, and I vowed to never return to LAYN. We went to another drop-in program instead, several miles away. We both showered, and when I stepped out of the bathroom in clean clothes, a policeman was waiting for me. Scarecrow was already in handcuffs. We were both being arrested.

The officers led him away first, and then it was just me and them. I felt the coldness of the metal as the cuffs went on behind my back, and I knew I would never see him again. I hadn't even been given a chance to say goodbye.

One of the two officers that was standing in front of me asked if my bag had any weapons. I shook my head, shock flooding through me. I was in handcuffs. Why?

"Why am I being arrested?" I asked, my voice suddenly loud and angry.

"You are a runaway," he told me matter-of-factly. I followed him obediently to the car, where I slowly slid onto the thick backseat. I watched as he threw my backpack into the trunk, and then the car began to drive. I bounced around slightly, as I had not been seatbelted in. I felt small and lost again.

We arrived at the Hollywood police station, where I was fingerprinted and photographed. My belongings were recorded on a piece of paper and then shoved into an envelope. I had less than twenty dollars left. How much Tomy's had we eaten? I hadn't been counting my money very well.

The officers took me back to their car, and we drove away from Hollywood. Away from Tomy's, away from LAYN, away from Cahuenga Boulevard, away from stars on the sidewalk. Away from Scarecrow. Away from the girls that told me to, "Go home, girl."

We merged onto the freeway. I watched as passengers in other cars turned to peer at me, the hardened criminal. The girl in the back of the police car. I wanted to cry, but I didn't.

I watched as we drove past a mural in downtown Los Angeles, with smiling faces of children playing a variety of sports. "They painted that for the Olympics," one of the officers was saying. They were trying to start a conversation with me, but I was angry, and I'd never felt so betrayed. Why had the drop-in shelter turned me in?

They drove me towards a large building that they called *Los Padrinos*. L.P., I didn't know what those words meant. And I didn't ask.

A large metal gate with spikes on top opened, allowing the police car to enter the fortress known as L.P. I tried to right myself up in the seat as much as possible; tried to see what mess I had gotten myself into.

They delivered me to a waiting guard, who collected my belongings and took me inside. They removed my cuffs and wished me good luck.

The guard was a middle-aged woman. I waited for her to tell me what would happen to me. I probably looked terrified, although I tried to keep a brave face.

I heard my dad's voice playing through my head, taunting me, telling me I'd end up in jail like my older brother had. Saying that I was "just like Kevin."

Here I was, in jail.

That hadn't taken very long at all.

I was instructed to take off all my clothes for a shower. When I did, I was sprayed with anti-lice spray and I had to squat in several different positions to prove that I didn't have any contraband. I'd never used drugs and had not had beer since I stopped hanging out with Melissa.

"Hurry up," the guard told me as she stood in front of me while I showered. There was no curtain, and I had three minutes to clean myself. The cold water did little to wash away the lice spray.

I put on the orange jumpsuit that she handed to me. The fabric was stiff and heavy.

"You're a 601," she told me. I did not know what she meant.

Another guard was suddenly standing beside her. "It's okay," she told her friend. "We'll get her on a 602 next time."

My eyes darted from one guard to the next. They were both women, strong, with weapons attached to their belts.

They led me down a long hallway, which curved and brought us to a separate ward. At the end of each hallway was an immense locked door. When we arrived at our destination, a girl's ward, we were buzzed inside. I followed them halfway down the hall before they stopped in front of a nondescript white door.

A loud buzzing sound announced the opening of the cell door. I stared inside at the tiny metal bed and small quarters. I bit down on my lower lip, uncertain.

"Go in."

I glanced back at them. Was this really happening? But the looks on their faces convinced me that I belonged in that cell. I took the few steps forward that separated me from them, and the door swung shut behind me.

An echo reverberated through the room after the door was closed. I stood just within the doorway, taking stock of my new surroundings. Small room, even tinier than I could have imagined. Small metal bed with a too-thin mattress, against the wall. No pillow. Thin sheets.

To my left, a tiny metal sink. No mirror, no soap, no paper towels. Off to the side, a metal toilet. The discarded remainder of an old roll of toilet paper.

Above the bed, a small window with long metal bars crisscrossing it into an impossible checkerboard. I crept across the cell, nervous, and stood on the bed to look out the window.

Outside, there were sterile sidewalks and the wall of another building, with no windows facing back at me. Nobody was out there.

I was trapped, inside of a concrete jungle. I stood and watched for a while, wondering if I was alone here. Were there other kids like me? Other 601s?

I jumped back down and looked at the door. It immediately reminded me of the isolation room at the hospital. Less than an inch at the bottom to peer underneath. A boxed window at the top, which was sealed from the outside.

They could see me, but I could not see them.

Every nerve fiber in my body was buzzing with a strange new sensation. I was trapped. I had been locked in a small cinder block fortress and they took the keys with them. I didn't know if I should scream, or cry, or vomit. The room spun around me in circles as the tears began to fall.

I was a caged animal. I was trapped.

And I had no clue what a 601 was. And why was a 602 worse?

Eventually, I laid down on the bed and let the fight fall away. I'd been locked up before, when my dad left me in the mental hospital two summers earlier. A part of me stayed behind in that unforgiving place when I was released. We never talked about what had happened to me there; he only mentioned the hospital when he threatened to send me back for small offenses. Uncleaned dishes. Not wearing socks. Talking back to my stepmom.

I hated small spaces. The hospital's isolation room had taught me that I was powerless. I buried my head in the pillowless, thin mattress and tried not to think about how many other broken girls had been trapped in this same room.

Tears fell until I had none left to cry. Day became night. At some point in my frantic crying, I fell asleep.

When I awoke, my thoughts of dread returned. Where was I? What would happen to me? Where was Scarecrow? Would my dad come looking for me? Would they place me in foster care?

A low whistle broke through my thoughts. "Hey, new girl," I heard someone say. I sat up, then stood. I looked out the window, but the concrete walkway was still empty. There was a trace of light coming in from under the door, so I laid my body onto the cold floor and listened for the voice to speak again.

"Hey," said the voice again. I laid down on the floor by that tiny crack at the bottom of the heavy door. Through the small half inch of freedom, I whispered back.

"Hi," I answered. Timid. Frightened.

Her voice was young, hollow. "What did you do?" she asked.

"I ran away from home."

"What did they charge you with?" she inquired. I grew quiet. She rephrased her question, "What number did they book you with?"

"601."

I heard her rustling around in her room, perhaps changing position. "That's good." I let out a low, deep breath. How was that good? Nothing good had happened all day.

"But what's a 601?" I asked.

"It's when you run away, but they've got nothing to charge you with," she told me. "But if you get caught for something else and you're a runaway, they call it a 602."

Apparently, being in juvie made kids experts in legal code. I nodded slowly. I was a 601. No wonder the guards were mad. They had nothing else to charge me with. Good, I told myself.

"What did you do?" I asked.

"I'm here for a 602," she told me. "But they have to treat me well. On account of me being pregnant," she confided.

I froze. Pregnant. That would be terrifying.

And sex makes people pregnant.

"How old are you?" I asked.

"Twelve."

Whoa. "I'm thirteen," I told her.

Her curiosity feigned, and we both went back to bed. I laid down, staring up at the ceiling. I couldn't fall back asleep now. Too many thoughts. 601s and 602s and pregnant twelve-year-olds who were stuck in juvie. Bad men at bus stops and dads who expected everything and nothing, all in one breath.

I awaited morning.

And somehow, morning came. They buzzed me out of my room, and I followed the guard's directions to walk down to a room I presumed was their dining room.

I noticed some girls had orange jumpsuits, and some had green. I asked another girl with an orange jumpsuit to explain the colors to me. "Orange is for serious offenses," she told me. I bit my lip slowly, thinking this over. Running away was serious, apparently.

"What did you do?" I asked her.

"I raped my four-year-old brother," she told me.

I stared at her uncomfortably, but I didn't say anything. I accepted my cereal and milk and ate slowly. I watched as several girls with large bellies demanded extra food. "I get extras, I'm pregnant," I heard one of them saying. I recognized her voice from our late-night chat.

"Hi," I said to her. She smiled back and sat next to me. She was so tiny; perhaps five inches shorter than me. African American, light skin, short hair, and a broad smile. She had extra milk on her tray. She told me her name was Josephine, or Josie to her friends.

Josie and I chatted about nothing until breakfast was over. There was no obvious structure to our days. The choices seemed to be eating, sitting outside, or staying in our rooms. Some kids were pulled away to go to school. She told me that kids who had been sentenced went to school, and the rest of us who were waiting for our court dates did not.

We went back to the same room for lunch, and then we were sent to our rooms for thinking time. Later, we had dinner, followed by more three-minute cold showers without shower curtains. Everything under the watchful eye of the guards. I finished in two.

The days repeated like this, and after a few weeks, I had gotten used to the routine. And that was the day that everything changed again.

As I stood up from lunch, Josie whispered to me, "You started your period."

I shook my head. No, I didn't. I was late, but still. I hadn't felt anything.

I told one of the guards, who said I could go back to my room to change. She double-checked on my offense and told me that someone had made a mistake. I should be in a green jumpsuit anyway, not orange.

I accepted the green jumpsuit and went to my room to change. I had never bled so much in my life. Something was wrong.

The next day, when it still hadn't stopped, I asked Josie. She told me I was probably miscarrying a baby. I thought about it and realized she might be right. We calculated out how far along I could have been, by my last menstrual cycle. I should have been at least four weeks.

I imagined what it would have been like, to have that baby. Was it Scarecrow's? Was it... that other man's baby; the guy from the bus? I cried for this loss and cried for all my other losses. They were my first tears since the night I'd arrived. They fell like rain, and I knew I would never fully recover from this what-if. I decided to name her, a little secret for myself. My little angel. A brief part of me that was gone too quickly; just another broken part.

The following day was my court date. The judge asked me to sign extradition papers. He explained to me that extradition meant I would go back to my home state and they would figure out what to do with me. He told me if I didn't sign paperwork for the state to fly me back to North Carolina, then they would change my 601 to a 602. Because they had spoken to my dad, and they were going to press charges for the theft if I fought extradition.

I had been wondering if I would go to a group home here or if I would be in L.P. until I was 18. I guess I finally had my answer.

As soon as I signed the extradition papers, they moved me to another detention center. They said it was closer to the airport, and that I would be flown home soon.

Home.

I didn't have one anymore.

They hadn't looked for me.

I wasn't the same person who I had been just a few weeks ago.

The next morning, the guards thrust an evidence bag to me, and I found my clothes inside of them. They smelled from being left in a tight container, and it was clear that there was no time or place to do laundry. I changed back into my clothes and they handed me my backpack. The officer removed my handcuffs when I was at the entrance of the plane. They were sending me on a direct flight from Los Angeles to Charlotte, North Carolina. No cuffs, no guard.

How could I escape?

I dreamt of how I could change out of my clothes, and maybe exit the plane with one of the other passengers. The officers on the other end were expecting me to arrive in my purple pants and white shirt. I could disguise myself. I could pretend to have a family and rush out of the airport.

I could find a way back to California.

An older gentleman was seated next to me, and he had seen the cuffs before I had boarded. Everyone had.

I stood up to grab my backpack at some point during the flight. He asked me what I was doing.

And told me not to.

"You have to face this," he told me. He didn't know me, but it's almost like he did.

The plane landed on time in Charlotte. I had never flown before, and my entire first experience was tainted. I waited until all the passengers in front of me had exited, and then I built up my courage. It was time. The old man walked a few feet behind me.

I walked to the exit, fear settling into the pit of my stomach. When I walked out of the long corridor, I tried to walk straight. Wanted to keep walking past the officers. But they called out my name, pulled me aside, and cuffed me.

Handcuffed again, I walked between the two officers, ashamed. I didn't understand why what I had done was so wrong. I wanted to be free; I wanted a reason to live. And my trip had cost me dearly, in ways that would haunt me for years to come. The secrets that I would start to keep to maintain my composure were beginning to form.

I followed them to the waiting police car, and by now, I knew the routine. I ducked my head and slid across the seat.

They tried to make conversation with me, but I couldn't find the words. I watched as the familiar path back to my hometown unfolded before me.

I watched as they drove me past my hometown, towards a nearby town. They drove me down a road that I'd never seen before, and then turned left onto a long road that led to a small building.

The sign in front said Detention Center.

I went through the motions of following them inside, getting uncuffed, getting sprayed with lice spray, showering, and getting checked in. I followed the guards to a room where a dozen or so other kids were spread out, seated around tables. I sat at an empty table.

I ate my meals when I was told to, showered when I was told to, and went to my room when they said it was time.

My dad didn't visit.

I met an older teen who was from New Mexico, also a runaway. We sat together for several hours, and I quizzed her on how she'd gotten to North Carolina. She tirelessly explained to me the intricacies of hitchhiking and how to get from one location to the next. While we chatted, she casually told me she'd left home because her dad and brother had been molesting her. We had very different reasons for leaving, but neither of us felt like we had a home anymore. She didn't judge me for my reasons.

She left a few days later, after her court date. I had hoped to keep talking with her, but she was on to her next destination.

I waited. I watched as other kids had visits from their parents.

Mine didn't come.

The day before my court date, we had a church group come in to talk to us about Jesus and church. I didn't really like church, since my family had only started going when my dad married Terri. But there was someone in their group that caught my eye.

He was a little older, holding a guitar. His face was familiar.

I kept staring at him, wondering.

And then I remembered the face. It was my older brother, Kevin! The one who had been sent away to foster care. I hadn't seen him in a few years by then.

I smiled at him. My brother had come to see me! He smiled back.

I watched intently as they played music for us and then passed out small Bibles. I accepted one from my brother, who passed them out on my side of the room. "Thank you," I said to him, afraid that I might cry again. And I couldn't cry in the dayroom, in front of the other teens.

"Be safe," he whispered as he kept making his way around the room.

Kevin had come to see me. I held the Bible tightly in my hand as the group made their exit.

Maybe everything would be alright.

The group left, without giving me a chance to really talk to my brother. I retreated to my room at the end of the evening, my new Bible in hand.

The officer smiled at me before locking me into my cell. "That's a good book," she told me.

I shrugged. I wasn't so sure, I thought. But if Kevin wanted me to have it, it must mean something.

I laid face down on the metal bed and opened the pocket-sized book, starting on page one. As I read, I thought about the day that Kevin had left. My parents hadn't warned me, and he was suddenly in a car outside and I couldn't say goodbye. I'd watched from the window as his new social worker drove away with him.

I was five, and my brother was gone. He was replaced so quickly, and no one talked about what had happened.

That was how we were. We never talked about what happened.

And that was why I was so lost. I needed to get these feelings out of my head, and I had no one to confide in. My dad always told me to get over it if I wanted to talk about what had happened at the hospital. Or with Kevin. Or my mom.

I couldn't get over it. I was racking up losses and breaking inside.

I suddenly felt like I was five again. Kevin was gone again and I'd never gotten a chance to say goodbye.

Kevin had come to see me. I hadn't seen him for several years. He had lived with us briefly a few years ago after he'd been sick and was released from the hospital, but not since my father remarried. He lived with my mom a bit too, but I had no idea where he was living now. He'd spent the rest of his teen years in foster care, but he was an adult now.

I read several chapters of the small pocket Bible, but I didn't understand it. I eventually fell asleep, wondering if my life would ever make sense again.

The next morning, I was told it was my court date. My belongings were placed in the waiting police car, and I was instructed to get in. I watched as we drove back towards my hometown, and I recognized the building where I was. We were at the county courthouse. I'd never been inside before. Everything was so new and so frightening to me.

After meeting for two or three minutes with my public defender, I was led into a courtroom. There was a judge sitting at the front of the room, my father at the other table with his briefcase, and my public defender. I sat down when the lawyer instructed me to sit.

The judge read the charges. Running away, extradited back from California. He asked my father if he would take me back.

My dad stood up and methodically began to open his briefcase. I'd seen that look on his face before; that dispassionate expression he used when he talked about my brother and all the things he'd done. He started to speak about what a difficult child I was, the mistakes that I had made.

I stood up. "No, I won't go back," I said. I had yet to learn courtroom etiquette, but that was enough for the judge. I was suddenly placed in the state's custody, and I would not be going back to my father's home.

He looked at me, a stern look across his face. I didn't care. I couldn't live in that house anymore. Memories started flooding back into my mind. I remembered what had happened when I was eleven.

I was escorted out of the courtroom, but not before I recognized the bailiff. He was my basketball coach from a few years ago. Shaking his head slowly, with a disappointed look on his face.

How could I explain to him, or to anyone really, what it was like at my dad's house? How I had to walk on eggshells around this new wife of his, who was so apt to break under the stresses of this world? Who frequented the mental hospital for deep depression, hated children, and clearly despised me? How could I explain that my life was falling apart, and that I needed some sense of control over something, anything? I couldn't explain, because I had no way to verbalize what I needed or even why. It would take me years to understand what was driving me away.

I followed the lawyer out of the room. Nobody cuffed me again. I was introduced to a social worker, who explained that she was now in charge of my case. I asked her if I could live with my mother.

She shook her head. "Absolutely not," she told me.

13
FOSTER CARE

The social worker led me to her car. A standard, state issued car. I was not forced to sit in a backseat with handcuffs. I sat in the front seat, next to her. I rubbed absently at my wrists where the handcuffs had been as she drove. Soon, we were in a neighboring town, where I was taken to a large brick house. This was a group home, I was told. There were several other kids here.

I was introduced to the adults who ran the program. They showed me to my room, and then explained the rules. My social worker asked me what school I wanted to attend.

"Can I go back to my old junior high?" I asked.

Yes. I could. Relief mixed with slight trepidation.

"Can I see my mom soon?"

"No," was her answer. My father had been my guardian, so it was his call. Which literally made no sense, considering that I was now a Ward of the State.

There's something hard and cruel about suddenly becoming a foster child. I remembered when my brother had been taken away. I remembered the multiple visits to my house by CPS when I was growing up, and them deciding to leave me with my father. I cursed at my social worker and hurried off to my new room. No, I had not returned to North Carolina as the same person, and the new me was angry and ready for a fight.

My former junior high was located along a major road in my hometown. Typical for the region, there were two churches on opposing corners across the street. Adjacent to the school was the nature museum that I'd wandered through when I'd run away locally a few years earlier. Across from the museum was the library. The school bore a striking difference to those I'd seen during my brief California visit; there were no fences or walls.

The school was designed as an open campus, a throwback to safer times. Grade levels were organized in separate areas, and it was rare for kids to cross from one region of the school to another for their classes.

When I arrived at the office with a staff member from my new group home, stacks of new paperwork had to be completed and filed. I was suddenly a foster child. I'd missed a month of school by then; I'd started my eighth-grade school year as a seemingly normal teen from a respected family and returned as a broken shell of my former self.

Reality set in as I was escorted back to my first period classroom. I was twenty minutes late. Every eye in the class turned to face me, and the teacher had a strange look on her face. It was immediately apparent that the kids knew I'd left for California. That meant that my brother Nick must have said something.

The teacher directed me to my old seat. It was weird to think I'd only sat in it for one week of the school year before leaving, and then it had remained empty.

Waiting. But not really waiting; life had gone on. These kids had continued learning about math, science, English, and history. My education had been painfully different.

I sat down in my desk and tried to ignore the giggles from a row of popular girls. One of the ringleaders, Kylie, whispered loudly, "When I went to California, my parents took me to Disneyland."

Another girl teased from behind me. "Where did you stay? I heard you were homeless."

I sunk down into my chair and squeezed my eyes shut. Time and distance had made me forget how much I'd hated this school, hated these kids. My childhood tormentors. Fellow students who picked on the weak, and I'd certainly been weak when I'd tried navigating a world that didn't make sense. When I'd been fighting publicly with my brother since elementary school. When my strange mom had picked me up in her giant blue car, her hands always shaking as a side effect from a medication given to treat another side effect from a psych med. I stared at the blank piece of paper in front of me and found that for once, I had no pictures to draw. No story to write.

The rest of the day continued with the same hushed whispers and taunts. "Did you meet any movie stars?" someone snickered. I bit down on my lip and wondered what Scarecrow was doing. Had he found a new girlfriend? Would he still be there when I got back? I remembered he told me his family lived in Alaska. Would he go back to them, after he got out of jail? The officers had placed handcuffs on him, too, back at the drop-in shelter. It had been a crime to hang out with me.

I ran into Nick during passing period, but he passed by like he hadn't seen me. I called his name and he kept walking. Apparently, my leaving had severed our tenuous connection to each other. Part of me had hoped that he understood, but the heavier part of me, the one that always bore the weight of my father's harsh criticisms, knew that it wasn't safe for him to talk to me. Nick had learned to keep his mouth shut and move forward. A safety mechanism that kept him in good favor with our father. But it was a mechanism that would continue to divide us.

By the end of the day, I was certain of two things. I did not belong here. And I did not plan to stay.

When I got back to the group home that evening, I took an inventory of what little belongings I had left. I packed everything I owned back into my backpack and remembered what the girl from the detention center had taught me. As I fell asleep, I tried to recall the locations of all the states in my mind. I retraced the states the Greyhound bus had driven me through and figured I could at least follow that path.

14
GONE AGAIN

Night became morning, and I awoke with purpose. I got dressed, ate a large breakfast, and carried my full backpack to the awaiting minivan. The group home worker was behind the wheel, waiting for each kid to get into the van. I was the last one.

By the time I was dropped off at my school, my stomach was in knots. My plan would require me to walk past my old neighborhood and across a busy intersection to get to the highway. What if someone saw me?

I hesitated and walked into school instead. When I sat down in my first period class, one of the kids whispered loudly about me living on the streets in Hollywood, and a small chorus of laughter erupted. I rolled my eyes and stared down at my paper. I hated this school and these kids. I hadn't fit in before I left, why would I expect things to be different? Why had I asked to come back here?

The bell rang, and I threw my backpack across my shoulder. As soon as class ended, I hurried off campus and made my way towards the highway. It was a brisk two-mile walk. I tried to focus my eyes straight ahead as I walked. Hopefully, no one would try to stop me.

Time to try out this hitchhiking thing. I did not have another one hundred and twenty dollars. And I wanted, needed to be anywhere but here.

I clutched the strap of my backpack, which by now contained the last of my possessions. It was too late to turn back; certainly, my group home and social worker were already aware of my absence. I hadn't arrived in my next class, and it was probably already third period by the time I made my way onto the highway. I'd made a split-second decision to go South, since I didn't have a map and I wasn't sure where I needed to go.

Cars whizzed past me, accelerating to get onto the interstate. I kept walking, certain someone would stop for me. I walked just past the entrance lane and turned to face oncoming traffic. It was now or never, I thought nervously. I had to get away.

Thumb outstretched, like in those old movies I'd seen long ago on television, I pleaded for someone to pick me up. One of these cars would stop, I told myself. If not a car, then a truck.

Cars were driving by quickly, their occupants rushing forward on their morning commutes. I started to doubt if this would work, but I kept my outstretched arm facing towards them. The hitchhiker's thumb. Someone would see me and decide to help.

I'm not sure how long I waited, but a truck did finally pull over. The tractor trailer slowed to a halt perhaps fifty yards past me. I bit down hard on my lip, fighting that forever internal debate, but chose to dash towards the waiting truck. I examined the outer structure of the door, uncertain how to proceed. The driver must have sensed my innocence and opened the door from the inside.

"Where ya headed?" I heard him asking me, in a thick Southern accent.

Middle-aged, white, more belly than hair. This would be my first ride, and the guy smiled kindly enough.

I smiled brightly, feigning confidence that I didn't have. I needed to appear older, wiser. "California."

He let out a low whistle. That was three thousand miles away from the southbound I-85 where he was picking me up. "Alright," he said. "I can drive you eighty miles or so."

Once I had climbed up into the cabin and put on my seat belt, the older man started asking me what highways I was planning to take. He must've smelled my lack of experience and started to tell me about the different roadways that connected the country. "First thing that you have to learn is all the even numbers go east to west, and the odd numbers go north to south," he said, explaining the highway numbers to me. I nodded, grateful for the lesson. "Why don't you look at that atlas I have back there?" he offered, pointing to a giant road atlas that he kept in the cabin just behind us. I peered back, noticing there was a separate sleeping area behind me. I was in awe; he could actually live in his truck.

I reached for the book and began flipping through it, until I found the large United States map. I stared at the picture, trying to memorize the pathway. I-85 south to the I-10 in Florida. Or I could cut across Georgia and get there faster. My eyes circled on a city. Atlanta.

I could memorize city names and tell drivers city by city, I thought to myself.

Atlanta. I'd never been there before.

The driver offered me a soda from his ice chest and chatted with me about truck stops and his favorite diners. When he dropped me off in the middle of South Carolina, I thanked him for the ride. He was heading down a different roadway, and he wanted me to stay on course.

Immediately I felt my heart begin to thud heavily in my chest again, full of fear and nervous anticipation. Who would pick me up next? I still couldn't believe how easy it had been to go eighty miles.

I could've done this instead of stealing from my dad. That two hundred fifty dollars was the only leverage the judge had over me in the Los Angeles courtroom. I wouldn't have signed the extradition papers if I hadn't been worried about becoming a 602.

Three rides later, I was in Atlanta. Night had fallen, and I arrived at a large truck stop shortly before midnight. I wandered inside, not sure who to ask for my next ride. The truckers had been asking on their CB radios if anyone would take a girl west, but then some of them had started asking if I was pretty or if I was willing to pay for the ride. I cringed and had not accepted any of those rides.

I went into the bathroom and straightened my hair. It was a bit frizzy, and I didn't like the way that my dirty blonde roots were starting to show. I'd been dying my hair regularly for the past two years, and it was overdue.

When I stepped out of the bathroom, a security guard passed by. I felt my palms begin to sweat but forced myself to walk the short distance to the convenience store. One of the drivers had given me ten dollars, so I had enough to buy something small. I hadn't been able to pack any food, since the people at the group home would have figured out I was leaving.

I walked through the store slowly, considering my options. I finally purchased a pack of cheap crackers with cheese; those unnaturally orange square crackers that come six to a pack. I clutched them in my hand and walked outside, towards the large lot full of awaiting tractor trailers.

I greedily ate my first cracker while wandering around. There were a dozen rows of trucks. I made my way down the third row and started to look for any drivers near their vehicles.

A finger suddenly tapped on my shoulder. I turned around, startled. It was the security guard from inside.

"What are you doing?" he asked.

"Um…" I paused.

"Come with me," he told me. He grabbed my arm and dragged me inside, where he marched me into a small office and told me to sit down. I sat in a plastic chair and swallowed hard.

He picked up the phone and called the police.

My eyes darted towards the door. He glared at me.

"Nope," he told me, confirming what I already knew. I was trapped.

A short time later, the police arrived. They asked me for identification, which I didn't have. They made me tell them my name, age, date of birth. The security guard folded his arms over his chest. "We're pressing charges," he said.

"What?" I asked, incredulously.

"Criminal trespass," one of the officers said. I felt my eyes grow wide. No. No. Not a criminal charge.

Handcuffs slid onto my hands, and just before the second hand was cuffed, my backpack was expertly removed from my back. "Let's go," one of the officers told me.

I nodded, following in step with him. I knew the drill already.

He drove me across town, to their juvenile detention facility. It was a tall building, across from the Atlanta Braves stadium. I went through the routine I'd come to know too well; interrogation, shower, change into whatever outfit they made the juvies wear, go to cell. I was locked into my cell and began my countdown to court.

It was a process that would repeat several more times before my hometown judge would grow sick of me. I would get extradited, flown home, and placed back in the detention center. I would go to court, get released to foster care, and leave again.

My next stop was Tennessee, then New York. I spent a week at a woman's apartment in the Bronx, freezing and starving, before I ventured out to the city. I tried to stay at their teen shelter, called the Covenant House, but I didn't like it. I wandered into Manhattan and found my way to the train station. I had just enough for a bus to New Jersey, so I took it. There was snow on the ground and I was cold. At least the lady in the Bronx had given me an old coat to keep me warm.

I hitchhiked across New Jersey. I was thirteen still and so sure of myself. After all, don't all thirteen-year-old kids know everything? I had walked across the tallest bridge I had ever seen, which bordered Pennsylvania and New Jersey. I crossed into the Pennsylvania side, grateful that I was so close to a resting place. I had slowly passed the signs announcing the upcoming Pennsylvania Welcome Center and could almost feel the warmth. As I approached, I clutched my last coins between my fingers, anxious to buy something to eat. I was new to hunger, and still trying to adjust to going days without eating. Compounding the situation was the amount of walking required when nobody stopped to offer me a ride. At times, I felt like I would have to walk the whole way to California.

Somehow, I conquered my fear of heights and made it over the bridge, but I hadn't prepared myself for what would happen next. After I had gone inside and changed clothes, freshened up a little, and bought a snack with the last of my change, I went outside to find a ride.

And walked right past a highway patrol officer. He wasn't like the other officers that I had met; he was angry and let me know it. What right did I have to be so far away from home? What if I got myself killed?

Didn't he know that I didn't care? That I didn't see an end in sight for myself? Who would I be, when I was from a family who despised me? Who could I become, besides the daughter of a crazy woman? That was what they expected of me, so why not give them what they wanted? It was the self-fulfilling prophecy of my youth.

The officer had slapped the cuffs on my wrists, harder than I was accustomed to. Pain seared through my arms. I twisted and cried, trying to break free. But there was no escape. I reluctantly followed the officer to his patrol car and watched in horror as we approached an older building that looked more like a fortress than a juvenile detention center. I spent the next week in a cold juvenile hall in Wilkes-Barre before getting sent back to North Carolina again.

This time, the judge was livid. I was costing my small town a lot of money in plane tickets. "We'll try something different," he told me. He sentenced me to the state's mental hospital, all the way in Fayetteville. I shuddered. That would be hard to escape from, I thought to myself. And buried in the middle of the state.

15
LAST CHANCE

When I arrived at the hospital, I was immediately struck by how different it was from the one I'd been in at eleven years old. The other kids and I were all there on court orders, and no one seemed all that crazy to me. Everyone had a story about trying to escape something or someone, and many of them had been in and out of juvenile halls for a while.

On my third day, I was informed I had a court hearing scheduled to determine if I had to stay in the hospital. Confused, I followed the group of newly hospitalized teens to an awaiting van. They drove us across town to a courthouse, where we would each sit in front of the judge and plead our case.

I waited for my turn and saw the judge wasn't really listening. He agreed with every sentence, some even before the teens spoke. I felt anger coursing through my body. Fine, I thought.

A younger girl, Jennifer, was standing next to me when I saw it. I turned to look at one of our orderlies from the hospital. "Hey, I need to go to the bathroom," I told him. The judge had ordered a thirty-day evaluation period for me, and there was no way I was willing to stay in a hospital for that long.

She saw a strange look on my face and said, "Yeah, me too. Girl stuff."

We only had two male orderlies with us, but several of the kids were still waiting to see the judge. "Go ahead," the one closest to us said. "But hurry up."

"Okay," I said, and darted down the staircase to a bathroom just at the edge of his peripheral vision. I opened the door quickly and made sure it closed loudly. Jennifer was on my heels.

"Now," I said, and we immediately crept back out. I glanced up. The orderly wasn't looking. No one was. We hurried down the rest of the stairs and exited the building.

When we got outside to the street, we both inhaled the free air. "We have to run," I said to my new accomplice.

And run, we did. We darted across town, in between buildings, until we'd arrived in a small neighborhood. We sat down for a few minutes to catch our breath.

"Now what?" Jennifer asked.

I smiled. "We find a ride."

We asked an older guy where the interstate was and begged for a ride. He eyed the two of us suspiciously, but obliged. Soon we were at the interstate.

No backpack, nothing more than the clothes on our backs. "Let's go," I told her. I thrust my hitchhikers' thumb out and she copied me. We watched as cars passed us by, and eventually one stopped for us.

"Where to?" the driver asked. He looked us over carefully.

"Durham," I said. I knew by now that I could never say anything far away, like California. People wanted to hear nearby locations, or they got nervous and asked how old you were. That was probably a few hours away, but far enough that the driver would drop us off "along the way" instead of at an actual destination.

Because we had no actual destination.

My mind was still reeling that we'd gotten away. And that I was suddenly traveling with a twelve-year-old.

Several rides later, we arrived in Asheville. It was night, and snow was falling in the mountains. We'd been traveling since our escape from court in Fayetteville that morning. "Where do we go?" Jennifer asked.

I shrugged. I watched as she bummed a cigarette from an older guy and flirted with him. I'd never smoked before, but something about the warmth of a cigarette suddenly appealed to me. It was freezing outside, and we weren't dressed for this weather.

"Here," she said, passing me one. She explained to me how to inhale, and I tried. After a deep breath, I let out a fit of coughs. She laughed. "You'll learn," she teased.

We started walking through downtown Asheville, trying to figure out where we'd stay for the night. It was too late and too cold to stand by the interstate.

"I'm hungry," she said.

I nodded. Hunger was becoming my companion. All these trips, and I'd learned to ignore the gnawing feeling in my stomach. "I have a few dollars," I told her. We'd managed to get rides with a few kind people who had offered us cash for the journey.

We went into a pizza shop and split a small pizza. We both had tall glasses of ice water for our drinks to save on the cost. When we finished, I paid with exact change. There was no money for tipping when you were a runaway, I thought to myself.

We started to walk down the road, and Jennifer lit another cigarette. As soon as the cigarette touched her lips, an approaching car flashed its blue lights at us.

"Damnit," I muttered. The officers hadn't expected to find two runaways; they thought they would be writing a delinquency ticket for teen smokers. We ended the evening in separate rooms of the local detention center, in the middle of a snowstorm.

A week had passed. Quiet filled the courtroom. Everyone could feel the judge's anger towards me. I stood silently next to my court appointed attorney. There were no family members here to observe my downfall. The people who had come to know me too well, but only on the surface, bore witness to my sentencing. I recognized the stenographer, the judge, and the bailiff. They were more than tired of seeing me hauled into their courtroom, handcuffs in place, wearing wrinkled clothes that had been sealed in an airtight bag for the past few days while I'd been in detention.

"You have cost the county a lot of money," the judge said. My head hung downward and I stared at the old wooden desk in front of me and the attorney. I felt the attorney nudge my elbow, so I forced myself to face the judge. Older white man, bald head, steely gray eyes. His brow was furrowed and his face set with hot anger. Jet black robe flowing around his aging body.

"I expect that you will learn a thing or two at C. A. Dillon," I heard him say. I could feel my eyes widen with shock. Dillon was the worst possible juvenile hall. I'd been hoping for another chance, or at least, I'd hoped for somewhere less harsh. If they'd placed me at the one near Asheville, I might've even been able to escape again. But they wouldn't do that, not after I'd escaped the hospital so easily.

The judge was still yelling at me. "Two years maximum sentence," he said in the middle of his tirade. I watched his lips move around the harsh words, wondering what it must be like to sit up there, high above young people like me. When he finally seemed satisfied with his pronouncement, he lifted the gavel and smacked it across the desk.

I nodded my head slowly, accepting my fate. The bailiff indicated for me to follow him out the door, and I walked the short distance from the desk to the doorway. I followed him into the hallway, where two officers were waiting for me. Disappointment clouded the bailiff's eyes as I was escorted away. I tried to separate my memories of him as my former basketball coach; there was no way he would ever understand why or how I'd ended up in so much trouble. I hung my head down and refused to make eye contact. As I walked between the two deputies who would escort me back to detention, I realized the bailiff's opinion of me had been the only one that had affected me in that courtroom.

Resolved to my fate, I slid into the familiar back seat of the patrol car waiting to bring me back to detention. The officers told me it would be a few days before I was transferred upstate.

I watched the familiar scenes of my hometown pass by as we drove back to the detention center. Away from the town that had already forgotten me. Away from my father and stepmother. My emotions were heavy, and I needed to get back into my cell as fast as I could. I didn't want to break down in front of the officers.

A solitary tear slid down my cheek, but my hands were locked behind my back and I couldn't wipe it away. I bit down on my lower lip, trying to imagine what two years would feel like. Who would I be in two years? I'd already become someone completely different from who I'd been just a few months earlier. Desperate for anything that would make me feel safe. Desperate for a place to belong. And that belonging wouldn't happen here. I couldn't verbalize how broken and traumatized I'd already become, but I was lost and searching for anywhere I could belong.

I'd been awarded a consolation prize in a twisted game of life. Two years in maximum security. I squeezed my eyes shut and ignored the sting of tears that fell for the rest of the ride. The officers probably noticed but didn't say a word.

16
C.A. DILLON

The long car ride to Butner, North Carolina felt like an eternity. I watched the road closely, memorizing the distance from here to there. It was what I did; I captured my surroundings in my memory and always sought an exit strategy. I bit my lip, realizing I'd been searching for an escape ever since the mental hospital two years earlier. Maybe even before that, when I'd mailed off for all the brochures about boarding schools.

No one had asked me what was making me run. I was just a spoiled kid costing my county too much money. I'd never had anyone sit me down and try to figure out the cascade of events that had set everything into motion.

When the patrol car finished its three-hour journey in front of the fortress that would become my new home for the next two years, the officer turned off the engine and turned around to face me. He had fatherly eyes, but harsh words. We hadn't spoken much during the ride. Most of the officers in my hometown had grown tired of driving me everywhere, and there had been times when I'd been mean and told them how I really felt.

"Well, you got what you wanted," he said. The officer beside him nodded his head in agreement.

"No, I didn't," I interjected.

"Let me finish," the officer said. "You're the one that kept running away. This is the one place you can't run away from. It's time for you to figure out how to stay out of trouble," he said.

I bit down on my lip, angry and afraid that I might start crying again. They opened their doors and walked around to the trunk, retrieving a folder to explain my history to my new captors.

The driver opened my door and helped me out. I instantly felt the coldness of the wintry air as I stepped outside. It was early December.

I stood and tried to stretch my arms, but they were still trapped together by an unforgiving pair of handcuffs. They'd tightened during the ride, but the officers had refused to pull over and loosen them. "Are you trying to escape?" the passenger had asked when I'd asked for him to help, chuckling.

They walked me towards the administration building, which was the front entrance. The building was older, unassuming. It was a light-colored brick building that looked more like it should house offices and business people, rather than serve as an entryway into hell. We had driven down a long road to arrive here, and the roadway and the prison were surrounded by oak and elm trees, as well as a forest of evergreens and other foliage. "There's quicksand out there," the driver had told me, laughing softly. "If you try to escape, you won't make it very far."

A thick fence with rows of coiled barbed wire at the top surrounded the compound, and the only break in the fence was the main building. We slowly marched up the steps, and I sucked in my last breath of not-quite free air before we stepped into the small building.

"Got one for you," the second officer said, handing the paperwork to an awaiting guard. He flipped it open and nodded. "Have a seat," he told me, and I moved slowly to the row of chairs against the wall. The driver stood by me, restless. I was an escape artist. He would not leave my side.

I wondered for the first time if the orderly in Fayetteville had gotten into trouble because of me. I glanced up at the officer. It had been almost a month by then. I would've been released from the hospital soon, if I'd stayed. Instead, now, I was awaiting the start of my two years.

And those two years wouldn't begin until I was taken to the other side of this building.

My heart sped up and I felt breathless. How could I make it in there for two years? All the other kids at the detention center had warned me that Dillon was the roughest prison in the state.

And I'd been sent here for misdemeanor larceny. In the end, they'd charged me with theft from my dad. He'd helped them place me here.

I glanced up at the officer again. He was grinding his teeth. Waiting to deposit me in my cell and drive away. My eyes traveled the room; to the guard, sifting through my court orders, to the second officer, to the doorway. There was no escape. Quicksand. We were a long way from the interstate.

Butner. I was a long way from home. California was calling, and I couldn't go there for at least two more years.

I bit down harder on my lip, this time drawing blood. Since when had I been picturing California as home? I hadn't even realized it until that moment. But yes, that was home. There was nowhere else I'd felt free. Nowhere else I'd felt like I could just be me.

Finally, the paperwork phase ended. The officers stood near me, between me and the door. I wanted to tell them, "Don't worry. I know I can't run this time," but I didn't. I waited impatiently for the cuffs to come off.

The second officer removed them slowly and let out a low whistle. "These were on pretty tight," he acknowledged as he wrestled to get them back off.

When the thick metal bracelets were removed, I rubbed the bright pink circles on my wrists. Pain seared through my wrists to my hands, and my fingers started to regain their feeling. I'd been feeling pins and needles in my fingertips for the past hour.

"Do better," the driver told me.

"We don't want to drive you anymore," the second officer said.

I nodded slowly. Their send-off speeches left much to be desired. I swallowed hard and turned to face the guard in front of me. The officers stood behind me until I was taken across the building, and out the back door.

Beyond the fences, there was a long field of frostbitten grass and scattered trees, and several smaller brick buildings. They were distanced from each other. I would learn later that there were three cottages; one for girls and two for boys. Each cottage had a central room with windows that could view each of three dayrooms, or "wings." Each dayroom housed one set of girls, with industrial sofas, a small table, chairs, a bookshelf, and a television mounted on the wall. The dayroom was attached to a bathroom, replete with three toilet stalls and a connected shower. The shower could accommodate three girls at a time. There was a large window along the shower wall, so that the guards could watch the girls while they took showers. An adjacent door connected to a long hallway, with individual cells located on each side. Each wing of the building could hold fifteen inmates. The guard walked me to the first cottage.

The only other two buildings on the property were a small church near the front of property, and the largest building towards the back, which was the school. There were sidewalks connecting the buildings to each other, and a large grassy field with a baseball diamond behind the school. Every building sat far enough away from the tall fences that everything was visible, and the lawn was well manicured. Rumors soon confirmed what the officers from my hometown had told me; there were numerous pockets of quicksand in the forest beyond the compound, and the guards would tell stories of attempted escapees who would wander in circles until being apprehended. This was maximum security, after all. We weren't meant to leave before our time.

The guard oriented me to the program and told me that I would stay up to two years. That was the first time that I'd heard that phrase. "I can stay less than two years?" I wanted to know.

"There's a point system, based on good behavior. Since you have a conditional sentence, if you make it to level five you can leave early."

"Really?" I asked, a strange feeling beginning in my chest. The beginnings of hope.

The guard explained the point system to me, and I listened eagerly. Either I made it to level five, or I stayed for two years. How hard could that be, to behave? I had never really been too much of a troublemaker, just a lost soul. I listened as the guard continued explaining different types of sentences.

Everyone started on level one, and they could only leave if they were level five and if they had a conditional sentence. Like mine. People with obligatory sentences until age eighteen or even twenty-five knew that no amount of "good behavior" would ever grant them leniency. There were no parole hearings for minors; each sentence was carved in stone.

It was my first day; a chilly winter evening in my new prison home. A prison of my own making. I had waited until after all the other girls had left the bathroom before I entered the cold, tiled room that evening. I could still hear the chatter of voices on the other side of the thin wall, and the guard passed by the shower window and yelled out a ten-minute warning. Whether I liked it or not, I had to move forward. And moving forward included showering in public.

I slowly undressed in one of the bathroom stalls. I could hear the turn of the key in the lock outside of the dayroom, which was adjacent to the bathroom. I wrapped myself in a towel and crept towards the open shower. There was a window on one side, which revealed the dayroom. The other girls had begun their task of cleaning. One was sweeping, one was wringing out the mop.

My trembling hand reached for the dial, and a spray of cool water began. I glanced at the window again, grateful that no one was watching me. I removed my towel and moved forward.

As my hand reached upwards to lather cheap shampoo into my scalp, I felt the first sting of hard wood against my back. Suddenly I was surrounded, and I was bombarded by fists, brooms, and mops. I whipped my body around, ready to fight, but I realized that I was outnumbered. "Bitch," I heard one of them snarl at me. I crouched down into the fetal position; covering my head with my arms and endured their continued blows. Minutes passed, or maybe just mere seconds. When they finished, I quickly turned off the water and wrapped myself with my now-wet towel.

"Five minutes," I heard the guard call out. I quickly redressed, rubbing the towel against my face to dry my tears. I walked slowly out of the bathroom, tossing the useless towel into the dirty clothes bin as I left. The girls were clearing out of the dayroom and heading towards their cells for the night.

I did not let my eyes meet with those of the guard. I wasn't ready for what I might see. Instead, I wrapped my arms over my chest and walked down the short hallway to my cell.

Thirteen years old. As the lights went out for the night and I heard the click of the lock as I was closed into my new cage, I finally let myself cry freely. Quietly. I hadn't even made it through the first day before getting beaten down. How would I survive two years of this awful place?

17
FREEDOM IN SPADES

The next day brought more of the same fists and curses. I was a target; the youngest in the group, and obviously very white. The girls let me know immediately that they ruled over me. I felt their fists against my back, my head, my stomach. If I went to the bathroom, I was cornered. They sneered under their breath when guards weren't paying attention. The leader of the group, Rashida, had pronounced to everyone that I was a stupid white bitch and they would break me.

The beatings continued every day and every night for the first two weeks. I couldn't remember a single night I hadn't cried myself to sleep, and I still had one hundred and two weeks left. I didn't even want to calculate how many days that was.

At least when I went to school, nobody hit me. We were intermingled with the other groups, so I was slowly meeting the other girls from my cottage, as well as the boys. I befriended a fifteen-year-old boy, Reggie, and during free play time I sat in the gym playing cards with him and some of the other guys. He had tight, curly black hair that spread freely in all directions, with a tall comb pushed deep into the afro. He was planning to get it braided that evening, he'd told me. I imagined that if it had been another time or place, I could've had a crush on that boy. He was getting released soon, so he kept his head low and behaved. And here I was, starting out my two years.

Reggie shuffled the cards, then began to deal them to the four of us. I sat across from him, his tentative partner in a battle of spades. They'd been teaching the game to me over the past week, and I was getting good at following Reggie's signals. I watched as he dealt the cards quickly around the table, his hands interchanging cards faster than our opponents could see. He had "stacked the deck," again, and made sure he had the best cards for himself, and a few good ones for me.

We each picked up our cards and I stared pensively at my hand. Reggie raised an eyebrow and I nodded slowly. "Ten," he said. The other team bid five. Someone was going down. I glanced at my hand, then at Reggie. Four spades, but all low numbers. Ace of hearts, ace of clubs, ace of diamonds. I'd seen him set the deck, and I knew he had the high spade. He winked at me discreetly.

Kareem was sitting on my right. He threw down his first card. Queen of hearts. He was gauging who had which card. I smiled and tossed my ace on the table. Reggie tapped the table once. I nodded and tossed out a low heart for the next round. He won the round with his King of hearts. We went back and forth, winning books.

Clubs were up next. Reggie threw out a seven of clubs, waiting for me to win the round. I tossed down my ace of clubs, ordering my hand to grab the book. But then Brian, who sat to my left, threw a five of spades on the table. Crap. He was out of clubs.

Reggie shrugged and watched as the next cards came out. He won the next round, then led with spades. Ace. King. Queen. Jack. Everyone ran out of spades, so we took the rest of the books. Our opponents had their one book, and we had twelve. "Great hand, partner," Reggie said. I beamed at him. If only the entire next two years could be spent in this gym, away from the beatings I'd been receiving in the cottage.

As we played, we chatted. From that small table in the gym, my nickname emerged. The boys thought it was hilarious I'd run away to California, and they told me I would be known as "Lil Hollywood" from that point on. I laughed, grateful someone finally understood that my heart was elsewhere.

A whistle blew from the edge of the gym. Automatically, we each stood and pushed our chairs under the table. Reggie gathered all the cards quickly and replaced them in the box, shoving them into his pocket. I smiled again. If only, I thought to myself. Different world, different circumstances.

I lived in fear for my first few weeks. Beatings were common and unpredictable. But I wanted to go up on my level. I wanted freedom.

One day, one of the guards asked me to come sit with her in the central area between the three wings. Glass walls on all sides of me allowed everyone to see that she was talking to me. Bruises lined my arms, all in different stages of healing. Some were fresh.

I expected her to ask me who was hitting me. She didn't.

"You need to fight back," she told me.

"What?" I asked, my voice hushed.

"This won't stop until they believe that you're strong. To them, you're weak."

I stared down at my arms and pulled the sweater they'd given me down just enough to cover the bruises. "Are we done yet?" I asked, anger filling my words. I understood what she was telling me, but I also knew she was blaming me. The beatings were somehow my fault. My desire to earn points had made me a target.

"Think about it," she told me as she put me back on the A wing.

I marched across the room and sat against the wall, on the floor. I wasn't willing to sit on the sofas anymore; people could attack me from behind. I never went to the bathroom during the day anymore either; I'd been beaten in the stalls. I faced the other girls and waited. A shoe flung across the room and hit me in my chest.

I leaned forward and picked up the shoe from where it had fallen. If only I could throw it back at them.

If only I could just leave.

I set the shoe down beside me and stared straight ahead.

That night, I awoke with a strange feeling. Every part of me felt cold, but there was something else.

A chill burrowed deep inside my bones, and even when I squeezed my eyes shut, I couldn't imagine anywhere beyond these walls and these fences. I tried to remember warmth, and California sunlight. Nothing came to mind. I needed to remember anywhere but here.

My body ached. When I opened my eyes and took in the sight of those same cinder block walls, that same small box that I'd been caged inside of like an animal for the past several weeks, I felt familiar tears trickling down my cheeks.

Minutes dragged on slowly, as if time itself had cursed me. I allowed the beginnings of daylight to creep into the otherwise unlit room, and my eyes slowly adjusted to the familiar sights; wash basin, cold metal toilet, door, barred window above my head. Metal bed with almost nonexistent mattress underneath me. Large cockroach staring at me from the middle of my too-thin blanket that covered my chest.

I screamed and jumped up, needing to escape another giant "water bug." I flung the blanket away from me, hearing groans from some of my now-awakened neighbors. The sun promised light but no warmth, and I stood in the corner of the room shivering and crying. This was my punishment for trying to get away. I had to bear this punishment, this sentence, for up to two years. And now I'd pissed off the other girls again by screaming. They would pay me back in the morning.

"Sorry," I mumbled through the walls. "Cockroach scared me."

Tears fell like a waterfall after a hurricane. Crying was a common occurrence. I'd been called Baby by some of my fellow inmates, who swore I was lying about my charge. Thirteen years old and the youngest female inmate in the state's maximum-security juvenile prison. A flight risk because I would do anything to get away from the place that brought me so much pain. For misdemeanor larceny. For stealing two hundred and fifty dollars from my father so that I wouldn't starve when I ran away from my severely dysfunctional home.

I kicked the wall and stifled a cry in pain. It was useless; there was no one to rescue me from the tiny cage I'd entrapped myself in. No one understood my rage; everyone assumed my family was perfect, that I was just a bratty kid. No one heard my screams for help. I just needed to exist without being a burden to the rest of the world. I just needed to be free without being penalized for escaping a place that made me feel like my feet were already sinking into a shallow grave.

I sat down in the corner and watched another set of cockroach antenna poke up around the edge of the metal toilet. They were everywhere, and I could not escape them. I picked up my flip flops and went on a rampage, trying to kill every cockroach that I could see. I could kill them now, but I would never feel clean; never feel like I was in a room devoid of insects that would trample on me while I slept.

Christmas came. My social worker drove up from my hometown several days before Christmas to deliver me a present. She brought me a bag of clothes; nothing special, but much better than the three outfits I'd been living in since I'd arrived. I'd showed up with nothing more than the clothes on my back; I'd lost small pieces of my belongings all over the country, including my backpack in Fayetteville. My caseworker at Dillon had found two more outfits for me so I would have some clothes to wear until they found a better option.

My social worker told me she'd called my dad, but he'd refused to send clothes. I was a Ward of the State, after all. He'd complained he was a victim, and I'd stolen money from him. She'd decided to go shopping for me instead. She gave me several sweatshirts and sweatpants. A few t-shirts, new undergarments and socks. A pair of shoes. The cheap stuff that can be bought at Walmart. And they were all the right size.

I thanked her profusely. Her visit was the first moment of kindness I'd had in weeks. She raised an eyebrow when she saw my arms, but I quickly covered up with a sweatshirt.

A church group came to visit and they brought Southern style Christmas food and presents. I sat between two girls who had been beating me senseless and feigned a smile when they said their Hallelujahs and Praise Jesuses. I accepted a new Bible from the church group; I'd left mine in my belongings at Fayetteville.

When I was locked back in my cell that night, I realized the guard had been right. This would never change. The girls would never stop hitting me. We'd finished our Christmas celebration and I'd had to go to the bathroom. I couldn't wait until I was locked in my cell.

Rashida had met me in the bathroom and punched me hard in my gut. She'd then smacked the back of my head when I'd tried to turn away. Afterwards, I threw up my Christmas dinner.

I stared at myself in the mirror, trying to recognize the sad girl that was reflected at me. My head stung where I'd been punched, and my stomach still ached. My throat was raw from vomiting. I hated them, and I hated myself.

Yes, I would fight back.

18
SELF DEFENSE

It happened the following week. I was sitting in English class, and someone threw something at me when the teacher's back was turned. She had no idea I was being assaulted everywhere; in the cottage, in the bathroom, in her classroom.

I stood up and screamed. I was filled with rage. How many more beatings would I have to endure? I picked up the object from the floor; a book. They'd thrown a book at me?

The teacher turned around and yelled at me to sit down. "You're getting a major!" she yelled.

I glared at her. A major? A major violation for screaming? I'd been beaten for weeks. We were already in January, and I'd been suffering at the hands of my cottage-mates for over four weeks. No one had gotten punished for any of the things they'd done to me.

"Fuck you, you stupid bitch!" I screamed at her. "Nobody likes you, and you're a horrible teacher!" I yelled. I dropped the book to the floor and picked up my desk. It was one of those heavy desk and chair combos. I picked it up and threw it against the ground, probably not moving it more than a few inches. "Fucking bitch!" I added for good measure. "Give me my fucking major, I don't care!"

By then, the guards were in the classroom and they saw me standing up in the center of a shocked group of students. The quiet girl had finally lost it. The chair was lying on its side next to me, and the book had been kicked away as I'd beaten up the chair. Instinctively, I knew better than to throw anything at anyone, or to hit anyone in front of the guards. I was there on a misdemeanor. A non-violent offense. Everyone else around me was there on felony charges; some for assault, robbery, attempted murder, murder, criminal threats. And I was mixed in with the masses, for stealing money from my dad.

"Let's go!" one of the guards told me angrily.

I darted an exasperated look at the teacher again as they led me away. She was tall, thin, with short hair that reminded me of my stepmom. She was trembling in the front of the classroom. I smiled and waved goodbye. "Bye, bitch!" I called out before the door was closed.

They walked me back to the cottage. Two guards to escort me. I shrugged. "Whatever," I muttered as they told me I was in big trouble.

When we entered the cottage, the few girls who were on lockdown stood from each of their wards and walked to the window to see what was happening. The guards sat me down in the middle and began reprimanding me.

Then the guard who'd told me to fight walked in. "We can't put her back in the same wing now," she said, her eyes meeting with mine as she spoke. "Move her to the C wing," she told them.

I glanced at the other two guards, hopeful. They were going to move me?

"Alright," one of them said.

An older woman stood from the office and walked across the room. She walked slowly, her ancient hips carrying her across the room defiantly. She opened the lock on the C wing. "Go on inside, we'll get your stuff," she told me.

I nodded. "Yes, ma'am," I told her. I hurried onto my new unit, grateful and hoping for fewer beatings.

I couldn't hear what they were talking about, but I settled into one of the sofa chairs and smiled despite my situation. I hadn't felt safe in a sofa chair in the center of the dayroom since the day I'd arrived. Everything had changed, in just one violent outburst. Somehow, I'd been rewarded for throwing a chair.

It would take me two months to regain my privileges to get off the unit again. I'd gotten myself in a lot more trouble than I'd realized, but I didn't care. I read every book on the unit, and I befriended the other girls on C wing. We watched soap operas by day and ate microwaved popcorn by night. My social worker left me ten dollars a month for snacks, and I bought popcorn and Cheetos once a week from the machine. I poured the Cheetos into the bag of freshly hot popcorn and shook the bag, as I'd been taught by my wing-mates. We spent our free time playing cards, doing hair, reading, and watching television. And there was certainly a lot of free time.

My dad still hadn't visited. I called him once, and he told me that he wished I was home. I hung up the phone. If he wished I was home, he shouldn't have pressed charges, I later complained to my caseworker when she asked me why I'd hung up the phone.

"What do you mean?" she asked.

"My dad. He pressed charges against me for stealing money."

"How much?" she asked.

"Two hundred and fifty dollars."

She shook her head. "What were your other charges?"

I shrugged. The trespassing charge in Georgia had been thrown out when I agreed to extradition and had promised not to return. "Running away," I said.

"That isn't possible," she said. "This is maximum security."

I stared at her for a long moment. She was my caseworker, and she clearly hadn't even looked at my file. "Yes, it is," I told her. "That's all I did."

She stared at me, certain that I was lying. She let me back onto C wing and I watched her make a beeline to the office where all our files were kept. Afterwards, I saw her staring at me strangely, but she never spoke about it to me again.

19
REGGIE

When my two months of isolation ended, and I'd done daily extra chores to earn points, I was freed to go back to school. By then, I felt different. No one had hit me since I'd moved to C wing. The girls were calm, peaceful. Trying to live out their sentences or work the program. Most of us were in foster care, and only a few people were aiming to go back home.

I walked in the familiar line back to school. A few of the A wing girls eyed me curiously, but the girls on my wing had told them to leave me alone. I was quiet, harmless really. And there was that one incident where I'd lost it and thrown a chair.

I sat down in my new classes, ready for a fresh start. I'd been placed in typing class, Spanish class, English, math, and art. We were making silk-screened shirts in art class. And Reggie was in the class. "Hey, Li'l Hollywood," Reggie said when I'd arrived in class. I smiled sheepishly. It'd been too long since I'd been around my spades-playing friends.

The teacher walked around the class to check on everyone. I was standing next to Reggie by the art table, admiring his work. He'd made a silhouette of Martin Luther King, Jr, and it would be designed into a t-shirt with the "I have a Dream" speech. Each of us would get a shirt. "Very nice, Reggie," the teacher said as he passed by.

"I like it," I told him softly. He smiled.

And then he frowned. "I'm getting released next week."

I bit down on my lip. Everything good in my life always got taken from me, I thought bitterly. "That's great," I told him. "Are you excited?"

He shrugged. "Nervous, actually."

We finished art class and I headed off to Spanish class. The teacher began a lesson, and I struggled with the pronunciation of basic, three letter words. "Say it again," she repeated, staring at me. The girl who had thrown a chair. "*Muy.*" (m-we).

I mispronounced it a few more times before I finally got it right. "*Muy bien,*" she told me. I stared back at her, confused. She smiled. "*Muy bien* means 'very good.'"

After Spanish, we had gym time. I played a round of cards with Reggie and his friends. "You got better when you were on lockdown," one of the guys said. I looked up and smiled.

"Nothing better to do," I told him, laughing.

Reggie smiled. "I'm going to miss these moments," he told the group. A heavy silence filled the four of us, but it soon passed as the whistle blew. Lunch time.

I followed my group to the lunch room and continued making my way through my first day back. Math was easy. English was a relief; I'd run out of books to read in the cottage. Typing was a bit of a challenge, since I'd never learned how to type properly, and my fingers always plucked the letters individually.

The teacher whacked her ruler next to me when I lifted my hands from the keyboard. "Not like that," she demanded.

I replaced them on the keys and tried again, but then lifted my hands up, feeling air between them and the keyboard. The ruler smacked next to me again. I cringed. I couldn't do this.

At the end of the day, I realized I only hated one class; typing. At least my return to school had been better. They hadn't put me back in the same English class.

I was wearing my brand-new Martin Luther King, Jr. shirt and sitting at the table in the gym when I heard the news. Reggie had gotten out a few days earlier, and one of the guys came to our table and dropped the news onto us. "Did you hear about Reggie?" he asked.

I put down my cards. "No," someone said.

"He's dead."

The words hung in the air. Reggie? Dead?

"How?" someone finally asked.

"They say he had a heart attack when he was playing football."

"He loved football," one of the boys mused.

"He was using again?" another one said.

I stared at them all. The conversation was twirling from one guy to the next. The cards lay in the middle, forgotten. Reggie's deck of cards. He'd given it to the guys when he's gotten released.

"Cocaine," someone said.

The whistle blew, and we scurried to our separate lines. Our guard tried to calm us down. "Is it true?" someone said.

The guard nodded.

I bit my lip. I knew better than to cry in public.

But Reggie was gone.

I folded my arms over my shirt; the one that he had designed in art class. I looked back at the boys in another line behind our group. Everyone looked shell-shocked.

Reggie.

Gone.

20

GOOD BEHAVIOR

Another month passed. I went up a level, and my dad finally visited. He complained about the long drive and told me that Terri hadn't wanted to come because it was too far. He would visit my sister later that day, so he wouldn't drive all this way for nothing.

All this way, just to see me. I nodded. There was no point saying anything.

When he left, I forgot everything we'd talked about. It hadn't really mattered, anyway. He hadn't once asked how I was doing.

I was doing terribly.

Time continued to pass, and I wasn't sure what the future held. I was level three, and I was begging for any extra chores or assignments that could earn more points. I'd learned every chore and I was desperate for my freedom. I'd decided I would stay in whatever group home they sent me to.

But then, my caseworker announced to me that the state had given custody of me back to my dad. I couldn't go back to foster care.

I had to go back home. With him, with Terri.

I hadn't been expecting that.

One of the girls encouraged me to write a letter to my dad, telling him everything that had happened. I spent a week preparing it, and I mailed it to him. The next time I called him, I asked him if he'd received it. He changed the subject.

I forced myself to finish the phone call and ended with a polite comment. I had to make peace with them. I had nowhere else to go.

Months continued rolling by. I made it to level four, and I was permitted to join the swim team. I sucked at swimming, but there were only a few kids at level four with conditional sentences. Two guards took us to a local pool to practice swimming.

I didn't know how to dive in properly. Or any swim strokes. I knew how to swim and how to stay afloat, and I could jump in like a cannonball, but my skills were limited.

We practiced and realized we wouldn't win our upcoming competition. But we would compete.

I put on my MLK shirt and climbed into the van with the group. This was the great test for me; they were driving me off site and waiting to see if I would come back or not. They drove four of us in a van across state to Samarkand, another prison a few hours away.

The driver looked directly at me in the rearview mirror before taking us off Dillon's property. "They have quicksand there, too," she told me. I recalled a recent failed escape attempt of two boys that had left all of us on lockdown in our rooms until they were found, as well as a missing tool in woodshop that had caused everyone to stay in their rooms until it was located. In woodshop, right where the teacher had left it. I nodded.

Each of us smiled broadly as the van pulled off the property. It was my first time outside of the fences since December, and by then, over seven months had passed. It was summertime, and the trees were in full bloom. The world had continued without us.

We passed familiar towns, and then continued our trek into the countryside. Almost two hours had passed when we arrived at a road with a large sign that read Samarkand. It was a wooded area that looked more like a summer camp then a prison. A smaller fence surrounded the prison. A fence I could've climbed over.

The judge may have had a point in sending me to Dillon, I thought wryly.

We wove through the long, sprawled out parking lot until we arrived at a pool. There were dozens of kids standing around, waiting for the swim meet.

The four of us exited the van, suddenly nervous. "I suck at swimming," I confessed.

The other girl, Wendy, laughed. "Yes, you do," she said. "We all do."

We walked up a short hill and arrived at the edge of the pool. Each of us held a small bag with our new swimsuit and a towel, a gift from the prison. "Go change," the guards told us.

We turned to face them, confused. We'd never been allowed out of their sights. But they shrugged and pointed us towards the changing room.

Wendy and I studied each other in our new bathing suits for a moment. "Wait, fix the strap," Wendy told me, adjusting the strap over my back. I thanked her, and double checked her straps.

"Ready?" I asked nervously.

She nodded. We stepped back outside, into the bright sunlight. Summer sunlight, in bathing suits. It almost felt free.

I glanced around the pool, surrounded by guards. Almost free.

We joined our group and waited for our next orders. My sport would be first.

A whistle blew overhead. We were supposed to line up at the edge. The lifeguard threw an object into the pool, and we were told to dive in and collect it. Two other girls stood beside me. Each one smiled bravely. We were representing our prisons, after all.

I peered into the water at the object I was supposed to collect, then looked at the lifeguard. They would time us, and the fastest person won. Both girls went before me. I was last.

The whistle blew. I dove in, and suddenly lost my breath. I started to panic and twirled in a circle. What the hell was I doing here? I didn't belong here. I wasn't a swimmer. I started pushing water away from me, trying to find my way to the bottom. Or the top. Or anywhere. My hands swung out in front of me and I felt the bottom of the pool. I swept my hand across and found the target, grasping it tightly in my hand before spinning in another circle. Which way was up?

I swallowed another large gulp of water. My lungs burned, and I forced my eyes open. Where was the top of the water?

Everything stung, and I started swimming forward, hoping I was right. My hand hit the bottom again.

What the hell?

I flipped my body around and swam upwards. I broke water and spit up as much of what I still had in my mouth. The lifeguard helped pull me to the side, where I broke into a choking fit before I climbed out of the water.

One hand in front of the other. The hand that I raised first was the one with the target. I climbed out of the pool, and I heard the announcer speak into a microphone. "Third place, from C. A. Dillon!"

I coughed again, then threw up the excess water.

"What happened?"

I shrugged, looking at the guard who had rushed over to check on me. "I can't do this," I told her. "I don't know how to not be caged."

Pity filled her eyes, and she walked me back to where the group stood. Someone retrieved my third-place ribbon, and I sat on the towel with tears streaming down my cheeks. My one brief moment in freedom; freely swimming. But I knew I wasn't free.

"Good job," Wendy lied.

Level five. It was the end of September, and if I managed to keep my level, I could go home. My dad had driven up to Dillon to meet with the team and me, to discuss the plans for my upcoming release. I'd worked the program; I'd stayed out of trouble. Since Reggie had died, I'd poured myself into my schoolwork and the church activities. I hadn't wanted to misbehave. I'd just wanted to live. But as I'd worked my way up the program, the beatings had started again. I was level five. I would be leaving soon, unless I got a major infraction. Unless I fought back.

I'd been attacked in the school bathroom. I'd been punched in the stomach. The bruises were reappearing on my arms from quick punches in the hallway or in the lunch line.

"Her stepmom just got out of the hospital again," my dad said. "She isn't comfortable with Sheri returning home just yet."

My caseworker shuffled her papers, staring at my dad. "The other option is foster care," she said.

I sat up straight in my chair. "I'll go back to foster care," I said.

My dad shook his head. "No. They sent me a bill for the time you were in foster care."

I glared at him. "You don't understand. I worked my program. When you're level five, these girls will do anything, and I mean anything, to bring you down." I set my arms on the table, a fresh row of bruises showing. My dad looked away.

"We can set her up for foster care again," my caseworker said.

My dad paused, considering. "No, we'll take her. When should I come pick her up?"

"Next week," the caseworker said. First week of October.

I breathed a sigh of relief. He would take me back. But Terri had made it clear that she didn't want me to return home.

"As far as school," one of the teachers at the table began, "We'd like to place Sheri in the tenth grade," they told my dad.

My jaw dropped. What? They were advancing my grade?

My dad shook his head again. "No. That wouldn't be fair to her brother. He's

88

in tenth grade," he told them. "Sheri should stay in ninth grade."

"I kinda want to be in tenth grade," I said.

My dad stared at me. "No."

I shrunk back in my seat. My teacher spoke firmly, "We get a lot of students here. Sheri is one of the brightest kids we've ever had in our school." When I wasn't throwing chairs and cursing out English teachers.

"My answer is final," I heard my dad say.

"What day next week?" I asked. I could accept losing an opportunity to advance a grade, but I needed to get out of there. My back hurt from where I'd been hit that morning, and my scalp stung from having my hair pulled in the breakfast line.

"Tuesday."

21
CONDITIONAL RELEASE

Tuesday came, and my dad picked me up. I walked nervously outside, the free air feeling like poison to my lungs. I didn't know how to make it from the front door to my dad's awaiting van. Somehow, I got across the short distance.

I would apparently need to stay on probation until the end of my two-year conditional sentence. I'd finished ten months already. Which meant fourteen months of probation. Fourteen months of not running away again.

We were supposed to meet the probation officer the following morning.

I sat down in the front seat and took a deep breath. I could do this. I could be free.

As my dad drove down the long road that hid Dillon from the world, I kept reminding myself to take slow, deep breaths. Freedom burned. I was terrified and excited all at once.

Nick and Terri were waiting at home. Terri cooked one of her typical meals, and I forced myself to eat a few bites before asking to be excused. At least it didn't have any cockroaches in it. There had always been chunks of water bugs in our food at Dillon, and one day I'd found a whole bug in my breakfast, lunch, and dinner.

I wandered upstairs and listened to their conversation from halfway up the stairwell.

"Can you believe that they wanted to advance her grade?" my dad was saying.

Nick chimed in, "That wouldn't be fair."

Terri added, "It's like rewarding her for everything she's done."

Then my dad, "They said she was the brightest kid there. That isn't saying much. Those kids are-"

I shook my head and hurried up the rest of the stairs. I didn't want to hear the rest of his sentence. Fair or not, I would not be advancing to tenth grade. I would be back in my same stupid junior high with the kids that had been so mean to me before I'd left. For sure they knew I'd been to Dillon.

I laid down and tried to devise a plan for my return to school.

Sleep did not come to me on my first night home. I laid awake, listening to the sounds of cars driving by on the main road by our house. Birds and other animal life calling out. The rattling sound of wind through the trees. Just outside my window, a free world awaited.

A world I was not fully released to. I had an appointment to meet my probation officer the next morning. They'd already warned me at Dillon that any violation of my probation would mean fourteen more months. Even if it was at the very end of my two-year probation period.

When I arrived at the courthouse the following morning with my father, we were greeted by my new probation officer. She had an office down the hall from the same courtroom where I'd been sentenced all those times before. I studied her for a moment; she was an older woman with a permanent scowl on her face. Tight blonde curls, dark black blazer with starched blouse underneath and tight black pants. "If I catch you doing anything wrong, I'll send you back to Dillon," she told me.

Nice to meet you, too, I thought angrily.

Our next stop was re-enrollment in my old junior high school. I paused before getting out of the van in the now unfamiliar territory. "Dad," I said. "Tell them I was in boarding school. Don't tell them where I was," I begged.

"They already know," he told me, exiting the van decisively.

I nodded, then stood to follow him. We walked to the office, where I took a seat and waited to be processed. I was different now; I had shorter hair and my makeup style had changed when I was locked up. I'd gained some weight, thanks to months on lock down followed by many more months of limited physical activity. I would soon be the subject of the same bullying that had broken me before. Or perhaps worse.

After my dad left, I was escorted to my first class. PE. I froze in the entryway of the gym. Balls were being thrown in all directions. The staff member who had brought me there watched my face. I was pale, near tears. "What is it?" the woman asked. She knew I'd just been released from juvenile prison.

"I can't do this," I whispered. A ball flew in our direction, and I ducked too quickly. It was at least ten feet away. I turned my head, whirling around to make sure no one was coming. I was so used to being attacked that I wasn't ready for normalcy.

"Let's go back to the office," she told me. I followed behind her, still trembling from the not-so-close encounter with the dodgeball. She asked me to sit down while she made a few phone calls.

I took a seat against the wall, watching as students came in and out of the office. Not a care in the world. Comfortable clothes. Free air. Kids who had never been forced to shower in front of a guard. Kids that had never been raped. I chewed down hard on my lower lip, a bad habit. A familiar metallic taste filled my mouth. Instinctively, I reached up to blot away the trail of blood.

"Let's go," she said several minutes later. She had been watching me while talking on the phone.

I stood, following her down the hallway. It wasn't as familiar as it should've been. I'd attended all of seventh grade here, and less than two weeks of eighth grade. It was ninth grade now, my last year in this building before high school.

As we walked down the hall, she tried to make small talk with me. "How old are you now?" she asked.

"Fourteen." I fidgeted with the straps of my backpack as we walked, trying hard to focus on not biting my lip again. It still stung where I'd broken the skin.

"Do you like to read?" she asked.

I thought about it for a moment before responding. Books had kept me from losing my mind at Dillon. I'd read every single book on C wing, and I'd borrowed some from B wing when I'd run out of reading materials. I didn't ask for anything from A wing. I checked behind us before answering, "Yes." As if thinking about A wing could summons another attack.

"Good," she said, approaching a familiar doorway. "I arranged for you to work as a library assistant instead of PE."

"But don't I need PE credit?"

"The principal will allow this to count for PE credit for you. Special circumstances," she said.

I glanced down at my feet, noticing the fading bruises on my arm as I did. They knew. They were trying to make this right. "Thank you," I mumbled, afraid to ruin this kind gesture. "Ma'am," I added, remembering where I was.

The door pushed open, and I looked up. We walked in quietly, and she escorted me to the librarian's desk. "This is Sheri. She'll be your assistant for the rest of the year," she said. "In lieu of PE." A silent communication passed between them, but I pretended not to notice. They must have figured out a special rehab for broken kids like me.

"Hi," I said nervously when the librarian turned to face me.

"Have you ever worked in a library before?" she asked after the staff member had left.

I shook my head. We hadn't had a library at Dillon. Just random books on shelves in classrooms and on the wings of each cottage. Mostly old mysteries, romance novels, classics that had probably been sold at yard sales. Discarded books. Treasures during my ten months away, where I'd escaped in my mind to other worlds. Safer places.

"Well, then, let's start from the beginning," she told me.

Being a library assistant soon became my favorite class. I didn't have to interact with other kids, and I could predictably shelve books for the entire period. All I had to do was scan them in and shelve them. Eventually, she taught me to check them out, too.

The other classes weren't as comfortable. I was returned to mainstream junior high. Physical science with my brother's cross-country coach, who quickly made it clear that he knew my history. Math, English, History, and the elective wheel. I had missed my chance to get into a foreign language, and the twenty or so Spanish phrases I'd learned at Dillon wouldn't get me into a Spanish class. They were only offering French that year, anyway.

Returning to my old school had presented a new set of problems. Where had I been for the past year? Why had I left? I found it easier to lie and say that I'd been in boarding school. It was sort of like a boarding school. But with bars. And fences. And cockroaches. And too many angry girls with no chance for early release. Rashida's face flashed across my mind.

I gravitated away from the kids who I'd known since elementary school. No one would understand me anymore. At lunch, I ate alone. Afterwards, I sat by myself on the bench waiting for the bell to ring. I needed to avoid trouble for fourteen months. Each day was one day less of probation.

A girl I'd known for several years sat down next to me and asked me how I was doing. I felt comfortable talking to her, because she seemed nice. But the next day, she told me, "I told my mom about you. She said you're just feeling sorry for yourself." I watched as she walked away, surprised by how much her words hurt.

But I hadn't yet learned how to explain why I did the things I did. I just knew that I didn't want to hurt so damn much.

I fumbled my way through classes, finding that I was suddenly an outcast. The newness of not being locked in a cell was a stark contrast to my recent past. I didn't have anything in common with my peers anymore. I was constantly looking over my shoulder. I was so paranoid of whatever awaited behind me.

I began a quick path into complete isolation. Weeks turned into months, visits with the probation officer became detailed lists from my dad and stepmom, lodging their numerous complaints. "She won't wear socks." "Her room isn't clean." The same stuff. "She talked back to me at dinner." Nothing had really changed, I'd just become more withdrawn at school and I fought back against my dad and stepmom at home.

A few months passed, and slowly it dawned on me. I couldn't do this for another year. I couldn't live underneath the same roof as my dad and my stepmom. I couldn't handle being in a school where I was so isolated, and my only peace was in the library.

My stepmom wanted total control over me. She was picking me up from school, dropping me off, and watching my every move. In the same breath that she told my dad she couldn't tolerate me, she demanded to be the one who drove me everywhere. Even worse, sometimes she referred to her depression and said that she was afraid to hit kids with her car while driving. Yet, she was still supposed to drive me every day.

The streets were calling to me. Life hadn't returned to normal, because there had never been normal. I hadn't been welcomed back into a healthy, loving family, because we weren't any of those things. Nick and I were on edge. I just couldn't talk to him. Time had distanced us. Our older siblings were already gone.

I was grounded if I walked home from school. Grounded if I didn't wear socks. Grounded if I went to the library after school. I couldn't find a place to just pause. To figure out why my heart was beating so fast; why my eyes couldn't meet people's gazes. Nothing could heal the brokenness that had formed over the past several years.

22
RUNNING

One morning, I told them I would just walk to school. But my backpack didn't contain books, and I didn't walk to school. I turned left instead of right and found my way back to the interstate. It was simple, really. Just two blocks away from the place that was supposed to be my home. The interstate was calling to me. I had been feeling a certain itch; a desire for freedom. Every argument with my stepmom reminded me just how trapped I was. The house was thick with tension, and every simple conversation led to an argument. I was the volatile, yet deeply wounded, ex-inmate on probation. Everything that I did wrong put me at risk of violating the conditions of my release.

I glanced both ways before walking down the freeway onramp. Looked back, making sure there were no police. I could still turn around and get to school late, and I wouldn't be in violation of my probation.

I reached out my arm, nervously displaying my hitchhiker's thumb. It had been so long, yet the familiar feel of wind against my arm as I trudged forward and hoped that someone would stop for me surged within my battered soul. "I can do this," I told myself.

No one stopped, not at first. My face was too young, so I shielded it with my cap. My eyes would betray the confidence that I so desperately pretended to have. I walked forward, passing each tenth-of-a-mile marker. Each post represented another step away from the confines of my probation, the confines of my home.

I heard the truck's brakes begin to catch before I turned. Someone was stopping. I waited, hesitating for a moment. This was it. As the tractor trailer pulled into a parked position on the edge of the highway in front of me, I had two choices. I could stay, or I could go.

My feet carried me the short distance between where I was and where I needed to be. I climbed up the familiar side of the truck and accepted the open door. Hitchhiking was always a mystery; who would stop for me? Would I be safe?

Leaning over the edge of the large cab, I saw a man, grinning to himself. Grey hair, beard. Beady eyes. I realized that I didn't care about his motivations and climbed up into the rig.

"Where ya headed?" he asked, his Southern drawl thick.

"New York," I told him. Anywhere but here. I always needed a destination. A place to escape to. South led to Atlanta. I couldn't go back there. West let to Asheville, to Knoxville. Places where I'd been detained. North was my route. I would go the long way back to California.

I buckled myself into place, and he merged back onto the highway. I watched as we drove past familiar street signs, those exits going to places I knew. As the miles between me and my family grew, my heart slowed back to a normal dance. We continued north, and I accepted the stranger's offer to drive me as far as Virginia.

Good enough, I told myself. As long as I got out of here, and fast.

The wind blew against the truck's cabin. A wintry wind, the kind usually accompanied by rain or snowflakes. I lied my way through stories of where I was going. I had pictures of my nephew to back my cover story. Going to pick up my kid. Had to get him back. He really was a cute kid. And yeah, I was nineteen.

I'd learned that people liked to accept a story, even if there were holes in it. No one wanted to know the truth. No one wanted to see me. Fourteen, angry, lost, and running away again. Leaving this place that held no hope for me.

I took a series of free rides to New York. I didn't care what happened to me anymore, if it meant I was free. Each mile further from North Carolina gave me another olive branch of hope. I needed to get away. I was slowly withering away down there.

New York was decidedly cold and snowy. I got dropped off a few blocks from Times Square, and my feet carried me the short distance to the Covenant House. When I arrived, I realized they wouldn't remember me from a few years earlier. I gave a fake name and age, and said I was nineteen. I had forty-eight hours to prove it. I smiled in spite of myself. Warmth while I figured out my next step. I stayed one night. Two nights felt too risky.

One of the drivers had given me twenty dollars on the road to New York. I could take a bus out of the city, I thought to myself. All I had to do was get as far out of the city as possible, and then find a ride that took me west. As long as it soared past Wilkes-Barre. I needed to get somewhere warmer, fast.

For some reason, possibly because there was snow on the ground and it was below freezing, rides across New Jersey to Pennsylvania were easier this time. Or maybe it was the look of total despair that had come to reside on my face. Either way, I was in Philadelphia later that afternoon.

I was shivering by the time I walked into the Greyhound station in the center of the city. Night was approaching, and I knew I needed to get out of Pennsylvania, by any means necessary. I walked up to the counter and asked the ticket seller how far west I could go for fourteen dollars. I'd bought a small snack and paid bus fare out of Manhattan. That was all I had left.

"It's fifteen to get to Harrisburg," she told me.

She showed me a map of the state. That would take me to the middle of Pennsylvania. Far from the fortress where I'd been held over a year ago, but not far enough. "Will you let me pay fourteen?" I pleaded.

The worker paused. She was older, perhaps in her late forties or early fifties. Time had aged her, and small wrinkles had started to form around her kind eyes. Her wavy hair was cut in a short, simple style. Her uniformed shirt appeared ironed, immaculate. "How old are you?" she asked me quietly.

"Eighteen," I said.

"Are you in trouble?" she whispered.

I nodded. Yes, I was always in trouble. Just not the way she probably thought. She reached out her hand to take the fourteen dollars I had placed on the counter. "Alright, sweetie," she told me as she printed a ticket. "Be safe."

"Thank you," I told her, trying to bite back my emotions. If she realized I was fourteen, she'd probably think differently. But yes, I was in danger. If I got sent back to Dillon, I'd be in danger every day until I finished my sentence.

I hurried to the bus and took a seat near the back. As the bus filled up, a man with shoulder length hair and an easy smile sat down next to me. I smiled back, then turned to face the window.

"Harrisburg," I heard the bus driver calling out. Crap. I glanced out the window, seeing a thick dusting of snow on the ground. My jacket wasn't warm enough for what was coming.

I buried my head back against the window. Maybe he wouldn't find me, I prayed quietly. I hadn't had much use for prayer; I had prayed in juvenile hall that the beatings would stop. They did, but then Reggie had died. And then they'd returned. And then I'd been sent back to a place where words hurt more than fists ever could.

The bus driver woke up several passengers in the rows in front of me, demanding to see their tickets. I snored softly, terrified that he would find me.

"Who is my extra passenger?" the bus driver called out. He checked a few more tickets before making his way back towards the front, letting out a loud rant about people not paying for their rides.

The bus roared back to life. I exhaled the breath I'd been holding. I would at least make it to the end of the bus line. But I would not step off the bus until we arrived in Ohio.

The passenger next to me let out a low whistle. "It's you, isn't it?" he asked me, his voice just loud enough for me to hear him. I turned to face him. How had he known?

"Please don't say anything," I hissed at him. "It's so cold outside."

He nodded slowly, his blue eyes sparkling. "Anything you say, sweetheart," he told me. And then I forced myself to fall back asleep. I only awoke for a brief rest stop, but I didn't leave the bus. When we arrived in Ohio, I walked off the bus slowly. There was still a smattering of snow on the ground, and a chilly breeze blew small trails of snowflakes atop the already growing piles.

The guy who had sat next to me was waiting for me when I got off the bus. "What's your plan, sweetheart?" he asked.

I stared at him closely. Not too young, not too old. Weathered. His face told a story of a hard life. Wavy blonde hair, long enough to be a rocker or a rebel without a cause. Thick coat, flannel top, jeans. Pock marks on his face, from a long-ago ailment we'd defeated before my birth. "What do you mean?" I asked.

"Where are you trying to go?" he asked, as we started walking slowly across the icy sidewalk. He reached for my arm as my shoe skidded on the concrete, catching me before I could fall. I steadied myself but didn't pull away from the touch. This man could turn me in. Or help me.

"Los Angeles," I confessed.

"On a ticket to Harrisburg?" he asked me.

I shrugged. "I didn't have enough for a ticket back to California."

He sighed. "I'm going to Las Vegas. I have an apartment there."

I stared at him oddly for a moment. I'd never been to Las Vegas, but I knew it was closer to Los Angeles.

"Come with me, I have an idea," he told me.

He led me to the ticket counter inside and told me to play along. "Hey," he told the man behind the counter. "This girl was sitting next to me on the bus. She lost her ticket at the last stop."

The ticket seller glanced from him to me. "Is that so?"

"Yes," he said. "We were chatting on the bus, and she told me she was going to Las Vegas. She even showed me her ticket," he said.

"Well, Miss, where's the ticket?" he asked.

"I don't know, sir. I might've left it at the rest stop. We all got off for snacks," I lied.

The ticket man didn't look convinced. "Was it a printed ticket? Or a handwritten one?" he asked.

"I don't know? I mean, I'm pretty sure it was handwritten."

He stared at me for a moment, considering. "Funny how you're both going to the same place."

"Yeah, funny," the man next to me said.

I bit down on my lip, wondering what the ticket seller would do. Would he call the cops? Would he run me through that interstate database and find out I'd broken my probation? Would he ask me for ID?

"Okay," he said. "I'll print you a new one."

"Thank you, kind Sir," the man next to me said. I watched as the printer roared to life, and several pages of tickets printed out, showing each stop where we had to change busses. He handed it to me, his eyes darting from the man next to me and then back to me.

"Don't lose this one," he told me, his fingertips brushing against mine as I collected it. I nodded in agreement and thanked him.

After we walked away, the man next to me chuckled. "That was too easy," he told me.

23
LAS VEGAS

The ride to Las Vegas was long and cold. There were traffic jams, slow moving traffic due to large snow banks, and construction. When we finally crossed into Nevada, I breathed a sigh of relief. We were almost there; I'd made it almost to my destination, on fourteen dollars.

The man who had helped me out on the bus chatted with me for the whole ride. His name was Chris, and he had been in New York visiting family. He'd taken a bus from the city and ended up on a bus with me.

"You can stay with me for a few days," he told me. I had agreed, since I didn't have any other plans. I just needed to be somewhere safe, and each day was a slow pace towards adulthood. Somehow, I had to keep myself as far from North Carolina as possible. Just until I turned eighteen.

I needed to turn fifteen first, I thought.

"Okay," I told him. I'd figured out that my "free" ticket from Pittsburgh had come with a price, and I'd mentally psyched myself up to deal with that price when we got to Las Vegas. What I didn't expect was to find that Chris's apartment was really a one room studio, more of a converted hotel room than an apartment. He lived a few blocks off the Strip. His place was small, smelly, and there were no personal touches. Who was this man?

Every time I tried to sneak away to find my way to Los Angeles, he stopped me. A few days passed, and he finally decided to go for a walk with me. I grabbed my backpack.

"You shouldn't go to Los Angeles," he told me.

I paused and looked up at him. We were on the Las Vegas Strip, walking past casinos and working women. "Why not?" I asked.

"There's too much time between now and when you're an adult," he told me. "You'll never make it. It's too long."

"What do you mean?" I asked. We were walking side by side, me holding the straps of my backpack, him with his hands buried in his pockets.

"Think about it," he said. "All you did was run away. You can go back."

I stopped in the middle of the sidewalk and stared at him. "No, I can't."

He shook his head. "Yes, you can. Think about how great you were in Ohio. You were flawless with that ticket agent. You can do the same thing with a judge. Make them forgive you for running. Tell them what they want to hear."

"But I'll go back to juvie," I said, the words coming out rapidly. "I can't."

He took his hands out of his pockets and placed them squarely on my shoulders. "You're a bright kid. You come from a fucked-up place. And you need to go back." His eyes were bright, sad. "I know about the hard life. You need to go back."

I stared at him. The years had been unkind to him. He was thirty-two but looked to be in his forties. He'd told me a little about his family, and I knew that he meant the words he was telling me.

"I'm scared," I whispered.

"I'll walk you to the police station. It's time to turn yourself in," he said.

I nodded slowly. Maybe he was right. My birthday was three months away, and then I'd still have to wait three more years. And what if these charges followed me into adulthood? I watched as a heavyset woman passed by and winked in my direction. She was a working girl. I didn't want that life.

"Okay," I finally said.

So close. I sat in the small confines of my cell in a Las Vegas juvenile hall, on mandatory lockdown for the first three days of my capture. I'd come so far, gotten so close to California. I wasn't sure what had caused me to give up my fight. Why I had listened to Chris, who had immediately walked me down the strip to the police station after convincing me to turn myself in. But not before convincing me to spend a few nights with him.

I couldn't understand why I'd given up. I knew that I was on probation. I knew I was going to be flown back, again, on yet another extradition flight to North Carolina. This was it. I was going to have to finish my two-year sentence. I'd only made it three months in my father's volatile house before giving up and leaving again.

I laid on the flimsy mattress waiting for my chance to go out into the general room. To be free from the cinder block fortress that trapped me in the middle of a desert. So close to the place that kept calling to me. I could feel it in my bones.

I closed my eyes and drifted off to sleep. The sound of metal releasing metal woke me, and I turned to see two female guards at my door. "You can come out now," one of them said. She was eyeing me suspiciously. Her face was set in a permanent scowl, and I was the subject of her annoyance for the moment. The woman behind her seemed equally serious, but her face was somewhat softer. She said nothing but patted me down before allowing me to leave the cell.

When I walked out of the tiny room, I was finally able to see where they'd taken me. A small dayroom was laid out in front of me, complete with circular tables where other incarcerated teens were seated. Everyone wore the same outfit; a white t-shirt and grey pants. I surveyed the tables, deciding. There was one with an empty seat, so I strolled over slowly. I knew better than to move too quickly, or to act presumptuous. I'd learned my lesson with the almost daily beatings during my first several months at Dillon. Damn it, I really didn't want to go back there. If I could only get a job and pay him back, just so that it might be forgiven. I wasn't ready for another stint in maximum security. I wasn't ready to be beaten again. And again.

I smiled faintly, silently hoping they'd offer me a seat. A Latina girl with an enormous belly smiled back at me. "Go ahead, you can sit," she told me.

I was so relieved to be out of my cage, I wasn't really paying attention to the television at the side of the room. There was breaking news, but I told myself I didn't care. The pregnant girl asked me what I was in for.

"I violated my probation," I said softly, eyes downcast. I had given up everything, for a little over a week away from my father and my stepmother. What had I done?

She nodded. "Yeah, me too." No further questions. I'd already said enough to indicate that I knew how things worked. She shuffled a deck of cards and started dealing. Spades. I knew this game.

An hour passed, and after losing more than winning, it was time for school. We walked in a single file line to another room, where we were led in a grammar lesson. The teacher was focusing on spelling rules. "I before E, except after C," he kept telling us. I watched him walk around the room and as he asked each person to spell words. Believe. Achieve. Ceiling. Some of the girls struggled, and I heard a few of them whispering in Spanish.

I stared at my paper, where I'd been writing down each word. I started to doodle on the edges, bored. Same broken girl, wandering along the roadside. Same backpack. Same sad eyes.

Class ended, and we walked back to the dayroom. A guard came for me shortly after, and I was taken to the courtroom that was built into the juvenile hall's structure. There, I was informed that I would be extradited back to North Carolina the following day.

The judge raised an eyebrow, not quite finished. "If you come back to Las Vegas before your 18th birthday, we will keep you until you're an adult. Got it?" he asked.

I nodded slowly. No more Nevada. Got it.

The day passed by slowly, and I kept watching the clock, knowing that my time in Nevada was ending soon. When they locked me in the room, I stared at the ceiling. The c-ei-ling. Waiting for another flight, another time to stare at an angry judge who would just see a screwed up defiant kid. Nobody had ever bothered to ask me why I kept leaving home. In over three years of running away, no one had wondered if there was a reason. It was always my dad's word against my own.

The following morning arrived, and the guards came for me early. I was given my clothes to change back into, before handcuffs were locked onto my hands. I forced a stoic look back onto my face as I walked through the airport, with people staring at me. The guards only removed the handcuffs at the gate, when I was pre-boarded onto the plane.

I knew this part. I was going to be sent back to the Charlotte airport, where another set of officers would be waiting for me. With another set of handcuffs.

When the rest of the passengers boarded onto the plane, an older gentleman sat next to me. He'd seen the handcuffs and knew I was in big trouble. He wanted to know why.

"I was running away, on my way to California," I said, tracing the pink lines on my wrists. The handcuffs had been too tight, again. I glanced out the window, not wanting to talk anymore.

"It's a good thing you didn't make it there," he said to me. I looked back at him, curious. "They just had a major earthquake in Los Angeles."

The Northridge earthquake. I would have been there, probably in a faulty building, if I hadn't turned myself in. I squeezed my eyes shut and ignored the man next to me for the rest of my flight home. I didn't want to talk about Los Angeles anymore, not right now. I didn't want to talk about anything, actually.

After the plane landed, after the police retrieved me from the airport and escorted me to their waiting car in handcuffs, after they drove me the twenty or so miles back to the detention center where I'd wasted too much of my childhood, I sat at a table in the tiny dayroom and let the weight of my decisions sink in. I was going back to C.A. Dillon. There was no way to stop the series of events I had started by running away again.

"You're back, Sheryl," one of the guards drawled in her thick Southern accent. "Where did they find you this time?" She refused to call me Sheri.

I let the air seep out of my chest in a deep sigh. There were so few expectations for me at this point. Stay or leave. Not much else. I glanced up at the woman. Curly red hair, thin face, too much makeup. "Las Vegas," I responded.

"Good thing you didn't make it to Los Angeles," she chuckled. I sank a little lower in my chair. I'd already been chastised on the plane by my elderly seatmate. I wasn't ready for another lashing. "Yeah," I mumbled quietly.

Eventually, the guard moved on to taunt another inmate. I stared at the cement walls. The fortress that surrounded me. This was the one place I would never dare to try to escape from. I knew we were at the end of a long dirt road, off a two-lane highway in the countryside. Deep red dirt screamed from underneath mounds of grass. It wasn't surrounded by the quicksand that was rumored to exist near Dillon, but it had enough muddy pockets and distance from everything else. I squeezed my eyes shut and pretended I wasn't falling back into despair.

"Hey, new girl," someone said. I opened my eyes and surveyed the young girl who'd taken a seat next to me. Cocoa skin, thick hair in braids. Mischievous eyes, dancing with some secret knowledge.

"Hi," I said. "I'm Sheri."

The girl smiled. "Latasha." She motioned to the guard that had been bothering me earlier. "She's a riot," she told me. I laughed.

We fell into an easy conversation. She ran through who everyone was; which kids were going to juvenile hall and which kids would probably get released. She raised a perfectly manicured eyebrow before telling me, "The tough judge is on this week."

"Damn," I whispered back. There would be no leniency. There was no way that I would get off easily.

24
RIOT

Loud noises announced a change in the guard. I stood from my slumber and crossed to the door, where two teens stood and peered into my cell through the square glass window. "We beat up the guards and took the keys!" one of them declared.

"We can let you out," his friend told me.

I shook my head. This was serious. Until that moment, I'd only been charged with a misdemeanor. I did not want to have anything to do with whatever they'd done.

An alarm started blaring overhead. "Leave me in here!" I told them harshly. "The judge is going to let me go," I added. A lie. There would be no leniency with that judge.

"Suit yourself," the first one said. I heard him shuffle off with his keys. I tried to see through the window, but I was at the far end of the corridor, and there was zero visibility of the dayroom from where I'd been placed.

I hurried to the window, frantic for details. Were they really going to escape? Had I made a mistake by turning myself in? What would happen to us?

The glass windows were thickest at the bottom, making everything look distorted. I stood on the metal bed frame in the center of the room and hopped up, trying to see through the regular window at the top. I saw blue flickering lights; a sea of them. We were surrounded.

I sat back down on the metal bed frame, ready to face whatever was coming next. I'd done nothing wrong.

As long as those boys didn't open my door.

I moved from the bed to my door and leaned back against it. I didn't want them to come in. I could hear them hollering in the dayroom, and they'd been announcing a play by play for me and the other inmates to hear.

"We made sandwiches!"

I didn't want out. Not for a sandwich. Not for anything, really. Those were not my criminal charges. I was not a part of whatever was happening.

"Give yourselves up!" I heard over a bullhorn. "The detention center is surrounded."

I cradled my head against my knees, which were clenched tightly against my chest. I would have preferred sitting in a broken building in Los Angeles at that moment. Or back in the Las Vegas cell, waiting to come out for the first time. Or wandering the streets of New York, in the snow. Almost anything was better than that moment, as the police stormed the building and tackled those boys.

We stayed locked in our rooms for hours while the damage was assessed. Those boys weren't going to see freedom for at least another lifetime. I shivered at the thought, recalling the first night I'd been attacked in the shower. I couldn't stomach going back to Dillon.

Hours passed before the police addressed those of us who were still in cells. We'd heard through the thin walls and the small space under the doors that the kids had been arrested, the guards were alive, and that we had to wait.

When the door opened, there were several officers with guns drawn. "Hands behind your head," they commanded. I nodded, terrified.

They patted me down and handcuffed me. "Let's go," they said. I walked side by side with the one that grabbed my arm. His hand was a little too tight, but I said nothing. We stepped over broken wires, ruined furniture. The boys had destroyed everything.

They marched me over to an awaiting police car and told me to get in. I did. I slid into the backseat next to two other girls. The door slammed shut.

"What's happening?" I asked quickly as the officer rounded the car.

"The building is ruined. They're shipping us all over the state."

That was alarming. I had court the next week.

"Where are we going?"

"Fayetteville," said the girl next to me.

I leaned my head against the window. It was nightfall already, and it was not an easy drive. "And the boys?"

"They're dumbasses," the girl against the other window said. "All they got was peanut butter and jelly and more charges."

"Yeah, stupid assholes," the girl next to me chimed in.

The officer who had dragged me out of the building opened the front door. "Ready?" he asked. He didn't have a fellow officer to ride with him. Apparently, there were too many of us and they had to move us right then.

"Yes, Sir," one of the girls said. I glanced over at the rearview mirror, where he was studying us.

"Were any of you involved in that mess?" he asked, watching our faces.

Three heads immediately bobbed from side to side, along with a chorus of "No, sir."

The engine turned on and we began our long trek to the eastern side of the state.

Three weeks passed before I was able to go to court. My mom visited once, braving the long distance in her rickety old blue car. That car had been with her since she'd divorced my dad.

"How are you?" she had asked. Her hand trembled some as she spoke, a mixture of medication side effects and concern. I felt awful for making her worry.

"I'm okay, Mom," I told her. I wasn't, but I couldn't tell her that. We were overcrowded, and it was my turn to sleep on a sheet on the floor. There were three teens per room, although each room was designed for one girl at a time. The space was full. We ate in shifts. They didn't want another uproar like they'd seen at my local detention center, and they didn't seem to believe us telling them we weren't involved.

"Where did you go this time?" my mom asked me. My dad hadn't told her much, apparently.

I sat back in the chair and studied her. She was the kindest, most broken woman I'd ever known. Fragile. But deeply affectionate. I thought back to the cemetery for a moment. "New York," I said quietly. "Then Las Vegas."

"I went out west once, when I was a little girl. My family took a road trip," she said. "It was nice."

My family had never had a nice road trip. I smiled anyway. "With Grandpa?" I asked.

A strange look crossed her face. "Yeah." She looked away.

"Mom," I said softly. "I need to tell you something." I had thought a lot about what Chris had told me in Las Vegas, and suddenly my mom was sitting in front of me.

My mom turned back, her pale blue eyes bright with an unspoken emotion. "Mom, I shouldn't have left this time," I began. She leaned forward, waiting for what I was about to tell her.

"What happened? What did your dad do?" she asked.

I shook my head. "No, this was my fault. I ran away because I thought I was pregnant," I lied. Quickly, I filled her in with my carefully constructed story. "But when I got to Las Vegas, I started my period. I wasn't pregnant. I'd given up everything. And for a mistake."

Her eyes widened. "Oh, no," she moaned softly.

"I know. I have to tell the judge. They need to know why I left. And why I turned myself in."

I'd never turned myself in before. My story was believable. She hugged me and promised to come to court the following week. I thanked her for driving so far to come see me. "Mom, you should go. It's a long drive, and it's hard for you to drive in the dark."

"I love you," she said.

"I love you too, Mom," I told her.

Looking back, I think that's the only time she ever hugged me in my childhood. I held my arms across my chest after she left, remembering the feel of her arms around me long after she'd gone.

25
GUILTY

"All rise," the bailiff said.

I stood beside my court-appointed attorney. We'd just met a few minutes before the case.

The judge sat down. I didn't know her. It was a her! She had never met me before.

I glanced around the room. My dad was there. My stepmom. Their minister. My mom. Apparently, my "confession" had gotten their attention. My mom must have called them. That would've been a hard phone call for her, I realized. A guilty feeling crept over me.

After all, I was guilty.

The trial began. Usually, my trials were quick. Me, saying sorry. The judge, yelling at me. Sentencing me to foster care, or a hospital, or Dillon.

My probation officer was seated behind my parents.

Crap.

"I understand you have something you need to say," the judge said to me. I nodded. She pointed to the witness box. "Come and have a seat." I stood and slowly crossed the room before sitting in the box. I could see the anger building on my probation officer's face.

The bailiff approached me after I'd sat in the chair, facing everyone. "Do you swear to tell the whole truth, and nothing but the truth, so help you God?" he demanded. I placed my hand on the Bible and replied, "I do."

The truth according to the story I had constructed, I thought. "Well, tell us," the judge said impatiently.

"I turned myself in when I got to Las Vegas," I began, trying to think of something sad. Dillon. Beatings. Reggie. Oh, God, Reggie. A tear rolled down my cheek. "Because I realized I'd made a mistake."

"Why?" the judge asked.

I turned to face her. She had grandmotherly eyes. Well, if I had a grandmother who gave a damn about me and invited me over for tea or something. Not my dad's mom, who uninvited me to a family trip when I was eleven. Or my mom's mom, who I'd never met.

"I ran away because I thought I was pregnant, but," and I literally choked out the rest of the words between sobs, "I started my period in Las Vegas, and I realized I'd made a mistake," I cried out. I could hear a loud groan from the direction of my probation officer. Crap. She knew I was lying.

The grandmotherly judge's eyes softened. "And you were afraid to tell your family you might be pregnant?" she prodded.

Crap. Don't say anything bad. Don't say anything. It's a trap, my brain screamed. "I didn't know how to tell them. So, I ran," I said.

"Your honor," I heard my probation officer calling out from the audience. I glanced at her; her face flushed and her tight blonde curls bobbing as she spoke,

"She violated her probation."

"I'm so sorry," I sobbed. I bent forward and put my head in my hands and cried. Cried for Reggie. For me. For the thought of my angel baby that I wasn't sure ever existed. For every damn time no one had heard me. For fear of returning to Dillon. I broke into ugly tears, and I couldn't stop. "I'm sorry, I'm sorry, I'm sorry," I kept repeating. I couldn't stop; I was on repeat by that time.

My dad's minister started crying, and then my mom broke down. The probation officer groaned. I had always known she had hated me, but right then, she would lock me away until eighteen if she had the choice.

The gavel struck against wood beside me. "Sheryl," the judge said. "Look at me," she told me.

I rubbed away tears and lifted my head, turning towards her. "I understand that you made a bad choice. And you made one good choice, by turning yourself in," she said. Her eyes were watery; she was fighting back tears. Guilt stabbed at my heart, so I thought again of the many things that had broken me. "I'm going to grant you one last chance. But if you find your way into my courtroom again, you will finish your sentence at Dillon. Tears or not."

I nodded, the tears still flowing. Mucus drained from my nose, and I had nothing to wipe it away with. "Thank you," I said softly. The gavel swung down again.

My court appointed attorney looked shocked. She hadn't expected me to win. I dared a glance in the direction of my probation officer. Her lips formed one word. "Liar," she mouthed to me from across the room.

I stood and followed my parents into the hall. This would not be an easy day.

After I returned home, I was grounded. My probation officer started calling every few days to check in. I wasn't allowed out of the house except to go to school. Every afternoon, I hid in my room after returning from school. The kids at school had grown tired of my antics, and it wasn't even interesting to them anymore when I returned from wherever I'd been this time.

After a week home, I collapsed into despair. I couldn't handle the isolation, the anger, the battles with my stepmom. My dad worked late, and when he came home each night, he screamed at me for whatever I'd done to piss off Terri.

One night, I went to the kitchen to get a cup of water. She was cooking, and another war ensued. "You can't come in here when I'm cooking!" she shouted.

I used to have rights in my house. But now, there was a woman in charge who despised me. I didn't resist. My will to fight had gone out. I took a cup from the cabinet and walked away. I could fill it with water upstairs.

I went up to my room and poured all the pills from my three pill bottles on the bed. Probation loomed over me. If I left again, I'd get caught. They'd send me back to Dillon, and I couldn't prove those officers right. Everyone was so sure I'd be back. I knew I was too young to reach eighteen without getting caught somewhere. The most I'd survived without being detected was a few weeks. At fourteen, I couldn't work yet. I couldn't hide in plain sight. I was just too young.

I shoved a handful of pills in my mouth and chased them with a long sip of water. I had to force back a sudden gagging sensation before repeating the motion two more times. Once all the pills were swallowed, I laid down on my bed. It was time for everything to end. I'd been fighting for too long.

When I awoke, everything looked hazy. My dad was yelling at me. They must've figured out that I'd taken the pills. He made me stand up and dragged me down the stairs. He put me into the front seat of his van and told me to buckle myself in. I complied, under the fog that was descending over me. I felt so tired all of a sudden.

The next time I opened my eyes, we were on the road. He had skipped the local hospital and was on the interstate. Where was he taking me?

Again, I drifted off. Again, I awoke. He had pulled in front of an emergency room doorway, and someone was bringing me a wheelchair. I felt arms on me, lifting me from the seat. I felt too heavy to move myself from the van's tall chair to the wheelchair below. Everything jolted and swayed for a moment, but then I was closer to the ground.

Chatter surrounded me. Conversations were happening, but they all felt so far away. A sharp sensation in my arm caught my attention for a moment. Something was pressing down on me. I couldn't see it.

More voices, more movement. Coldness filled me, and I felt myself shivering. I was placed on a flat surface, and a blanket was pulled over me. I couldn't understand the words that anyone was saying. My dad's muffled voice was somewhere in the background, probably telling them some other story about some bad thing I'd done.

I attempted to roll my eyes but fell asleep instead. When I awoke the next time, I was being lifted from the bed and placed back into a wheelchair. A bright ray of light crossed into my field of vision, and then more movement. I didn't hear my dad anymore.

Chirping sounds. They were taking me somewhere. I felt an upward pull and then everything shifted again. They were rolling me out of an elevator and then down a hallway. I wasn't sure how many of them were with me. Were they afraid I'd run? Would they carry me and tie me down, like when I was eleven? I shivered again, suddenly afraid. I hadn't died. They were going to lock me in a little room again.

Something dark brown was in front of me, but then it pulled away and bright lights tried to enter my sights. The people continued to wheel me forward.

The wheelchair stopped. Everything was still so fuzzy, and the movement hadn't helped. I felt dizzy and unfocused. "Can you stand?" someone asked. The first words I'd understood.

I wasn't sure how to answer them. Could I? I didn't think so. My mouth went slack and I said nothing. I felt arms on me again, lifting me. Lowering me. They placed me on a mattress that felt like it wasn't very high off the ground. I reached out a hand, curious. I needed to know where land was; everything was swaying. My hand immediately met with the cold, concrete floor. Good, I was not going to fall. Good.

Bad; I hadn't died. Bad; I was back in a psych ward.

Good; I wasn't at home anymore.

Someone was talking to me, but I closed my eyes and chose quiet instead.

26
FAILED ATTEMPT

"Good morning," I heard someone say.

Fog filled my vision again. I hadn't dreamt it. I'd really swallowed three bottles of pills. "I'm tired," I said gruffly, irritation filling my voice. I rolled back over in the bed and dozed back into sleep.

Hours passed. Every so often I tried out my vision again. Hazy. I'd done something to my eyes.

That wasn't the plan. I hadn't wanted to go blind. What the hell had I taken? I tried to remember but could only recall the bottle of naproxen. Useless stuff, really. Everything in my body hurt, even after a bottle of pain pills. Especially my head and my heart. I rolled back over and stretched my hand back to the cold floor. The certainty of knowing I was close to the ground made me feel safe. I left my hand there, to absorb the cold. To melt the fear and anger.

Another hour or so passed. I'd lost track of time. How many days had I been here? Why wasn't I hungry? My stomach felt like it was on fire. I wanted to try my eyes again, but I was becoming scared.

My hand scratched the surface. It was a little grimy, a little rough. A bit like me. I smiled despite my blurriness and all over pain. They'd tossed me on the floor and expected me to break.

"Good evening," I heard another voice tell me.

I hesitated, then opened my eyes. I saw a woman standing in front of me. Curly hair, wiry glasses, scrubs. I could see her.

"Hi," I said softly.

"How are you feeling?"

I wasn't sure. Was unexpectedly alive an answer?

"Tired," I said finally.

"Would you like to eat?" she asked.

I shook my head. No, I didn't want to eat. I wanted to sleep. Sleep was peaceful. It was quiet. Waiting for whoever this woman was to get tired of me and walk away, I squeezed my eyes shut and ignored the rest of her questions.

When I finally reopened my eyes, I was aware that time had passed. The ground next to me didn't feel so cold when I reached out my hand to steady myself. I finally made my way out to the dayroom, where I learned that I was in a different hospital than before. "Can I call my mom?" I asked.

The nurse shook her head. "No phone calls until the doctor gives you permission."

I sighed loudly. More of the same. I sat down in a dayroom chair and let my eyes focus on my surroundings. I was still fuzzy from the pills, but at least I could see again.

My stomach rumbled, so I walked over the counter and helped myself to a piece of fruit from an awaiting fruit bowl. Apparently, our only readily available snacks were apples, oranges, or bananas.

When I sat back down, a nurse approached me with a small paper cup. "Here are your pills," she announced.

I glanced up at her, still drugged from my suicide attempt. "What?" I asked.

"The doctor ordered these pills for you."

"No," I said.

"You have to take them," she said.

I glanced around me. I hadn't seen an isolation room. In fact, I hadn't seen the other kids yet. They must've been in group or school or something.

"No," I repeated.

The nurse put her hands on her hips and glared at me. "You'll take them," she told me confidently.

The other youth arrived from play therapy. Apparently, there was a gym down the hall. I smiled, grateful I'd get to meet some of the other kids. But just as I was ready to introduce myself to a girl with long blonde hair, my nurse came back.

"Come with me," she told me.

I stood and followed. This should be interesting, I thought.

A mattress had been placed on the floor in the hallway, next to what appeared to be a nurse's station. "Sit," she told me.

"What?" I asked.

"You are going to stay here until you take your pills."

"I'd like to talk to the doctor first," I said loudly.

"No."

"Then I'd like to talk to my mom."

"No." More firm this time.

"I have rights," I told her defiantly.

"No, you don't. You take the pills, or you stay here."

"For how long?" I asked.

The nurse shrugged. "Until you take the pills."

I shrugged. Whatever. I could sleep on the mattress. I laid back down on the mattress and tried to fall asleep, but the bright hallway lights shot rays of artificial light down on me.

"Damn it," I muttered, and covered myself with a sheet to block out the light.

Hours passed. The nurse came back to offer me a sandwich for dinner.

"Don't I get a regular meal?"

"Take the pills," she told me.

I shook my head. Whatever.

Nighttime came. Kids passed by me, but they looked straight ahead. "Hi," I called out to one of them. A night nurse stepped back over to me.

"They can't talk to you while you're on punishment," the man told me.

"I won't take the pills," I said. "I have rights."

Everyone went to bed, and I sat up on my mattress in the middle of the hallway, wondering what hell I'd been dropped off in.

The next day came, and the cycle continued. I couldn't talk to anyone. I couldn't see my doctor. I couldn't call my mom. I didn't want to talk to my dad, so I didn't ask. I stayed on my mattress, except for very brief moments when they escorted me to a private bathroom.

Each day repeated with a demand for me to take the pills. I counted as the days passed. Two. Three. Four. Five. Six. Seven.

On the seventh day, I said to hell with it. "Give me the damn pills," I muttered to the nurse. She triumphantly handed them to me.

I popped them into my mouth and pushed them to the side, then took a quick drink of water.

"Show me," she said.

"Huh?" I asked.

"Open your mouth," she demanded. I opened my mouth, and she saw the pills. They began to taste bitter. "Swallow them," she commanded, handing me another cup of water.

Frustrated, I took another sip of water and swallowed the pills. "Done."

"Great," she said. Hands on her hips.

"I have to go to the bathroom."

"Nope. You are not vomiting those pills," she told me. She told me to sit there for thirty minutes, and then I'd be free to join the other kids.

I stared at the white paint on the wall across from me, noticing the small fleck of dirt on the wall that had entertained me for seven days. Damn it, I thought. I was not winning this battle.

I fell into a routine. Breakfast. Go to the gym. Group therapy. Lunch. Go to school. Sometimes my doctor would visit and change my medicines around. He wouldn't really talk to me, but he flipped through my chart and told me the changes he would make.

"Can I call my mom?" I asked.

"No," he told me as he read through the nurse's notes.

"Why not?"

"You need to work the program," he told me.

I stared at him. What program? They'd been force feeding me pills since I'd arrived. Apparently, the program was pills and way too much therapy.

Weeks passed. At the end of a month, without really rehabilitating me, I was told I was being released. "Okay," I said quietly. My dad final came to pick me up. The nurse explained their Partial program to him. I would go to a day program each day for my first week home. It was a "partial" release back to my regular life.

He took me for the first day, but after that, he didn't take me back. "Insurance doesn't cover this," he told me when he picked me up. I nodded.

"You have to go back to school tomorrow."

I groaned. I hated my school. "When do I meet with my probation officer?"

"Oh." A long pause. "They called while you were here. They cancelled your probation last week."

"What?" I asked. "Why?"

"They got really upset that you took all those pills. Told me to keep taking you to therapy."

I nodded. Okay. Strangely, I was too crazy for probation.

27
NEW BEGINNINGS

When I returned home that evening, I pleaded with my dad to let me try a different school. He listened to my concerns, and decided it wasn't a bad idea. He agreed to let me go to a different junior high school across town.

I wasn't on probation anymore, so it wouldn't be too big of a deal if I had to wait for him to get off work to pick me up. Terri was refusing to drive me anymore.

My first day at the new school was quiet. I sat in math class and realized I had fallen behind in my studies. I'd missed too much school, and it was starting to show. I tackled the first set of math problems and struggled.

The kids were curious about me. No one knew me, so they didn't know about all the times I'd gone missing. They didn't know I'd been gone for a very long time, to whoever knows where. They didn't know my past.

I began to excel in my new school. I turned fifteen, and life started to calm down. Three more years, I kept telling myself. I could make it.

And then it happened.

One afternoon, I arrived home and Terri was in a characteristically bad mood. It was just me and her. Nick was at school, doing one of his many extracurricular activities. He was an expert in finding ways to not be home.

Terri started yelling at me. I yelled back. "Stupid bitch!" I was tired of walking on eggshells for her. She'd been provoking arguments with me for weeks.

She stretched out her arm and smacked me hard across my face. I paused, then smacked her back. "No," I told her automatically. "My mom doesn't hit me. You're not my mom. Don't you ever, ever hit me again!" I yelled.

I ran upstairs and grabbed my backpack. To hell with this place. I'd tried it their way. I'd behaved, gone to school, gotten good grades. The school year was almost over.

I thrust a few meaningless items into my backpack. Some clothes, a notebook, a pen. A small road atlas, which I'd kept just in case. Angry, I took the stairs two at a time. This was the only time she would ever hit me, I told myself as I rushed out the door. I hurried down the road, towards the highway. The one that was always waiting, always ready to offer me an escape.

And my dad pulled up next to me in his van.

"Get in," he told me. His face looked tired.

I paused. "No," I shouted. "Terri hit me."

"And you hit her back."

"She's not my mom!" I reminded him.

"Please, don't go," he told me. "It isn't safe." I paused. He hadn't ever told me to stay. How many times had I left, wanting him to tell me to stay?

"I can't deal with her anymore," I told him, my voice losing its edge.

"We'll figure it all out later." He stared at me, and I noticed a smattering of gray hairs along his forehead. "Just get in."

I nodded and climbed into the front seat of the van. He drove us the short distance back home, and I went to sit in the side yard. "I'm not ready to go in yet," I told him. He nodded and went inside the house.

I wandered to the area where I'd played as a child, before everything fell apart. The dogwood tree I'd climbed so many times sat to my right, in full bloom. I'd even found an opossum once and released it up onto a branch. I chuckled at the memory. At times I'd been fearless. Other times I'd been just plain stupid.

The backpack sat beside me. I took out the notebook and my pen and began to sketch the trees in front of me. Tears rolled down my cheeks. I didn't know if this was home or not.

Hours passed by. Doors slammed, and a car engine started in the driveway. Something was happening, but I stayed in my little world. I wasn't ready for whatever mess I was about to walk back into.

Finally, Nick came to get me. "Terri left," he said.

I turned to face him. "What?" I wasn't sure if he was smiling or not. It was always so hard to read his subtle expressions. "What happened?"

"Dad chose you. And she left."

"But it's the only time he's ever chosen me."

"She said she's filing for divorce."

I nodded slowly. It was over. The last four years had been hell. Ever since she'd moved in and unbalanced our house. "Good," I said.

Nick picked up my backpack and we walked inside together.

Terri drove down to Atlanta with her sister and they maxed out every single credit card before she filed for divorce a few days later. By the time the paperwork reached my dad, he was furious. There was no turning back. It was over.

My dad was quieter, but at least the arguing stopped. He went to his room a lot more than before and sat down on his rocking chair playing solitaire.

"Dad," I said one night. "I'm sorry she left you." I wasn't, but he was.

"It's okay," he said. The mask he wore wouldn't let me in. He shuffled the cards.

"What are you playing?" I asked. I already knew, but I wanted him to talk to me so badly.

"Solitaire." The game of loneliness.

"I used to play a lot of cards in Dillon," I said quietly, searching for commonalities.

He paused and set the cards down, not looking at me. "We don't talk about that place."

I nodded. Right. We don't talk about anything, I thought. He'd told me that when I'd been away, I was erased from his conversations. First there was Kevin. Five minus one. "I have four kids," he would tell his friends. Then there was me. "I have three kids," he would announce. How easily he had excluded me.

"I got an A on my math assignment," I told him.

He nodded. "Good."

I always got As. I didn't know how to earn less than an A. Less than that would surely anger him. Grades had always been important to him. "I joined a club at school. Civil Air Patrol. They said if I do everything they ask, I can fly an airplane."

He glanced up at me. "That's a good group."

"Yes," I told him. I'd joined so he would like me again.

"When do you fly?" he asked.

I stared at the cards, which had made their way back into his hand. He had turned his attention back to his game and was dealing out another round of solitaire. "I have to go through some sort of weekend survival thing first. It's this weekend."

He let out a quiet laugh. "That should be easy for you."

I bit down hard on my lower lip. "Alright. I'll go do my homework now," I told him.

The strange, new quietness that filling the house was eerie and peaceful. My dad spent his evenings in his room, and Nick stayed late at school almost every day. I started driver's ed classes, since it was the last year they'd be offered for free at the local schools. I went to my survival weekend but quit when they told me to eat spoiled food. I had my limits, and clean food was something I couldn't deviate from, not after all the uncooked meals. Even if it meant disappointing my dad and never flying a plane.

Life after Terri was calmer. More peaceful. My dad and I quickly settled into a routine that kept us from interacting with each other, so life became safe for a while. I was almost finished with ninth grade, and Nick would be leaving at the end of the summer for the North Carolina School of Science and Mathematics (NCSSM). A path had been set in motion for me. Melinda had gone to that school. Nick would be leaving soon. My dad wanted me to apply too. Perhaps that was what I would need; a proper, acceptable escape from the family.

Summer came and went, and I began to mentally prepare myself for high school. I would be going to the local high school, the one where kids from both junior highs merged into one school. I would be surrounded by kids who knew what I'd done, and kids who hadn't formed strong opinions against me yet. Anything could happen.

Nick left, and I started tenth grade. He had been a fantastic runner on the cross-country team, and my dad always talked about how wonderful it was that he was following in his footsteps. Running was important to him.

I decided to try out for cross country. I was overweight, and I showed up in the wrong shoes and denim shorts. I'd made the decision in fifth period, when I'd realized it would give my dad something to talk to me about. Lately, he'd been devoting thirty-seven seconds per day to me. There had been a news segment talking about the decline in parenting in the United States, and they'd averaged that parents spent thirty-seven seconds per day with their kids. He'd made it into his new goal.

I wanted more. The coach remembered me from physical science class in ninth grade, before Las Vegas and the suicide attempt. I was known to be a quitter. When things got rough, I didn't just quit, I packed my bag and left. I was an expert at quitting. "You have to show up every day," he said, raising an eyebrow in my direction as he spoke to the team on the first try-out.

The team started stretching, but I'd arrived a few minutes late. I had been trying to find a pair of shorts to wear but decided to just use the denim shorts. "Alright, take a lap around the school," he commanded.

And we took off running. Immediately, I was out of breath. I forced myself to make it around the corner before pausing. I could feel my dad's disappointment. Couldn't even make it past the corner, I imagined him saying.

I swallowed a deep breath and kept running. Everything hurt. I kept going. My belly ached, my legs cramped, and my face was beet red by the time I rounded the final corner. Everyone else was already in the next sequence of exercises, but I didn't care. I'd made it.

The coach looked at me strangely, then told me what to do next.

Each day was like that. I showed up, and he didn't cut me. I ran hard and finished last. For some reason he kept me on the team. Long after I would've cut myself.

And my dad was so damned proud that I was running. It was almost like he'd forgotten I was slow and fat and I'd never win a race. He was talking to his coworkers about me. He had four kids again!

I made a few friends on the team, and they brought me to their youth group. Life started to make sense again. The youth pastor talked about hard times, and it was like he was talking directly to me.

I shaped up. I kept my room clean. I wore socks, just so that my dad wouldn't get mad at me. Some mornings, I ran before school. He dropped me off, I pushed through my classes, and he picked me up after cross country.

When the season ended, I gravitated towards a kind woman at the youth group. She volunteered every Wednesday at the local homeless shelter, and she was looking for teens to join her to prepare the meals.

She didn't know my past, or why I was so eager to go help. I started showing up every Wednesday and worked hard to prepare tasty meals for the occupants. I really wasn't a great cook, but there were enough helpers in the kitchen to make sure I didn't mess up too much. On the days when I wasn't cooking, I cleaned the donations closet and sorted the pantry. There was something freeing about giving back.

My dad and I existed on two different planes. It was just him and me. We barely spoke. I counted myself lucky that he took the time to practice driving with me and when my birthday rolled around, I got my license.

He announced I could borrow his spare car. Apparently, he'd been counting down the days until he didn't have to drive me to school anymore. I rejoiced and rushed over to the local shopping center after school. By the time I returned home on the evening of my sixteenth birthday, I'd found my first job.

Life moved on. I began working full-time and staying up late every night to do my school work. He kept reminding me to apply for NCSSM. I didn't argue. The new me was calmer, quieter. I wouldn't tell him I hadn't applied until after the deadline. I wouldn't tell him that I was sinking, because he wasn't listening.

What I didn't realize, what my eyes didn't see until after the fact, was that my dad was distant because he'd started dating again. He had already found The One. And I was the last kid at home. Our quiet existence was about to unravel.

116

28
FALLING

Eleventh grade began. I went to work after practice, and kept pushing to be the perfect student, the perfect daughter. Even though I'd worked extra hours over the summer and finally repaid my dad the two hundred and fifty dollars that I'd stolen, it wasn't enough. He was simmering that I hadn't applied to NCSSM.

Nick was doing well, and he'd started his senior year. I was the wild card, the one that didn't fit. I was supposed to be gone already. My eleventh-grade year was a reminder to my dad that I had turned down an opportunity. He was furious that I hadn't even applied but didn't ask me why.

I was struggling to maintain all As. For the first time, I couldn't keep up with my coursework. The classes were getting harder. My dad didn't know that my pre-calculus teacher had made me promise to never take calculus at my high school before offering me a decent grade. It was a weird foreign language to me, and I couldn't understand all the new math terms and why the hell I needed to learn about limits or derivatives.

Work was too much. One of the older guys had been hitting on me, and it was making me uncomfortable. An older woman that I worked with had noticed, but when she asked me about it, I denied everything. The part of me that never told resurfaced. I must've done something wrong to attract his attention.

I wanted to find a different job, but I didn't have time. The hours were too long, and I was struggling to keep it together. I felt like I was imploding. When the second semester began, and all my classes shifted because we were on block scheduling, I decided I'd had enough. I wanted to take a semester off. I needed a break. After all, I'd calculated the number of credits that I needed to graduate, and I knew I'd still be able to finish with my class.

So, I stopped going. School was too much. The high school had adopted a tardiness policy that penalized students who were late. If I arrived even a minute late, I couldn't go to class. Instead, I had to sit in a tardy room. Didn't they understand I was up late, working, followed by drinking coffee and studying to maintain my perfect GPA? But there was no absence policy. If I couldn't race to school fast enough, I would turn around and go home. There was no point sitting in the tardy room.

"This is ridiculous," my Spanish teacher told me when she saw me in the hallway one morning. I'd been ditching classes for only a few weeks at that point. "Are you even coming to class today?" I shrugged. I was exhausted, and I felt like nothing I ever did was enough.

I ditched class after lunch, not willing to face my Spanish teacher. Instead, I went to see some new friends. My church friends had turned away from me when I'd started skipping school. I was falling apart at the seams, but the only people who noticed or even gave a damn were the outcast kids. I went to a new friend's house, where we sat and drank wine coolers while complaining about our parents. I'd turned back to my old friend, the bottle.

I still went to work, but usually after several cups of coffee to reverse the effects of liquor. Life didn't make sense anymore. Sometimes when I lay on my bedroom floor late at night, I tried calling the teen crisis hotline. But the feedback was always the same. Talk to your parents. Go to church. Everything works out if you follow the rules.

But the rules did not apply. Nobody recognized the telltale signs that I was in trouble. My dad wouldn't speak to me; he spent most of his evenings locked in his bedroom or out in the garage working on his trains. On weekends, he went out on dates with his girlfriend. Things were getting serious with her.

One afternoon, everything boiled to the surface. I was struggling under the weight of everything. I went to the youth office at my former church, desperate for someone to talk to. The crisis line hadn't helped. And the help that the church group offered was the opposite of what I needed. They called my dad. They didn't understand that he only knew one way to fix things.

He finished his work day; he wouldn't take a few hours off to help his kid in crisis. When he finally arrived, he had a look of disgust on his face. I had seen that look before, back in the courtroom. He told me to get in the car, so I did. He drove me into Charlotte, where we sat in his insurance company's office while they tried to determine what to do with me. His troubled daughter, the girl with a history. I'd fallen to pieces and I didn't know why. "Dad, I need to go to work," I kept pestering him.

"No," he commanded. I shrunk back into my seat. I began picturing all those nineties television commercials, advertising hospital programs to "fix" broken kids. I was broken, but did I need to be hospitalized?

"I really need to go to work," I repeated. I was buzzed, but not drunk. Wine coolers mostly. I'd been pretending to myself that those didn't have that much liquor in them. I'd skipped the past three days of school, but I hadn't missed any shifts at my job. Although my dad was clueless about my school attendance at that point. Blocking the school's auto-dialer from calling my house had been too easy.

After much deliberation with the insurance rep, they decided to send me back to the same hospital where I'd spent a month at fourteen years old. After I'd downed a few bottles of pills in my failed suicide attempt. Except this time, I wasn't suicidal. I was mad as hell, frustrated, and beginning to wonder if I should leave again. But I wasn't suicidal.

That didn't stop them from placing me on a 72-hour hold. My dad convinced them I was at risk of harming myself, and the intake nurse was quick to take my dad's version of events. She didn't ask me a single question. Once we finished the intake process, my dad left.

When I walked onto the familiar hospital unit, everything looked different. I saw everything through the eyes of a jaded sixteen-year-old kid, well worn by the years that had elapsed. Awareness had finally set in. No one would listen to me; everything depended on the words that came out of my dad's mouth. How long had we played this game? How many times had he bullied through parenting, to control the outcome? I was sixteen, yet, how many of his kids had even stayed in the house until sixteen?

Now, I stood at a crossroads. My dad wanted me to be labeled as crazy. I saw things differently. I was a screwed-up kid from a screwed-up home. My mom was bipolar, my first stepmother was depressed. They had the same damn psychiatrist. I had tried to pretend I was fine after everything that had happened, but I wasn't. Signs of stress from all the previous trauma were creeping back into my life. The nights I had wandered, the times I'd been locked into a small cell. The previous hospital stays. The man who raped me when I was thirteen. All those subjects were taboo to talk about in my house; a lifetime of pain I had to pretend hadn't happened. I was screaming for help, but not this.

I was not suicidal. I was not a danger to myself, or anyone else. I hadn't taken a bottle of pills. There was no reason to be admitted this time. My eyes took in the familiar yet long forgotten environment. The nurse's station flanking the unit. The hallway where I'd stretched out on a mattress for a week when I refused to take pills. The small dayroom, where I'd spent meal time and free time. The rows of patient rooms lined around the dayroom like a u-shape, each room with space for two crazy kids.

29
72 HOURS

The nurse went through a long questionnaire to assess my mood. I'd done these before. The questions would repeat themselves every so often, to make sure that you were answering honestly. When I finished, I stared hard at the nurse. "Can I at least call my work and tell them I can't make it to my shifts this weekend? I can't lose my job."

The nurse shook her head. "No phone calls until you've seen the doctor."

"Can you please at least call the doctor to ask? Please?" I pleaded.

It was uncharacteristically cold outside, and there were predictions of an impending ice storm. I waited for several hours, my arms held squarely against my chest to maintain my composure and keep warm. While waiting for the doctor, I sat in the dayroom.

Another young man was sitting near me, and his arms were wrapped in thick white gauze. He was a tall, angry white boy, with a hint of desperation in his hazel eyes. "Where do you work?" he asked after the nurse walked away.

"Chick-Fil-A," I told him.

He grinned despite his mummy arms and obvious discomfort. "Me too. I work at one here in Charlotte."

"Really?" I asked. "That's cool."

I wandered across the room for a cup of water and returned to sit across from the tall boy. "What are you in for?" he asked.

"My dad told them I was suicidal."

"Are you?" he asked. I noticed a hint of blood on the edge of his gauze wrap.

I shook my head. "Not for the past few years." I took a sip of the water before meeting his eyes. "You?" I asked.

"I tried to kill myself." He peeled back a little of the gauze, and I saw a thick cut on his wrist. The wound was sewn together haphazardly. Like they'd had to rush to save him.

My eyes were fixated on the wound. "You're still here," I told him.

He laughed. "Yes, I am."

"I guess you had to live so we could talk about working at Chick-Fil-A and being crazy?" I asked. He laughed again.

My eyes darted to my own wrists, wondering what kind of pain would bring a person to slice through their own flesh. I thought I had an idea. But it was a memory so far removed from who I'd become.

"So, what are you going to do?" he asked me.

I looked up, remembering the moment. "I don't know. Wait for my three days to end, then go back to work?" I wasn't sure. I probably wouldn't even have a job after missing my shifts.

"After that?" he asked.

I laughed this time. "I have no idea. I wanted to stay here until I go to college, but it's looking like I might have to make a new plan." I gulped down the rest of the water, then stood. I paced the room for a moment, finally settling on staring out the window. Darkness had fallen, and small dots of snowflakes had started to fall.

"I think I'm going to take a bike ride across the country," he said.

I nodded, still seeing the outside world. Trapped again. "I think I'll go to Mexico," I said softly. "If nothing else works out, I could always become a topless dancer." I laughed, knowing that I'd never do that.

He laughed too. "Then I'll ride my bike to Mexico and find you at a bar."

"I need a drink," I admitted.

We chatted about everything and nothing, until it was time to go to our separate rooms.

The next morning, there was a light dusting of snow on the ground. The roads were iced over, in a gentle North Carolina version of black ice. My psychiatrist wouldn't be in to see me. People were staying home. I sat lazily in the dayroom and watched Saturday morning cartoons, feeling freer now that I'd spent a night out of my dad's house.

Breakfast had come, but there was no coffee. No matter how much I begged and pleaded the case of my caffeine headache, they said that it would stunt my growth. "My growth spurt finished a few years ago," I pleaded, but I spent the morning sipping on water and milk. Nothing to curb the sudden shock of a coffee-less, alcohol-less existence.

I went through the motions of group and told my peers I was not suicidal but had been drinking and skipping school. Since my dad was clueless and couldn't figure it out, he'd called my behavior suicidal. I called it, "taking a break." The therapist recognized me from my previous stay, and he didn't push too hard. I was rational and was able to explain my feelings. I'd done some growing up over the past few years.

"What is your plan?" the therapist asked.

"Well, I've been working for almost a year," I said. "I guess I'll have to research emancipation," I told him. The other youth followed our conversation, obviously curious about the mystery arrival from the previous night. I absently stared out the window again. Wind carried trails of lazy snowflakes. The wintry storm continued, and I was trapped in the psych ward. "Although, this is purely sabotage. No one will let me call my job to tell them that I can't make it."

"They should let you call," the Chick-Fil-A boy said. I glanced back at him and smiled gratefully. The other kids chimed in.

"I shouldn't have been drinking. I shouldn't have skipped school," I stated boldly. "But no one ever asks or cares about what I need. No one has heard me. I need a break. I'm tired. I'm pushing towards a goal that doesn't make sense. I have enough credits to still graduate on time, even if I take this semester off," I heard myself saying. "My dad doesn't listen. He only cares about what makes him look good, and he doesn't want to be a dad. He's the one that keeps saying he only wanted four kids." I paused dramatically, staring at each face before I finished my sentence. My eyes locked with the counselor when I added, "I'm number five."

121

Monday finally came. The last day of my 72-hour hold, and the first time that I met with my psychiatrist. He was a young Indian doctor, perfectly manicured and wearing an expensive suit. I sat across from him, waiting to hear what meds he was planning to prescribe me. Lithium, or perhaps something else. How ironic, since my dad was a chemist working for a lithium plant.

He had asked me a series of questions, but many of them were different from the ones I'd been asked before. What did I want to do? He'd heard about me asking for information on emancipation. He'd read the counselor's notes from group. He was probably about to label me as defiant or some other willfully stubborn term used to describe screwed-up kids.

"I'm so sorry," he said. My ears perked up and I met his eyes. "It sounds like you shouldn't be here. Your dad is the one that needs help."

What? My heart soared as I realized what the psychiatrist was telling me. I wasn't crazy. I wasn't. I was living in a dysfunctional environment that was breaking me down, but it wasn't me. He was the first adult who ever spoke so strongly against my father. He told me that I could go home, and that I should pursue more information on emancipation. He thought I had a case.

I thanked him and went back to my room to gather my things. When my father arrived to pick me up, I glanced back at the other kids. "Bye," I whispered to the Chick-Fil-A boy. He still had that look of desperation in his eyes. I winked. "Mexico," I told him, and he laughed again. I needed for my last memory of him to be filled with laughter, because underneath all my own struggles, I recognized that he would probably complete his previous attempt.

My dad waited outside of the unit, and he wore a scowl on his face. My shoulders slumped somewhat, realizing that nothing had changed. He quickly led me back to his car and drove us to another place. A therapist's office.

"Come on," he said gruffly. I followed him out of his car and into yet another sanitized office. We didn't talk while we sat in the small waiting room.

"Sheri," I heard my name called from a doorway that had opened at the side of the room. I obediently stood and crossed the room, my dad walking beside me.

A female therapist stood in front of us; her hair was short and brown, her face stern. She wore thick rimmed glasses and a khaki pantsuit. Her perfume reminded me of my first stepmother. I followed her to her office, where she and my dad began questioning everything I'd been doing. Apparently, my dad had now learned about the absences.

"What were you thinking?" my dad asked.

"I need a semester off," I said quietly, finally saying it out loud.

"No," he said. One clearly spoken, flat word. It hung between us.

"I need to find my own way."

The therapist smiled and made eye contact with my dad briefly. Weird, I thought. "If you try to apply for emancipation, the judge will find out you were in the hospital this weekend. You won't win," she declared.

What? How had they known? I stared at her for a long moment but did not engage. "Fine," I finally said. "Are we finished? I need to go to work."

My dad begrudgingly paid the therapist and walked me back to the car. On the walk to the car, he ranted about co-pays and how much my trip to the hospital was going to cost him. I ignored the small patches of ice on the ground and shivered from the chilling cold. My dad was wearing a warm winter coat, but he hadn't thought to bring me one. I climbed into the car and stared out the window, wondering what to do now that my world had begun to implode.

30
WHITE VAN

I didn't have to wonder for too long. Nick came down for a visit from school later that week, and my dad told him, "Get ready, let's go have dinner." I was eager to see my brother and ran upstairs for my jacket. When I returned, my dad and my brother were standing in the dining room. My dad looked at me, that same harsh scowl that he'd been wearing far too often when he faced me. "Not you," he said. I was excluded, again. "You're not going with us to dinner. You've been causing trouble lately. And you know what, I don't care if you're here or not when we get back."

Our eyes met, and I held his gaze. Fine. He didn't want me here? I watched as he walked out the door with my beloved brother, the brother whom had learned from a young age how to stay on my dad's good side. Nick was smarter at this than I was. I'd always managed to push every button, to infuriate my dad both intentionally and unintentionally. I stood with the door open, watching them back away in my dad's van.

After they left, I screamed at the top of my lungs. One good, solid, this-sucks-more-than-words scream. I slammed the door as hard as I could and ran up the stairs, two at a time. I threw a few outfits into my backpack and hurried back down the stairs. My job had cancelled all my shifts for the week because I'd left them shorthanded during the snowstorm, which turned out to be their busiest weekend all year. People with no power had come in droves looking for food.

I threw my backpack over my shoulders and strutted out of the house, fueled by anger and hopelessness. I got to the edge of my yard and paused. Now what? Did I get back on the freeway and leave again?

I found my legs taking me in another direction. Instead, I walked through my neighborhood, down the winding roads to the park. When I arrived at the park, I sat on the merry-go-round, lazily kicking it into slow circles with my thick shoes. I glanced down at my feet. No socks. My dad always yelled at me for not wearing socks. I shrugged. What did he know?

My next stop was the gas station on the corner. It had a pool table and a Ms. Pacman game set up in the back room. I looked inside, but none of my new friends were there. No one to crash with for the night. I dropped a quarter into the Ms. Pacman game and began darting ghosts and eating white dots. There was a standing contest that if anyone beat ten thousand points, you could win twenty dollars. But the game was set to hyper speed, and I only made it to eight thousand points. I sighed heavily before pushing my hands back into my pockets.

One of the girls I'd driven home from school a few times lived down the road from there. Maybe I could crash at her house for the night? I tried to recall her name. Lisa? Liz? Lila? I wasn't sure. Would she be home? It was at least ten o'clock by then, and the traffic passing beside me had diminished.

I exited the gas station and continued walking, but by now I'd gone at least five miles. My heel was starting to hurt. I paused, glancing down to see what was wrong with my foot.

No socks. I'd formed a blister and popped it on the back of my heel. "Idiot," I muttered to myself. I traced the small pool of blood with my shivering fingers. Why had I let myself get into this predicament? My father had always told me to wear socks, and I had argued vehemently against him. Yet here I was, bleeding from a broken blister on my sockless foot. I cursed my father for being right while I shoved a shredded piece of tissue into the back of my shoe.

As I adjusted my shoe, a white van pulled up next to me. A middle-aged man with slightly balding hair stared out at me. "Want a ride?" he asked.

I shrugged. What the hell, I thought to myself. I had managed to hitchhike back and forth across the country when I was only thirteen, and nothing had happened to me. Besides, I was older, stronger, smarter. I was sixteen years old. Why not, I told myself. "Okay," I said nonchalantly.

The man reached across to open the door. I lifted myself into the high seat, and then sat timidly in the chair. An unwelcome chill ran down my back. Stay calm, I cautioned myself as I closed the door, even though my heart rate had just doubled. The back of the van was bare, and there were no windows. I shrugged. This is nothing, I told myself. Just a few, short miles.

"What's your name?" the man asked in a friendly tone. I sighed. I had been worried for nothing. I told him my name, and then answered his next few questions about where I was going, where I went to school, and where I worked.

We were almost to my friend's house. I watched the street signs, still anxious to arrive. "It's the next left," I told the man.

He nodded. I waited, but then he missed the turn. "Hey!" I exclaimed, almost a little too loudly. "You missed the turn."

The man sighed. "I'm sorry, little lady. Let's turn down the next street, and then we'll go back." He stared at me for a moment before turning left onto the next street.

I stared straight ahead. I watched as we turned and approached the street to my friend's house again. And again, as he missed the turn. Before I could think, or speak, the man grabbed my neck. His strong hand dared to pull me closer to him. I screamed, and tears began flowing down my cheeks.

My eyes darted around the van. What could I do? I had to get away somehow. "Let me out, or I'll jump," I heard myself saying. Suddenly, the man had let go of me, and he began to accelerate.

"I'll fuckin' jump. I mean it," I shouted. The man laughed, a cackling sort of laugh that you only hear in movies. The speedometer approached forty, then fifty miles.

Swallowing hard, I pushed open the door. The van was moving so fast, and the door felt so heavy against the force of the cold, February air. "Go ahead, bitch," the man was saying. "You'll die if you jump."

I'll die if I stay, I thought. All my life, I'd heard urban legends of bodies being found in the woods, and my hometown was full of woods. I stared at him for one hard moment, and then threw myself out the door. I fell to the ground, knees against concrete, backpack against my chest, the floor pad from his van at my feet. The van skidded to a stop for a moment, and I screamed. With all the strength I had left, I sat up, trying to stand. Tears streamed down my face, and I was frightened of what could happen next.

The man looked back at me one last time and then drove away. He accelerated quickly, making it impossible for me to memorize his license plate number. I watched as his taillights faded away down the long, two-lane highway.

Get up, that inner voice inside of me screamed. He might come back. I struggled to stand, and then felt my body thrust forward into a clumsy run. I sprinted to the doorway of the first house I saw and began knocking hysterically. Nobody answered.

Dogs barked, lights turned on, but nobody opened their doors. I ran from house to house, knocking and crying, begging and screaming. Nobody came outside.

I crouched down next to the curb, my face a mixture of tears and sweat. Blood dripped from my knee, and there were rips in the fabric of my corduroy pants. My loud, frightened moans finally brought somebody to their doorway. A woman came outside, soon followed by her husband. They helped me stand up and walked me into their house.

"What happened, you poor little thing?" the woman drawled in her thick, North Carolina accent. "Are you alright?"

"No," I heard myself saying. "That man tried to kill me." I repeated my story several times until she understood what had happened. I must've been unintelligible the first few times, since the tears would not stop flowing.

The woman wrapped a jacket around me. "Let's call your parents," she suggested.

"No, I can't." I shook my head in protest. "My father kicked me out. I can't go back."

"When did he kick you out. honey?"

"Tonight." I shivered at the memory of our conversation just a few hours earlier. He'd said he didn't want me there, and I'd left. Was it only a few hours? It seemed like days, or weeks, had passed. So much had changed for me, all in a matter of minutes. I probably could've been stubborn and stayed, but for what? Maybe he'd find a different psychiatrist who would be willing to keep me hospitalized for a few months. It had worked before. I thought back to those two months and ten days that I'd been locked away when I was eleven. What was the justification for that? Had it mattered? He'd gotten away with it and had miraculously made sure I was cured in time for school to start. So that nobody would have to know.

I finally agreed to call a friend from work. While I was waiting for her to arrive, a police car drove up, apparently summoned by neighbors who had mistaken me for a burglar. My friend parked her car behind the patrol car and rushed over to me.

The police officer asked me to repeat my story and questioned me in detail about the man's description. "I don't know," I cried. What color was his hair? His eyes? His clothes? What type of van was it? "It all happened so fast."

The officer relented. "Alright. Let me take you home." He refused to let me leave with my friend, insisting that he take me to my father's house.

"But my father won't want to see me. Please don't take me home," I begged.

I stood nervously behind the police officer as he rang the bell. My backpack was still clutched against my chest. Not here, anywhere but here, I wanted to scream. But I didn't. I was more terrified of the police than of my father.

My father opened the door, and the look in his eyes said it all. As we followed him inside, he said, "Officer, she's always getting into trouble. I knew eventually something like this would happen. She's been giving me a lot of problems lately."

My eyes surveyed the room. My sister, Melinda, and my brother, Nick, were both sitting in the living room behind my father. Even my four-year-old nephew was listening.

"She's been through a terrible ordeal," the officer said. But someone interrupted him, citing yet another mistake I had recently made. The officer shook his head in frustration, before turning his back to my family. He faced me, saying gently, "If you remember anything or need to talk about what happened, call me." He gave me his business card, and then left.

I stood in front of my family, unprepared for their onslaught of insults. My little nephew noticed I was crying and asked me if I was alright. I bent down to answer him, but my sister cut me off. "I don't want you around my son," she told me.

I shook my head in disbelief. Only a four-year-old had bothered to ask me if I was okay. And of course, I wasn't! How could I be? I ran upstairs and slammed the door to my room. So be it, I told myself. If the police wanted me to stay here for the night, I would. But first thing tomorrow, I would start looking for someplace else to go. Anywhere but here.

The door opened suddenly. Nick came in, angry at me for causing yet another problem while he was visiting from school up north. "You wanted something like this to happen," he told me. I yelled at him to shut up and get out, and he did. I just wanted to be left alone.

No one came to check on me. Late into the night I lay in bed, trembling in fear. My mind replayed the horrible event again and again, but I couldn't see the man's face. What did he look like? Would I be able to recognize him if I saw him again?

"Wake up," my father was yelling from downstairs. I sighed, squeezing my eyes shut. I hadn't even slept. How could I? My entire body was still shaking, at times violently, but now it maintained a reminiscent tremble.

I quickly put my corduroy pants back on and found a different shirt. The pants were comforting and reminded me that I was a survivor. I traced the piece of thread that was broken at the knee, where I'd fallen. The fabric held traces of blood from where I'd scraped my knee. I had been through worse, so much worse. I could get through whatever was coming next.

Dressed and ready to conquer the world, I went downstairs to face my father. He mentioned the psychiatric ward, a continual threat he'd been using over the past few years. He'd used it to control me. He thought it still would. But somehow, his spell of control had broken. My scraped knee screamed a different story. He didn't have power over me anymore. I would stay for the moment, only because the officer had made me come back. His business card sat in my pocket, and I traced the edges with my fingertips. Someone wanted to hear what I had to say; if only I could remember.

He drove me to high school in the same awkward silence that had enveloped our house over the past few years. Finally, we arrived, and he turned to me to ask if I was working that evening. As if nothing had happened. What else could I have expected, anyhow? My family's policy about less than desirable events was to leave them in the past. Never talk about them; never try to work through problems. But the stain would remain forever. I could picture the distasteful glare I received whenever I brought up my ten-month stint in Dillon. Of course I shouldn't bring up last night's events. Talking wasn't necessary, since our actions screamed what our words would never say.

"Yes," I lied. "I'll get a ride home."

He drove away, and I walked down the small hill connecting the school's property to the adjacent convenience store. Some of my new friends were already congregating in the parking lot.

Sammie was there. I'd met her a few weeks earlier. She was a year older than me and had a way of commanding everyone's attention. "What happened to you?" she asked, immediately noticing my broken pants.

I stared absently at the road as I told her the previous night's events. When I finished describing what had happened, she had a serious look on her face. "My stepdad started molesting me again. I need to leave," she said.

Indecision crossed my face. I hadn't been planning to leave yet. Maybe summer, I'd thought. But my dad wasn't going to allow me to do this the legal way. Emancipation was out of the question.

Out of the corner of my eye, I saw it. A windowless white van, passing by us slowly. A driver, whose face I couldn't remember and couldn't forget, meeting my eyes briefly before driving past us. I turned back to Sammie, my heart racing. Breathless, I told her, "When can we leave?"

School ended. It had been a terrible day; I'd shifted from class to class and realized just how much work I'd missed. I wouldn't be able to catch up, and my teachers weren't cutting me any slack. My chemistry teacher gave a lecture about the attributes of students who fail. He stared at me while speaking. A classmate that I'd befriended when I was attending the nearby church whispered harshly to me, "What are you going to do, drop out?" before walking away. No opportunity to speak. I watched as she was enveloped by a crowd of students during passing period.

I called my work and begged for a shift. I needed money. They finally relented, perhaps because they knew my situation, but more likely because they needed another warm body selling southern style chicken.

My dad had taken the car, so I was suddenly without transportation in a small town with limited bus schedules. I went back to the convenience store and asked each person with a car if they could drop me off at work. I finally begged someone that I didn't know to take me to Chick-Fil-A.

As soon as I got to work, I changed and clocked in. I needed every penny. I volunteered to wash the large stack of metal pans, and afterwards was transitioned to the front line. They gave me a register and asked me to do what I did best. I'd been highly successful in "suggested sales," and I was usually able to convince people to add a slice of lettuce and tomato for a small cost, or to upsize their drink and fries. I got into the rhythm of work, forcing myself to forget the previous night's events. Forcing myself to forget a certain white van.

We hit a brief lull in customers, so I turned away for a moment to make a fresh pot of coffee. I would need a cup soon, and I was sure that at least one customer would want fresh coffee. When I turned back around, there was a customer at my register.

Head bowed down, hat covering his head. Thick jacket. I walked the short distance back to the register and smiled.

Our eyes met. I froze.

His menacing eyes were looking back at me. A creepy smile spread across his lips. Those lips that had tried to kiss me the previous night. "I'll have the number one special," he said, then winked.

I paused, not sure what to do. I was alone at the front of the store. The cook was busy in the small space behind me, and he wouldn't hear me unless I yelled. There was no panic button.

He pulled a five-dollar bill out of his wallet and handed it to me. I took it from him, almost dropping it when his fingers touched my hand. Was he going to kill me? Did he have a gun?

I quickly made change and grabbed his food. I glanced through the metal slots where the cook always passed me fresh sandwiches, but he was preoccupied preparing the evening's chicken. I scooped fries into the paper carton and placed them on his tray with a shaking hand. When I turned back to see him, he was still staring wildly at me with that awful grin.

It took an eternity to fill the Styrofoam cup with coke. When I passed him his completed tray, he winked again and said "Thanks." I watched as he strolled to an empty seat directly across from me and stared at me as he took each bite.

Frozen in place, I watched him. Idiot, I told myself. It was my fault he knew where I worked, where I went to school. He could follow me home and figure out where I lived. I hadn't seen a white van in the parking lot when I'd glanced out the window, so he must've brought a different vehicle. He was anonymous, but I wasn't.

Each bite, each sip, he stared at me. I hovered over the center cash register, not quite sure what to do. Should I run? Should I get my boss? Should I pick up the phone and call the cops? I thought about the officer's card in my pocket, but still wasn't sure.

Another coworker rounded the corner and noticed me. I was trembling, and he would later tell me that I'd gone pale from fright. "What's going on?" he asked nonchalantly.

I lifted a finger to point at the man, my trailing fingers shaking as I stared at him. The man quickly stood and left the restaurant as I tried to explain myself to my coworker. When he finally understood who that man was and why I was so afraid, he ran outside.

But the man from the white van was gone. A dark car sped away, and my coworker hadn't gotten plate numbers.

I quickly took a break and called Sammie. When she picked up the phone, I told her I wanted to leave the next day. We agreed to meet at the convenience store, and she said she'd have a ride waiting for us.

I hung up the phone and forced myself to go through the motions of smiling at customers, selling meals, and cleaning until my shift ended. A coworker drove me home, and I watched the rearview mirror for any sign of someone trailing us. Nothing seemed out of the ordinary, but I was afraid nonetheless. He'd found me twice already. It wouldn't be long before he found me alone.

31
ESCAPE

Morning came swiftly again. Too fast. I yawned as I made myself a cup of gas station coffee, then hovered in the doorway of the convenience station waiting for my new friends. I didn't dare go back outside. White vans without windows were obvious, but a small dark car? Escape would be impossible if my attacker showed up, because I didn't even know what I was looking for.

Halfway through my stale coffee, Sammie arrived. She was in a small jeep, with a guy I didn't know. I chugged down the remaining coffee and tossed the Styrofoam cup in the trash. My fingers intertwined in the loops at the bottom of my backpack, holding the satchel tightly against my body. This was it. This was the vehicle that would take us to safety.

I pushed open the convenience store doorway, the chime of bells above it signaling my exit. Sammie smiled when she saw me. I'd never seen her smile like that before. Freedom soared across her face.

We drove the short distance to my house, and I grabbed two more bags from my room. My dad's words from the other night ricocheted in my memory. "I don't care if you're here or not when we get back," he had told me. Anger fueled my movements as I rushed down the stairs with my belongings. I engaged the door alarm and locked the door before leaving. He'd surely change the code as soon as he knew that I was gone for good.

The only thing between us and freedom was the open road. Sammie's friend turned up the music as we merged onto the interstate, and Sammie turned around to look at me. I'd taken a seat in the back and was finally starting to feel my heartbeat returning to a normal rhythm. I'd been on high alert since I'd met the man with the white van, and every time I closed my eyes I could almost see his face. But the features clouded over and morphed so quickly that I couldn't identify anything about him except those eyes.

"Florida?" she asked.

I shrugged. My bags were neatly tucked beside me in the chair, and I lazily twisted the strap from my backpack between my fingers. Florida was the one southern state I'd missed in all my escapades when I was thirteen. It was time to see if sunshine and new opportunities could set me free.

She laughed loudly. Of course, Florida was fine. I'd agreed to pay the driver to take us there. I wouldn't be able to pick up my last check until later and was thinking that I could ask for them to mail it to me. For now, I had three hundred dollars. We figured that would get us a hotel for a week or so while we tried to figure it out.

I closed my eyes and let sleep come to me. I hadn't been sleeping well for too long. I'd been running on sheer adrenaline and bad coffee.

Florida arrived sooner than expected. I slept throughout the day and when I awoke later that evening, we had arrived in Daytona. Sammie was flirting with the guy next to her, and he seemed to be enjoying it.

We stopped at the first cheap motel that we saw, hoping for a cheap weekly rate while we looked for jobs. When I went into the office with Sammie, we found out that there were no vacancies.

Race Week had come to town. We couldn't have picked a worse week to pack our stuff and move to Daytona. As we traveled down the main boulevard, we saw signs declaring no vacancies. On a side street just outside of town, we finally found a cheap motel. But the price was almost sixty dollars per night. Sammie's friend checked us in, since he was over eighteen.

Sammie's friend helped us carry everything inside before falling asleep on the sofa. We each took a bed and fell asleep as well. "It'll work out," Sammie murmured as she drifted off to sleep. I stared across the room at our sleeping driver, still on edge from the other night. My eyes grew heavy and sleep finally won.

Our driver collected his payment in the morning and promptly left. He had to get back to work. As he drove away, I stared around our hotel room. We each had several bags. And no transportation.

"We need jobs," I said.

"Let's get started," Sammie agreed.

We both got dressed in our most business-like clothes. Nice blouse, dark pants. Well-combed hair. We were ready.

"We need a phone number," I said as we started to walk out of the hotel room. I had a key and a pen in my pocket, and Sammie double checked the lock. Our temporary home was secured.

"Let's ask in the office," she told me, and we walked to the hotel office. An older woman sat at the desk, a bored look on her face.

"Are you checking out?" she asked.

Sammie shook her head. "No, we paid for three nights. We're looking for jobs here, so we will need the hotel's phone number," she told the woman.

The woman nodded unenthusiastically, scribbling the number onto a scrap of paper. We accepted it and hurried out.

"Now what?" Sammie asked.

I pointed to a fast food restaurant down the road. My stomach growled loudly, and Sammie laughed. "Food?" she asked.

"Food and jobs," I confirmed. We made our way down the long block and began looking for work. The fast food restaurants were not looking for employees. A convenience store on the corner was hiring adults only. Sammie would be eighteen in a few weeks, and I was still sixteen.

By noon, we'd been told no by a few dozen potential businesses. We sat down in front of a McDonald's and stared up at a tall hotel that overlooked the ocean. I shrugged. "Why not?" I asked.

Sammie nodded. "Let's do it."

We went into the hotel and asked for human resources. We were directed towards an office in the basement. An older woman with a terse expression sat behind a desk, filling out paperwork. "Yes?" she asked.

"We're looking for work," Sammie proclaimed.

The woman shook her head slowly. "We don't have anything for you here. All we have is maid work right now."

"That's fine," I said quickly.

The woman narrowed her eyes at me. "You have to clean hotel rooms after our guests," she said, her words slow. "It's hard work."

Sammie smiled. "We like to work hard."

"Have you worked before?"

"I've been working for a fast food restaurant for the past ten months, so I know how to work hard," I told the woman. She nodded slowly. I watched as she pulled two fresh applications out of her desk and handed them to us.

"Alright, that will do. Fill these out," she said.

We obediently stepped outside and completed the applications. When we returned to the office, she smiled hesitantly. "You can start on Monday," she said.

Sammie nodded. "Great," she answered back. "Just one question. When is the first paycheck?" It was Thursday. We had two more nights at the hotel.

"That takes a few weeks," the manager told us.

Sammie nodded, and replied, "Okay." I could hear the hollow resignation in her voice. This wasn't going to work. We would run out of money long before we would get paid.

We thanked the woman and exited the hotel. When we were back on the main road, Sammie shook her head. "This won't work," she told me.

I nodded. "Yeah. It's race week."

"We could put our stuff in storage, and sleep on the beach," she said.

I stared past the hotel, towards the white, sandy beach. I crossed my arms over my chest, letting the light ocean breeze blow against my face while I faced the ocean. "Maybe," I told her.

We set our plan in motion. Sammie called the local storage units, deciding which one we would use. Our plan was to drop everything off the following day. We had two more nights, and work wouldn't start for several more days.

Restless energy exuded from both of us. "Let's find something to do," Sammie said. I nodded. We both got dressed in fancy dresses that I'd managed to shoplift from the mall in North Carolina. Afterwards, we wandered down the main street looking for something to do.

The 7-11 on the corner was a logical first stop. We each bought a soda but filled our pockets with snack food. "They'll forgive us," Sammie said when we were walking down the street. "We have to be careful with our money, since we only have a little bit left."

Yes. Our money. I shrugged. I was safe. There were no white vans down here without windows. I'd watched every passing car, my eyes vigilant for any signs of my attacker. But he wasn't here.

Darkness fell, and we wandered aimlessly for a while, chewing on cheese crackers and cookies. Sammie was eating a pack of Vienna sausages. They looked like mini hot dogs to me, and I still hated hot dogs. I tried one, but it made my stomach feel queasy. It reminded me of Terri's cooking, and suddenly I decided I was done eating meat. It was like a switch had turned on inside of me with that one harsh memory.

Afterwards, we stopped in front of a laser tag parlor. "I've never done that before," I said.

Sammie laughed. "Me either." We were both wearing short dresses, mine black and hers bright red. True to form, I had shoes without socks. She was wearing sneakers with socks. "Let's do it," she said.

I walked up to the ticket counter and paid for a pass for each of us. We started chasing after each other, shooting each other with combat guns and hollering whenever one of us got shot. A group of boys showed up, so we weren't alone in the arena anymore. We switched for a second game and formed our own team. The battle of boys versus girls ensued for the next hour. Finally, a young employee with a bad case of teen acne let us all know that it was closing time.

"We could go drinking," Sammie offered. I shook my head. Our game had cost forty dollars. We'd gone on a whim, but money was flowing like water.

"Let's go back to the motel," I told her. The mental math over our spending was making my head hurt. We wouldn't be able to do this again.

The next morning, Sammie and I sorted our possessions. We each narrowed our stuff down to one small backpack of essential items. Sammie called a taxi, and we took it over to a storage unit. We paid a month advance and left most of our belongings in the unit. We left behind most of our clothes and anything that we couldn't carry in our backpacks. I left behind childhood photographs and a small coffee pot that I'd found in a secondhand store; a relic that I'd been planning to use in my future apartment.

Afterwards, we navigated our way back to the motel using the city bus system. They had cheaper fares for students, so we smiled and pretended that we had not just skipped town and dropped out of high school.

We wandered along the beach, trying to figure out where we'd sleep. There wasn't anywhere obvious. Everything looked fairly secured, with lifeguard towers and nearby hotels in sight. "I don't know how this will work," I said.

"Me either," Sammie said. "Maybe we should try Miami."

I shook my head. "What about our stuff?"

She shrugged. "We can come back for it."

I stared at the beach, watching families playing together in the sand. A little girl was building a sandcastle. Her father bent down to help her with the design. I glanced away.

"How will we get there?" I asked.

She shrugged. "You said you've hitchhiked before, right?" she asked.

Yes, I had. I sighed. "Okay. We can leave in the morning," I told her. We had one more night at the hotel. One more night of safety, before the unknown.

32
MIAMI

Morning came too soon. We packed our backpacks, and as we walked out of the hotel, frantic energy filled me. We were leaving all our stuff, going somewhere else. I had a bad feeling about this plan. How would we get back to Daytona?

"Miami will be better, you'll see," Sammie told me. I turned to look at her. She had a hopeful look in her dark eyes. Hope was an emotion I hadn't felt for a long time. I couldn't bear to tell her how frightened I was of hitchhiking, after what had happened the previous week. Whenever I closed my eyes, I saw half of that man's face. Never enough to recall details. As if my memory was protecting me from something.

I nodded. "Let's go."

We took a city bus back towards the interstate. When we got off, I led the way up the onramp, feigning strength that I didn't have. I could do this, I thought to myself. It had been a few years, and I'd grown up some since the last time I'd hitchhiked. But nonetheless, here we were. I hadn't hitchhiked with a partner since I was thirteen, and that hadn't turned out so well. The end of that trip resulted in ten months at Dillon.

When we were standing beside the asphalt, I raised a shaky hand and bared my thumb. "Here we go," I said softly. Sammie smiled. She was almost eighteen, had lived abroad, and was ready for something better. To me, she was fearless. I was the one who was building up a mountain of fears.

We stood on the side of the interstate for almost twenty minutes before a car pulled over. It was a small vehicle, white color. I cringed, thinking of the man with the white van. I quickly pulled the hotel's pad of paper and pen out of my pocket and jotted down the make, model, and license plate number as Sammie climbed in.

"What is she doing?" the driver asked Sammie.

Sammie shrugged. "She got attacked last week. She writes down details to stay safe," she told them.

The man nodded with understanding. I climbed into the backseat, my ears tingling from hearing their brief conversation. Sammie was in the front seat, making herself comfortable. She was so free, I thought to myself again.

Our driver pulled back into the traffic on the interstate. "I'll take you as far as I can," he told us. "I'm taking the 1 south as far as Melbourne."

We both nodded, pretending we knew Florida's geography. I quickly flipped through my pocket atlas from my seat in the back of the sedan, reviewing landmarks. "Thanks," I said, noticing that he would keep us on our path to Miami.

True to his word, our elderly driver took us as far as Melbourne. Our next ride took us further, to Pompano Beach, and our last driver took us into Miami. We found our way to the train system and took a ride to a random destination in downtown Miami.

"Let's start here," Sammie said, eyeing a row of strip malls. We needed jobs, and they were a reasonable place for us to start. We hurried off the train and down the tall staircase, returning to street level. Our only possessions were the small backpacks on our backs. We had left everything else in our storage locker in Daytona.

We walked with purpose across the street. When we arrived at the first row of stores, we saw only one "help wanted" sign, in the window of a yogurt shop.

Sammie smiled. "That's our chance," she said. I shrugged. "Okay," I told her.

We went into the store and asked about the job. A teenager stood behind the counter. "You can fill out an application," he told us.

Sammie shook her head. "We don't have a phone number or address. Is the manager here?" she asked.

His eyes grew a little wider. He looked like he wasn't older than eighteen or nineteen, and his slightly blemished face and casual t-shirt pointed to a simpler life. I sighed, knowing already we didn't have a chance here. We'd never fit in at a frozen yogurt store.

"You can fill out an application," he said, but we both stood staring at him. How? With no address or phone number to leave behind, Sammie and I realized at the same moment that we were in trouble.

"Thanks," I said softly, and we walked out.

"Now what?" Sammie asked.

"We keep trying," I told her. We pushed onward and stopped in every single store along the strip mall, inquiring about work. No one was hiring, or they wanted to call later, or the manager wasn't there.

When we finished visiting all the stores, I saw Sammie was starting to look nervous. "It's okay," I told her. "Let's take a bus somewhere else. This isn't the right place," I told her.

She nodded. We walked across the parking lot and approached a bus stop. "Where to?" she asked.

I shrugged. "Anywhere."

We boarded the first bus that arrived.

Hours passed. We ended up in a bad part of Miami, and I instantly regretted it. This was not a good choice. We should've stayed in Daytona, where we could've taken jobs as maids. Or we should've gone west, to California. Instead, we'd blown all our money at a Daytona hotel during race week.

We sat down on a bus bench, feeling defeated. "What do we do now?" Sammie asked. It was early afternoon, and we hadn't planned far enough ahead to figure out where we would stay.

I shrugged. "There's probably a teen shelter here," I said quietly. "We could check the phone book."

Sammie nodded. "Let's go," she said.

We stood and walked a block towards the nearest phone booth. There was no phone book attached, so we walked another block. And another. When we finally found one with the yellow pages, I thumbed through it. I searched "runaway," "homeless," "teen," and "shelter," and then I found it. The Covenant House.

I sighed with relief. I'd been to the Covenant House in New York when I was thirteen. I knew it would be safe.

While Sammie stood beside me watching our surroundings, I dialed the number. A man picked up on the other end.

"Hi," I said quietly. "My friend and I, we need a place to stay," I told him.

"How old are you?" he asked.

"Sixteen and seventeen," I told him.

He quickly asked me a series of questions. Where were we from? Where were we now? I looked up at the road signs and told him the two cross streets for where we were.

"That's a bad area. We'll send a van as fast as we can. It'll be at least thirty minutes, though," he told me. He asked me to describe what we were wearing and told me we should wait at a bus bench. A marked burgundy van would pick us up, and the driver would identify himself as Gary.

"Okay," I said. "Thanks." I hung up the phone.

Sammie looked at me expectantly. "Well?" she asked.

"They're sending someone to get us. They want us to wait on a bus bench," I told her. Sammie nodded, looking relieved. We were both on edge, I realized. We walked back towards a bus bench near where we'd be picked up. "It's a guy driver," I told her.

Sammie nodded. It didn't worry her the way that it worried me. I'd been fidgety with every single man that we'd encountered during our trip. Something about being assaulted had burned its way into me, making me afraid of everything.

The van arrived almost an hour later. It was a burgundy van labeled The Covenant House, as the man on the hotline had promised. "Hi, are you two Sammie and Sheri?" the man asked. "I'm Gary," he told us. Sammie and I stood up, and Sammie moved closer to the van to talk to the driver. I trailed behind her.

What was wrong with me? I'd fearlessly made my way all over the country several years earlier, but the hair on my arms was sticking straight up and I was tense from meeting new people. This wasn't like me; I was normally fearless.

Now, I was just afraid. I took the long way around the van, quickly jotting down the license plate number on my notepad. I heard Sammie explaining my actions to the driver when I climbed into the seat behind her.

He glanced at me through the rearview mirror. Older, wiser eyes bearing into me. "You're safe now," he told me. I nodded, but I didn't feel safe.

We buckled ourselves in and watched as the driver guided us away from downtown Miami and back onto the freeway. He entered the northbound lanes. My breath caught. That was the wrong direction.

"Where is the shelter?" I asked suddenly. Sweat beaded along the back of my neck, and my hands grew clammy.

"Fort Lauderdale," he answered. He must've noticed my nervousness and started peppering us with details. "It's a little north, near the beach. The program is safe," he told me again.

"I've been to Covenant House before," I said, then looked away.

"Which one?" he asked, curious.

"New York. A few years ago." Twice, I thought to myself.

Why had we come to Florida? This wasn't what I'd wanted.

I tuned out the driver and watched the road. Sammie picked up the conversation, and I heard her telling him about our search for jobs and running out of money.

An hour passed before the driver pulled the van off the freeway. Traffic was heavy in both directions. We'd apparently called for help during rush hour, and they'd stopped everything to come for us.

I watched as the van looped off the freeway and drove towards the ocean. Palm trees dotted the streets. When he reached the final street alongside the ocean, he turned. We drove a few more blocks, the sight of sand and crisp blue water to our right. I turned my eyes towards the water. Usually, the ocean filled me with peace. But right then, a tidal wave of doubt overcame me.

"We'll get you guys settled in for the night," the driver told us once he had pulled the van into a gated building. A guard sat at the gate and pressed a button to let us in. The gate closed behind us, and I shivered at the sound of the wrought iron fortress closing us in. "And we'll go over the program with you in the morning."

I nodded slowly. Right. They had to call our parents.

When we were inside, and Gary had taken us to a waiting room, I turned to Sammie. "I don't like this," I told her. "I feel trapped."

Sammie had never spent ten months in juvenile hall. She'd never been in countless dangerous situations. She didn't sense danger in the same way that I did. But she had been listening to me and had been trying to understand how deeply my intuition ran.

"We need to give it a try," she said. "We have nowhere else to go tonight."

I nodded. An intake counselor came and introduced herself to us, and after some basic questions, she showed us to two separate rooms. "This one is for seventeen and younger," she explained. "And we have another one for eighteen-year-olds. We're a little short on space in the minor area, so we'll move Sammie in with the adults, since her birthday is next week."

"What?" I asked. We were both minors. And they were separating us.

"The program here is a little different than New York," the lady started to explain. I watched as Sammie was escorted away. Once I was finally alone, I sat down in an empty room, awaiting my roommates, whoever they were.

Dinnertime came. Sammie was seated in the dining hall, with two guys sitting next to her. They were laughing and must have been talking about something funny, I decided. The boys were listening to her intently.

I wandered through the cafeteria's assembly line. Rice, vegetables, fruit. I ignored the chicken that they were serving; I was serious about my sudden vegetarianism. With my tray in hand, I wandered towards the drink station. They had juice, milk, or water. No coffee.

Coffee would've been amazing at that moment, I thought to myself. I needed to keep myself alert, ready for anything. I felt trapped.

After I poured myself a cup of milk, I walked slowly towards the table where

Sammie sat with her new friends. "Hey, that's my friend," I heard Sammie say loudly to the boys.

I nodded and sat next to her. "Hi," I said, my voice heavy. It was too early to make friends, I thought to myself. Sammie was too trusting.

"I'm Nolan," the white boy said. "This is Joey," he told me, pointing to the light skinned boy with glasses.

"How's your room?" I asked Sammie. Mine was a smallish dorm room with three other girls. She smiled.

"This place is great," she told me. "They said that when I turn eighteen, I get to stay out until eight. Or later, if I find a job."

The boys were smiling. They had been pumping Sammie full of info about the program. I pushed the vegetables around my plate absently with my fork. "What is it like for sixteen-year-olds?" I asked.

"Oh," Joey said, shaking his head. "They'll probably send you back with your parents."

I shook my head. "No," I told him. I wasn't going back. Especially not after the guy with the white van found me at work.

"We'll see what they say," Sammie told me, taking a long sip of her juice. We had both eaten very little since we'd left North Carolina, and although I was starving, I didn't want to eat with these boys at the table.

"Sammie, I need to talk to you," I said. I glanced at both boys. "Privately."

Sammie rolled her eyes but told the boys to leave.

"This won't work," I told her. "I think we need to keep going. We should go to California."

She shook her head. "No. This is a good program for me."

"Not for me," I told her. "I won't go back to my dad's house. He told me to leave, and besides, he's getting married again."

"Look, you're the one that needed to get away. Let's try this for a few days."

I shrugged and took a bite of food. "Fine," I told her.

She nodded, and we finished our meal in silence.

"You're right, this won't work," Sammie said two days later. I hadn't given my dad's phone number, and I was planning to hitchhike to California by myself. Sammie had been thinking about finding a job, until she found out that there weren't any good adult school programs in the area.

"We both need to finish high school," I reminded her.

"I should call my mom," she told me.

My jaw dropped open a little. That was a surprise. I stared at her as she walked to the office, where she asked to use the phone. While she was gone, Joey came to sit next to me. "Have you decided to stay?" he asked.

I shrugged. "Doubt it," I told him.

"Where will you go?" he asked.

I smiled. "Probably California," I told him. It was just a dot on the map to me, but often, when I closed my eyes at night and tried to imagine where I belonged, my mind wandered back to my brief stay there when I was thirteen.

"I've never been to California," he said quietly. I shrugged. I didn't care where he had or hadn't been. But Sammie liked Nolan, and Joey had been hanging around me. It was as if we were pairing off as couples.

When Sammie came back to the day room, she had a big smile on her face. "My mom said she'll buy us bus tickets back to North Carolina," she said.

"I don't want to go to North Carolina," I told her.

"To Charlotte. She'll pay for a week in a hotel for us, while we look for jobs."

Nolan sat down beside Sammie. "What about me and Joey?" he asked.

"You can come with us. I'll ask her to buy two more tickets."

Joey's eyes widened. "She'll do that?" he asked.

"Sure," Sammie said. "She doesn't want me in the house, but she still wants me to be happy."

I stared at her for a moment. Something wasn't right. She'd needed me to pay for our trip to Florida, but now her mom was buying us four bus tickets? I waited for her to share more details, but she didn't. There were a lot of things I didn't know about Sammie. I knew she'd been abused by her stepfather, and her mom had let her get married and divorced when she was sixteen. I knew she had lived abroad, in Turkey, and she wore an Arabic necklace on her neck with her name spelled in foreign letters.

What I didn't know was why her mom was suddenly willing to spend money she hadn't seemed to have a week ago.

"What about our stuff?" I asked.

"We'll buy a car and come back for it before the month is over," Sammie said.

I shook my head. "That's a long drive," I told her. I asked the boys if they knew how to drive, and they didn't. Among our new group, I was the only one with a license. It would be a long trek back.

"We should stop in Daytona," I told her.

"She's buying the tickets to Charlotte," Sammie said firmly. I squared my shoulders, ready to argue, but then I remembered my new fear of hitchhiking. I wasn't ready to take a solo trek alone across the country. I wasn't willing to go back to my dad's house. And I didn't want the Covenant House to call him, so I had only one remaining option.

"Okay," I said.

"Great. We leave tomorrow morning," she told me.

33
CHARLOTTE

That's how we ended up taking a bus trek with two boys we barely knew. We left the shelter with Nolan and Joey. The shelter workers tried to convince each of us to stay, but Sammie was determined, I was angry, and the boys were ready for an adventure. Nolan's relationship with Sammie had blossomed; they were holding hands all the ways to the Greyhound station. Joey reached for my hand, but I wasn't sure I was ready to start a relationship with anyone. I let my hands fall into their usual place, burrowed deeply into my pockets.

Nolan and Sammie sat together, one seat in front of me and Joey. Somehow, he'd won the aisle seat, trapping me against the window. "Hey," he said, trying to get me to calm down.

"I can't go back," I said, toying with the straps of my backpack that was resting on my lap. "And what about my stuff?"

"It'll be okay," he said softly. "Tell me what happened."

I'd been vague in my descriptions of that night, up until right then. We had a long bus ride ahead of us, and I knew I was stuck with this group for now. I looked out the window, watching intently as the bus pulled away from the station and merged onto the interstate. Northbound, the opposite of where I needed to go. I needed to get away, not return.

"My dad told me to leave," I said softly. "So, I did. I could've argued, I could've stayed, but I was over it all by then," I said, speaking of the events from a few weeks ago like they were long ago. "And when I tried to walk to my friend's house, this guy offered to give me a ride. And like the dumbass that I am, I said yes," I told him.

I looked up at Joey and saw that he was actually listening to me. Concern etched across his face. "He missed the turn. Twice," I told him. "The second time, he tried to grab me." I shuddered, reliving the moment. It was burned into my skin; the feel of his hand on my arm, his mouth coming close to my face as he leaned in to kiss me. The feel of his lips on my hair as I'd turned away, shocked and frightened.

"He started to accelerate, and I pushed the door open anyway. And then I jumped," I said, the memory flooding my brain. A tear rolled down my cheek. "But then he showed up at my work the next day."

I felt his arm wrap around my shoulder. I wanted to pull away, but it felt good to have someone care about me. My head involuntarily leaned against Joey's shoulder, and I continued to talk. "I had to leave. And Sammie needed to get away, too. So, we paid for a ride to Daytona."

Joey nodded. "It's okay now," he told me. "That guy won't find you. Sammie says Charlotte is far enough away from your hometown."

I wasn't so sure. I closed my eyes and tried to map out all the ways between where it had happened and Charlotte. He still could find me.

My dad hadn't cared. I remembered what he said to the officer. "She's been getting into a lot of trouble lately." Not, "Are you okay?" Not, "It'll be alright, you're safe." Not, "I'm sorry I told you to leave."

We were incompatible as daughter and father. Neither of us was willing to cross that bridge and say what we really needed to say.

"I haven't seen my parents in years," Joey said, and he confided in me a story of growing up in foster care. "Nolan hasn't either. It's the way it is sometimes," he told me.

I closed my eyes and let this new stranger hold me as I fell asleep. It would always be my choice, I told myself as I drifted off to sleep. I would decide who to care for, who to give my heart to. I wasn't willing to share my heart yet but leaning against this stranger was better than being alone.

The road to Charlotte grew shorter and shorter. I let myself relax with Sammie's friends. After all, she seemed happy. I could at least try to be happy, too.

When we finally arrived in Charlotte the following day, we took a taxi to the hotel that Sammie's mom had arranged for us. One week was paid in advance, as she'd promised. We could use the hotel's address and phone number while we looked for jobs.

After we checked in, we surveyed the room. Two queen sized beds. Apparently, I was sharing a bed with Joey. I looked at Sammie curiously. Her mom was okay with this?

While the boys settled in, Sammie and I walked down the block to the grocery store. We were down to our last twenty dollars, and everyone was hungry. I wondered yet again why Sammie's mom had agreed to this. We bought two loaves of bread and the cheapest peanut butter and jelly they sold and headed back to the hotel.

The boys had showered and made themselves comfortable. We placed our purchases on the table and began making ourselves sandwiches. Sammie made one sandwich for each of us, and when Nolan asked for a second, I shook my head. "We're almost out of money," I said.

"Sammie's mom will give us more," he said confidently, and reached for the plastic knives to make another sandwich. I glanced at her, and she shrugged. She'd told me at the market that she really liked him. The look on her face told me to let it go.

I sat down on my side of the bed that I was going to have to share with Joey. He seemed nice enough, I thought to myself. He sat down too, and we both quietly ate our sandwiches.

"Tomorrow, we'll all look for jobs," Sammie said.

I nodded. We'd find something fast, I was sure of it.

34
DAVID'S HOUSE

A week passed. I called my brother David in a moment of weakness, and he had offered to let me stay with him. We hadn't found jobs yet, and the situation between us and the boys was falling apart. Sammie was sitting outside smoking a cigarette when I told her my brother was coming to get me.

"Fine," she said.

I nodded. "Fine." My arms were crossed over my chest. "The boys need to look for jobs too, you know," I told her. We'd been out every day, trying to find any place that would hire us. But the boys hadn't been looking. Sammie had agreed to stay at a different hotel for the upcoming week; a dirtier, cheaper hotel. I didn't want to keep doing this. I needed stability.

"Call me, okay?" Sammie said when my brother arrived. I nodded. Of course, I'd stay in touch with her. She'd saved me from the man with the white van.

David started to tell me what bad decisions I'd made as we drove away. I sighed heavily. This wasn't going to be easy. He told me I shouldn't have gone to Florida and everyone was worried about me. I didn't want to disagree with him or ask who "everyone" was, so I kept my mouth shut.

When we arrived at his house, Denise was waiting in the kitchen. Their house was a few blocks from my dad's house, in a loop through the neighborhood that allowed the corner edges of their properties to touch. "Dad wants your key," he told me after I'd set down my backpack.

I nodded, reaching into my backpack to search for my keychain. When I found it, I silently pulled the key off the chain and handed it to my older brother.

"There will be rules," he told me. "You have to go to work or school," he said.

School was futile at that point. I'd missed half the semester, and there was no way I'd catch up and maintain a decent GPA. I could always get a job at the mall, I thought to myself.

"Did you drop out of school?" Denise asked me, her voice high pitched.

This wasn't good. I sat down at the table and let them tell me how I'd ruined my future and how I was making all the wrong choices.

I'd made a mistake. I shouldn't have agreed to come here, I thought to myself.

"I'll take the semester off, and I'll still have enough credits to graduate on time," I said finally. "I can get a job for now," I told them, meeting their eyes.

"Alright," David said. He seemed satisfied with my answer. "You can start looking for work tomorrow."

I played with their young son for a few hours. Geoff was my second nephew, and he was four years old. Years earlier, I was playing cards with David at his house, and I had a bag of M&Ms. When I got down to the last three, David said he wanted them. I agreed, but "only if I can influence your firstborn son." He'd said yes. It had been a long-standing family joke. And then his wife had found out she was pregnant. I joked about being an influence on him but knew I wasn't doing well yet.

I wondered what he would think of me as he got older.

I put down the toy car I'd been holding. I couldn't be this person. I would have to figure out a different plan. "Goodnight, Geoff," I said, kissing him firmly on his forehead.

The next day, I went to the mall and convinced the Chick-Fil-A manager to hire me. He recognized me from the freestanding restaurant across town. I'd been a great worker until I'd been attacked, and since it was the same family that owned both restaurants, he decided to give me another chance.

When I walked back to David's house after finding a job and scheduling myself for the next day, I took the back way to avoid my dad's house. I walked behind the shopping center to the small opening in the fence that indicated an old stairway and walked slowly down the path that led to David's street.

I arrived at David's house to find Denise playing with Geoff in the backyard. She waved at me, so I approached.

"I found a job," I told her proudly.

"What about school?" she asked cautiously.

"I'll go back in the fall," I lied. I knew I'd leave before then. I was already calculating how much money I could earn by summer. I knew this wasn't going to work. Geoff smiled up at me from his sandbox.

"So, tell me about the job," she said.

I told her the details. I'd been re-hired by Chick-Fil-A, and I would work the morning shift. They were expecting me there at eight o'clock the following morning.

She nodded, suddenly quiet. "Alright," she told me finally. "Your brother will be home soon."

I swallowed hard. I'd taken my time at the mall and wasted part of the day, just to avoid being in the house. Something just didn't feel right.

When David returned home, it was obvious he'd already heard my news from Denise. He handed me a list he must have typed at work. "What's this?" I asked, confused as I read the first few lines.

"Well, since you're going to work instead of school, we've decided you have two choices. You can pay rent, or you can earn your rent. These are the chores you'll need to do so you don't owe us anything."

I read through the list. Clean the house. Pick up the laundry. Potty train Geoff. What the hell, I thought. This really wasn't going to work.

"Um, why?" I asked. "I thought you wanted me here."

David sighed. Denise didn't say anything. I turned to look away, and Geoff passed by me at that moment. I couldn't do anything to harm this kid. I wasn't fit to stay with them. Somehow, I had to come up with a better plan.

I calculated how long I'd stayed in the system previously. How long I'd spent in juvenile hall and random detention centers. I could make this work until summer. "Okay," I said softly. What other choice did I have?

The next day, I left for work early. Not only did I want to be prepared for my first day, but I felt like I needed a fresh start. I'd struggled to get through my chores the night before, and Geoff wouldn't sit on the toilet. There was no way I could hold a full-time job and complete the chore list. But I tried anyway. I begged my previous boss to hire me back, too, and began working at both restaurants. In my spare time, I tackled the chore list.

Ultimately, the decision wasn't up to me. When I arrived back at David's house from work a few weeks later, Denise was standing in the living room with an envelope. She yelled at me; told me that she knew.

"What did I do?" I asked.

David filled me in. Sammie's mom had called them and told them I was planning to leave. They'd withdrawn my recent paychecks from the bank.

"Since you're leaving anyway, just go," Denise told me.

I nodded slowly. Right. I was going to leave anyway.

I picked up my backpack and filled it with clothes. Then, I sorted through my belongings I'd retrieved from my dad's house. "Fine," I said, a half hour later when Sammie's mom arrived. Her mom kept darting angry looks in my direction as she drove. There was a boy I'd never met in the back seat with them.

"Let's go," Sammie told me.

I stared at her strangely. "You got me kicked out," I told her.

"Well, let's go. You kept telling me about California. Let's go."

I glanced over at the pale, skinny boy in the backseat next to me. "Who are you?"

"This is Hunter," Sammie said. "He needs to leave too. You have enough for three tickets, right?"

I did.

"I wasn't going to go until summer. I wanted to save up for a car."

"You owe me," she hissed.

Her mom drove us down familiar streets to the bus station. I glanced over at Hunter, wondering what his story was.

"I guess we're going to Hollywood," I finally said.

35
BACK TO CALIFORNIA

Hollywood.

I was finally home.

Inside of the taxi, I glanced at the others; suddenly aware of how awkward I felt, sharing this moment with them. The city I had dreamed about for the past three and a half years loomed before me, and the sweet smell of the thick air filled my lungs. The dirty city streets looked like streets of gold to me. I imagined I felt the same joy as newcomers had felt when they set their eyes upon New York City for the first time, back when people left everything behind for a chance in a new country.

Home had only been three days away; at the bargain price of one hundred and twenty dollars for a one-way ticket. The price hadn't changed. And I had finally arrived.

We arrived at our first destination; Hollywood Self Storage on Argyle and Franklin. We would not leave behind our last possessions as Sammie and I had done in Daytona, several months earlier. I would not live out of a backpack ever again, I thought. We were better equipped this time.

The sign said that we were still too early; Hunter and I decided to guard our belongings while Sammie bought a dozen donuts from across the street. We were so hungry; it had been too long since our last real meal.

The streets had an acrid odor, but to me, it smelled like a field of wildflowers. I felt free; finally safe from white vans and police officers waiting to arrest me for being underage. We had made it!

We gleefully ate the donuts, one after another. They tasted so much richer than the donuts we were accustomed to. They were thicker, doughier. They would give us the false sensation of fullness. We even shared them with the treacherous man who had accompanied us from the bus station. I ignored him; the others were fully aware of my opinion of him.

I paid for three months of rent for a small storage locker, and we carefully hauled all our misshapen bags and boxes to our new locker. We crammed everything inside, keeping only the bare necessities in each of our backpacks. I noted down the hours of the storage, so that we could get back in when we needed to. Then, I slid the key onto my empty keychain, and shoved it into my pocket.

"Time to get to our hotel," Hunter reminded me. I groaned. I had a really creepy feeling about the strange man that he'd met on the bus and I didn't care who knew it. That bad feeling that I usually got was screaming at me to watch myself.

"It costs too much," I said, reminding them that it was my money.

Sammie leaned in closer to me, whispering in my ear. "You owe me. Please do this for me. This one little thing."

She begged, and I gave up my reasoning. "Let's go," I finally agreed.

We took yet another taxi where we found a cheap motel. "Give me forty dollars, and I'll pay the other forty, so that we can have the room for two nights," the man told me.

I shook my head. "I don't like that idea."

"Come on, I'll need to sleep after I get drunk."

"Aren't you paying Hunter to watch over you? Shouldn't you also pay for the room?" I countered.

He shook his head. "There's three of you and one of me. I'm paying half."

I looked at Sammie. She mouthed to me, "Give him the money."

The man went inside and paid for the room, while we waited outside. We didn't want the clerk to charge us extra for having more than one person in the room so it was logical to stay out of sight.

After twenty minutes or so, a side door opened. The man beckoned to us, and we followed him inside, up the stairs, and into the waiting room.

Sammie relaxed, sitting down at the table with Hunter. The man sat down on the bed. Only I remained standing.

"Let's order food. How about you give me twenty dollars and I'll buy us some lunch?" the man said.

I shook my head. "Do you even have any money?"

The man smiled. "Of course. Look, I have forty dollars right here." He waved forty dollars in front of my face.

"That doesn't impress me. It's my money." I glared at him, the fight building up in my eyes. Sammie grabbed my arm. "Why the hell would I be impressed when you're showing me my money?"

"Well, if you guys don't want to work for me," the man began.

Sammie looked up at me, pleading. Hunter's face seemed to shine with desperation. "We need the money," he told me. I shook my head again.

"Forget it. You two can stay if you want," I said, throwing my backpack across my shoulder again. I walked outside, and after a few minutes, Sammie caught up with me. "Let's learn the bus system," she pleaded with me. "Hunter is already working. And we can use the money."

I shrugged. "Whatever. But don't make me tell you I told you so," I told her. "You know if I don't follow my instincts, something bad always happens."

"I know, I know," Sammie told me, putting her arm around my shoulder. "I just think you might be wrong this time, and we really need the money."

"If you say so," I said, thinking of the one hundred or so dollars our fund had dwindled down to.

We walked up the street to Hollywood and Western. The street didn't seem so glamorous anymore. The excitement had faded, and had been replaced with a cold, nauseous fear.

Something bad was going to happen. I could feel it in my bones.

We rode the 217 line all the way to its last stop before exiting. We were on the corner of Washington and Fairfax in uncharted territory. The area seemed a little dirtier, and it reminded me of when we had gotten lost in Miami. "Let's go back," I told Sammie.

She smiled faintly. "You're right. Let's just go to the McDonald's over there and use the bathroom first, okay?"

I nodded. "Good idea."

We went inside, where Sammie and I went to the women's restroom. Sammie stepped outside to ask the manager something, and he came into the restroom where I was checking my hair in the mirror. He leaned back against the door and smiled at us. I turned to look at him; he was a small man and of an unknown ethnicity. His hair was dark and wiry, and his skin was copper colored. A pressed uniform hung loosely over his small frame, and a sickeningly sweet smile hung across his face.

I raised an eyebrow. What was Sammie up to now? "We need money. Do you know where we can get jobs?" she was asking.

The man pulled down his pants, still smiling. "Forty dollars," he told us.

I shook my head. "Ew!"

Sammie mimicked my reaction. "Let's go," she said, and the manager shrugged. He moved out of our way, letting us pass by.

"Your choice," he said, still smiling. Laughter seeped out of his filthy little mouth.

The 217 bus back to Hollywood picked us up quickly, yet it wasn't fast enough for me. I felt so angry and violated. I couldn't get away fast enough.

Sammie and I spent most of the bus ride "window-shopping" for ideal apartment buildings or places to apply for work. We pointed at interesting buildings and laughed about shared memories of our job hunt in Daytona.

"We can find work as hotel maids or in a restaurant," Sammie said.

"Yeah. Or maybe we could work in a store. I'd prefer retail to greasy fries any day." I smiled. "Well, if there is a Chick-fil-A out here, I'd get the job for sure. I already have a year's experience."

Sammie and I laughed. "Yeah, and you still have the name tag."

Our jovial mood changed slightly when the bus turned on Hollywood Boulevard. "I'm not going back to the hotel tonight, Sammie," I told her, motioning towards the backpack that I had brought with me. "I have a really bad feeling about that guy. I just don't trust him."

Deep brown eyes pleaded with me, but I shook my head, even as Sammie spoke. "Well, then we'd have to meet up in the morning. Where will you go?"

"I don't know. I'll just walk around or something."

36
THE FIRST NIGHT

We said our goodbyes, and I exited the bus at Vine and Hollywood. Tall buildings loomed above me at all sides of the intersection. I was standing in front of a pizza shop, which looked less than inviting. Across the street was a liquor store, and diagonal was a small Mexican restaurant. It was painted bright orange and had specials advertised in Spanish.

I liked Mexican food, and I had studied high school Spanish for two years. It was time to see if I had learned anything.

I crossed both streets and then walked the final few steps to the restaurant. The lunch area was smaller than I had imagined from outside; there was a small counter that seated around four or five patrons.

When I entered the tiny space, I noticed there were already a few customers lining the wall. There was a small space, but I would not fit there. Either I would have to wait or eat outside.

With a shrug, my eyes began to search the menu. *Carnitas*, I thought. Well, that probably meant meat. Now that I was vegetarian again, that was not something I could eat. This wasn't the first time I'd given up meat; I'd spent several months avoiding meat under the reign of Terri. I recalled all the times I'd had an upset stomach from her uncooked meat. Oh, why hadn't I paid more attention when we had studied the food chapter in my Spanish class?

I couldn't remember the word for beans, but I figured they understood English. "Can I have a bean burrito?" I asked the cashier.

He smiled, a big, toothy grin. "*Solo uno?*"

"Um, sure." I glanced back at the wall.

While the cook prepared the food, the parking lot attendant came inside. He smiled at me, attempting to flirt. But he didn't know English and my Spanish sucked.

"*Un burrito de frijoles, listo.*"

I glanced away from the parking attendant, focusing on the cashier. He signaled me to pick up my food, which I obediently picked up. As soon as the food bag was in my hand, I walked rapidly towards the exit, grateful for a chance to escape the leery eyes of the cook and the parking man. At least the cashier had been somewhat friendly, although very intent on smiling at me. What, had they never seen a redheaded girl from North Carolina before? Or at least, a fake redheaded girl?

I sat down at the bus stop in front of the taco stand. When I opened the bag, I saw that the food had been packaged in a foil container, and that it was relatively warm. Peeling back the top, I found my burrito was filled with refried beans, cheese, an orange-colored rice with peas and carrots in it. I inhaled the aroma of the food, realizing I was finally eating authentic Mexican food.

The food was surprisingly good. When I finished, I realized the parking attendant had been watching me eat. He sat down next to me at the bus bench.

"What is your name?" he asked slowly, his words thickly accented.

"Sheri."

"Cheri?"

"Close enough."

"Want to have some cerveza, Cheri?" I looked at him closely. He had dark hair, tied back in a ponytail underneath his attendant cap. Young eyes, perfect complexion. He seemed friendly enough. And I was lacking better options.

I smiled. Beer. I could drink a few beers, I thought. Why not? It had been a long day, and I had no place else to be. Darkness had started to fall, and I needed to feel numb again.

Tossing my wrapper into the metal trash can beside the bench, I followed the parking attendant to the back of the restaurant. We entered the kitchen, where the cook was grinning solicitously at me as he uncapped a glass bottle of Corona.

With a twist of the hand, he squeezed a lime into the narrow end of the bottle. I reached out for the beer that was offered to me and took a quick swig. The alcohol numbed my throat, and I chased the bottle down as fast as I knew how. It was becoming too easy for me to do this, I thought sadly. The angrier, heartbroken part of me pushed forward. Why the hell not?

Both men cheered me on. They handed me another beer, and another. I drank them recklessly, increasingly bitter that I was stuck in Hollywood alone for my first night back. The men continued handing beers to me until I was completely drunk, and then I sat down in the hot, perfumed kitchen. The cook began cleaning the kitchen around me, preparing to close for the evening.

Dripping in sweat from the heat, and still unaccustomed to the climate of Los Angeles in April, my body was simmering. I stood up, but quickly realized that my feet would not work properly. The parking attendant approached me from behind, catching me before I could fall.

"Enough. You need *café*."

I stood, propped against the kitchen counter, my hands desperately clinging to the chrome. The cook prepared a thick, dark instant coffee for me. They gave it to me, forcing me to drink the warm liquid.

"*Ya me voy*," said the parking attendant to the cook. He took me by my arm and helped me walk away. I was too tired to care and too drunk to ask where we were going. He carried my backpack for me, as well as the half of my body that would not obey my commands. I leaned against him, grateful I could follow someone's lead for the moment.

We walked for a few blocks, and the cooler night air was able to refresh me. It was such a contrast to the steamy kitchen; I was beginning to feel a little like myself again.

The man stopped in front of a small hotel, still clutching my waist. "Is this okay?"

I shrugged. "Yeah," I said, not really caring anymore. I had never been so reckless before, but who cared, anyway? I had nowhere to sleep, and no one seemed to give a damn about where I was. Not even my so-called friends that had accompanied me to California. "This is okay."

The next morning, I awoke with a sharp headache. The man from the night before was sitting next to me, smiling. How long had he been watching me sleep?

"Good morning," he said.

I rubbed my eyes, and then glanced at him again. It took me a moment before awareness flooded over me. I wrapped a sheet around my body and glanced around the room. Fear. Vulnerability. "Where is my backpack?"

He pointed to the doorway. I glanced at the bag, glad I had not lost it during my momentary touch with reckless insanity.

"I need to go find my friends," I heard myself saying. My head was pounding, and I was exhausted. I really shouldn't have been drinking. He looked like he wanted something from me, but I didn't care. I needed to find my friends, even more than I needed to get away from the stranger next to me.

"Cheri –" said the guy. I didn't even know his name.

"Sheri."

"Cheri, I like you."

I shook my head. "I have to go."

I gathered my clothes and my backpack. He stood by as I escaped to the bathroom, where I quickly showered and got dressed. When I emerged, he was waiting for me. Ready.

"I will walk with you." He seemed nice. Safe. At least, as safe as a man could be who gets a sixteen-year-old girl drunk and takes her to a hotel.

We walked side by side, the distance between us growing as he escorted me back to Hollywood Boulevard. Somehow, I was supposed to find Sammie and Hunter on Hollywood Boulevard. I turned to look at the man who I had spent my first night back in Hollywood with, and flashed him a sad smile.

He kissed me on the cheek and we said goodbye. I sighed. It wasn't meant to be. Time to search for Sammie, I thought sadly. But I was less complete than when I had parted with my friends the night before. I kept losing pieces of my heart, one by one.

37
BACK ON THE STREETS

I walked a few blocks, noticing the intricacies of an early morning in Hollywood. Street sweepers were scrubbing down the stars on the Walk of Fame. People were huddling in groups at the bus stops. Closed storefronts were covered with thick, metal doors to protect them from would-be robbers. Tourists walked around anxiously, pointing at stars on the sidewalk or at other Hollywood memorabilia. I wandered down Hollywood Boulevard, wondering where to go next. It was early, and Sammie and Hunter weren't anywhere obvious.

Eventually, my feet found the familiar path back to LAYN. The Los Angeles Youth Network. The place where I had stayed when I was thirteen. Also, the place that had called the police on me when I was thirteen, starting a cascade of events.

I paused in front of the building. The white paint had been replaced with an eerie bright blue, and a mural showing a distorted Dorothy from the Wizard of Oz. A tragic mural; kids searching for home in a place that wasn't.

I paused, deciding. And rang the bell.

"Why are you here?" I heard the tall, lanky man ask me in his thick Middle Eastern accent. There was a hint of annoyance in his tone. He was staring at me from behind a desk, fingers hovering over a small intake packet, awaiting the answers that would explain my very existence. He introduced himself as Jonah, one of the drop-in shelter staff at the Los Angeles Youth Network.

I slid down in the chair, suddenly feeling uncertain. Why was I there? How could I answer a question I would not fully understand for another twenty years? I froze, chewed down on my lower lip. How could I explain the forces that drove me westward, again?

Our eyes met for a moment, but I could not hold his gaze. There was too much judgment in his dark brown eyes. I quickly glanced out the window, to the parking lot, where a puff of cigarette smoke rose from the group of teens that were hanging out behind the building. "I knew I could come here. I've been here before," I told him.

He scribbled something onto the intake packet and waited for me to speak. I stared blankly outside for a while before turning back to face him. He was clearly waiting for me to continue my story. I sighed heavily and added, "I ran away when I was 13 and I came here for a few days."

"From North Carolina?" he asked.

I nodded. Yes, from North Carolina. That place I never wanted to return to; the place where I had experienced so much pain.

The conversation continued as a series of terse questions and short answers.

Was I abused? No, not physically. Was I ever in jail? Sure, 10 months in juvie when I was 13. Foster care? Yes, after I ran away when I was 13. Not anymore, and never again. Did I want to go home? Are you kidding me, after he told me to leave?

Nope. Was I sexually active? Not your business. Fine, yes. Where was I planning to stay? Wherever, but not in the shelter. Was I thinking about going home? What, why? I just got here. I was here to stay.

I sensed this man did not like me. That was okay, I supposed. I didn't really like me most of the time. I shrugged it off and stood up once the intake was finished. Finally, I was free to relax.

I followed Jonah down the hallway, towards the dayroom. A heaviness of nostalgia and regret filled the air. The walls held photographs of a long-ago celebrity softball game. A distant part of me remembered the layout of the shelter from my brief stay there in 1992. The dayroom was essentially the main open space for the homeless youth who lived at the shelter and those who dropped in during daytime hours. Since all the youth were hanging out in a cloud of Marlboro and Newport smoke behind the building, I had a few blissful moments to eat my breakfast in peace.

I was absolutely starving after spending last night on my own. Well, not really on my own. But at least not with the two so-called friends that had traveled with me from North Carolina.

After filling a Styrofoam bowl with corn flakes and milk, I sat down at one of the two circular tables and allowed myself to relax a little. I was finally here. Finally, back in California, the place that had captivated me at 13, the place I had dreamt of returning to over the past several years. The place where I would finally have a chance to get my life together. The only place in my sixteen years that had ever felt like home. Reggie's voice echoed through my mind. "Lil Hollywood." I wondered if he would've been proud of me for making it back.

As I ate, I had a chance to study my surroundings. A large TV sat in the corner, barely audible and showing a news segment. Same black sofas, although more worn since my last visit. In fact, the whole building was starting to show signs of aging. Many lost teens had passed through this building; who knows where each of them had ended up. The wall was lined with a long table and several archaic desktop computers. Behind me was a payphone, a bulletin board full of scattered papers and messages, and a window to the outside world. There was a small kitchen space connected to the dayroom, and Jonah was standing there. Watching me.

I sighed again. This was my life now. I finished the bowl of cereal and tossed the temporary bowl in the trash. I had rested, and perhaps now I could start looking for Sammie and Hunter. I had briefly forgotten my traveling companions. I was still furious with them.

I stood, almost ready to leave, when the front door opened and closed loudly. A heavyset Latina girl with a thick jacket came into the hallway suddenly. Her hair was slicked back into a fierce ponytail, and anger furrowed her brows. I watched as she crossed into the dayroom and picked up the pay phone. She made a few quick calls, and then noticed me after she hung up.

"Are you going to stay here?" she asked.

I shook my head. Nope. No shelters for me. At least, not yet. I wanted to explore my options. "I'm Sheri," I told her.

"Michelle," she told me.

I stared at her for a moment, wondering if we would be friends. Maybe, I thought. I shrugged and asked her, "Want to go shoplifting with me? I'm thinking about getting a new shirt."

She shrugged and agreed, so I put my backpack back on and we walked together back down the long hallway to exit the building. We wandered up the road and turned onto the Boulevard.

There was a small boutique, and we entered with ease. I chatted with the salesgirl for a few minutes, and then nonchalantly folded a few shirts up and buried them under my arm. Easy for me. I waved goodbye to the saleslady, who was completely unaware of my theft. We left the store a few shirts richer, and we divided up the loot before we went our separate ways.

I settled into a slow stroll, trying to reacquaint myself with the city that had captivated me for so long. A small triumphant smile formed on my lips. Sure, I'd come back earlier than expected, but nonetheless, I was back. I was home.

And I was homeless. I took a deep breath and considered my options. I had wandered for several blocks already and was now back at the corner of Hollywood and Vine. I could see the burrito stand from the previous night, and while a part of me wanted to see if that guy was back at work, the broken part of me was ready to move on. I decided to take a seat on a bus bench in front of a pizza parlor, on the furthest corner away from the restaurant.

I watched as traffic moved by in front of me; cars and city buses. It was a warm spring day, and everything seemed bright and hopeful. Mothers walked by with small children. Twenty-somethings on their way to work bustled past, their eyes focused and their clothing crisp. I settled onto the bench, my faithful backpack resting beside me.

Perhaps twenty minutes had passed by when a police car drove down the street and stopped in front of me. "Get on the next bus or get up and walk," the officer shouted from the window. Startled, I grasped the handle of my backpack and stood up.

I was clean. I had showered in the morning, before leaving the hotel room. I was wearing clean clothes; my hair was combed. I wondered, how did they know? How had they picked me out of the lineup so quickly?

That uneasy feeling that I used to get when I was younger had returned. I strapped my backpack on and began walking slowly. Where would I go? I didn't know where Sammie or Hunter were, and I was seething with anger now. We'd had a plan. And that plan did not include them blowing half of our remaining money on a con artist.

I glanced down at the bright pink stars on the sidewalk as I walked. Apparently, there would be no rest stops. I read names of actors, producers, and musicians. Some names I recognized, but most I did not. That's the problem of having an interrupted childhood, I mused. I was clueless about so many things.

38
THEIR FIRST NIGHT

"Sheri!" I heard someone calling my name. I paused, searching for Sammie. I saw her across the street, standing with Hunter. I waited for the light to change before running across the street to join them.

"We've been looking for you everywhere," Sammie started, her voice higher pitched than normal. Hunter was uncharacteristically quiet.

I shrugged. It wasn't their business how I spent the night. They didn't care where I was going to stay when we had split up the previous day. I made a face, daring them to question me further.

"That asshole raped Hunter," Sammie blurted out. That got my attention.

"What?" I demanded. We were walking now, back towards the cheap motel they had stayed at.

They filled me in quickly. The ex-con that I'd been wary of was just as dangerous as I'd suspected. I had met men like him before and knew he was trouble. We had argued about the hotel room and the money and Sammie had tried to make me feel guilty. I wished that I'd been wrong, but my intuition rarely failed me.

"So, what are you going to do?" I asked. Nobody said anything for several long minutes.

We walked down Hollywood Boulevard, past where the stars stop lining the streets, past the decaying buildings. We turned onto Western Avenue, and when we arrived at the motel, I waited outside. It was a typical sketchy motel, and I couldn't go in because I hadn't stayed the night.

Sammie and Hunter went back in and gathered their belongings. I could hear them arguing with the man inside but I couldn't quite make out their words. In that moment, I was grateful for my intuition. Nothing good could come from not following my instincts.

When they came back outside, they both had their backpacks strapped on their backs. Sammie was angry, and her face was flushed. I could see Hunter was starting to perk up a little. His cheeks looked a little pinker as we walked back to the Boulevard. Away from that man, and back towards uncertainty.

We walked down the Boulevard for a few hours, watching the city wake up. Shop owners were spraying the sidewalks in front of their stores, thick metal gates were being lifted away to reveal the stores hidden behind them during the night. Hunter wanted to sit down to rest but I told them about the police officer that had shouted at me earlier in the day. We finally met a few other homeless kids, who walked with us to a small park. It was a few blocks away from the main boulevard. Sammie and Hunter talked to them excitedly, eager to learn anything that would make this trip worthwhile. I sat back, pensive.

That night, I stared up at the sky, wondering why I couldn't see the stars. I sighed deeply; the only stars in this place were the ones people walked all over as they hurried about their days. I wondered if I would ever get it together. Would I find what I was looking for, even if I didn't have any clue what exactly that might be?

My friends and new companions were passing around a bottle of alcohol, and I gladly took a long swig. Why not? I had already given up so much of who I was over the past few months. I was entranced by the circular conversation happening in front of me; the two homeless kids Sammie and Hunter had found were sharing a bottle of alcohol from a brown bag. Cigarettes were being passed out, and one found its way into my hands.

I'd never been much of a smoker although I'd known other teens who smoked. I shrugged and put the cigarette to my lips, letting a kid named States light it for me. I inhaled, coughing deeply. I'd given my lungs so much time to heal since those earlier escapades, and instantly the cough returned.

States was clearly the leader among the pair. He was younger, a fast talker. Camila wore her history on her face. These streets had claimed her. I wondered how long she'd been out here? I watched as she licked her lipstick stained lips, trying not to lose too much color onto the cigarette she slowly inhaled.

Camila and States were telling us about their trips to Mexico. They encouraged us to come along with them, saying there was plenty of work dancing at the topless bars. I took another drink as they talked dollars. Sammie and Hunter were leaning forward and taking it all in; I sat back and drank quietly.

When the liquor was gone, and the conversation was starting to dwindle, anxiety began to set in. Nightfall. No place to go. Down to my last hundred dollars, but I told Sammie we had only ten dollars left. She'd been wrestling with the numbers all day, trying to figure out if I was telling her the truth.

"We could introduce you to some people and get you down to Mexico this weekend," States was saying. I shook my head, but Sammie and Hunter eagerly agreed. We all stood to walk somewhere else, wherever States and Camila were planning to take us.

After exiting the tiny park, our small group began walking down the side streets that led us back to the main boulevard. My backpack bounced lightly on my back. I watched for "help wanted" signs in the windows of the businesses as we walked, but there were none. We passed by lingerie stores, souvenir shops, eateries. When we passed by the small Mexican restaurant I had stopped at the previous night, my eyes quickly searched for the parking attendant. I didn't see him. I wasn't sure if I even wanted to see him again.

Next to the small restaurant, we passed a tiny bar and a deli. The bar had a bodyguard by the door, protecting the occupants from minors like us. I peered in as we passed, my lips craving another drink. Another chance to forget, if only for a moment. Instead, we kept walking, past the entrance of an old theater called Pantages.

Inside the unlit foyer, there were dozens of people setting up their camps for the night. "People squat here," States was saying, testing our group to see if we understood the lingo. He was clearly seasoned, and he was leading us somewhere. My intuition started to kick in again.

"Sammie, we can stay here for the night," I told my friend, pausing in front of the theater.

Camila interrupted us. "Nah, this isn't a good place," she told us. "You should stay with us."

I kept my eyes on Sammie. I didn't want to get separated again, and I couldn't go back to the same spot from the previous night. Sammie hadn't even asked where I'd gone, but her night had been much scarier than mine.

"Let's go," States urged us. Hunter glanced at me, a wave of nervousness rolling across his face. He was so pale, so different. One night changed everything, I thought. Sadly, I knew exactly how that felt.

It wasn't the time for me to interject. I shrugged and fell back into step with the group.

We continued down Hollywood Boulevard, passing the end of the pink stars on the sidewalk. I was beginning to get my bearings, and I recognized the street sign for Gower. A few blocks down the road was the shelter where I'd met Michelle. Was I ready for a shelter? I wondered.

States was talking quickly, sharing details that were more like puzzle pieces. "Sometimes when we go down to Mexico, Camila makes a couple hundred dollars in one night." I raised an eyebrow. Interesting, Camila did the work and States did the talking. "We can talk to my friends, and maybe they'll help you go to Mexico with us."

I shuddered involuntarily. This wasn't good. "Sammie," I whispered as we walked. "We should go back to that squat."

She shook her head. "We need this opportunity," she told me. I shrugged. Fine, I would stick with them for now. But if things got bad again, I was leaving.

We rounded the next corner and stopped in front of a dilapidated apartment complex. There was a large wrought iron gate, and a metal box at the doorway had been set up to let certain people inside. I paused, thinking that the gate was in better shape than the building.

States pressed a series of numbers, and a voice spoke through the intercom. "Yo," said a man's voice.

"Let me in," States said, and then we heard a buzzing sound. It reminded me of the apartments in the Bronx that I'd spent a week in when I was thirteen.

Camila pulled the gate open, and we all followed States inside the complex. We walked to the back of the building and States knocked on a door. Three solid knocks, then a tap. "Yo," a large African American man said as he opened the door. "States, my man," he said, tapping his fist against States' own outstretched hand. The man eyed us carefully, his gaze falling indiscreetly over Sammie and me. "Come on in, ladies," he told us, stepping aside to allow us to enter his apartment.

"Hey, I met these travelers," States told him after we had all walked inside. The living room was sparsely decorated. There was a coffee table with no decorations or books resting in the center of the room. A tired yellow sofa sat against the wall, and a bean bag chair sat against the opposite wall. I cocked my head to the side, trying to see the rest of the apartment. It didn't look like anyone truly lived here, I thought to myself.

"Right, right," the man said. "Would either of you ladies like a drink?" he offered.

Sammie nodded. I shook my head. Nope, not here. I didn't feel reckless anymore.

"Have a seat," he said, as he wandered out of the room to get Sammie's drink. I peered cautiously at the sofa, which would only hold a few of us. Sammie and Hunter sat, with Camila beside them. She fussed with her hair quietly.

I stood against the wall, my eyes on the small kitchen. Our host brought a handful of wine coolers to the room. "You love those," Sammie exclaimed, looking at me. I glared at her.

The host paused in front of me, offering me a bottle. "No thanks," I said. I pointed to my head. "I've got a headache," I lied.

He laughed, a heavy sound. "Right," he told me. "What's your name?"

I stared back at him. He was obviously older than us. His eyes were deep brown and his skin reminded me of dark coffee. His smile was too relaxed, too sure. On an ordinary day, I would've thought he was a good-looking man. But I couldn't read his facial expression, and something about him made me nervous. I'd promised myself to follow my instincts after the man in the white van had attacked me.

"Sheri," I offered. There was no sense pretending I didn't have a name. I leaned against the wall with my arms crossed over my chest, ready to watch our meeting unfold.

"And you?" he asked, turning his attention to Sammie. She beamed. I thought back to when I'd met her at the convenience store next to our high school. Everyone listened when she spoke. She was larger than life. He'd read her well, I thought cynically. I felt my heartbeat begin to race.

I watched as he handed her a bottle, and she eagerly took a swig. It had been a hard night, and she'd been through a lot. Just the previous night, I'd needed my own release. New town, new life. There were so many things that each of us needed to forget. She paused for a moment, then said, "Sammie."

"Is that short for Samantha?" he asked in a charming tone. I sighed. This was too much.

States interjected. "Do you think they'd do well in Mexico?" he asked.

The man chuckled. "Yeah, they'll do alright," he said.

Camila sat up straight, presenting our host with a bright red smile. He hadn't told us his name, I realized. She reached for a drink also. He hesitated, but then handed it to her. "Do you have any clothes that they could wear?" Camila asked him.

Another laugh. He nodded. "Yeah, I'll be right back." He wandered out of the room, then returned with a large trash bag full of clothing. He set it in front of Camila, who quickly set down her drink on the coffee table and began rummaging through the bag.

"This is nice," she said, pulling a yellow tube top out of the bag and holding it in front of Sammie. "It'll make your boobs pop," she told her.

I watched as Sammie and Camila inventoried the clothes in the bag. My mind darted back to conversations I'd had just a few months ago, joking about dancing topless in Mexico. But this was serious. Camila really did dance at bars in Mexico.

"We're going to get regular jobs," I told our host. He turned back to me, still smiling.

"States, this girl is funny," he said, his eyes on me. I watched as he sized me up. I was wearing the shirt I'd stolen with Michelle earlier in the day. Had that just been this morning? I pondered. So much had happened. It fit snugly over my chest. And of course, I had on those damned corduroy pants. The ones I'd worn that night when the guy in the white van had picked me up. My eyes shifted downward, and I could still see the tear in the fabric over my right knee. Panic surged back into my chest.

"Sammie, we need to go," I said. She looked up at me, suddenly recognizing my fear. I was serious. This wasn't a good idea.

Sammie nodded. "Sheri gets these bad feelings sometimes," she started to explain. I shook my head. "We'll let you know," she added as she stood. Hunter followed suit.

"This offer will expire," our host said. States stood up abruptly.

"I'll talk to them," I heard him say as I took a step towards the door.

The man reached for my arm, catching it briefly in his outstretched hand. "Don't miss an opportunity," he told me.

My heart thudded in my chest. "Get out, get out!" it screamed. I pulled away, and the contact between us faded. "Thanks for the offer," I mumbled, rushing out the doorway. Once outside of the apartment, I took several deep breaths.

"Are you okay?" Sammie asked.

I shook my head. "Let's go," I told her.

States and Camila raced out of the apartment after us, but I turned around and faced them. Hunter and Sammie were behind me. "We're fine on our own," I said.

Ultimately, we walked away as a smaller trio, towards an unknown evening. I felt safer without them. I'd forgotten for a moment how little Sammie and Hunter actually knew about living out here. They'd been sheltered from the streets up until this moment. Sure, Sammie and I had spent several weeks together in February, when we'd been a haphazard pair traveling away from danger in North Carolina. But she'd never seen the things I'd seen. I reminded myself I needed to speak up sooner when we were in danger.

39
OUTSIDE

We found a quiet wooded area near the park to sleep. I awoke with the sensation that ants were crawling on me, which was one of my deepest fears after the time I'd spent at Dillon. While Sammie and Hunter slept, I sat up beside them and peered down the hill, overlooking Hollywood. We were too exposed up here; we'd slept only a few yards away from the fence for a hotel. Covered or not, I knew that we needed to find somewhere safer.

Daylight came, and Sammie stretched her arms. Hunter let out a low whistle. "The ground was rough," he told us. I nodded. Sammie looked at me, waiting to hear my thoughts.

"We should walk back to the Boulevard," I told them after they both sat up. The traffic had started to pick up below us, and the city was awakening. Sammie agreed, and stood to dust off the dirt and debris from sleeping on the hard ground.

Soon, we were strolling down the Boulevard, taking in the sites. The previous day had been too traumatic for all of us. I wondered when we would run into Camila and States again. We walked a few blocks before sitting down at a bus bench, aiming to get our bearings.

"I'm hungry," Hunter said. Sammie and I nodded. I knew what he wanted; he was hoping I'd buy us a meal. But our cash was running out fast, and we'd wasted too much on that con artist. If I thought about it for too long, I would realize just how angry I was with them for not listening to me.

"We could see if any of the drop-in shelters are open today," I offered. They both peered at me, curious. Sammie had been with me to the Covenant House in Miami, but our stay had been brief. She knew I didn't want to stay in a shelter again.

Hunter kept his eyes fixated on the passing cars. His voice shook a little as he spoke. "What do we have to do there?" he asked.

I explained what I'd seen at LAYN the previous day. "We could get a bowl of cereal or something," I told him. He finally turned to look at me, his features showing relief. "I think they open in a few hours, but we'll be okay for now," I told him.

Sammie stared up Vine Street, in the direction of our storage unit. "Maybe we should get more donuts?" she asked, hopeful.

My stomach growled loudly, battling with the harshness of our situation. "We don't have enough money," I said.

Sammie focused her eyes on me. "It was three hundred sixty for the bus tickets," she started, beginning to count the money we'd spent. "You said we spent two hundred along the way here. And we spent forty for the hotel."

I shook my head. "No. You paid the whole hotel and he took extra money. You guys weren't watching when he conned you," I told her.

Sammie wasn't satisfied. "How much is left?"

"Not enough," I told her. "We paid for storage, too, remember?"

We were about to battle when a girl walked up to us. "Are you new here?" we heard her say. I glanced up, grateful for a friendly face. Standing in front of us was a girl who was probably our age, with dirty blonde hair and bright blue eyes. Her hair fell to her shoulders, wiry and in need of a shower. She wore a tattered black shirt bearing the name of a heavy metal band I didn't recognize, and skin-tight black jeans that had several casually sewn on patches. A dog collar hung loosely around her neck, and she wore chain bracelets on both arms. Large chains, like the ones used to tie up vicious pets.

I smiled up at her. We probably didn't look very clean either, I thought to myself. The streets were already attaching themselves to our skin and hair. "Yeah," I told her. "I'm Sheri, and this is Sammie and Hunter," I said, pointing to my friends as I said their names.

"I'm Cobra," she said, her green eyes twinkling as she said her name. Cobra. It fit, I thought to myself. "Are you guys hungry?" she asked, sitting down next to Hunter on the bench.

Hunter nodded. She reached into the backpack she'd been carrying, pulling out a few bags of chips. "There's a burgundy van that passes out snacks on the weekends and sometimes at night," Cobra told us.

As we ripped open the chips and began to eat, Cobra kept talking. "The guy is nice, but he'll try to get you to go to a shelter. I mean, that's cool, if you want to go to a shelter, but most of us avoid that scene."

I tried to focus on the chips as she spoke. Great. Burgundy van. I hated vans. Vans spoke of danger and missed turns.

Sammie noticed the look on my face but turned back to Cobra. "What about drop-in shelters?"

Cobra continued. "Those are fine. There's a few of them. Teen Canteen opens at nine, and they have food and showers. You can do laundry there sometimes, too," she told us. She opened her own bag of chips and took a bite. "LAYN is a pain. They're pushy because they have a night shelter. The Way-In too," she told us. Chuckling, she said, "The Way-In showed me the Way-Out."

I laughed. "There's so many," I told her.

"Oh, and there's the Gay and Lesbian Center down the road," she said, pointing down Vine. "And My Friend's Place," she said, pointing westward on Hollywood, "But they don't let you sleep and they don't have showers." She began rummaging in her bag and handed us a folded card that said Services across the top. "You can have this. They pass them out everywhere."

I took the card and unfolded it. It was a service directory for homeless youth. Programs, times, locations, phone numbers. Places for legal help, medical care, shelter, food. "Wow," I said softly.

"Yeah, it's pretty organized," she told us. "I'm more of a San Fran girl, but some of us travel down here to Hollywood sometimes."

"Travel?" Sammie asked.

Cobra laughed. "Yup. We hop trains and they take us where we need to go."

Sammie looked perplexed. Shelters, squats, traveling on trains. This was not her world. But it would be. Cobra told us to try Teen Canteen first, in an hour. We thanked her, and before she left, Sammie asked, "Where do you sleep at night?"

Cobra smiled, pointing in the other direction, towards the Pantages theater that we'd passed the night before. "At Pantages," she said. I nodded. "You should come there tonight," she offered.

"Maybe we will," I said.

"We shouldn't sit here for too long," I announced after I saw a police car pass by on the opposite side of the street, recalling the officer from the previous day. They both immediately started to stand up and put their backpacks back on. We tossed the chip wrappers in a metal trash can next to the bus stop and examined our options.

"If we walk slowly, we can get to LAYN when it opens," I said.

Hunter raised an eyebrow. "Didn't Cobra say to go to Teen Canteen?"

I shrugged. "Yeah, but I know for sure that LAYN has breakfast."

Sammie shook her head. "Let's try Teen Canteen," she told me. I shrugged. We double-checked the map on the services handout and saw that they were both a few blocks down the road, off Gower.

When we arrived at Teen Canteen, we saw that it was a small white building that sat discretely between an apartment building and the back of a small shopping center. The program was housed in a two-story building and surrounded by a short black fence. A half dozen other youth were standing in front; some were obviously teenagers like us, and a few looked like they had passed twenty already. The handout that Cobra had given us listed ages of all the programs and only a few of them continued to see young adults into their early twenties.

"What time is it?" we heard someone say from the small group. Everyone had large backpacks and a telltale heaviness in their expressions.

"Five more minutes," someone else said. I glanced around, noticing the strange beauty of the group standing with us. A tall white boy with a long green mohawk stood at the front of the line, waiting to get inside first. His hair was bent slightly to the right, wearing signs of poor sleep and the need for a shower. In spite of the heat, he wore a black leather coat with metal studs affixed into it in the name of a band. He wore red and black plaid pants, and a metal chain hung loosely around his thin hips. I couldn't quite see the shirt he wore under his jacket, but I imagined it said something powerfully angry. Combat boots were tied loosely around his feet. I would later learn these boots were favorites among some of the homeless youth; the steel toes in the front delivered a powerful kick when there was a swift need for self-defense.

Beside him stood two similarly dressed teens with short hair and chain necklaces. One of them had a lock at the base of their chain necklace; a weapon. Their hair was not yet styled, and they looked like they'd been out partying all night. But they had easy smiles and spoke quietly together while all of us waited for our free breakfast and hot showers.

There was a young black girl with a short ponytail standing near them. She wore jeans and a white t-shirt underneath a blue jacket with LA imprinted on it. Her eyelashes were heavy with last night's mascara, and she looked like she hadn't slept much. Beside her were two Hispanic kids; both boys. They were also wearing jeans, and each wore a light-colored t-shirt. One of them had three dots tattooed under his left eye, and they both had short hair.

I thought about my own shoulder length red hair and the dry heat that I wasn't yet accustomed to. Was the goal to keep cool, or was there another motive for all the styles in front of us? I turned back to look at my friends. We all looked like we'd just stepped out of another time and place. Maybe we needed to rethink our appearances, I thought.

The door in front of us opened, and a young man with a clipboard stood in front of us. "Hey, guys. Sign in, and then go ahead and get something to eat," he said. Everyone walked into the building quickly, after confirming their names with him. When it was our turn, he paused. "New around here?" he asked.

"Yes," Sammie spoke for us.

"Not a problem. I'm Ron. Go ahead and sign in, we'll do a quick intake with each of you after you eat," he told us.

We thanked him and signed in. The process was easy. Name, whether you wanted a shower, laundry, or case management services. We each opted for a shower. At least we now had a place to do our laundry.

We walked inside, passing through a small lobby with four foldable chairs and a glass window that looked like it belonged in a bank. There was a door to the left, and then we were in a small dayroom filled with five small tables that each had three or four plastic chairs around them. There was a desk where another staff member sat, and a table off to the side with cereal cartons and milk, as well as a loaf of bread and jars of peanut butter and jelly. Interesting, I thought. We could prepare snacks for later. Along the back of the room was a small set of lockers. I quickly counted fifteen. Each one was small, like the ones that were used in high school. I was grateful for our storage locker once again.

Beyond the lockers, there was a door on each side marked as unisex bathrooms. I would learn later that one had a shower, and the other was only a bathroom. Along the side wall was a washer and dryer. There was another door, but I wasn't sure where it led. Probably upstairs, I pondered.

"Cool," Sammie said as she poured a large bowl of cereal for herself. Hunter stood behind her, his disposable bowl and spoon in hand. I set down my backpack at a table and joined them to pick up our breakfast.

We heard the water turn on in the shower. There were four kids ahead of us, and we'd been told the showers were maximum ten minutes each. I glanced up at the clock on the wall. That would be fine, since we had nowhere else to go.

"This is nice," Hunter said several minutes later, when we were all seated at the table and eating. I studied him for a moment. I hadn't really thought much about where he'd come from, but Sammie had told me he'd been living in her shed back home. He was so pale and thin and had already been through so much in just a few short days. This would be nice for him, I thought. Food, programs willing to help us, and new opportunities.

"Yeah," I agreed. "It's nice."

We each ate two bowls of cereal and packed a few sandwiches inside napkins for later. After we'd each completed a short intake with the guy from the door and after we'd showered, we stepped back outside to explore.

"What now?" Hunter asked.

"We need jobs," I said. "But first, we need to figure out what address and phone number we'll use on the applications."

"Or we could do that," Sammie said, pointing to a metal newspaper box alongside the street. There was a free sign on the box, so I walked over and pulled out one of the trashy newspapers. They had half naked women on the covers and offered escort services and other sex for hire options. I flipped through the magazine, seeing all the personal ads across each page.

I shrugged, handing it to her. "We could," I said, pivoting around and looking at her. "Or we could find jobs."

"Whichever," she told me. I thought back to our failed attempts to find jobs in Daytona, Miami, and Charlotte. We'd struggled in three big cities already. Yet I'd been able to find a job when I'd ventured off on my own. Maybe I would need to do that again, I realized.

Sammie was staring at some of the small printed ads in the back of the magazine. "One hundred dollars an hour?" she said, letting out a slow whistle.

I crossed my arms over my chest. "Yeah," I said, counting out loud. "Four guys a night, at one hundred dollars an hour, for one week… that would give us two thousand eight hundred dollars. More than enough for rent." She smirked a little as she recognized my sarcasm. "Maybe even a hundred guys a month? We could get a really nice place. You should totally do it, Sammie," I told her.

Hunter laughed. Sammie shoved the magazine into her backpack. "Let's look for jobs," he said.

40
PANTAGES

We wandered around for most of the day, acquainting ourselves with our new city. In the afternoon, we followed some other kids into a program on Ivar Street. My Friend's Place, the one Cobra had told us about. They had bologna and cheese sandwiches and fresh fruit for lunch. I sighed. "I'm a vegetarian," I exclaimed proudly. I sometimes strayed from my diet out of necessity, but for some reason, I was holding fast to it since we'd left North Carolina. I was angry and needed some sense of control over my life.

I took the bologna off my sandwich and handed it to Hunter, who added it to his. We sat in the dayroom and enjoyed another free meal before completing yet another intake session. The questions were simple. Name, age, where were we from, did we need anything? Afterwards, they reviewed local services with each of us.

We left the dayroom shortly after lunch. "That place is boring," Sammie said. They'd told us we had to be actively doing something or we had to leave. No sleeping, no sitting quietly, or pondering our lives. I shrugged. Free food was nice.

As the afternoon wore on, we wandered aimlessly around Hollywood. Eventually we found our way back to Hollywood and Vine. Something kept drawing us back to that intersection, and I kept my eye on the small Mexican restaurant that was lodged between the bar and the office building on the corner. On the other side of the bar was Pantages.

The sky started to change, and we needed to make a decision. "What do you think?" Sammie asked.

I nodded. "Yes. I have a good feeling about it," I told her as we stared at the theater. We'd seen people setting up camp. It was time to see if it could become our safe place for the night.

When we'd passed by the previous night, we hadn't been able to see the lobby as well as we could in the late afternoon. I stood in awe, amazed by the history in front of us. Pantages was an old theater, with ornate designs and a faded red carpet in the lobby. It was once a place of grandeur. But now, it had been converted into an open squat; a place for kids who had no place else.

Apparently, nobody cared if a bunch of homeless youth hung out there at night and slept in the outdoor lobby area. We settled into the corner and attempted to relax, but we would remain on edge for the rest of that first night. And for many more nights.

Over the next several nights, we grew accustomed to the darkness and sounds of the people around us. As time wore on, my back was starting to ache from my sleeplessness on the cold floor. Always watching, waiting. Sometimes at night, tourists would pass by and stare. Other times, people would bring containers of food, leftover from catered dinners or large parties. A van from the Covenant House would stop by and drop off chips with sandwiches to the younger homeless kids. Anyone under twenty-one.

We'd made a few fast friends. Zony, a frail girl who wore a spiky collar around her neck and painted angry lines along her eyes. Sometimes they looked like teardrops. Her short, cropped hair was hot pink, and facing the sky. She usually sat alone, but sometimes offered to sit near us. There was always a faraway look in her pale blue eyes. An older couple was there with their small child, Micah. Micah was a toddler, with long blonde hair and all-knowing eyes. He stayed near his parents, but sometimes wandered towards our group to watch us. His father was a war veteran, paralyzed. He was Native American, and he wore his hair long like his son. His wheelchair rested behind his family's blanket when he sat on the floor. Micah's mother was an older white woman, her body full from age and her hair speckled with gray. Everyone regarded them with respect; they'd become parental figures for many of the lost kids. We met Nora there also. She had long curly blonde hair, and she seemed like she was ready to take on the world with her bare hands. She confided in us she would be traveling again soon and spoke of a world full of other places where kids like us could go. Oregon. Washington. Canada. Australia. There were various kids with chains around their waists, necks, wrists. Mohawks, piercings. All in all, we were surrounded by our new dysfunctional family.

I was tired and I desperately wanted to sleep in a bed. The newness of our situation wore off quickly. After a particularly long night in which I'd been awakened to sounds of fights, police sirens, and I'd heard someone scream in the distance, I wanted out. I sat down with Sammie at our new breakfast spot; a small diner called Burger Factory that was located on the corner of Hollywood and Gower. They offered cheap coffee with one free refill, and they opened at seven in the morning. That was perfect, since the cleaning crew arrived at Pantages shortly before seven, but the drop-in programs didn't open their doors until later. We needed a place to be, a place to wait. And I needed coffee.

I was barely sleeping. I sipped the welcome taste of warm coffee and sighed heavily. Seventy-one cents per cup, so we shared one cup each morning. I was having the first half of the first cup, and it tasted heavenly.

"I think I want to go to the shelter," I said after drinking my portion.

Sammie's eyes grew wide. She was eighteen now. She'd have to go to the Covenant House, and Hunter and I were still minors. This would separate us.

"No," she demanded. "I don't want to go to the Covenant House by myself."

"Why do you have to?" I asked. She hadn't done an intake at LAYN yet. They didn't know she was eighteen. "Why don't you ask your mom to lie about your age?"

Sammie accepted the cup from me, taking her sip. "Hmm," she mumbled. "She would do that for me." I nodded. Of course, she would. Sammie's mom would do anything for her. Except kick out the man that she was married to; the reason that Sammie had run in the first place.

Hunter looked relieved. I could tell the past week had been hard on him, too. Circles were forming under his eyes, and he carried a haunted look with him everywhere he went. I remembered that feeling. I buried that feeling, somewhere deep and broken inside of me.

We agreed. After coffee, we walked the short distance down Gower Street to

LAYN, where we asked for shelter.

41
LAYN

Guillermo was suddenly my new case manager, a tall, Latino man with a shaved head and a somewhat serious expression. He was staring at me from behind his desk. I glanced around the office. It seemed even less inviting now than the previous week.

"If you're going to stay, we need to call your parents before 72 hours," he explained. Right. Emergency shelter rules were specific. I could stay for three days for free, but anything after that would cost me a telephone call to my dad. He would know where I was.

I shrugged. I hadn't lived with my dad for the past two months, and he was almost remarried. "Fine," I said. I wasn't ready to talk to him, but maybe I wouldn't have to.

"And we need to talk about your plan."

I sat up straight. Perfect. My seventeenth birthday was a few days away, and I was ready to get started on a job hunt. "I'd like to work and get an apartment," I told him.

Guillermo shook his head. "No. You need to go home. I'm placing you on the reunification plan."

I glared at him. What gave him the right to assume he knew what I needed? I shook my head. "No. I am not going back."

We stared at each other for a few silent moments. He would prove to be a stubborn adversary. But I was more stubborn. "We'll talk more about this later." He straightened the paperwork on his desk. "Group is at eleven, curfew is at 7 p.m.," he told me.

"Okay," I mumbled, standing.

"Send in your friend," he told me. I nodded and walked back out to the dayroom.

Sammie and Hunter were sitting at the dining room table, finishing another helping of cereal. Sammie's cap was turned backwards, and her face had grown thinner over the past few weeks. Hunter had already been thin, and those circles under his eyes were scary. They were both starved. I understood the feeling. "Sammie, your turn," I told my friend, signaling for her to go meet Guillermo.

Group. We sat down for our mandatory group session. The three of us, and four other youth. Michelle was already seated on the long sofa. Next to her was a skinny girl with shaved eyebrows that had been repainted, and her hair similarly slicked back. Andrea. Another girl sat on a folding chair, African American with her hair in thick braids. Laticia. Emma was the short, innocent-eyed white girl with thick hair that framed her face. Steve wore sunglasses and a cap, which he was quickly told to remove. He was African American, tall, and appeared more than a little high.

Dr. Gregory sat down in another folding chair, clapping his hands together to signal the beginning of group. Guillermo approached, and Hunter's case manager, Curtis, joined the group as well.

"Emma, please tell the group what the rules are."

Something uneasy crossed her face, but she sighed heavily and sat upright in her chair. She carefully recited, "Only one person speaks at a time. We will respect everyone. What happens in group, stays in group."

Dr. Gregory nodded in approval. "Laticia, tell us the confidentiality rules."

Laticia yawned. "Fine," she said, her disdain obvious. We all had somewhere we'd rather be. And nowhere to be. "Everything you say is confidential, unless you say you're going to hurt yourself or someone else. Or if you tell us you were abused."

"Great. Any questions?" Dr. Gregory asked everyone, his eyes surveying my group. Nobody had any questions.

"Alright, Emma, how are you doing?" Curtis began.

Emma glanced up at Curtis. "Fine. Except my stupid mother won't show up for family meetings." She stared back down at her hands, then began chipping away at her nail polish absently.

Dr. Gregory turned to Emma. "How did it make you feel when your mom missed the family meeting?" he asked.

"How the hell do you think I felt?" she groaned. She pushed a stray hair away from her eyes. "Angry. Frustrated. I'm rotting here because my mom doesn't want me back."

"Is that really the *only* reason that you're here?" Laticia asked, turning to face Emma.

Emma's shoulders sunk. There was history here, and we had just walked into a firestorm. "My mom uses, too," she muttered.

I watched as Emma crumbled into herself and recalled how it felt to be young and hopeless. As much as I wanted to tell her it would be okay, I knew it wouldn't. I turned to face Laticia, whose words had caused Emma to stop making eye contact with the group.

"Alright, that's enough for today," Dr. Gregory said. Laticia looked surprised. Apparently, group didn't end abruptly on regular days. "Emma let's talk in my office?" he added.

I watched as Emma followed behind him, her eyes on the ground as she walked.

"Do you have a cigarette?" Laticia asked our group after the caseworkers had stepped away. We all shook our heads. She sighed heavily. "I really need a cigarette," she told us.

Sammie nodded. "Yeah, me too."

I shrugged. I could use a beer, I thought.

42
EMMA

I stood in front of the mirror in the girl's bathroom, grateful for a quiet reprieve. It'd been days since my last shower, and I finally felt clean again. I wrapped the large bath towel around my body and stared at my reflection. My reddish hair was still bright enough, but lighter roots were showing. A new bottle of hair dye would be needed soon.

A gentle knock at the door indicated that someone else was coming into the bathroom. Knocking wasn't necessary, since there were three toilet stalls and two showers. "Come in," I answered automatically.

The door opened inward, and Emma entered. "Hi," she said, making her way across the room to stand beside me at the mirror. I held my towel tightly and glanced at her. She took off her beanie and tried to flatten her wavy hair against her head.

"I was thinking about dying it green," she said as she twisted a bobby pin into place. She had short cropped hair, but the bangs kept escaping from the pins. "What do you think?"

"Green would be nice," I said. "I'd like to try blue," I added, running my fingers through my damp hair.

"Manic panic is pricey, but I heard Kool-Aid could work," she told me.

I smiled. Thirteen was a tough age. "Whichever. I'll probably stick to red for now, though. I have to find a job," I confided.

"But didn't Guillermo say you were going home?" she asked, her eyes wide.

"Just like you're going home?" I reminded her.

She shrugged. "Good point." She glanced around the room, hesitant. "Do you mind if I play some music in here?"

"Go for it," I told her. "I'm just going to get dressed anyway."

While I changed in one of the bathroom stalls, I heard something heavy being placed on the counter. Alanis Morrissette's angry voice filled the bathroom. When I was fully dressed, I stepped out of the stall and sang "Ironic" with Emma. A CD player sat on the counter, the disk spinning wildly inside.

"Have you heard this one?" she asked, as a sad song began.

I paused. I hadn't.

"Sometimes is never quite enough... If you're flawless, then you'll win my love," the singer crooned. "Don't forget to win first place... Don't forget to keep that smile on your face," I heard the melodious voice sing to us.

Emma sang along with every word, her eyes heavy with unshed tears. I understood her pain; the shared song spoke of an upbringing like mine. "Your mom?" I asked her when the song finished. She nodded. "My dad," I offered.

"I have to go see her," Emma told me while she rearranged her short hair in front of the mirror. "Do you think you and Sammie could go with me?"

"Sure," I told her. "When?"

We agreed to take the bus to somewhere called Brentwood the following morning. She said they used to live in Pacific Palisades, but her mom had moved them into an apartment a few years ago. Apparently, her mom had missed several sessions with her, and Emma wanted to pick up some of her stuff and move on. "I might just go traveling," she said absently.

I didn't say anything, because I couldn't think of the right thing to say. Traveling was dangerous, but so was heroin. So was being thirteen, in a world where your mom missed your counseling session and you couldn't go home. "How long have you been clean?" I asked instead, eying her Narcotics Anonymous chip that was hanging from the wallet that she'd set down on the sink.

"A month," she said, absently scratching her arm. She watched my expression carefully, waiting for me to reprimand her for having used at all.

"Congratulations," I told her softly. "I bet it was hard."

She nodded. "Yeah." I think she wanted to say more, but just then, Laticia slammed the door inward and entered the bathroom.

"Turn that shit off!" she yelled loudly. She clearly didn't like Alanis's ballads.

Emma clicked the off button, and the music ended. We had gotten halfway through the CD. "It's my turn to take a shower," she said. "Let me use that box," she told Emma, gesturing towards Emma's CD player.

"Okay," she agreed quietly, clicking it open to remove her disc. I watched as she walked slowly out of the bathroom, the fight drained from her small frame.

I picked up my belongings and followed her out, just as Laticia turned the music up. A loud rap song burst from the bathroom, even after the door closed behind me. Emma and Laticia were polar opposites, but they managed to exist in the same broken space. A place for broken teens.

"How much further is it?" Sammie asked from the seat in front of us. She was staring out the window, watching the city change from apartments into a brilliant design of nightclubs.

"Another fifteen minutes," Emma said. She absently ran the NA chip through her fingers as we rode, occasionally scratching her arm. I pretended not to notice.

I leaned back in the seat and surveyed the other passengers. It was mid-morning, and we'd left the shelter over an hour ago. Emma had a stash of bus tokens and had begged Sammie to agree to come with us. She didn't want to face her mom alone.

We were on the number 2 bus, heading westward. As we rode, we passed by the UCLA campus. I held my breath for a moment, wondering what it would be like to study there. As the thought passed, the bus chugged down Sunset Boulevard, and the road became narrower after we passed over a large freeway.

"We're almost there," Emma said a few minutes later. I watched as she pulled the cord for the bus driver to stop, and we exited the bus. The scenery had changed again, and we were in an upscale neighborhood with condos and fancy houses. It was reminiscent of the television show Beverly Hills, 90210, I thought to myself as we followed her down the sidewalk.

After several blocks, she paused. "Do you see that building?" she asked. Sammie and I shook our heads. "That's where O. J. Simpson killed his wife," she told us. I glanced back at the building, wondering if Emma had lived here already when the murder happened. A discarded bouquet of flowers sat on the sidewalk by the building.

She didn't add any more details. Instead, she started talking about her sister. It was the first time she'd mentioned any other family besides her mom. "I don't think my mom will be home," she told us. "It'll probably just be my big sister."

"Oh?' Sammie asked, then turned to glance at me.

Emma paused dramatically a few blocks later. "It's up there," she told us, pointing to an apartment across the street. "Can you guys wait down here?" she asked us.

Sammie opened her mouth to say something, but I spoke first. "Sure," I told her. "We can just go stare at that guy's stuff over there," I said, pointing to a yard sale that was taking place at the corner. It was Friday morning, which seemed unusual for a yard sale. Sammie noticed something she wanted, and quickly agreed.

I watched as Emma took a deep breath and headed across the street. She was carrying an empty backpack, which she planned to fill with some of her essentials. When she reached the doorway on the second floor, she knocked timidly.

Sammie was already talking to the guy at the yard sale, so I walked quickly to catch up with her. "We need this," she told me when I got closer. I noticed she was pointing to a hiking backpack. It was older and bright red.

"Red probably will draw attention to us," I told her.

Sammie wasn't listening. The man was helping her try it on. I glanced back up at the apartment complex, only moments before I heard Emma and another woman start shouting. "Oh, no," I muttered.

"He says he'll sell it for twenty dollars," Sammie whispered loudly to me. She was now wearing the gaudy hiking backpack. "We need this," she repeated.

"No, we don't," I said, craning my neck to see what was happening upstairs. Emma slammed the door, and I heard a lock bolting into place. She was rushing back down the stairs, heading in our direction.

"Yes, we do," Sammie argued.

We were low on cash, but I wasn't willing to fight with her over a stupid backpack. "Fine," I told her, pulling out a wad of small bills and counting twenty dollars. "But now we're almost out of money."

"Thank you," she told me gleefully. She quickly paid the man and moved towards me with the large camping frame in her hands. "We need this," she repeated. I eyed her quizzically. We were staying in the shelter now, but was she already planning to leave?

Emma ran up to us at that moment, dividing my attention. Her eyes were heavy with tears, and the eyeliner she'd painstakingly painted on that morning was dripping along her cheeks. "I hate her!" she told us.

I glanced up, noticing a woman on the balcony. She was tall, thin, and wearing a flowing white gown or robe of some sort. Her hair flowed past her shoulders, dark like Emma's. "Your sister?" I asked.

"No," Emma sobbed. "That's my mom."

I kept my eyes fixated on the woman, who had folded her arms across her chest. This was the woman who Emma had been waiting for, and she had not come

172

to the meeting. I wondered about their history but didn't ask. I'd already learned some stories were better left untold.

"Let's go back to LAYN," I said softly. Sammie tried to hide her smile as we trekked back to the bus stop, and I watched Emma pull the sadness back within, trying to force a cheerful smile.

As we walked back, Emma had us take a different route. Not past the infamous murder scene, but instead, down a city street replete with coffee shops and newsstands. Sammie's backpack suddenly made it impossible for us to blend in like a small group of teens, hanging out in the city. Instead, it was as if "homeless kids" had been stamped across our shirts. Or perhaps emblazoned into our skin.

"I shouldn't have gone there," Emma said as we walked. She traced the letters on her NA chip as she rolled it around in her hand. "She doesn't want me back." Her hand trembled a little, and she shoved the chip into her pocket.

"She doesn't deserve you," I said.

Sammie nodded. "Yeah," she agreed. She was wearing the pack proudly and holding onto the metal rungs as she walked. As if the pack was already full of all her belongings and carrying a rolled-up blanket. Sammie was born to be a wanderer, I thought as we walked. It seemed like she was already on her own journey.

Emma paused at a newsstand, glancing at covers of magazines. Happy teens; dressed in bright summer colors. Newspapers from around the world, announcing current events. Tattoo magazines, with angry looking young women staring at us, covered in ink.

She traced the cover of one of the tattoo magazines with her finger, touching a tattoo along one of the women's arms. "I guess I'm on my own," she said, looking back at me.

I nodded. "It seems like you are," I told her. "Are you going to go to a foster home?" I asked, the words feeling like cotton in my mouth.

Emma stared at both of us, the older, more lost versions of her possible future. "I'm not really sure," she said, and shoved her hands back into her pockets. We started walking again, passing a mall and a few fancy restaurants. When we finally made it back up the hill to the bus stop, we were all lost in our own thoughts.

The ride back to LAYN was long and silent. Each of us had our own worries to ponder, and as we approached our temporary home, our problems gleamed in front of each of us even more.

43
SEVENTEEN

"Happy birthday!" one of the staff members said to me a few days later. I had just raced down the stairs to make breakfast before they would put everything away. I hadn't been able to wake up that morning, and Sammie was in a strange mood. She had told me the previous night I needed to hang out more with Hunter and her, instead of making new friends.

I glanced up cautiously, my eyes meeting the staff member's. Evan was his name. He was a few inches taller than me, Hispanic, and had tall hair that he combed to the side. His eyes always seemed to be smiling. He was looking at me from the kitchen as I hurried to pour myself a bowl of cereal. I had five minutes left before they would put everything away.

Seventeen. I felt like I'd entered a weird new twilight zone. Not quite an adult, but almost there. Only one more year until I would finally be free. "Thanks," I told him, forcing myself to smile. It was my second birthday I'd spent away from home; the first had been back when I turned fourteen at Dillon.

I shrugged off the weird feeling I'd been having for the past few days and sat down to my awaiting bowl of corn flakes. They had switched out the cereal choices to healthy ones, so I poured a large serving of sugar on top of the flakes before covering them with milk.

Evan started to collect the breakfast supplies as I ate. I grabbed the corn flakes container and refilled my bowl before he could take it back to the kitchen. He laughed. "I made you a cake," he said. "You don't have to finish all the cereal."

I glanced up at him. "You did?" I asked.

"Of course. It's your birthday," he told me. Curious, I abandoned my cereal on the table and stood up to see if he was telling the truth. I wandered towards the kitchen, where I saw a pan filled with chocolate cake sitting on top of the stove. There was a jar of frosting waiting next to it.

"Really?" I asked again. Something about the cake seemed so unreal. These people didn't even know me yet, and here they were, remembering my birthday and making me a cake.

Evan beamed. The part of me that had been breaking for so long couldn't find a reaction, so I said a quick thank you and sat back down. I stared at my full bowl of cereal instead.

"Are you okay?" Evan asked, sitting down next to me at the table.

I shrugged. "Sure," I said. But I wasn't sure.

"We'll have cake at lunchtime today," he told me.

I nodded. "Yeah." They'd had to call my dad already, since I'd been in the shelter for over three days. My dad hadn't mentioned anything to me about my birthday. Was that why I was upset? I glanced around the room. Sammie had walked back in from the parking lot, and she carried a trail of cigarette smoke with her. At least she'd left the gaudy backpack upstairs. Hunter was asleep on the sofa, his long-sleeved flannel shirt wrapped around him like a protective layer.

"Hey, birthday girl!" Sammie said as she sat next to me. She glanced over at Evan, who shared a smile with her before standing. Had she asked him to make me a cake?

I was overthinking things. "Hey," I told her. I took another bite of cereal, if only to keep myself from having to speak.

Guillermo walked in. "Seventeen!" he said as he saw me. "Happy birthday!" he called out.

Everyone was looking at me. I suddenly realized I didn't want this kind of attention. "Thanks," I said, standing. I tossed the bowl of cereal in the trash and headed outside.

Sammie followed me. We sat down on the back staircase, the one that served as an emergency exit from the girls' dorm. I stared at the parking lot and the row of chairs where a few other teens were chain smoking. "I need a drink," I said, licking my lips absently.

Beside me, Sammie nodded. I could feel the movement of her head next to me. "Me too," she said. She adjusted her glasses and pushed a strand of black hair behind her ear. "Do you want to look for jobs again today?"

"Not really," I said. I'd been all over Hollywood for the past several days, filling out applications and trying to find work. I hadn't had any luck yet. It just didn't seem like a birthday activity.

"Okay," she said, sitting back. "Hunter is resting," she told me.

"Is he doing okay?" I asked, turning to see Sammie's face as she spoke. I didn't really know him and I wasn't sure if Sammie did either. He was a thin, frightened mystery to me. A smallish teen who had been molested back home and hadn't fared well in California either.

Sammie shrugged. "I don't think so. He doesn't want to be here, but he doesn't want to be anywhere. I don't really know what he wants."

"He turns eighteen in a few weeks," I said, watching Sammie's face. "He has to figure it out pretty quick."

Hunter hadn't gone out with us to look for work. After we'd moved into the shelter, he'd stopped doing much of anything. He was constantly asleep on the sofa, or at other times he was in the back, chain-smoking cigarettes with the other teens.

"I'm not sure how we'll get a place if none of us have jobs," I said pointedly. We had thumbed through apartment magazines and had even toured a few apartments after we'd filled out our first set of job applications. They expected only one third of our income to be rent costs. We would have to make at least eight hundred a month each to get an apartment in Hollywood.

Sammie sighed. I realized again that she'd never had a real job. I wondered, not for the first time, if I'd made a mistake bringing them here with me. Her words echoed in my mind. "You owe me this," she'd told me.

The debt had been repaid, I thought bitterly to myself. The eight hundred dollars that I'd earned between the two jobs I'd held in North Carolina was long gone. I was grateful our stuff was in storage, but I'd need to come up with the monthly storage fees again soon.

"Happy birthday to you!" the song ended. I sat in the dayroom, staring at the cake that Evan had made for me. Chocolate cake, chocolate icing, seventeen cheap candles. I wondered if my family was thinking of me on this day.

The crowd of teens gathered around the table, smiling. Birthdays were bittersweet, I realized as I took in each of their faces. Times meant to be spent with family. For the first time, I realized that these kids were my new family. "Thanks," I said after I blew out the candles. Evan began to cut the cake, and everyone took a slice.

"Let's take a picture," Evan offered after cake. We gathered outside by the stairs. Me, in my favorite butterfly shirt. James stood next to me in his skater clothes. Emma smiled behind her wavy hair. Sammie turned her hat backwards, laughing. Michelle wore a thick jacket over her shirt. Hunter smiled weakly from his flannel hiding place. Laticia posed and grinned at the camera. We were a group of misfits, celebrating life together. One of the staff members joined our small group and Evan took the picture. We smiled like a group of old friends, not like a group of lost kids that had been haphazardly tossed together in a homeless shelter.

Seventeen.

I wondered what the next year would bring.

44
SPANGING

Over the next few weeks, I kept filling out applications and riding buses all over Los Angeles. I still hadn't had any luck, and my caseworker Guillermo kept bugging me about reunification. "If you won't go back home, you'll have to meet with a social worker for placement," he told me.

"No," I said. "I won't go back into foster care."

Our arguments were always the same. "You'll have to decide soon," he told me. "You can't just stay here indefinitely."

I shrugged. "Okay. I just need to find a job."

Sammie and Hunter weren't looking for work anymore. Sometimes we'd take a walk in the afternoon, and one afternoon we sat down on Hollywood Boulevard in front of an abandoned building. I was tired, and Sammie had been spending her days with Hunter, "spanging," or asking people for spare change and cigarettes. They'd been getting a few dollars a day, and usually had enough to smoke a pack of cigarettes between the two of them. I was tired from having argued with Guillermo, so I agreed to "spange" with them for the day.

I collapsed onto the ground next to them. We made cardboard signs and tried to figure out the cleverest slogans. "That other guy always writes – 'Why lie? I need a beer,'" Hunter told us. He'd been wandering the Boulevard sometimes during the day. He was getting nervous about turning eighteen.

I scribbled a catchy phrase onto my board, and Sammie took the boldest leap. "Stranded – just want to go home."

Mothers passed by with their little ones, tugging them away from us. Young men and women, mostly in their twenties, passed by on their way to and from work. Occasionally someone would stop and offer us a few coins, but more often, people would stop and try to argue with us. "Get a job!" one man blasted at us. I felt frustrated. That was what I'd been trying to do every single day for almost a month. No one was hiring. Most jobs I'd applied for had asked if I spoke Spanish, and I didn't. Others wanted to know if I'd finished high school. I couldn't find anyone who was interested in a seventeen-year-old with ten months of work experience and half of an eleventh-grade education.

Three hours and two and a half dollars later, an elderly couple approached us. "Do you mean that?" one of them asked.

We glanced up. "Yes," Sammie automatically responded.

"Where are you from?" the man asked.

"North Carolina," Hunter told them. "We really just want to go home." When he said it, it sounded genuine. It was the first time I'd heard him voice those words out loud. I knew we had to say it was real for people to give us their change, but he sounded so desperate.

"Why are you all the way out here?" the woman asked.

"We ran away from home," Sammie volunteered. A half-truth.

They paused and glanced at each other. "Are you sure you want to go home?"

the man asked.

"Yes," I lied. Why did they keep asking us that question?

"Well, I suppose we could buy you bus tickets home," the man offered.

What? All three of us suddenly stared up at them. "You would do that?" I asked. I hated myself for asking, with that lost sound erupting in my words. The sound of hopefulness. If they bought us bus tickets, and we sold them, we'd have almost enough money for a down payment on an apartment. Or at least enough to pay our storage fee for a few more months.

"Yes," the man said. He gestured to a car that they'd parked up the road from us. They must've seen us and pulled over.

We stood, all three of us caught in our own thought processes. Would we go home? Would we stay? Each of us had different answers to those questions. My thoughts never ventured eastward. I wanted to sell that ticket.

As we followed the elderly couple and sat down in the backseat of their sedan, we caught each other's eyes from time to time. Would they really buy us three tickets?

The ride to downtown Los Angeles was peppered with questions and false answers. Sammie and Hunter carried most of the conversation, as I stared out the window. This couple must be wealthy, I thought to myself. Who could afford to buy three bus tickets for perfect strangers? I watched as we passed by familiar landmarks on the freeway. Some of them reminded me of that fateful drive four years earlier when I'd been arrested for being a runaway. The mural was still there, bright and full of Olympic cheer. Downtown loomed before us, with tall buildings and concrete magic.

Once we'd arrived at the station, we followed the couple to the counter. They seemed shocked when they realized the price. Almost four hundred dollars. No discounts, no AARP, no AAA. The man turned around to size us up. "Are you sure you'll use these to go home?" he asked. He'd already asked the ticket man if it was possible for us to return them after he'd left. Apparently, they were non-refundable.

"Yes," we said in unison.

The couple spoke quietly with each other for a moment before passing their credit card to the man at the counter. The next bus would leave in four hours. He wouldn't be able to wait with us to make sure we were on it. "Okay," he said. Afterwards, he handed us each our individual tickets. "I don't want to see you on the Boulevard again," he told us. Then he gave us twenty dollars, for food along the way.

"Thank you so much," Hunter said.

"Yes, thank you," Sammie repeated. I mumbled a similar reply.

As we watched them walk away, we stood in silence for several minutes. I spoke first. 'Non-refundable?" I asked.

We walked out to the terminal and sat down, studying the tickets.

"It connects in Phoenix first," I said. A layover in Phoenix. "Maybe we could sell it to someone who only wants to go part of the way."

We wandered around, trying to find anyone heading eastward who hadn't bought a ticket yet. No such luck. After an hour had passed, and the security guard had started paying attention to us, we sat back down. "Well," I said. "If we can't sell it, we should at least get back to LAYN before curfew."

"We could save them," Hunter said. He had been staring at his ticket. They were good for sixty days.

"Yeah," Sammie chimed in. "Just in case we decide to go back."

I shook my head, confused. "Why would we go back?" I asked them.

They both shrugged. "Just in case," Hunter said.

"Whatever," I told them. We walked back to the counter and broke the twenty dollars into change for the bus. "Time to go back to Hollywood," I said.

45
KICKED OUT

A few weeks passed. No new jobs. We hadn't been back to the Boulevard to spange after the elderly couple bought us those tickets. The last thing we needed was for them to call the cops on us.

"I have to go to Covenant House soon," Hunter said. His birthday was looming in front of us.

"Yeah," I said quietly. I could tell he was worried about it.

We were sitting in the dayroom, chatting quietly about our situation, when Curtis stormed in. "Sammie, in my office, now."

"What?" she asked. Her eyes grew wide. Something had happened.

Sammie followed behind her case manager, suddenly afraid. "What happened?" Hunter whispered. I shrugged. I had no idea.

When she came back out, she was crying. "I have to leave," she said.

"What?" I asked.

"My mom called and told them how old I am," she said.

"Oh, no," I said.

"Sheri," I heard Guillermo's voice.

I followed Guillermo into the office. He spent the next fifteen minutes telling me how much the three of us had disappointed them, and that the program could get in so much trouble for having an adult mixed in with teens. "I'm sorry," I told him. "It's not my fault her mom lied!"

The result was sweeping. All three of us were being kicked out. We went upstairs and packed our stuff, with a staff member watching over us from the doorway. "I guess we're going back to Pantages," Sammie said, packing her big red camping backpack. She didn't appear too bothered by the change of events.

"I guess," I said, my hand shaking as I filled my backpack. I'd grown accustomed to the dorm style housing, availability of showers, and meals. "But why, Sammie? Why did your mom tell?" I continued to stuff the rest of my belongings into a trash bag.

Sammie sighed, rolling the last of her shirts into the pack. "I told her about the bus tickets, and she got mad I didn't use mine to come home."

"But she wanted you to come out here," I reminded her. Her mom had gotten me kicked out of my brother's house. She and her mom were the ones that had left me with no options.

"Yeah, well, people change," she said gruffly.

We dropped off our excess stuff at storage first. We'd each collected more clothes at the shelter, since there was a donation closet of clothes in the case manager's office. I'd been all over Los Angeles looking for work, and professional clothes would be important in securing our future apartment. While we were there, Sammie grabbed the blankets we'd received from a drop-in program a few weeks ago.

When we arrived at Pantages, we recognized a few of the teens. The older couple and Micah were there. They'd already set up their space for the evening, and Micah was dancing around their blanket barefoot. "Well look who's here," the father said.

Sammie waved. "Hey," she told them. Micah laughed and plopped down on the blanket.

"That's a beauty," he said, eying her backpack. He was seated on the ground, his wheelchair resting behind him.

Sammie started to set up her backpack against the wall. "I'll stay here," she said. "You guys can go get food."

"What?" I asked.

"From the programs. Go get food, and bring me some," she said. She wanted to guard our spot.

I stared down at her, the faded red carpet mismatched against her camping gear. She'd already sat down and begun to make herself at home. Hunter shrugged and sat down beside her. "I'll stay here too," he said, a hollow expression filling his eyes. He couldn't quite meet my gaze. Weird, I thought.

"Um, okay," I told them. I pulled my backpack straps tighter across my shoulders, my hands clasping the straps as I tried to figure out what to do. "So, you're both going to stay here?" I asked them.

"Yeah," Sammie told me. She looked frustrated. I wasn't sure if she was mad at me, or at the situation.

I shrugged. "Alright. I'll do my best," I told her. I paused before walking away. She had a strange air to her; comfortable amongst a sea of sadness, but also tense.

When I reached the edge of the foyer, I looked both ways, deciding. It was early in the afternoon. Turning right would take me to My Friend's Place. Turning left would take me to the Teen Canteen and the Way-In. I felt my feet carrying me to the right. Straight past the deli, the bar, and then the Mexican restaurant. It was too early for the parking valet to be working. I breathed a sigh of relief when I didn't see him in the parking lot. That would have been too much, I thought sadly as I continued walking.

I crossed Vine, then onto the other side of Hollywood Boulevard. There was a pizza shop on the corner, and the guy behind the counter waved. Emma had introduced me to him when we'd been spanging a few weeks earlier. He offered discount pizza slices to us for a dollar, and we'd each earned enough to buy a slice. He was a nice guy who had told us he'd been homeless before, and he told us he'd never turn us away if we needed a place to sit. I paused, thinking about it. But I needed to find food.

My feet continued walking, carrying me over pink stars before my brain could catch up. I didn't want to be back on the streets. I wanted to keep looking for work, and here we were, stuck on the streets again. We couldn't spange on the Boulevard, or the elderly couple might find us and call the cops.

I paused in front of a lingerie store. Maybe Sammie would want to go to Mexico again. I didn't want to go, but I wouldn't stop her if she asked again. She'd gotten me kicked out of a shelter and my brother's house. Deep down, I was fuming mad.

It was the middle of May. I'd been on my own for several months already, and I had eleven more months until I would finally be an adult. Only eleven months, I thought. I started walking again, reaching the corner of Hollywood and Ivar a few minutes later.

I crossed the street with the traffic. Behind the shawarma shop was My Friend's Place. I didn't even know what shawarma was, but they also had something called falafel that I'd heard was vegetarian. Someday, I would try it.

Down the long pink corridor that ran along the side of the shawarma shop and squarely behind it was the drop-in shelter. I paused, glancing into the room before entering. There were only a few youths sitting in the dayroom. One was reading, and another was filling out some paperwork. This was the program where we had to do something if we wanted to stay.

"Hi," said one of the staff members. I had met him the last time, but I couldn't remember his name. So many people had introduced themselves to me since we'd arrived in Hollywood. This man was in his thirties, and he had a little beard and brown hair. "Are you here for lunch?" he asked.

I nodded. "Can I get two extra lunches? My friends had to stay at Pantages to guard our spot."

The man glanced up at the clock. Three o'clock. "That's early isn't it?" he asked.

"We got kicked out of LAYN," I told him. He raised an eyebrow. He hadn't known we'd gone to a shelter. In fact, the last time we'd gone there, we'd said we weren't interested in shelters.

"Just this once," he said, reaching into the drawer and pulling out three sandwiches.

"Bologna and cheese again?" I asked sadly. I had been hoping for peanut butter and jelly.

He sighed. They almost always served bologna and cheese. I thanked him and helped myself to a handful of fresh fruit, which I stuffed into my bag.

"Did you want to sit down and eat?" he asked.

"I have to take it back to them," I said quickly. We'd spent several hours lugging our stuff to the storage and rearranging our belongings, followed by trekking back to Pantages. We'd missed lunch, and everyone was worn out. It was not turning out to be a very good day.

He offered me a cup of water. "Relax for a minute. Let's chat," he offered.

I couldn't think of a reason why not. It was hot outside and I was upset. I hadn't wanted to be kicked out. He saw my hesitancy and pulled out a chair for me at a nearby table. He sat on the other side and waited.

I glanced back at the doorway, always needing an exit strategy. I paused, like a wild animal trying to decide if I should fight or flee. "You can take it to them in a few minutes," he offered.

The cup of water was on the table in front of me. I was thirsty, I realized. I slowly sat down, placing the backpack on my lap. I glanced at the staff member, then picked up the water. After a long sip, I set it back down.

"What happened?" he asked.

I paused. Did these programs talk to each other? Probably, I decided. "Sammie lied about her age, and they found out."

"She's not a minor?" he guessed.

"Yeah," I said. "Her mom lied for her, but then decided to tell on her. Typical," I muttered, drinking the last of the water. My eyes wandered across the room, to the large fish tank against the wall. I hadn't noticed it before. A grey fish swam by slowly. He wasn't in a hurry. He wasn't homeless, I thought bitterly.

"So now all three of you are on the streets?" he asked.

I nodded. This was the most I'd said to any staff members since I'd arrived back in Hollywood. I paused. "When did this place open?"

He looked around the room, taking in the scenery that I was noticing. "We used to be up the road, in a small building," he told me. "But we've been here on Ivar for a few years."

"Was it small, in the middle of a big parking lot?" I asked, remembering something suddenly.

"Yes," he answered, eying me strangely.

"Huh," I mused. "I went there once, back when I was thirteen." I had started punching a design into the top rim of my Styrofoam cup, creating a jigsaw of lines around the edge. I stared at the fish tank as the grey fish rejoined a group of colorful fish, thinking back to that short trip. It had changed me forever, in less than a month's time. I'd never felt so free and cared for. And I'd been betrayed by LAYN back then, too.

I leaned back in my chair, finally glancing back at the staff member in front of me. "I should go," I announced, rising to stand.

"Do you want help finding another shelter?" he offered. I shook my head.

"Maybe later," I said wistfully. I wasn't sure what to do yet about Sammie and Hunter, but I felt like we were falling apart fast.

"Well, you know where to find us," he said. I nodded and gathered my belongings, quick to make my escape. I'd said too much. I'd revealed too much of myself, and I instantly regretted it.

I hurried away, aware of the feeling that the staff member was watching me as I exited. I wouldn't turn back to see the concerned look on his face. Instead, I rushed onward, back to Pantages.

46
ALONE

Several nights passed by, and each morning we got up when the cleaning man arrived. Sometimes I laid awake at night, listening to the sounds of people and cars passing us by. Most nights, a burgundy van from the Covenant House stopped by in front of Pantages and offered us sandwiches, chips, and juice. I knew that Hunter had been talking to them the previous night.

On the morning of Hunter's eighteenth birthday, he announced that he was going to go to the Covenant House. I was glad he was going; he'd become even more quiet, if that was even possible. What shocked me, however, was when Sammie announced she was going with him.

"But what about me?" I asked as the two of them prepared to leave to meet their intake counselor. The man with the van came around a lot at night, and he must have done a great job convincing Hunter and Sammie to get off the streets. I thought back to how much Sammie liked the Covenant House in Florida.

"LAYN will let you back in soon," Sammie said. "Besides, you're more streetwise than us," she told me, throwing my own words back at me. "You'll be fine."

I watched as they walked away. Anger, relief, sadness, and an overwhelming new fear filled me. I'd gotten what I had started to think I'd wanted. They'd left me alone.

And now I was alone.

I wandered over to Teen Canteen, where I went through the motions of taking my morning shower and getting breakfast. Lunches were spent at Teen Canteen, and dinner was at the Way-In. When I stood in line for my meal several nights later, I saw a familiar face.

"Emma!" I called. She was sitting at a table, staring at the macaroni and beef that they were handing out. I took my portion and sat down across from her, slowly separating the noodles from the beef as we spoke.

"Curtis kicked me out," she said.

I sighed. A lot of that was happening lately. "Why?" I asked.

"I refused to go to placement," she told me. "Fuck placement. I've done everything I was supposed to do, and my mom won't take me back."

She took a long sip of her drink. I waited. She was too young to get a job, and even I couldn't get one with work experience. How would she make it from thirteen to adulthood? "Now what?" I finally asked.

"Where are your friends?" she asked, suddenly aware of their absence. I shrugged, recanting the story to her. "That's messed up," she said after I finished.

"Yeah," I told her. It really was. We finished our meal and wandered back to Pantages. As we walked, she told me she was thinking about traveling up to San Francisco. Or maybe just across town, to Santa Monica.

"Do you want to come?" she offered.

I shook my head. I wanted to get back into LAYN, if I was truly honest with myself.

The next afternoon, as I set up my spot in Pantages, I saw Emma racing up the street. She ran into the foyer of Pantages, her eyes wild. "Someone tried to grab me," she said.

I let my backpack fall to my side, and I stood to look at her. "What?" I asked.

"I went to Beverly Hills. I was sitting near where my dad works, spanging," she told me. "He came out of his work, passed right in front of me. He wouldn't even look at me." She'd never mentioned a dad before, I thought as she spoke.

"I only got a few dollars, so I gave up and walked up the hill. I was heading back to Sunset, to catch the bus." It was a steep hill, one that made your calves hurt. I'd made the mistake to walk up that hill once before.

"And then a brown van pulled over."

"Shit," I said. We'd heard stories of a brown van, pulling over and trying to grab homeless girls. The drop-in programs had been warning us about the van all week, and they'd been begging us to keep our eyes open. To try to write down the license plate and give it to them.

"And there was a guy in the back. He grabbed me," Emma said, her words rushed and high-pitched. "He pulled down my pants, and he was going to rape me," she said, "but he got confused for a second because he saw my tampon string."

"Oh, thank God," I heard myself saying as she continued.

"I kicked him as hard as I could with my shit-kickers," she said, referring to her combat boots, "and I ran as fast as I could. I was holding up my pants with my hands while I ran," she said.

"Did you get the license plate number?"

"No," she said.

"Shit, there's two men," I said.

"Yeah." I sat down then, exhausted from hearing the story of her chase. Had he followed her to Beverly Hills? Homeless kids didn't normally go over there. Most of the sightings of the van had been in Hollywood.

She had asked me to go with her, and I'd said no.

That wouldn't even be the last time I would let her down.

185

47
AEWC

A few days later, I went back to LAYN and begged to be allowed back into the shelter. Guillermo offered me a week, but said I'd have to agree to placement or reunification by the end of the week. I shrugged. "Sure," I lied. There was no way I was doing either of those things. I would keep looking for a job instead. Sammie and Hunter were both at the Covenant House, and I hadn't seen them in days. Sammie was banned from LAYN and had been spending most of her time with her new friends at her new program anyway.

In the meantime, an older gentleman stopped by to tutor some of the other youth. He sat down at the table, working on English with a new kid, Amon. He was from Egypt, and he was alone in the US. Somehow, he'd found LAYN.

"Do you want to finish high school?" the tutor asked me.

I looked up. "Yes," I told him. "But I have to get a job."

"You could go to A-WHACK," he told me.

"What?" I said, confused. He spelled it for me. AEWC. Adult Education and Work Center.

He smiled, his thick mustache bobbing up as he spoke. "It's a continuation school. You pick up work, and you turn it in when it's done."

"Oh?" I asked. "And they'll let me enroll?" I had been worrying over my high school coursework, but usually a parent's signature was needed to enroll in school. I'd begun to feel like a useless high school dropout, and I didn't like that feeling.

"Sure. It's down the street, in the basement of a church."

"AEWC," I repeated, letting the name roll of my tongue. "Okay," I said.

He scribbled an address onto a piece of paper. "It's a short walk," he said.

I nodded. "I'll go see," I agreed.

Several long blocks later, I stood in front of an aging church on Gramercy Place. I hadn't ventured down Hollywood Boulevard in this direction since when we'd first arrived, and the area looked run-down. I paused in front of the church, thinking back to the time I'd spent with my old friends in youth group back home. Everything was different now.

I took a deep breath and entered the building. There was a glass window along one side, complete with a church office and a secretary. The woman behind the counter pointed me towards a set of stairs. I inhaled a long breath of the stale air before slowly descending the flight of rickety stairs. When I got to the bottom, I pulled open a solid wooden door, revealing a large room.

A woman sat at a desk by the door. She had short cropped hair and an easy smile. I walked over to her first, introducing myself. "They sent me from LAYN to enroll in school," I said quietly, trying not to let the other students hear me. The room had a half-dozen circular tables, and at each of them sat two or three students. There were a few other adults wandering around the room, presumably helping them on their assignments.

"Have a seat," she offered. I sat across from her as she introduced herself.

"I'm Valerie, and I'll be one of your teachers. Tell me about yourself," she said.

"Um, I'm Sheri, and I need to finish high school," I told her.

"Great," she said. "How much more do you need to do?"

"I was in eleventh grade before I left home," I told her.

She nodded. "Where was that?"

"North Carolina," I answered.

She eyed me curiously. "Do you have a parent who can sign your paperwork?" she asked as she began to pull some forms out of a file in her desk.

I shook my head. "No," I told her. I stared down at my hands in my lap. Of course, this wouldn't work, I thought miserably. I'd gotten so excited about the possibility of finishing school.

Valerie's kind voice brought me out of my trail of thoughts. "It's okay. I think we can make an exception for you," she told me. "Let's fill out some paperwork so we can request your transcripts."

She had me sit down at a table and fill out paperwork, and she made a photocopy of my driver's license from North Carolina. Afterwards, she went over the California high school graduation requirements with me, having me put a checkmark next to any of the classes I'd passed. She stared at the paper curiously. "Hmm. If this is correct, you'll only need a few more classes," she told me. "Let's start you in twelfth grade English, and we'll see what else you need when your transcripts arrive."

Another teacher came and sat next to me. "This is Roger, my husband," she explained. Roger shook my hand. "Sheri is going to be one of our new students," she told him. He nodded immediately.

"Great. And I see you're starting with English," he said, noticing the piece of paper in front of me. "This is a course contract. You complete each of the assignments, and then turn them in to be graded. If you pass all of them, you finish the class," he explained.

I nodded. That seemed easy enough. "Okay."

They walked me over to a long wooden structure that I hadn't noticed earlier. It was like a raised office space, and there was a woman sitting behind a long desk with cabinets opening on her side. "English 12A," Roger said.

The woman opened a file cabinet and pulled out several assignments. They were photocopied stories with questions at the end of each packet. "Each packet is an assignment. When you complete the assignments, bring them back, and we'll give you more," Valerie explained.

"You can do your work here, or at home," Roger offered.

Home. The word felt weird to me. I nodded. "Thanks," I told them, accepting the packets. Valerie handed me an empty manila folder to place them into.

They reviewed the hours with me and told me they were excited I was joining their class. I thanked them and placed the folder in my backpack before getting ready to leave. "I have to go back," I told Valerie. "Thanks."

I still had a chance to finish high school! I hurried out of the building and back to the main road. When I finally reached the shelter, Guillermo asked me what I'd been up to.

"I enrolled at AEWC," I told him proudly.

He shook his head. "Reunification," he reminded me.

I shrugged. There was no point fighting about plans, I reminded myself, before I wandered back to the dayroom so that I could get started on my homework.

48
SANTA MONICA

Several days passed. I completed my first homework packet, but then I got distracted. I decided to go out and look for work again. Each day, I wandered in a different direction, seeking work opportunities. Each afternoon, I came back empty handed. When I came back at the end of my first week back, Guillermo was waiting for me in his office. "Are you ready to go home?" he asked.

"Home?" I repeated blankly. "Oh, you mean with my dad? Nope."

"Foster care?" he asked.

I shook my head again.

"This isn't a hotel," Guillermo said, his eyes glaring at me. "You can't just check in and check out whenever you want."

I glared back. I didn't want to check in and check out, I thought to myself. I wanted to stay. "I want to look for a job," I told him. "I enrolled in school. I want my diploma."

"No. Your plan is reunification."

This battle had been repeated in many ways over the past several days. I shook my head. "No." I crossed my arms over my chest, trying to control my rage. "My plan is independent living."

"Well, you can't stay here," he told me.

"Fine. Fuck this place," I said, standing up.

"And you can't come to the drop-in center either. You're out."

I felt the last piece of my heart ripping into pieces. "I don't care," I told him. "I'll find a job anyway." I stood up and stared at him one last time. "I'm not going back."

He shook his head. We were both angry, and this was a battle neither of us could win. We were both stubborn but standing on opposite sides of a chasm. He wanted me to go back to North Carolina. Or go into foster care. I would rather sleep outside and take my chances.

I gathered my belongings and marched out of the office. "I don't need you or this place!" I yelled.

"Bye," he said. In our battle of wills, we were both aiming to win.

I grabbed the edge of the door in between my fingers and made sure I slammed the front door as I left. My backpack felt weightless on my back as I waited for the reverberation from the door hitting too fast against the frame.

Standing in front of the shelter, I let loose a string of expletives. Who cared, right? I didn't need this shelter. I could just go back to panhandling. And maybe I would join some of the Travelers and head to San Francisco. Or Oregon. How hard could it really be to jump onto a moving train?

I trudged up Gower Street to the restaurant on the corner. I figured I'd buy a cup of coffee while I tried to figure out my next move. The restaurant always had decent coffee available and they didn't pressure their patrons to buy anything else. At least it would give me a few minutes to ponder my options.

Sitting at the corner table, I sipped my tan colored coffee. There was something magical about cheap coffee with one free refill. I could stop moving. I could get my bearings.

I'd missed the morning rush, because I'd spent my morning battling with my case manager. That hadn't turned out well at all.

My plan had been to come back to Hollywood and get a job. I lazily traced a map of the United States on the orange table top with my finger, wondering where I would go next. Or if I would even go anywhere at all. I'd been confined mostly to Hollywood, although I'd heard there were squatters in Santa Monica, too.

I pulled out the long-forgotten homework and finished another packet. Something satisfying passed through me as I finished it. After it was complete, I shoved it back into my backpack. I shouldn't go too far, I thought to myself. AEWC was offering me a chance to finish high school.

My second cup of coffee was almost finished. I glanced up at the bus stop across the street. Which bus would take me to Santa Monica? I wasn't sure. I had picked up a few bus tokens from Teen Canteen to look for work, and I had a few dollars left over from spanging the previous week.

I stood up, ready to try something new.

An hour later, the bus stopped. I had expected to ride the 2 bus all the way to the beach, but I still had a lot to learn about the bus routes. "This is the end of the line, kid," the driver told me.

"But I thought this bus went further," I told him.

He pulled off a transfer ticket and handed it to me. "Simple mistake. Where are you trying to go?"

I hugged my backpack more tightly to my chest. Would he call the cops if he figured out I was a minor? I didn't answer him. Instead, I quickly accepted the transfer ticket and rushed off the bus.

The sky had begun to darken and I was in a new place. I didn't recognize my surroundings. The bus had passed UCLA again, but it had turned instead of going straight. I was now standing in front of a row of businesses, and people were passing by in all directions. Crap, I thought.

I walked up to the bus stop sign and started reading through the options. Which one would lead me to Santa Monica? I wondered.

A blue bus stopped across the street from me. Whoa, I thought. The guy who had given me directions was right. The bus said Santa Monica Blue Bus. Maybe I was already here?

I turned and asked the woman next to me if we were in Santa Monica. She chuckled.

"This is Westwood," she told me. "You can take a city bus or a blue bus to get there." She saw the transfer ticket in my hand and directed me to Wilshire Boulevard. "Walk three blocks that way and get on one of the buses that says Santa Monica on it."

I thanked her and hurried down the road, feeling dizzy from the sudden change of environment.

Several blocks later, I found Wilshire Boulevard and located the correct bus stop. I boarded the next bus and took it to the last stop, Santa Monica Promenade. I sat in the back and waited to exit last, wondering what to do. It was already night, and darkness covered the city with its mysterious veil. Where would I sleep?

I wandered around, not sure where to start. Where did the homeless kids meet up? I'd heard people talk about the promenade before, so I knew it would be a good start. I wondered if Emma was already down here. I hadn't heard from her since I'd gone back to LAYN.

Feeling overwhelmed, I decided to enter a toy store. I walked around the small space, eying old-fashioned toys and trying to figure out what to do at the same time. Where would I go? I hadn't seen any street kids.

When I walked back out, I saw an older man and a teen with a skateboard. They were holding a sign, asking for change. Finally, I thought to myself. "Do you know where people stay at night?" I asked the teen.

He glanced over at the older man. Maybe they were related, I thought to myself. He stepped away and conversed quietly with him. He had greying hair and some wrinkles around his eyes, but otherwise looked like he couldn't have been more than fifty. The teenager had wiry black hair and he kept his bright yellow skateboard tightly against his side.

"Sure, kid," the older man said. "You can camp with us tonight."

I smiled gratefully. It had been a long day, and after getting lost in Westwood, I'd begun to feel desperate. The old man nodded. "We'll leave in a few minutes," he told me.

When we started walking, he took the lead. I walked alongside the teenager. "Call me Falcon," he said, his eyes darting away from me. Like a bird of prey, I thought to myself. How fitting. We exited the promenade and headed a few streets away. I could smell the ocean, and suddenly felt calm. I hadn't felt calm all day. That tense feeling that I always got right before something bad happened had been brewing since the early morning. The ocean air helped begin to put me at ease.

We walked across a large road, towards a park. I could see darkness beyond the park. No more buildings. The sound of waves crashing against the beach filled the air. Night fall had come, and the waters were restless.

Next, he led us across a bridge. "That's the Pacific Coast Highway," Falcon said. "It's safer to cross it over here," he told me.

We continued down the bridge, reaching a sidewalk on the other side. The older man stayed several feet in front of us, and Falcon asked me basic questions. What was my name? Where was I from? Was I alone?

"Yes, I'm alone," I said softly, staring out at the darkness that sounded like ocean. Sandy beaches were mildly illuminated by streetlights, but I couldn't see the water. We continued walking for a long time, even passing through a few tunnels under the road and then up a hill. The tunnels had taken us back to the other side of the highway.

We began climbing a steep hill, with rugged terrain stretching out in all directions. The sound of cars passing by rapidly overshadowed the relentless sound of the waves. I was mesmerized by the sounds and smells.

Finally, we came to a campground on the mountain. I wouldn't have realized this was here, I thought to myself when I arrived. There were two tents. "You can sleep in my tent," Falcon said. He spread out a blanket for me on the ground by flashlight.

"Thanks," I told him. Exhausted and emotionally spent, I quickly fell asleep.

49
PEPPER SPRAY

A burning sensation caused me to awaken. I started coughing, and my eyes wouldn't open. What was happening?

I felt a hand unzipping my pants and I screamed. "What the hell?" I shouted, kicking and screaming against the man who was trying to undress me. I stood abruptly and threw my backpack over my shoulders. When my eyes finally opened, I saw the old man sitting on the ground, hand over his crotch. I'd kicked him hard.

I reached down and grabbed the familiar bottle out of his hand. "How dare you spray me with my own spray!" I shouted, squirting pepper spray in his face and kicking his outstretched arm. "Asshole!"

"Fucking bitch!" he called out after me as I ran down the mountain. I hadn't seen Falcon again, and a part of me worried that he'd jump out and grab me. It was early morning, shortly after sunrise. I raced back down to street level and hurried alongside the highway. The tunnel was too risky; they would expect me to double back the way we'd come. I trekked along the edge for several miles.

My arms were shaking violently, and tears were running down my cheeks. At some point I'd realized that I needed to zip my pants, but I still couldn't shake the feeling of his fingers on my skin.

I stopped walking long enough to throw up. My eyes still burned, and my stomach was empty. A day ago, I'd awoken in a bed at LAYN. "Damnit," I muttered. I hadn't wanted to be back out on the streets again so soon. These streets were literally trying to kill me.

An hour later, I arrived back at the Promenade. I found a bathroom in one of the parking garages and rinsed my eyes and my mouth. The water brought back the sense of being pepper sprayed again, and a fresh wave of sobs escaped my mouth. Finally, the tears stopped coming and I was able to calm my tremors. "Asshole," I said again, remembering the old man and his greasy hands.

I wouldn't make that mistake again, I told myself. When I walked out of the parking lot bathroom, I had resolved to find a safer place to stay.

Eventually I found my way to the center of the promenade. There was a large cement structure with two opposing benches. On each end, there was a manicured plant with a metal dinosaur head. It was like a freakish design from Edward Scissorhands, and I immediately loved it. I paused in front of it, wondering what my next step would be.

"Hey," a small voice called out. I glanced up.

"Emma?" My friend from the shelter was right in front of me.

"What are you doing here?" we both said at the same time.

"I'm squatting with some friends," she said. She introduced me to another girl that was standing beside her. Ava was her name. She was about the same age as Emma.

I smiled and introduced myself to her. Ava smiled back. I was taken aback by her sweet young smile. Such innocence on that face, I thought to myself. She must have been new on the streets. Her hair was shaved bald except for two wispy bangs falling on each side of her face. She wore a grey sweater that was torn at one end. "Hi," she replied.

"Is there a place to get coffee?" I asked.

Emma shook her head. "Everything's expensive down here," she told me. "And there's no services."

I sighed. We sat down between the two monstrous dinosaurs and I told them about the previous night. "I think I'll go back to Hollywood," I told her. "I don't think I should be here, after what happened last night."

She nodded. "We'll walk with you to the bus stop," Emma said.

We agreed to meet up again in Hollywood the following week, and I waved bye to them as I rode away on the bus.

When I returned to Pantages that afternoon, I felt like I'd grown older and wiser. My encounter with the old man at the beach had brought back my earlier fears. Men in white vans. Men in campsites. Men at bus stations. I had a lot of reasons to be wary of men.

People were starting to set up. I saw Micah's dad, sitting in his wheelchair. He was crying. His wife was next to him.

"Where's Micah?" I asked suddenly.

"They took him," the man said, tears rolling down his cheeks. His wife was seated on the floor, her face peeking out from underneath a river of messy hair.

"They wouldn't let us have him because we don't have a home," she cried.

"We're Native Americans, this is our land!" the man shouted. "My people used to live in tents, and they wouldn't let us have our son because we live off the land."

They collapsed against each other, broken by the world. I felt tears streaming down my own cheeks yet again. I'd cried so much in one day, but there was no way my tears measured the number these heartbroken parents were crying.

"Can't you get him back?" I asked.

"They won't let us have him unless we have a place," the woman said.

I sighed heavily. So much was dependent on following the rules. But there were no jobs for me, and I imagined it would be harder for a disabled man and his wife.

My pain needed an outlet, and I turned to what was familiar. I'd begun scribbling words on paper when I felt lost. Words became poems, poems became a small booklet. I drew a cover page and imagined myself selling copies on the corner of Hollywood and Highland. Somehow, even at seventeen, I felt people needed to know how hard it was to be a homeless kid, on the streets one week, in a shelter the next.

I'd started sitting on the giant cement construction blocks on Hollywood and Highland, debating between spanging and selling those booklets. But I never made the photocopies, never prepared them, because I got scared someone would notice

194

me. What if they noticed the not-quite-an-adult girl, perched on the cement rock on the corner? What if someone decided I was better back in the system, when I'd fought so long to avoid it?

There was energy in the movement of tourists, locals, and the construction crew. The corner was changing, and I wasn't sure I was ready for all the commotion. The red line of the subway was being expanded, and construction crews were working day and night to connect downtown Los Angeles with Hollywood, and then to tunnel further, to the San Fernando Valley. One of the new metro stops would be on the opposite corner, behind the chain linked fences that the workers had set up.

I sat on the cement block, pondering life. A notebook was often found in my hands, and words fell freely onto the pages as I counted down the days left of being seventeen. The poems chronicled my downfall; one took me back to lazy summers before my mom had gone crazy. Another showcased my alcoholic tendencies. Yet another screamed for independence against the outside forces that prevented me from moving forward.

I must've been lost in thought, because I didn't see the security guard until he was standing next to me. The city had invested in a series of security guards to monitor traffic on the boulevard. Specifically, to keep the homeless kids moving and help beautify the city.

"You can't stay here," I heard a man say. I looked up, and my eyes met with those of a security guard that I'd seen a few times. He was in his late twenties, Hispanic, stern features juxtaposed with kind eyes.

"I'm writing," I told him, passing a page from my booklet to him. He scanned the page, saw the crude drawing of a woman drinking her liquor alongside my tragic poem.

He sighed. "You still can't stay here," he repeated.

"Sometimes it's hard," I said softly. "Sometimes I can't keep moving, and I need to just stop. It's the weekend; there are no services anywhere tonight. I have nowhere else to go," I told him.

Our eyes connected for a long moment. It was getting dark, and I knew I'd have to go somewhere eventually. But for that moment, I felt safe. I was on the corner, exposed, but a wild creature surrounded by many watchful eyes. I was untouchable.

"Alright, I'll give you thirty more minutes," he told me. "But then, you have to go."

I nodded, grateful for a brief reprieve from the endless walking. I didn't like walking without a purpose. I wished I'd been able to stay at the shelter, but I was constantly battling with Guillermo, and he only saw one plan for me. I'd have to wait a few more weeks before trying again.

I sat, staring at the foreign tourists staring at the ground. Pink stars littered the sidewalks, and people traveled from afar to see a city that didn't match their expectations. Hollywood wasn't beautiful. It was dirty, lonely, harsh. Hollywood was a broken city filled with sadness, invisible people, and the people that followed behind them with plans to exploit them.

50

SAM

The following week, I wandered into the deli next to Pantages. I was hungry, broke, and uncertain. When I entered, a young man sat behind the counter.

"Hi," he said. "I've seen you around." I nodded. Everyone had seen me around. I lived around. The streets had become my home.

"Can I get a cup of water, please?" I asked. Most places refused to give out water to homeless kids. The guy looked like he might too, but something in my face must've caught his attention.

"Okay," he told me, filling a paper cup with ice water.

He came out from around the counter and motioned for me to sit. I sat down across from him. "I'm Sam," he said. "This is my family's deli."

I nodded. The implication was strong. Don't mess with the family's business. I drank the water quietly, my head spinning from everything that had happened over the past few weeks. I still hadn't heard from Hunter or Sammie. They must have settled into their new lives at the Covenant House.

"You sleep at Pantages?" he asked.

"Sometimes," I said, my eyes darting back towards the doorway. Exit strategy.

"Hmm." He sat back in his chair.

I stared up at him, suddenly curious. He was young, with an angular face and dark hair. Emerald green eyes. His skin was slightly darker than mine, and his words carried a slight hint of an accent. He'd told me that his name was Sam. "How old are you?" I asked.

He paused. That was not the question he'd been expecting from the young homeless kid who had begged him for a cup of water. "Twenty one," he said.

"Twenty one. If I was twenty one, I'd buy myself a drink," I told him. "Three actually. Or maybe more."

He stared at me. I was hurt, angry. My brokenness had risen to the surface, and he picked at it. "You should be looking for a job," he chided.

"That's all I've done since I got here," I retorted. "Nobody wants to hire me. I'm just some stupid street kid." The words hung heavily in the air.

Sam's mouth gaped open for a moment, but he caught himself. We sat in silence for several long minutes, until a customer came in. I started to stand up, but he asked me to wait.

He walked back behind the counter and prepared a sandwich for the customer, then returned to sit across from me. "I'll buy you a drink," he said.

I looked up at him, surprised. "Really?"

"Sure," he told me. "I get off work at ten tonight."

I eyed him curiously, wondering if the drink would come with a price.

The shattered part of me bubbled up with a surprising realization: I didn't care. I wanted a drink. I wanted to begin to forget. So many memories were flooding back into my mind; Micah, my friends, the man with the white van. I remembered the way Micah's parents had wailed at his loss.

Nobody was crying for me like that.

"Ten," I repeated, realizing how good looking that Sam was.

"Ten," he said again. I nodded and stood, tossing the empty water cup into the trash.

At ten o'clock, I walked back to the deli. I hadn't set up my spot at Pantages yet, and I wasn't sure if I wanted to go back into the depressing tomb again that night.

Sam waved from behind the counter and raised one finger. Just a moment, he implied. The lights began to turn off, and soon, Sam emerged at the front of the building. He had changed into a regular shirt. "Walk with me to my car," he told me. I nodded, following alongside him.

We walked a few blocks until we arrived at his car, a large grey car with soft black seats. I sat down next to him in the front seat, suddenly aware I hadn't ridden in a car for several months. I glanced over at him, uncertain.

He sensed my discomfort. "Let's go buy you that drink," he told me. I nodded and fastened my seatbelt. It felt strangely tight around me. My backpack was rested securely on my lap. I fidgeted with the straps, even when it was in front of me.

"Don't be nervous," he said to me as he drove me down the road. When we got to a convenience store on Sunset, I walked inside with him. "Pick something," he told me.

I glanced at my choices. I picked a beer and a wine cooler.

"That's two," he laughed, taking them from me.

"What about you?" I asked.

He shook his head. "I don't drink." I paused for a moment, watching him replace my wine cooler on the shelf and pick up a pack of four instead. I followed him to the register and waited while he paid.

When we got back to the car, I eyed him curiously. "You don't drink?"

"I have one condition," he told me.

Fear flickered through me. "Really?" I asked, my eyes intent on his.

"Yes. I don't want you to go back to that theater tonight, not if you drink these," he told me, handing me the bag. "It isn't safe."

"But I don't have anywhere else to go," I told him, annoyance creeping in.

"I'll get you a hotel room," he offered.

"What?" I asked. That sounded like strings attached.

Sam shook his head. "Relax. I've seen you around," he told me. "You just look so sad sometimes."

I couldn't argue with him on that. This man must have seen me. I leaned back in the chair and considered my options. "Okay," I finally said.

Sam drove me to a nearby hotel and paid for one night while I sat in the car. He had taken his car keys with him, obviously very aware that I was still a street kid, not to be trusted. Afterwards, he walked upstairs with me.

I put my backpack down and stared at him. "What do you want?" I asked nervously.

"Nothing," he told me. He sat down at the table. "I want you to be safe."

"Why?" I asked.

"I don't know," he told me.

I nodded slowly, glancing over at him. "Okay. I guess I'll take a shower," I said, picking up my backpack and walking to the bathroom.

Once the door was closed and locked behind me, I took a deep breath and set my backpack on the floor. I turned on the shower and let the steam of an impending warm shower begin to flood the room. The humid air was inviting, and it had been too long since I'd had a shower in a regular bathroom without somebody telling me to hurry up.

"Damnit," I whispered to myself as I stepped into the shower. Sam was waiting outside. He seemed nice, and he had fulfilled his part of an unspoken deal. I lathered shampoo into my hair, trying not to think about what he would ask of me.

When I finished showering, I towel dried my hair and then wrapped the towel around myself. I swiped away the moisture from the bathroom mirror, I peered sadly at my reflection. I still had that too-young face that made it hard to blend into the crowd or hide from the police. My fading red hair hung loosely around my shoulders, begging for the attention that only a bottle of hair dye could provide. I wouldn't be a dirty blonde again. Deep down, I could never shake the feeling of being unclean.

My eyes. They were staring back at me, sad pools of blue that struggled to conceal emotions. I knew when I smiled, it never reached my eyes. I'd lost my reasons to smile too long ago. I couldn't think of the last time I'd been truly happy. Laughing, yes. But happy?

I tried not to think too much about the man that was waiting for me in the hotel room. He had not protested when I'd disappeared into the bathroom. After all, he knew I was one of the street kids who slept on the cold, aged red carpet in front of a forgotten theater. The streets were a part of me, and he must've seen it. Why else would he have brought me here?

Wiping away nervous beads of sweat from my face and chest, I kept trying to convince myself that I was unbreakable. I'd gnawed on my lower lip and combed my hair several times before I realized I had nothing left to prepare. When I finally decided that I couldn't prolong it anymore, I opened the door to the awaiting hotel room and walked out to greet Sam.

Wrapped in nothing but a towel, I stepped into the room. I instantly was assaulted with the change in temperature. The room was cooler, as the motorized air conditioner was humming to life in the corner. Sam was seated at the table, staring at me.

"Okay, I'm ready," I told him. I had spent most of the half hour staring at myself in the mirror, trying to psych myself up for whatever was coming.

Sam stared at me, his eyes suddenly wide. "I'm sorry," he told me. "I didn't mean…" his voice trailed off.

I glanced down at the towel, embarrassed. He hadn't come here to take advantage of me? He didn't want me?

I held the towel more tightly, my cheeks suddenly burning against the sudden pain of rejection. Sam stood, crossing the distance between us. "I'm sorry," he repeated, and wrapped his arms around me in a gentle embrace. "Really, I am."

He released me and stared at me for a moment. I darted my eyes down to the floor, trying to hide how much he'd managed to undercut my feelings with those two words. *I'm sorry.* He pressed his lips against my forehead in a very platonic kiss, before stepping back. The distance between us was growing.

Sam placed the hotel key on the table and gestured to the door. "Lock the door. Check out is at eleven," he told me.

I watched as he let himself out, and from the window, I peeked out and saw his car pull away. My fingers automatically reached for the lock, and I bolted myself inside the small room. Without another thought, I walked across the room and opened my first bottle. "Damnit," I said out loud.

When I awoke, the bottles were gone, and I had the beginnings of a headache. It was a strange feeling, realizing I'd been turned down and protected all at once. At first, I searched for the bottles under the bed and in the trash can. No bottles, although the brown bag from the liquor store sat empty on the table. Next, I walked to the door, and realized I'd unlocked it at some point. What had I done? I quickly bolted the door shut. Where were the bottles? I couldn't remember anything from the previous night. Well, anything after Sam had left and I'd been alone. I remembered opening the first drink, but that was where the memory abruptly stopped.

I wandered back into the bathroom and drew a bath. I'd wanted one for so many months, I told myself. I eased into the water, hoping it would help my head stop pounding. Afterwards, I found the cheap motel coffee pot, and brewed an entire pot. I drank one cup after another until it was finished. When I was fully dressed and ready to leave from my temporary shelter, I glanced at the digital clock across the room. Nine o'clock.

Backpack firmly across my shoulders, I hurried down to the lobby to turn in the keys. "Room 209," I said quickly as I dropped the keys on the desk and rushed away.

I found my bearings and started walking, realizing I was close to school. "Why not?" I muttered to myself, crossing Hollywood Boulevard and approaching the old church.

I went down the stairs two at a time. When I got to the large wooden door, it opened in front of me as I reached for it. A young Hispanic boy with a shaved head and gang tattoos stepped out, walking quickly past me. I waited.

When I walked in, Valerie saw me. "Hey," she called. I walked over to her and sat at her desk. "I got your transcripts," she told me. She pulled them out of a thin folder that had been waiting on her desk.

I nodded, rubbing a spot on my temples absently. I was clearly hungover. I'd finished all five drinks, and they'd been my first drinks in a few weeks. I was already trying to figure out where I'd find more.

"You did surprisingly well at your old school," she said, pulling out a page where she'd calculated my credits. "Your GPA is the highest our school has ever seen," she told me. I knew that it was high, but that was a surprise to me. I scanned the document. 4.8 weighted, 3.9 unweighted. They had ignored my failed attempt at second semester.

Quietly, I stared at her. I wasn't sure what she wanted me to say. "My dad kicked me out," I said finally. "I'm homeless and I just want to finish high school."

"Have you thought about college?" she asked.

Roger approached. They must've been waiting for me to return. "No," I admitted. "I stopped thinking about things like that a long time ago," I told them both. My eyes felt heavy. "I just want to survive to eighteen," I said, looking up at them both.

"Are you still in the shelter?" Valerie asked.

"Yes," I lied. I didn't need them worrying over me. Or calling child protective services. And besides, I was clean today. I had showered and taken a bath. I hadn't quite washed the feeling of that greasy old man's hands from my skin from the beach trip, but I was clean.

They kept staring at me. I started to feel nervous, so I reached into my backpack and pulled out the folder with my work in it. "I finished my packets," I said. Valerie nodded, taking them from me. "Let's get some more work for you," she told me.

We walked together to the counter across the room, where I turned in my work and collected several more packets. "You'll graduate soon," she told me. "You're so close."

I nodded. "Thanks," I told her as I shoved the work into my backpack.

I left, feeling like my world had been rotated slightly. It wasn't completely upside down, but it was different. I was different. I walked down Hollywood Boulevard with a new sense of purpose and stopped at My Friend's Place when they opened for lunch.

A young Korean woman sat behind the desk. "Peanut butter and jelly?" she offered. There was a stack of bologna sandwiches beside a smaller stack of peanut butter and jelly ones. I smiled and accepted it.

I sat down at one of the desks and ate my sandwich and apple. Kids ate and left. When I finished eating, I opened my backpack and pulled out the packets. I began reading through the assignment and answering the questions on the notebook paper they'd given me at school.

A few hours later, the woman sat down across from me. "I'm Suzie," she said.

I nodded, looking up. I'd finished all the assignments. Maybe I would get more the next day, I thought. The course required twenty packets, and now I'd finished six.

"Are you in school?" she asked.

"Yeah," I told her. "AEWC. I'm going to earn my diploma."

"That's great," she said. "And then what?"

I paused. That was the second time in one day. It must've been a sign. I shrugged. "I don't know. Turn eighteen?"

After I packed up, I wandered back down Hollywood Boulevard, away from Pantages and the deli and Sam. Away from the Mexican restaurant with its parking guy. Away from the heartbroken parents whose kid would now be raised in foster care. I needed a break from everyone. Absently, I wandered down the street, reading some of the pink stars with names forever burned into them.

Several blocks later, I stood in front of a small sandwich shop. I glanced over, seeing the sign at the lower edge of the glass. Help Wanted. I walked in, suddenly ready to try anything.

51
HIRED

I walked up to the counter of the sandwich shop and asked for an application. A thin Hispanic guy stared at me from behind the counter. "Can you fill it out now?" he asked. "The owner will be here soon."

Gratefully, I accepted the application and sat down in a booth to complete it. When I was almost finished, a small Indian man sat down across from me. "Hello," he said, extending his hand to mine. I looked up and immediately forced a smile. Something about the way his eyes focused on my chest made my stomach flip with unease. I shook his hand; he turned my application to face him.

"Great, great," he said as he read the application. "I see you've worked in food service before." He read through the schooling information. I was now able to include the name of my new high school. "What are your hours for this school?" he asked.

"It's independent studies," I told him.

"Perfect." He paused, looking at me too closely. His eyes met with mine, and I felt my body tense. I could feel his knees touching mine from underneath the table. "I'd like for you to work at my Gardena store, so that we can work closely together," he said.

I shook my head. "That's too far. Can I work here?"

He sighed, something crossing over his face. "Alright," he told me. "You can start tomorrow."

"Manuel," he called over his shoulder. The man from behind the counter came to join us. "This is Sheri. She starts tomorrow. Make sure that her paperwork is all in order."

"Thank you, sir," I said.

He reached out to shake my hand again, this time holding my hand longer than he needed to before releasing it. I forced the smile to remain on my lips. I needed this job, I told myself.

The next day, I arrived ten minutes early for work. I had a mixture of first day jitters and moderate discomfort from meeting the owner the previous day. Hopefully, he wouldn't work with me too much, I thought to myself.

Manuel was already standing behind the counter. He began training me on how to cut the bread. When I didn't cut it exactly right, he quickly reached for my hands and moved my hand underneath his to make the cuts. The deep-seated sense of nervousness rose up in my belly again. Damnit, I needed this job, I thought to myself. I ignored the bad feeling passing through my body and focused my knife on the bread. Cut, cut, stop. I glanced back at Manuel for his approval. He smiled, a little too widely. My smile faded, and I looked away. Damnit.

I quickly memorized the menu and worked hard to prepare sandwiches for each customer. Manuel stood beside me as I prepared my first orders. "Good,

good," he told me. "Remember, only three olives per half sandwich," he added on when I sprinkled a few extra olives on a sandwich at a customer's request.

"Okay," I said, removing one from each side of the sandwich.

I wrapped the sandwich and offered chips or a cookie. The customer added chips to his meal and paid. I could see Manuel smiling from my peripheral vision, but instead of making me feel pleased, I felt uneasy.

After my first day, I went back to Pantages and fell asleep in the corner. In the morning, I rose early and went to Teen Canteen for a shower and breakfast. I glanced down Gower, my eyes not able to see LAYN, but I knew it was there. I wanted to go back. The shouting match I'd had with Guillermo replayed in my mind and I groaned. I'd ruined my chance.

On the second day of work, one of the squatters came in and tried to get me to give him a free sandwich. "Go away," I hissed. Manuel came out of the back and approached us.

"Just trying to see if you're hiring, Sir," the guy with the mohawk said.

"No, we're not," Manuel said. Fortunately, the guy from Pantages left. I would plead with him later that night to leave me alone at work. We weren't friends, and I didn't want to lose my new job for giving people free sandwiches.

I continued my day, making sandwiches for customers and offering add on items. In the afternoon, Manuel taught me how to make cookies and bread. I prepared a fresh tray of cookies during a slow period.

"Do you live around here?" Manuel asked during down time, his arm bumping into mine as he spoke. He was standing too closely.

I nodded, trying to step away. I reached over to pick up a stray piece of lettuce on the counter. When I turned to toss it in the trash, Manuel had shifted his body in front of me. I glanced up at the video camera on the wall. What would the owner say? I stepped back and waited to see what Manuel would do.

He glanced up to see what I had been looking at. The video camera. He tilted his head back at me for a moment, then flashed me yet another toothy smile. "I'll go prep more vegetables," he told me.

I nodded. I needed this job, I told myself again. I could do this.

Later that afternoon, I saw the staff members from My Friend's Place pass by the front. One of them did a double take and walked in. "Hi!" she said. It was Suzie, the woman that had talked with me last time.

"Hi," I said, my eyes darting to the back door. "Um, I'm working," I said. I saw Manuel pass by the door and peer out. I waved and turned back to her.

"That's great!" she told me. She reached into her bag. "Do you need a sack lunch?" she asked.

I shook my head quickly. "Not now. They don't know I'm homeless," I whispered. "Please."

Suzie apologized and hurried away. I returned to tidying up the counter.

Manuel came back out. "She didn't want a sandwich?" he asked.

I stared at the space where Suzie had been before answering. "No, she was asking for directions to the Hollywood Sign," I lied. He shrugged. Tourists were common around here, so it was believable.

At the end of my shift, Manuel let me make myself a sandwich. He rolled his eyes when he realized I wasn't eating meat. I prepared a veggie and cheese sandwich and thanked him.

"See you tomorrow," he said, winking at me.

I nodded. "Thanks, see you tomorrow."

During my fifth shift, Manuel asked me to go back to the freezer to get more bread. Another person was working with us at the counter. I nodded and went to the freezer for the frozen bread rolls. I bent down and started reading the boxes along the wall, trying to find the wheat bread.

The door opened to my right. My only exit. I stood up straight and faced whoever had entered the freezer with me.

Manuel.

"Hi," he said, his voice syrupy. "I've been wanting to kiss you all week."

I backed up a few steps, until I was cornered between boxes of frozen cookies and vegetables. The temperature was low and cool. I felt the icy box behind me. I was trapped. My manager descended into my space and pressed his hot lips against mine before I could react. When his hands started groping me, I pushed against him. "No," I said. My knee began to quiver. Should I fight back? Could I? A memory from my time in juvenile hall flashed into my mind; a too-small room with bugs crawling everywhere. No one would believe me. No one would believe a homeless kid with a criminal record. My leg straightened, and my knee went slack.

He pulled back and looked at me closely. "Do you want to work here or not?" he asked, dangling my job in front of me. His eyes were steely gray and his face was contorted with rage. I felt a myriad of emotions; anger, fear, helplessness. Nothing that happened here would change my situation. I stared at the doorway, then back at him. I was still homeless, lost, and broke. This was my first job in Hollywood, after months of searching. I wrestled with my decision, but when it came to me, I spoke quickly.

"I quit," I said, pushing past him. I hurried out of the freezer and back to the front, where I tossed my visor on the counter. "I don't need this," I told Manuel, who had followed me back from the freezer. My hand absently scrubbed away the feel of his lips on mine. I reached down below the counter and grabbed my backpack from the cabinet where I'd hidden it. "I'll be back next week for my paycheck."

With that, I rushed out the door and didn't look back. I quickly put distance between myself and the sandwich shop, and that space helped cleanse me from the onslaught of emotions that followed. Years later, I would see a news story about a female employee being assaulted by the manager at their nearby store. I wouldn't feel surprised, just sad.

52
BACK TO THE BEACH

When I returned to Pantages, Sammie was seated in her old spot. Hunter was sitting next to her, an exasperated look on his face. Between them was her camping backpack, red and full. A blanket was bundled up in her typical fashion. "We missed curfew," she said, throwing her hands in the air in defeat. Hunter had an indecipherable look on his face.

"Right," I said. I'd been on the streets, off the streets, and back on the streets since the last time I'd seen them. A world had crashed down in between us.

"I heard you got a job?" she asked, raising an eyebrow.

I shrugged. "I quit," I told her.

"Why?" she asked.

I sat down and told her about the owner and Manuel. She shook her head in disgust. We'd both seen our share of predators over the years, but it seemed this city had the highest number per capita we'd ever encountered.

Leaning back on my elbows, I recanted some of the lighter stories from my weeks. Finally, I turned to them and said, "Let's go to the beach." There was safety in numbers, and they already looked worn out by what was in front of them.

Sammie's eyes perked up. I remembered what she'd told me in Florida; the beach calmed her. It usually calmed me too. Except when I had pepper spray in my eyes and a strange old man's hand reaching into my pants. An involuntary shudder crept over me.

"Okay," she said.

"Great. Let me go turn in some school work and then I'll be ready," I told her.

Sammie eyed me strangely. "School work?" she asked.

I smiled. "Oh, yeah! I enrolled in an independent studies program," I told her. "Do you want to go there?" I glanced at Hunter's face. Neither of them looked very interested.

"Not yet," Sammie said. "I'm thinking about starting back in the fall."

"Alright," I said. "Why don't you guys go pick up some snacks at the drop-ins and we can meet back here in a few hours?"

Sammie nodded, standing. Hunter stood beside her, his face still pale. "I think I'll hang out here," he told us.

Sammie and I exchanged a look. Sammie looked concerned, but I shrugged. I'd survived on my own. Who was I to tell him what he could and couldn't do?

A few hours later, Sammie and I sat on a city bus to the beach. Hunter truly had decided to stay behind in Hollywood. During the ride, Sammie was telling me about all the drama from the Covenant House. "I liked the one in Fort Lauderdale better," she told me.

I knew that. She'd complained to me about leaving Florida for months. It was why she'd told me I owed her a trip to California. Perhaps it was why I'd felt like I did owe her. But my debt had long been repaid.

When we arrived at the Promenade, Sammie was eager to explore. We walked around, looking at different shops and ogling the tourists. After a few hours, we wandered back to the center. There were a few street kids seated between the dinosaur plant-metal things, and I recognized one of them. "Hey," I said to a girl with fiery red hair and heavy makeup.

"What's up?" said the small girl. She was thin, dressed in tight fishnet stockings with red and black plaid pants that had been torn into shorts. She wore a thin black tank top and a chain link necklace. Emma had introduced me to her when I met Ava the previous week.

"This is my friend," I said, pointing to Sammie.

"Lizard. My name is Lizard," Sammie said. I glanced back at her, slightly amused. When had she picked a street name? And why hadn't I been able to pick one for myself?

"Hey, Lizard," said the too-thin girl. She smiled faintly. "I'm Sparrow. Got a cigarette?"

Sammie nodded, pulling a pack of Marlboros out of her pocket. Interesting. She had money for cigarettes somehow.

We sat down next to Sparrow. She was dainty and quiet, bird-like. I decided I liked her nickname. "Have you seen anyone else?" I asked, wondering where Emma and Ava were. The girl asked me who I was looking for, and I told her.

"Nah, they went traveling for a bit," she told me. Traveling. They could be anywhere. I sank back against the cement structure, inhaling another puff of smoke. I was a casual smoker and only smoked if someone offered me a cigarette. But Sammie always teased me that I didn't really inhale right.

The day dragged on slowly, and other street kids passed by. Sparrow was waiting for someone, but I wasn't sure who.

"Do you know of any squats?" I finally asked Sparrow. She nodded. Night had come, and we'd been quiet companions for most of the day. Sammie had gotten up to explore a few times, and I could see her looking at a display of sterling silver jewelry across the promenade. She wasn't good at shoplifting, so I secretly hoped she wouldn't try.

"Old timers sleep down on the beach," she told me. "Don't do that. If you sleep on the sand, you'll get smashed by the sand machines." I nodded. That sounded horrible. "The lifeguard towers are usually occupied." She looked over at me again. I was wearing an army fatigue shirt and old jeans, and my hair was wiry and thick from sweat. I'd gotten the shirt at the same store that sold pepper spray. I was tattoo-less, and my clothes didn't fit the crowd. "I might know of a squat where you guys could stay," she said softly.

As the evening passed on, I figured out how the kids ate down here. Couples passed by with Styrofoam packages, wandering home after date nights. I heard one of the other kids asking for their leftovers, and when they came and sat back down with us, they proudly shared a box of fettuccine with chicken. They offered me a few bites, which I gratefully accepted. I skipped over the lumps of chicken.

Sammie came back, suddenly aware there had been food. "It's easy, Sammie,"

I explained to her. "We just ask for people's leftovers."

She grimaced a little but walked with me as I began making my way through the crowd. After asking a dozen people, I managed to get a small box of spaghetti and half a cheeseburger. We returned to the center and shared with everyone, which we'd quickly realized was customary with this group. An older street kid who looked like he belonged in an 80s metal band winked at Sammie. She beamed back at him.

At the end of the evening, Sammie and I followed Sparrow back to her squat. We winded down long sidewalks and between buildings until we arrived at a building that was under construction. "Almost everything from the earthquake has been repaired already," she said regretfully. It had been three years since the Northridge quake, and squats were being refurbished into upscale housing. Three years since I'd been stuck in Las Vegas, just out of reach of the earthquake's devastation.

We crawled through a crack in the chain linked fence and snuck around back. Sparrow let out a low whistle. A door opened. Inside, we saw a dark room with debris and trash all over the floor. "Quick," she whispered, and we entered the room behind her. The door closed shut, and a flashlight came on.

"Who did you bring?" a man's gravelly voice asked, a light shining over our faces. We couldn't see him, but he could see us.

"Two new friends. Lizard and another girl," she said. I didn't have a pseudonym, so I didn't fit. I scratched at my arm absently.

"Alright. Show them the back room," the voice said from behind the light.

Sparrow walked us down a hallway to a room in the back. This had been a larger apartment, I noted as we made our way to our hiding space. We laid down on the blanket Sammie always carried under her pack. Sparrow settled in near us, and as the night progressed, several other kids showed up and camped out on the floor.

I awoke in the middle of the night to chatter in the next room. I sat up slowly, a dizzy sensation of déjà vu filling me. Years ago, I'd been awakened by my mother when I slept in a stranger's house. I had always hated myself for not walking into the other room to see what was happening. I stood and walked to the other room. A low light and harsh whispers guided my feet.

"Hey," a tall guy said, eyeing me in the doorway. A group of guys was standing in the room, drinking. They were all dressed in black and had metal chains hanging from their necks, waists, and wrists. Always ready to defend.

"Hey," I said softly, leaning against the door frame. My eyes were heavy from poor sleep. "Spare a beer?" I joked.

One of them laughed. "Yeah, come on in."

I sat down next to them and drank a beer, listening to their stories about traveling. They'd just gotten back from Arizona and were heading up north in the morning. "Do you want to join us?" one of them asked. He had sad eyes.

I shook my head. "I'm kinda trying to finish school," I told him.

Laughter erupted from the group. "Okay, schoolgirl," one of them said. Another one handed me another beer. They kept talking, and I eventually fell asleep on the floor near their group. None of them made a move on me, and for some reason, I hadn't expected them to.

53
86'ED

We spent a few weeks at the beach, until finally our skin was too sunburnt, and I was ready for a real shower. The public bathrooms by the pier had an odor that could only be described as homelessness, and there was just no way to get clean enough under the gentle spray of water that the beach showers offered. "I need to turn in my schoolwork," I told Sammie. I had finished each of my packets already, and I hadn't been to school for too long.

We boarded the bus and headed back to Hollywood. On arrival, we headed to Teen Canteen, where we both took showers. Afterwards, we waited while our clothes washed in the machine. "I wonder what Hunter is up to," I mused.

Sammie's eyes widened. She'd clearly forgotten about Hunter.

That evening, when it became clear that he wasn't coming to Pantages, she started asking about him. "Has anyone seen him?" she asked. She described her frail blonde friend with terror in his eyes. Someone had seen him, turning tricks on Santa Monica Boulevard. I cringed. That wasn't what I'd expected to hear.

The next day, Sammie went to look for him. When she came back, she was high. I was sitting in Pantages with Nora when she returned. "Damnit," I said. "What did you use?"

She giggled. She fell into the corner, her usual spot, and didn't unpack her blanket. The next few days continued like that; Sammie was always high, and I had returned to the bottle. I was annoyed with her for deciding to start using again, but I had my own issues. I'd been drinking too much, and it was starting to catch up to me.

Later that night, I'd gotten drunk and started kissing a boy, and then another boy who liked me had walked into Pantages and seen me.

"That's it!" the boy, Joker, had shouted at me, angry. Nora took a few steps back.

I sat up, still drunk but worry forming in my head. "What the hell?" I asked, pushing the boy aside. "Why are you mad at me? I thought we were just kissing," I said, confused. The boy I'd been fooling around with grabbed his stuff and took off.

"You'd better leave Hollywood, or I'll kick your ass," he told me. I stood up, wobbling a little as I tried to walk towards him.

"Hey, you don't have to be mad. Let's have a beer," I said, then started laughing.

I plopped back down on the ground and opened another drink, which I guzzled down in front of him. He bent down and stared at me in my eyes. "Stupid bitch," he told me. I laughed again. His cold hand suddenly crashed against my cheek, and my beer bottle fell to the floor.

"Hey, leave her alone," Nora said. "She's drunk."

Tears began to flow from my face. "You broke my beer," I said, eying the shards of glass and yellow liquid that had erupted over the floor. "Damnit, I wanted to drink that," I said, reaching over to touch the liquid. A shard of glass sliced into my hand.

"You're 86'ed," he said, kicking my thigh.

"No, you're 86'ed," I said, laughing.

Nora stood in between us. "I'll tell her when the alcohol wears off," she told him. He must've left, because the kicks eventually subsided.

Morning came. I awoke with a sharp headache and a stabbing sensation on my face. Everything hurt. My thigh hurt, my hand hurt, my cheek hurt. How much had I drunk last night?

"Good morning, stupid," Nora said.

"What?" I asked. I stared at her. She'd changed her hair over the past few months. She now sported a tall blonde mohawk. I hadn't decided if I liked it or not yet. But it did command authority.

"You got yourself in big trouble last night," she said.

I sat up quickly, rubbing my temples. "I feel like I got run over by a train."

Nora shook her head. "Nah. You just got the shit kicked out of you by your boyfriend." She helped me pull myself up into a standing position. The world spun around me as I stood.

"Oh, my head hurts," I told her.

"Well, he did bitch slap you."

My hand immediately went to the throbbing place on my cheek. "My face hurts," I told her. "What happened?"

Nora recounted the argument from the previous night and told me that I'd been kissing the wrong guy. I cringed. "I said that?" I asked. Maybe I had been drinking too much, I thought for the first time.

"Coffee. Now," Nora said, dragging Sammie off the floor. We both followed her obediently to the Burger Factory a few blocks away. "You've got to get out of here," Nora told me.

"Why? He'll change his mind," I said, two cups of coffee later.

"No," Nora said. "He's part of the Hollywood Dogs," she told me.

I was confused. Hollywood Dogs? What the hell was that? Nora filled me in. They were a local gang, and they were a group of tough ass guys who meant what they said and did whatever they wanted. "What's an 86?" I asked.

"It means you've been kicked out. You can't stay here anymore."

"But why?" I asked. My head was still swimming, and my face hurt. I needed to look at my leg to see what the damage was. I'd already seen my hand, and there was a deep cut that had fortunately closed on its own.

"It doesn't matter why," she said. "But you have to leave."

I shook my head. "No. I have to finish school."

"Not if they kill you," she warned.

I sat up straight. "Wait, what?" My eyes widened. "Why would they do that?" I vaguely remembered Joker telling me about visiting his family for the holidays and watching an episode of Cops on TV. When he'd looked up at the screen, he'd realized he was the criminal being chased on the episode.

"You do what they say. Trust me, you need to leave." Her eyes were frightened. She must've seen them do something before, I realized. She glanced at Sammie, who was coming down from something harsh. "Besides, does she really need to be out here, like this?" She'd been using serious drugs, not just simple stuff like marijuana. I recalled Joey's concern about her using heavy stuff back in Charlotte.

"Okay," I said quietly. I opened my backpack and searched for my bus ticket. I pulled it out, checking the dates. It had expired a few weeks ago. Crap. "My ticket won't work," I told her.

"Well, you're a drunk and she's on drugs. I'll travel with you," she told me.

I nodded, accepting what she was telling me. I needed to leave. Sammie needed to leave. She would go with us.

"We can hitchhike," I told her. Three people is safer than one.

"Okay," she said. "Where do we catch the freeway?"

I thought about it for a minute. I wasn't sure where the Hollywood freeway went, but I doubted it would be easy to catch a long-distance ride there. "Santa Monica," I told her.

"We leave tonight," she said.

54

TRAVELING

That was the beginning of our cross-country trip. The three of us stood along the side of the 10 freeway at its origin, in Santa Monica, later that evening. Sammie, with her smoke-filled, wiry black hair and glasses. Me, with a large bruise on my cheek, and others hidden under my clothes. Nora, with a green mohawk and a stern look on her face.

I remembered the tattoo I'd gotten earlier that week when I was drunk. I'd gone to a parlor on Hollywood Boulevard and lied about my age. They'd let me buy a cheap, small tattoo for forty dollars. Now, I was the proud owner of a blue and purple pair of drama faces. Because the past week had been nothing but drama.

I stretched out my thumb and attempted to summons a ride. An hour later, someone finally pulled over. "Where are you ladies going?" a man asked. It was late, perhaps ten or eleven at night. Sammie looked like she was starting to withdraw, and her skin had broken out in a cold sweat.

"Vegas," I said. I'd learned many years earlier to never tell the whole truth to a stranger. The man chuckled and said he could take us to Riverside.

"That's fine," Nora said. She knew the area better than us, and apparently, Riverside was on the way.

Nora was clear-minded, so she sat closest to the driver and chatted with them. "Yeah, we're just on an adventure, you know?" she said. He was laughing with her. "Like back in the sixties, when people used to travel the country to see where the road would take them."

"That sounds fun," he said. "Too bad I can't take an adventure with you," he told her with a wink. She shrugged. Her newly dyed mohawk made her look mean and domineering, but her laugh was young and carefree. Nora was a girl who I'd only chatted with a few times up until that morning. I decided that I liked her.

We rode into the night and ended up close to a place called Rialto by the next morning. "I used to live here," she told us, and we went to a Carl's Jr where a friend of hers worked. She chatted with them for a few minutes and came back with plates for the salad bar.

"Don't overdo it," she told us. Sammie and I nodded. It had been weeks since we'd had a solid meal, and we were confronted with an overflowing salad bar.

Sammie filled her plate with salad, potato salad, and chocolate pudding. I smiled. "I love their chocolate pudding," I told her. I grabbed some too, along with cottage cheese and a large salad. We sat down and ate our first portion, and then returned to the bar for more. Nora was in the front, chatting with her friend. When she came back, she shook her head. "We have to go," she told me. "I know these people. You can't eat that much."

"Oh," Sammie said, finishing the food on her plate quickly. I took my last few bites, too, and then grabbed a handful of the crackers at the bar to stuff into my backpack.

"Sorry," I told her. It was the middle of June, and the last full meal I could remember had been when I was at LAYN in early May.

We followed Nora back outside, and a friend of hers offered us a ride back to the freeway. "Thanks," Nora said, eying us. "Nothing weird," she told us. She glared at Sammie, who had been reminiscing about using acid years ago.

"Right," I said. We sat in the back seat, with Nora in the front. I tuned out their conversation, my eyes fixated on the small desert town. Who would want to live in such a desolate, hot place, I wondered. I already missed Hollywood.

We just needed to drop Sammie off, and I'd go right back.

After we were dropped off by the freeway, Nora's friend handed her some cash and told us good luck. "Be safe!" she told us. Nora thanked her.

We walked back down to the freeway. We were close to Vegas, Nora had told us. Our arms outstretched in unison, attempting to summons a ride from the passing motorists. A few people passed by with forlorn expressions and cars too full for three girls, especially since Sammie had that giant backpack. Finally, a small pickup truck pulled over and we climbed in.

"Where to?" the driver asked.

"Vegas."

"Right on," he said, spinning his wheels and lurching the truck forward. I immediately regretted the cottage cheese. Hours later and after much forced small talk, he dropped us off near the Nevada border. "Here's twenty bucks, just in case," he said, handing us another bill. We smiled and thanked him.

"Cool," we all said afterwards. Nora held onto the twenty, since Sammie was an addict and she told me I drank too much. I laughed. Why did she keep saying that?

When we were close to Las Vegas, a sudden fear washed over me. Crap. I'd forgotten what the judge had told me when I was fourteen.

"I can't go to Vegas," I said quietly, so that only Nora and Sammie could hear. We were in the backseat of a car, and a couple sat in the front, telling us how awesome it was we were traveling the country.

"Why not?" Nora hissed.

"Got arrested there when I was fourteen," I whispered back.

"Okay," she told me.

Once we entered the city, she asked if we could be let off near the outskirts. After the car pulled away, but not before the couple handed us thirty bucks, we surveyed the area. "We can sleep out there," she said, pointing to a long patch of desert that wasn't overlooked by any large hotels.

"Sure," Sammie said.

We set up camp on the dry ground between succulent plants and spiky short cacti. "Let's just hope there's no snakes," Nora said as we laid down to sleep.

We stared at the sky above us. Just on the outskirts of Las Vegas, we were able to see a full sky of shining stars. "It's beautiful," I said. I couldn't remember the last time I'd seen stars in the sky.

"Los Angeles is covered with smog," Nora told us, yawning. "Good night."

"Good night," I told her. We'd been lucky so far. Our journey would probably

212

take a few more days, but we'd get Sammie to North Carolina soon enough.

I tried to piece together the fragments I remembered from the other night. I remembered kissing a boy, but I hadn't realized it was the wrong boy. Maybe Nora was right. Maybe I was drinking too much, I thought soberly.

The next morning, we found a Del Taco on the Strip and they bought cheap tacos. I searched the menu for a cheap vegetarian option, then ordered a quesadilla. "Wow, this isn't that bad," I told the girls as we ate.

"I can't believe you've never had Del Taco," Nora said to both of us.

We started to walk down the Strip, but I stopped the girls. "I can't be here," I told them quickly. "We need to leave, now."

Sammie recognized the haunted look in my eyes. "Why?" she asked me.

I quickly recanted the entire story of my last visit to Vegas. "We need to go, now. Please."

We walked back to the freeway and turned to face oncoming traffic. Sammie looked worn out from the heavy drugs and travel, Nora had a mohawk, and I had fared somewhat better after sleeping in the desert. "Stand in front," Nora commanded. "They'll pull over faster."

"I hope you're right," I told them. I was suddenly afraid of going back to juvenile hall, back to North Carolina. But that couldn't happen, I tried to tell myself. Kids could leave home at sixteen in my home state. They couldn't extradite me anymore.

But they could still keep me in juvie here until I turned eighteen.

I outstretched my arm and thought of all the things that could go wrong.

For once, none of them did. A car pulled over a few minutes later, offering us a ride out of Nevada. The driver was going all the way to Utah.

It was my turn to sit in the front and make awkward conversation. Usually I freaked out, but at that moment I'd do anything to get out of Vegas.

We arrived in Utah later that afternoon. We re-counted our cash and decided to share a salad bar meal at the local Wendy's.

Sammie went first. She filled up the plate with salad, pudding, and fruit. I reached over and took a bite. As soon as the food crossed my lips, the manager came over to our table and started yelling. "I see what you are doing here! Get out now or I'll call the cops!"

"What?" I asked incredulously. She hadn't even eaten yet. "We paid for that!"

The manager shooed us out of the restaurant; Sammie clutched the plate in her hands as we hurried outside. "We need to go, now!" Nora said.

I nodded. I took another quick bite of the very expensive unlimited-but-just-one-plate of salad and let the girls finish the rest as we raced back to the freeway. We hid behind a thicket of trees for a few minutes before deciding the cops probably weren't coming. When they'd finished the salad and we'd all caught our breath, we walked back to the side of the road.

"We need a ride, fast," Sammie said. I nodded. I suddenly despised the entire state of Utah.

"That was five whole dollars," I protested as I pointed my hitchhiker thumb towards traffic.

"This sucks," Nora said. We had spent fourteen dollars already; if our next ride didn't give us money, we probably wouldn't have enough to make it across the country.

The next day, we arrived in Colorado. By the time we got to Denver, we realized we'd arrived during a special event. People were dancing in the streets, drinking and singing. They were awaiting a parade. "What are you celebrating?" I asked a guy with a cooler full of beers.

He smiled. "You're not from around here, are you?"

I laughed. "Kinda obvious, isn't it?" We were each decked out in backpacks, and Sammie's was an oversized hiking backpack. Nora was the only girl on the block with a mohawk.

"We won the tournament," he told me. Hockey or something.

"Awesome!" I told him. "Can we celebrate with you?" I asked, eying the cooler.

Nora nudged me from my side. "You don't learn, do you?" she asked.

I shrugged. "Come on, you know you want to give us each a beer," I laughed, flirting with the guy. He smiled back and handed us each a glass bottle.

"Have fun, ladies," he said, winking at me as we hurried away.

We walked through the streets, quickly guzzling down our drinks so we wouldn't get caught for underage drinking. "We should find more," I said, tossing my bottle in the trash.

"No, we should stop drinking and find another ride," Nora said, glaring at me.

I shrugged. We were standing in front of a mall, and the stores looked empty. Everyone was out on the streets, partying. "They threw a party for us," I joked. "They must've known we were coming to town."

Sammie laughed. "She has a point," she told Nora.

We walked into the mall, grateful for the sudden blast of cold air on our faces. "Let's go shopping," I said.

Nora rolled her eyes. Sammie grinned. They knew I had no intention of paying for anything.

Our first stop was a homemade soap store. Nora started chatting with the store clerk, who was overly excited when she realized that we were hitchhiking across the country. "That's so cool!" the young girl said. "I've never been anywhere outside of Colorado. What an adventure."

As the sales clerk went through the cabinets and selected some free samples, Sammie and I grabbed a few larger sized bars. "This one smells like coffee," I said, sniffing an oval shaped bar with brown flecks in it. The sales clerk turned back to talk to me, while Sammie grabbed another bar.

Nora rolled her eyes again. "Let's go, girls," she told us.

I smiled at the clerk. "Thanks for everything," I told her.

"Be safe!" she called out after us, as we hurried away to another shop.

By the time we made it back to the freeway, Sammie was laughing hysterically. "She was so clueless," she told me.

We inventoried the soaps, clothes, makeup, and snacks that we'd accumulated. I'd even managed to snag a bottle of blue hair dye. "You're good," Nora told me. "I'll at least give you credit for that."

I nodded. At least I was good at something.

Our rides took us further north than we'd wanted. We eventually passed through Kansas. After standing by the side of the road for hours, we found a ride to the rest stop. All of us were tired of traveling by then, and we'd run out of snacks. We were down to our last twenty dollars and trying hard not to spend it.

"I have an idea," I said. We went into the girl's bathroom and covered our hair with the blue hair dye. Sammie's jet-black hair didn't change at all, but mine and Nora's took some of the color. I laughed again. "I got a polaroid camera at the mall," I announced, showing them another item I'd managed to shoplift.

"No way," Nora said.

"Yeah," I told her. "I'm good, remember?"

We took a series of photos of ourselves, with awkward bluish-greenish hair and bright colored makeup. After we'd finished the pack of film, I shoved the camera into Sammie's bag and we divided up the pictures. "For the memories," I proclaimed.

"For the memories," the girls cheered.

We went back to the road, no longer caring about the endless miles of corn fields and flat land. We would always have this trip; this journey to drop Sammie back off in North Carolina. I knew I wasn't planning to stay. I wasn't sure what Nora was planning to do next.

We found a truck driving duo that took us across several states, and they bought us dinner at the truck stop. We took turns sleeping in shifts, since the back could only hold three people and the front was made for two. When one of the truckers slept, I made sure to move back to the front seat. Too many bad things had happened to me in trucks by that point. I only rested when both girls were beside me.

"Why Los Angeles?" the driver asked me as we crossed into Tennessee. Everyone else was sleeping.

I stared at the long, unfamiliar road in front of us. It was late, and there were only a few other trucks on the road. Regular people were tucked away safely in their beds at this time of night.

"I don't know," I said, my voice taking on a faraway tone. "There was this map, and I opened it up and said, 'That's far enough.'" I glanced over at the driver, whose eyes were on the road in front of us. "I guess Hawaii was too far to travel by truck?" I joked.

He chuckled. "You've been through a lot," he said after a few minutes had passed. "I've got a teenage son. I'd hate for him to be out here like you guys. You're lucky to have found each other."

I nodded. Perhaps. Although, here I was, taking a one-way trip with girls I wasn't sure I'd ever see again. The return trip back to Los Angeles wouldn't be as safe. I was already beginning to dread the journey.

"He's a lucky kid," I said softly.

The driver took us to his home in Memphis and introduced us to his family after he dropped off his fellow trucker. We had a family meal and met his teenage son. His wife prepared us several sandwiches and a bag of snacks before he took us back to a nearby truck stop.

"Be safe," the older man said gruffly. He handed me two twenty-dollar bills. "And find somewhere to settle down. You really shouldn't keep crossing the country like this."

I nodded. The others hadn't seen us chatting. I pocketed the forty dollars and headed over to where they were standing.

"Did he give us any money?" Sammie asked.

I shook my head. "No. But at least we got to rest, and his wife made food for us."

Nora sighed heavily. "We've got enough for another meal, but we really need to make it to Sammie's house soon."

I nodded. "We can get there by tomorrow."

Five days had passed already. We were getting closer each day, but the journey took double the time it would have taken on a Greyhound bus. Again, I regretted letting our tickets expire. Sammie should've gone home months ago.

"Let's go," Sammie said, her eyes bright. "I think I'm finally ready to go home."

55
DAVID'S, AGAIN

Sammie's mom actually hugged me when she saw us. Sammie had called her collect from Kansas to let her know we were on our way. She had wanted to buy us bus tickets, she later told us. But her husband didn't have any money to spare.

The same man who had been abusing Sammie.

I shuddered at the thought. But it was still safer than what she'd been doing in Hollywood.

Sammie's mom agreed to buy Nora a bus ticket to her family's home in New York and told me she was going to drop me off at my brother's house.

"But I don't want to go there," I said.

"They're expecting you. I called them to let them know you're coming."

"No," I protested.

Her mom didn't accept my response and told me to get in the car. She was mad at me for taking Sammie all the way to California, even though she'd literally dropped us off at the bus station. I fumed all the way to my brother's house. "You're lucky I even gave you a ride," Sammie's mom told me angrily when we arrived at David's. "Don't call Sammie anymore."

I nodded. "Okay," I said. It didn't really matter, I told myself. I was going back to Los Angeles anyway. There was no way I was staying here.

When I started to walk up the sidewalk in front of David's house, his wife opened the doorway and called my name. They'd been expecting me.

"Alright, I should get going," I told my brother. "I need to get back to the bus station."

"Why?" Denise asked.

I was planning to pay for a ticket as far as forty dollars would take me. I could hitchhike afterwards. I just wanted to get away from this town and all the memories it contained.

I shrugged. My little nephew came and sat down next to me. "We want you to stay," he said quietly. His speech was too perfect, too practiced.

"You have to stay," my brother told me.

I shook my head. No. This wasn't what I'd wanted. They'd told me to leave.

"I'm going back," I told them.

"Stay," David said, his voice strong and authoritative. "If you hate it, I'll buy you a ticket back."

"When?" I asked.

"Give it two weeks," he told me.

I reached out my hand and forced a handshake from him. "Okay, deal."

What I didn't know, what I couldn't have anticipated, was what they told me the following morning. I awoke, feeling groggy and disoriented. I hadn't slept in a bed for a long time. When I went to the kitchen for breakfast, David was standing over the stove cooking.

"Oh, you don't work today?" I asked.

He shook his head. "No, we leave for our vacation today."

"What?" I asked. Cool. I'd have the house to myself.

Denise stood up from the table, where she'd been sitting next to Geoff. "Yeah. We're driving to Canada. We've been planning it all year."

I smiled. That would be fun for them.

"But if you don't come with us, we'll just cancel it."

I could feel my eyes grow wider. Wait, what? "You didn't say anything about that," I told my brother.

"Well, we're going. Get your stuff."

My shoulders sank. This wasn't good. I went back to the room and stared at my backpack. Should I just leave? Did I really want to hitchhike?

The idea of a bus ticket providing safe passage back to California was enticing. But the idea of spending a vacation with my brother and his wife, when they were pissed off with me? Crap.

I walked back into the living room, backpack over my shoulder. "How long did you say this trip would last?"

"Two weeks," David told me.

It was a road trip I wasn't ready for. Two long days to get to Canada, in a car with my brother, his wife, and their four-year-old son. They hadn't designed a trip that included me. I felt like an awkward, closely watched, fourth wheel.

David and Denise made efforts to connect with me, but they also made it clear they didn't approve of any of my choices. When I pulled out my homework packet and started working on some of my school assignments, David grew angry.

"What are you doing?" he asked.

"I'm almost finished with high school, back in California," I told him.

He shook his head. "We're giving you a place to stay. You don't need to go back."

But I did. The tension in the car on the drive made me feel panicked. It had already been several months since I'd left, and I had no plans of returning. I'd only come back to drop off Sammie.

And to lay low from the Hollywood Dogs for a few weeks.

We stopped at Niagara Falls on our way to Canada. I peered out at the great divide between the U.S. and Canada and saw the similarities with my own life. I was a part, but not a part, of this family. I couldn't overcome the chasm that had been forming since I was eleven. Since I'd spent the summer in a hospital, for reasons I still couldn't understand. For the ten months I'd spent at Dillon. For the countless times I'd pleaded for a way out. Boarding school. My mom's house. Anything would have been better than the chaotic home where I'd been living.

I wanted them to understand, but every time I tried to talk to David or Denise, they became defensive. They were angry and hurt that I wouldn't stay.

We went to Toronto, and I stared down at the city below from the glass floor of a tall building. We traveled to small cities, and my eyes sought out the street kids, toiling through their lives. Wandering. I was like them. I was hiding among them. They were me.

The southward drive took us through Maine. We went out on a boat in the Atlantic, and I felt like that other ocean was calling me. The Pacific.

"I need to get back to school," I said to my brother one evening over dinner. We were in Vermont, at a bed and breakfast.

"You need to stay in North Carolina," he told me. I watched as he drank his Samuel Adams, and I craved my own drink. No, I needed freedom. I needed peace. I couldn't go back to the way things had been.

I couldn't go back to the impossible chore list, the rent, the same high school where I'd been an outcast.

In North Carolina, I saw no future for myself. There was a solid dead end in front of me. At least in California, I could finish high school. A path had already been set in motion for me.

They went to the Ben and Jerry's tour; I stayed behind at the bed and breakfast. I walked outside and breathed in the fresh mountainous air. At least the scenery was beautiful. And my nephew was cute. But I was broken.

And no one knew how to put me back together, especially not me.

They argued on the drive back to North Carolina, mostly about me. By the time we were back at my brother's house, I knew what I had to do.

I went to his room and asked him for the bus ticket.

He sighed heavily and said fine.

The next day, I boarded the Greyhound and left again. I was becoming an expert at leaving.

56
GOING HOME

Three days later, I pressed the button for the buzzer. "Hi," I said when the door opened. Guillermo was standing in front of me, his arms across his chest.

"Hi," I repeated timidly. I saw a familiar face pass behind him in the hallway.

"How can I help you?" he asked me, his voice serious.

"I was wondering if I could come back yet?" I asked.

"Are you ready for reunification?"

I shook my head.

"Foster care?"

My head shook even more quickly.

"I don't think we can help you."

I bit my lip, looking away. My eyes felt heavy with unshed tears. Why was this so hard? I just wanted a place to say. When I looked back at him, my heart was pounding too fast. "Please," I said quietly.

His facial features softened for a moment. "Not yet," he told me.

My shoulders slumped. "Can I at least have breakfast?" I asked him. I felt a familiar metal taste on my lips. I'd bitten down too hard.

He continued to stare at me. Over a month had passed, and the sun had turned my skin a few shades darker. My hair had recovered from the failed blue hair attempt while we'd been in Kansas, and I'd managed to re-dye the red roots while we were traveling. The time I'd spent in Canada and the northeastern U.S. had given me a little more perspective. "Okay," he said, stepping aside so I could enter.

"Really?" I asked. He glared at me. I rushed inside, afraid he would change his mind. Quickly, I hurried back to the dayroom, where I found the familiar set up that had begun to feel like home to me.

I sat down at the table and ate a bowl of cereal, then pulled a fresh packet out of my backpack. When Guillermo passed by to check on me thirty minutes later, I was almost finished with my homework.

He pulled up a chair and sat down next to me. "Where's your friend?" he asked.

I paused, putting down my pencil. When I glanced back up at him, the time and distance must have passed across my face. I'd always had a hard time concealing my emotions, and that moment was no exception. "I took her back to North Carolina," I told him.

"Interesting," he said. "Why?"

"She started using, and it wasn't safe for her to stay," I answered.

"Why didn't you stay in North Carolina?" he asked.

"I don't have a home there anymore," I told him, forcing down the memory of the look on Denise's face as I'd left. The look of disappointment in David's eyes as he'd paid for my bus ticket. That wasn't my home. I wouldn't go back again.

"But you don't have a home here, either," he said.

I sighed. "Yeah," I told him. "You're right. But I'm going to graduate from high school soon."

He nodded. "I see that. How many more classes do you have?"

"Only five or six," I told him. "I'd finish faster if I could stay here."

He shook his head. "Not yet. Let's just reinstate your drop-in privileges first."

With that, he stood and walked away. I wanted to yell back at him, but I was running out of options. I couldn't go back up on the Boulevard, and I had to hide from the Hollywood Dogs, so I needed better to behave and stay out of sight for a few hours.

57
RED

Hollywood Boulevard was off limits, so I ventured a few blocks south instead. Frustrated, hot, and still exhausted from the arduous journey back to Los Angeles, I settled in on a bus bench on the corner of Sunset and Gower after drop-in services ended for the day.

Bored, I struck a match, watching the flame burn and sizzle before it went out. Red to orange to white to black smoke. I stared for a moment, then pushed the hot ember against my arm.

My skin turned red, then blanched. I felt nothing.

I closed my eyes, allowing myself to fall back asleep on the bus bench.

When they reopened, I saw the sky had changed. It was dark now. And a man was seated next to me.

"What's up, Red?" the man asked me. I turned to look at him, sizing him up in a few short seconds. He was dangerous.

"Nothing," I mumbled. I allowed my vision to focus on the cars passing by. There weren't too many of them at this time of night.

"Want to go for a ride?" he asked. I noticed a sedan pass by and recognized it. It had circled past a few times since I'd awoken.

I stood up. I quickly secured the backpack strap over my shoulder. "I'll walk."

The man stood up as well. I turned to the west and began to walk. He fell into step next to me.

Danger. My senses buzzed. I had to get away.

I continued walking at a brisk pace down Sunset Boulevard. He kept offering his ride, and the car passed by us every five or ten minutes. The windows were tinted.

"Where are you going, Red?" he asked me.

I shrugged. "The beach."

He laughed. It was a deep, roaring laugh. "That's a long walk."

I continued walking, saying nothing.

"I'll keep walking with you," he said. "If you don't mind."

"I do mind," I said, picking up the pace. It was late, sometime after 2am. The buses were infrequent at this hour. The only people out on the streets of Hollywood at this time of night were up to no good. Or hiding from it.

Danger.

I could feel his nearness. He could grab me quickly, and I'd be in that car and injected with something before I could react. This is how it happened. This is how all those poor girls who walked the streets got taken. A smile, a kind gesture, an offer for a car ride.

We walked down Sunset Boulevard, passing the high school on the corner by Highland Avenue. Past the late-night strip clubs. Past La Brea, and Fairfax. We'd walked several miles, and he kept trying to talk. All the while the sedan kept creeping by.

"You look tired," he said.

I sighed. I shouldn't have let myself fall asleep on that bus bench. This was my fault; I'd left myself out in the open. In the den of wolves.

"It's not too far," I said bravely. My words had to remain strong; confident.

We kept up the charade for at least four miles. I noticed the change in scenery as we transitioned from Hollywood to West Hollywood. I was a moving target. If I stopped, anything could happen. How many people were in that sedan? Certainly, they were stronger than me.

We passed dozens of empty bus benches. Closed shops. Businesses. An older homeless man, asleep atop a cardboard box. Empty parking lots. I read each street sign, trying to think. How would I escape?

And then I saw it. The police station on the left; the gas station across from it. Diagonal from me. Daylight was coming.

Time was passing as we walked down the Boulevard. My legs felt heavy. I knew I had just this one chance.

I timed my steps with the streetlight ahead. I could make it across at just the right time. The walk light beckoned to me, and I devised my plan.

We crossed the street, and immediately I pivoted into a different direction to make it across the Boulevard. He was close enough to grab me, but he hadn't expected me to change course.

I had run cross country for two years. I had strength in my legs that I'd forgotten. My walk became a run, and I raced into the convenience store at the gas station. The bells jingled from the door as I entered.

"Help me," I begged the store clerk.

He glanced up from behind the counter. There was a look of indecision on his face; would he protect me? He saw me, then my pursuer.

The man entered the store and saw the store clerk picking up the phone. He quickly turned around and left. The sedan pulled up and took him away, just moments before the police car arrived.

Crap.

Danger.

I stared at the officer, a pudgy gentleman who probably needed less donuts or more gym time. "What happened?" he asked.

I froze. Old hoodie, faded t-shirt, secondhand jeans. Well-worn shoes. Backpack. Wild red hair. Everything about me screamed who I was.

No, no, no. I was so close to adulthood. Why was it so hard to be seventeen? If I had been eighteen, I could stand tall and tell him the truth. But at seventeen, I was out of place. Free but not quite. Always chained to that number.

He asked me to join him across the street, at the station. I felt the beads of sweat rising on the back of my neck as I was escorted to sit in the back seat.

Not handcuffed. I looked up at him curiously, and the door slammed shut.

He walked around to the driver's side and sat down. "Are you okay?" he asked.

I nodded. Danger.

He drove us across the street. The sedan was gone. It was just me, an officer, and I was surrounded by the expansive police station. He parked behind the building.

No escape.

I waited for him to open my door and fumbled at getting out. I hadn't gotten out of many police cars without handcuffs on. This was different.

He led me inside. We passed a reception area and I followed him to his desk. We both sat down. He logged onto his computer before turning back to look at me.

"Name?"

"Sheri," I said softly. My voice cracked. This was it. I clasped my hands together, trying to make them stop trembling.

"How old are you?"

I looked up at the wall, noticing the pictures of this officer and his family. Pretty wife, cute kids. A normal family. "Seventeen," I answered.

"Show me some ID," he demanded.

I nodded. Of course. I realized my backpack was still strung across my back and slid it around so that I could open it.

Did I have anything illegal with me? I tried to remember if I had any cigarettes left. I certainly had matches, I thought, remembering my arm.

I unzipped the backpack as little as I possibly could and pulled out my wallet. When I opened it. I saw the worn edge of my North Carolina driver's license underneath my bus pass. Oh, man. I wished I was old enough to get a California ID instead.

I started to reach for the driver's license, but my hand stopped. Danger.

I pulled out the bus pass and quickly closed the wallet.

"Here's my student bus pass, sir," I told him. It had come in the mail while I'd been away, and I'd just put it in my wallet earlier that day. Blue, emblazoned with a Metro symbol and my name, it read 1996-1997 school year and it was just in time for the beginning of a new year.

He looked at it closely. My full name was listed on it. But not my age. I was seventeen. I wasn't legally required to carry ID until eighteen years old.

I looked at him, my eyes brimming with tears. Please, they pleaded. I glanced back at the picture of his happy family. That teenaged daughter of his would never have to fall asleep on a bus bench. That little boy of his would never be sent away to foster care. The mom in the picture was probably not bipolar, just a few missed pills away from a manic episode.

Damn it.

He took the blue laminated card in his hand and sat back in his chair, obviously pondering his next move. Indeed, it was a Los Angeles student bus pass. Correct location. As long as he didn't realize I was from someplace else.

He held my gaze. "Who was that guy?" he finally asked.

"I don't know, but he was following me."

We both knew I had been pursued by a bad guy. A pimp, most likely. They were a dime a dozen out here. And once they caught you, they owned you.

No one owned me.

He stared at me, and perhaps really saw me. I was terrified.

Danger.

He typed my name into the computer, searching.

224

"Date of birth?" he asked. I told him.

The computer searched, and I tried to remain calm. My hands had somehow changed position, and they were digging into the sides of my legs like claws. I couldn't feel it. I saw my knuckles turning white and released my death grip on my thighs. That would be a nasty bruise later, I thought.

The search ended. Nothing.

All that history, hidden. The states didn't communicate well, as the internet was still new, and databases were not fully connected. He wouldn't know about Dillon. And he didn't even see I'd been arrested in Los Angeles four years earlier.

He looked at me again. Those eyes, so very knowledgeable and concerned. He slid the bus pass back to me. I thought to myself, he was probably an excellent father.

"You're up very early for school," he told me. He lifted an eyebrow, inviting me to follow his lead.

My pulse quickened. Yes. School. I had a school bus pass. I nodded.

"Be safe," he said kindly.

I stared at him, not sure if this was really happening.

He stood up, and I did also. "I'll show you out," he told me.

I swung the backpack back over my shoulder. My feet carried me behind him as we walked down the hallway, towards safety. My body ached from the journey I'd taken. My heart screamed thank you, but the words could not be spoken aloud. The meaning behind them might make him change his mind.

Safe. But danger was never too far away.

As I exited the police station, I knew I had to get as far away as possible. Before the computer realized I was an unaccompanied minor or before the pimp came back for me.

I walked back to Sunset Boulevard and looked both ways. It was early morning now. I could see a bus driving towards me from the west.

I raced back to the bus bench, where I greedily awaited my safe passage back to Hollywood.

I boarded the bus and sank into a chair in the back.

58
ELIJAH

When I returned to Hollywood, I went straight to school and switched out my coursework. A police car passed me while I waited for the bus near my school. My body flooded with anxiety and I recoiled at the memory of sitting in the back of a police cruiser early that morning.

The car kept going, oblivious to my panic on the corner. I continued to wait for the bus, hoping for a safe passage through Hollywood and out of sight of any of the Hollywood Dogs. When I exited the bus at Ivar, I rushed across the street quickly, trying my best to blend in with pedestrians.

I passed the shawarma shop and My Friend's Place, hastily reaching my destination. The public library. Homeless people were known to frequent this library, but usually they were older and alone. I found an empty cubicle near the back of the building on the second floor and pulled out my homework assignment. I needed to read a book called *A Raisin in the Sun*. The school didn't keep books on hand and expected us to go to the public library if we needed copies of novels for reading assignments. Calmer now, I wandered through the stacks until I found what I was looking for. Gratefully, I found that it was a small book.

With the book in hand, I walked back to my cubicle and settled in, ready for a long day of reading. I opened it to the first page and let the words come alive on the pages.

After I closed the book later that day, I thought for a long moment. Why had they given us this book to read? What meaning was I supposed to derive from it? There was one quote going through my head, over and over: "Sometimes it's hard to let the future begin."

Was it hard? Or was it impossible?

I stared at the closed book for a while before I answered the set of questions and fumbled through the required essay. I put all the loose pieces of paper back into my backpack and stared at the time. The library would close soon, and I needed to figure out dinner. I'd missed sandwiches from My Friend's Place because I'd spent the whole day reading, but that was better than strolling in when there was a large lunch crowd. The Way-In was where a bunch of Hollywood Dogs went for dinner. Now it was approaching night, and I hadn't eaten.

My last meal had been the previous day, when I'd sat through LAYN's drop in hours. Realizing I needed to find food, I reached into my backpack. At the bottom of my bag, I found the crumpled blue services card I'd been given when I'd arrived in Hollywood several months earlier. The only other nighttime meal today was a once weekly church service on Cahuenga. We had nicknamed that place Children of the Corn and nobody I knew went there.

I shrugged. No better options tonight. Most people don't go back to the same places where they'd been threatened. But I was determined to finish my high school classes before I moved on again. If nothing else had come out of my argument with my family, I was resolved in my plan to finish my diploma.

After placing the book where I'd found it, I walked downstairs and peered out the window. No gutter punks. I breathed a sigh of relief, then took a side street across to Cahuenga. When I arrived at the address on the services card, I paused. There was a small sign announcing the weekly meal.

I pulled open the large metal door and climbed a flight of stairs. When I arrived at the doorway, I heard someone strumming a guitar and singing a song that I recognized from when I was younger.

"Hey, come on in," a voice called out to me.

"Oh," I said quietly, startled. I walked into the room and looked around. There was an older woman, a few college-aged kids who looked like they were volunteers, and some other youths I didn't recognize. I didn't think any of them were Dogs. I hoped that they weren't.

I went through the motions of a short youth sermon and then picked up my meal. It was home-cooked; I filled my plate with pasta and vegetables and moved towards a seat in the back.

The guy who had been on the guitar came and sat near me. "Hi," he said easily. "I haven't seen you here before."

I stared at him cautiously. He was a good-looking man, and he looked too kind to understand my life. "I haven't been here before," I answered back. He smiled.

"Elijah," he said, offering his hand.

I hesitated but shook his hand. "Sheri," I told him.

"What's keeping you on the streets?" he asked pointedly as I took a bite of my pasta. I choked a little, then looked up at him wildly.

"What?" I asked.

"Well, what is it?"

I set down my plate on the empty chair next to me. "I don't have a place to live," I told him.

"But why not?" he asked, his eyes gazing through me.

"Um, I need to be an adult before I can get a place," I said.

He shook his head. "That's an excuse. Why aren't you in a shelter?"

"What?" I asked. "I…" my voice trailed off. Because Sammie lied about her age? Because I refused to go to foster care? Because I knew my dad and I weren't compatible, and he was engaged to be remarried? Because I'd argued with Guillermo?

"Do you use? Drink?" he asked.

"I drink," I told him. Nora's words echoed in my head. "Maybe too much."

He nodded. "Are you ready to quit?"

Our eyes locked. How did he know? I nodded. "I probably need to," I told him.

"Do you want to go to AA with me?" he asked. His eyes were electrified as he grilled me.

I had never been. Alcoholics Anonymous seemed terrifying, and I was only seventeen. But then, my mind flashed back to the night when I'd been 86'ed, and even earlier, to the times when I'd gotten drunk and blacked out. I remembered almost getting shot in North Carolina when I'd been drinking and cheating badly in a Spades game. I paused, thinking about Emma and her NA chips. She was only thirteen and she was in NA. Seventeen wasn't too young for AA, I mused.

"How old were you when you had your first drink?" he asked.

"Eleven," I answered back. My voice was hollow, my throat raw. I didn't want this. I'd come here for a free dinner.

"There's a meeting tomorrow night," he told me. "Do you want to go?"

"How do you know there's a meeting tomorrow night?" I asked.

He reached into his pocket and pulled out an AA chip. Aha. He knew it when he saw me, because he saw part of himself when I'd walked into the room. "Okay," I stammered.

We set a meeting place and he agreed to pick me up the next night. I fumbled through the rest of my meal and the service before walking away nervously. Damnit. This was serious. Even strangers could tell I was drinking too much.

59
A.A.

The next night, Elijah picked me up just as he'd said. I sat in the passenger seat and felt constrained under the seat belt. I'd changed over the past six months. We were approaching the end of July, and I'd never wanted a drink more than I wanted one on that long ride. I tried to get comfortable, but my back hurt from sleeping on the bus the previous night. I'd taken the four line, back and forth, Los Angeles to Santa Monica. Not fun, but safer than the unknown in Hollywood.

"I go to UCLA," he told me as he drove. "There's a big open meeting once a week near the campus," he explained.

"Open?" I asked.

"Open means everyone can attend. Closed means that you have to admit you're an alcoholic to attend," he told me, casting a glance in my direction as he drove.

I sunk down in my chair. Sure, I drank a lot. But was I really an alcoholic?

He parked in front of a large church, explaining to me that AA meetings often met in churches or other public buildings. "A lot of people here smoke and drink coffee, to get over the cravings from alcohol," he told me as we walked inside. He'd encouraged me to leave my backpack in his car. It felt weird to walk inside without my stuff.

"It's okay," he'd told me, more than once. We settled into seats in the middle, and several people said hi to him and introduced themselves to me.

An eternity later, it seemed, a man approached the podium. "Good evening, everyone," a man said. By then, I'd started my third cup of coffee and I'd gone through a circle of hello's and congratulations for attending my first meeting. I wanted to melt into my chair and hide. "My name is Leroy, and I'm an alcoholic," the man announced.

I froze. Wait, what? Around me, everyone chanted in unison, "Hi, Leroy."

"I've been asked to tell you a story about my drinking. I didn't believe I was an alcoholic," he began, his eyes darting around the room from the stage. He spoke into a microphone, since the room was enormous and filled with hundreds of people. "I didn't think I could be, since I've only ever gotten drunk four times in my life."

The man paced across the stage as he spoke, my heart pounding as he told his story. "The first time I got drunk, I was in college," he said. "I was at a frat party, and when I left, I drove myself home. Or at least, I thought I could drive myself home." He paused dramatically. "I woke up in the hospital. They told me my car had hit an oncoming driver, and she died instantly."

I sat up in my chair, horrified. Wait, had he really just said that?

"I was sentenced to ten years for manslaughter. I got out after five years, and I found a job. I'd lost my spot in school already. Instead, I tried to get my life in order. I was doing great. I wasn't an alcoholic, I told myself. I'd only ever drank one night in my life."

He went on to describe how he had found a job, fell in love, and had gotten married. "We were on our honeymoon when it happened," he told us. "I got drunk again. I didn't realize I needed to stay away from alcohol. I couldn't have been an alcoholic," he told us. "But I got drunk, and I slept with my new wife's best friend. She left me, and I'm pretty sure they stopped being friends." He continued his tale, adding that the next time he got drunk, he lost his job. The final straw was when he crashed his car into a tree and ended up in the ICU.

"I only ever drank four times in my life," he repeated. "And alcohol took over, all four times. I lost my ability to reason. I lost my control over my life." Another pause. "I took a life. I ruined other lives."

He stared around the room, his eyes locking with mine for a moment. "My name is Leroy, and I'm an alcoholic," he repeated. "I've been sober now for 864 days."

The audience stood and began clapping after he finished speaking. I stood next to Elijah, terror coursing through me. My life was currently in danger because I had gotten drunk. Was I an alcoholic?

Afterwards, he walked me back to his car. "What did you think?" he asked.

"I think," I said, licking my lips. "I think I might have a problem," I whispered.

"A few of us go out after the weekly meeting and have dinner. Do you want to join us?" he asked.

"I don't have any money," I said automatically.

He smiled. "I'm inviting you. Do you want to go?" he asked.

"Okay," I said quietly.

I went with him to Denny's, where I met three of his friends. Two were recovering alcoholics, one was a supportive classmate. "Hi," I said quietly from my seat next to Elijah.

"Hey," said one of the girls. She introduced herself as Lana, and she was a beautiful blonde with dazzling eyes and a great smile. She stared at me intently. "Tell us about yourself."

I looked around the table. Cara was seated between Lana and Rebecca. Cara was an Olympic contender in gymnastics, and she was tiny and fierce. Her curly black hair was pulled back tightly into a bun, as if she'd just come from practice. She stared curiously at me. Rebecca was an older woman with a metallic jacket and bright red lipstick. She smelled like stale cigarettes and too much perfume. She had introduced herself as Lana's sponsor.

"Oh," I said softly. I wasn't sure what to say among this group. What do you say when you're seated next to a star athlete and three self-proclaimed alcoholics? "Um, Elijah brought me to the meeting," I said and shrugged helplessly. My gaze slipped down to my lap where I was fidgeting with my fingernails. I had painted them black a few days ago with a stolen bottle of nail polish, and the paint was chipping. It was falling apart, just like me.

Elijah jumped in. "I met Sheri in Hollywood," he told them. They all nodded.

"Oh, like at that program you volunteer at?" Cara asked. "Are you a volunteer?"

I looked up, meeting her dark eyes. "No," I said, my throat suddenly hoarse.

"Just a homeless kid who probably drinks too much."

Nobody reacted harshly to my statement. In fact, Lana leaned closer, and Rebecca nodded. Cara spread her hands across the table, grabbing mine in her own small gymnast hands. "How long has it been?" she asked me.

A confused wave crossed my face. "Hmm?" I mumbled, trying to figure out the question. How long had I been on the streets? That was complicated.

"Since your last drink?"

I stared at the table, unsure. We'd been in Vermont at a cabin, and my brother and his wife had left for the day. It was one of those bed and breakfast cabins that belonged to someone else, and we were renting the room. I'd found the owner's stash of beer and helped myself while they toured the Ben and Jerry's ice cream factory. I was an opportunistic drunk. If it was available, I drank it. "Maybe a little over a week?" I said. Had it really been that long? I licked my lips. Yes, it had.

"That's great," Elijah said, a little too quickly.

Rebecca knew better. She sat forward and looked at me closely, her older eyes catching mine for a moment. "You need to go to meetings," she told me. "I see that wild look in your eyes."

I stared back at Elijah. "I'll get her a meeting guide," he told her.

"And this homeless thing. You need a place to stay," she continued. I watched her hands move as she talked. They animated her words, and the massive stash of rings and bracelets that she wore glittered as they moved.

"You make it sound so easy," I said bitterly, just as the waitress arrived with our food. Everyone else had ordered dinners, and I ordered a typical kid meal. Pancakes, at close to midnight.

Elijah nudged me from my side. "It isn't," he said. "I have no idea how hard it is," he began, commanding my attention. I set down my fork and knife and listened to him. "I never had to sleep on the streets. I came close, but I never did. I have no idea what it's like for you."

Lana confided, "I've done some scary things for alcohol. I regret so much. I let alcohol take control of my life."

"I don't think it's got control of my life," I answered quietly. "I mean, I like it, and I drink when I can, but I think I'm okay."

Rebecca was next. "Are you okay?"

I stared around the table. They wanted to know if I was okay. We were in the middle of a very serious discussion. About me. Was I okay?

"I will be," I said boldly. "When I'm eighteen. For now, I'm not okay." My hand trembled a little as I began to cut my pancakes. Everyone was staring at me, and I felt like they really saw me.

"Have you ever blacked out?" Lana asked. I nodded. I'd woken up in some frightful places.

"Has your drinking ever gotten you in trouble?" Rebecca asked. I nodded again. Joker's face flashed through my mind, and I automatically reached up to touch my cheek.

"Did you ever drive while drinking?" Elijah asked from beside me. When we'd been driving over, he'd asked if I knew how to drive. I nodded slowly, thinking back to a brief period of drinking that set everything into motion all those months ago, back when I was in North Carolina. I'd been driving a car, and there were a handful of classmates in the car with me. We were all buzzed. I tapped the bumper of the car in front of me at a red light. They'd laughed it off and let me go. No one else knew about that moment.

"Tell me the worst thing that happened because you were drunk," Lana said.

I looked up at her, my eyes shiny. "Um, I'm not sure which one is worse," I said. I put down my fork. They weren't going to let me eat, I realized. "Well, once, I got drunk, and I was playing a card game with some guys in the projects. When I tried to set the deck, one of them pulled a gun on me and told me not to cheat."

"When was that?" she asked.

I thought about it for a moment. "About six months ago," I said quietly.

"You said you weren't sure," Lana continued. "Tell your other story."

I stared down at my hands. "A few weeks ago. There was a boy who liked me, and I thought he was okay. I kissed him but didn't realize it wasn't him because I was drunk. The real guy, he came back and found me kissing some random guy. He beat me up and told me I was 86ed from Hollywood."

"What does that mean?" Elijah asked. "To be 86ed?"

I looked over at him. "He'll kill me if he finds out I came back."

"But why would you come back?" Cara asked.

"I didn't know where else to go," I answered her.

Elijah nodded. He stared at me for what felt like a long time before he spoke again. "I think, if you think about it, you'll realize that alcohol has a hold over your life."

I stared at the pile of shredded pancakes on my plate, wanting to eat them. I wanted everyone to stop focusing on me. I was hungry and emotionally raw. Exposed. "Maybe," I said.

"Tell you what. Why don't you go with me to another meeting tomorrow?" Elijah offered. "It can be a smaller meeting."

I hesitated. "Maybe," I said. It was getting late, and I was starting to worry about making it safely through the night. I would probably have to sleep on the bus again. Hopefully, it wouldn't smell too badly.

"Okay?" Elijah asked.

I nodded, returning my thoughts to the group in front of me. "Yeah, I'll go," I said quietly, reaching for the syrup. I absently poured it onto my pancakes in the shape of a sad face. I used to make happy faces, I thought. Realizing what I'd done, I replaced the syrup bottle in the middle and stirred the pancakes again with my fork. Elijah raised an eyebrow at me. He'd seen what I'd drawn.

After dinner, Elijah led me back to his car. "We have two options," he told me.

I glanced up at him from the passenger seat. "Two?" I asked.

"Well, one is I could drive you back to Hollywood, where you're in danger." He turned to face me, his eyes serious. "The other is something that AA people do sometimes, when people are struggling. You could couch surf for a little, while you get on program."

"Couch surf?"

"Yeah. You could stay with me for a couple of days while we try to figure out something more stable."

I glanced at the clock. It was after midnight. I remembered the pimp from a few nights ago. "Okay," I said quietly. "I want to sleep on a couch." Bus benches were dangerous, buses were risky. An annoyed bus driver could always call the cops, and I was still a minor. But a couch; that offered possibilities for real sleep.

He drove us across town, to a large flat off Olympic Boulevard. He explained that he had several roommates, and they were all supportive of him working the program. He also explained that he really shouldn't have me over, since he was still working the steps, but that he didn't know what else to do. I nodded, not sure what I was supposed to say.

His living room was expansive, and sure enough, had a nice couch. He brought me a stack of sheets and pillows. I curled up on the sofa with my backpack beside me, just within arms' reach.

Elijah's house was nice, but temporary. His roommates would only allow me to stay for a few days, and I was getting anxious anyway. I didn't know how to let a guy just be nice to me, just because they wanted to be nice to me. I was awkward and fumbled my way through his house and his routine. A few meetings and a few days later, he returned me to Hollywood. "Good luck," he told me, scribbling his phone number on a sheet of paper for me. "Will I see you on Tuesday?"

I nodded. Dinner at the "Children of the Corn" or whatever that place was actually called.

"Thanks," I told him.

"Call me if you get the urge to drink," he told me.

I nodded. Maybe I would, I told myself. He was doing well, in spite of his past. Maybe I could become sober, get my crap together, and go to UCLA too. I almost laughed at the thought, but another one pushed through more strongly. Maybe I could.

I went to LAYN for breakfast, but Guillermo was off for the day. I couldn't get permission to stay if he didn't approve me. Evan sat down next to me, his serious eyes catching my attention. A lot of people had been trying to figure me out lately, I thought.

"How have you been?" he asked.

"Okay," I mumbled. Teens moved in and out of the room around us.

"I heard you left town."

I nodded. "I did. I came back."

"What are you up to today?" he asked.

I shrugged. "I have to stop by school, and I figured I'd try a one o'clock meeting this afternoon."

He looked at me closely. "A meeting?"

I glanced up, our eyes meeting. It was dangerous to admit something so personal to someone else. "AA."

"Very good," he told me. "I'm proud of you."

I nodded again. It was a safe answer. I was sometimes amazed by how little I could get away with answering peoples' questions. I'd been expected to say much more when I was under lock and key in the mental hospital. But here, when I was scurrying down a path of self-destruction, I could burn my skin with matches and drink and nod yeses and nos.

"Okay, then," he said when he realized I was done talking. I watched as he stood up and made his way back to the kitchen to tidy up the breakfast supplies.

60
APOLOGY

Hours later, I returned from an awkwardly quiet closed meeting in the basement of a church off Fairfax. I got off the bus at Ivar, ready to hurry over to My Friend's Place, when I ran into him.

Joker. The boy from the Hollywood Dogs.

"Wait," he said. I waited. My hand immediately traced my cheek, which had hurt for a week after he'd slapped me.

"I'm sorry," I said quickly. I cowered in front of this boy, who had been wielding power over me. He was only a few inches taller, thin but strong.

He crossed his arms over his chest, waiting. "I told you to leave."

I stared into his eyes. Eyes of a boy that had liked me, and I'd thought I'd liked back. But he'd hit me and kicked me and threatened me. "I did leave," I told him. "But I came back."

"Why?" he asked. He cocked his head to the side, his dark hair shifting with the movement.

"I didn't have anywhere else to go," I told him. He continued to stare, his fists forming as his arms shifted to his side.

"I could have you killed for crossing me," he told me.

I stared down at my feet. I hadn't noticed that my shoes had a hole in them. Or that my jeans were unevenly frayed at the bottoms. "I'm working the program now. I started going to AA," I told him. I lifted my gaze, meeting his eyes again. A tear rolled down one cheek. "I know I was drinking too much."

"That's good," he said softly, something changing across his face.

"I'm trying to be better," I told him.

"You need to be better. You drink too much," he told me. I remembered very little of the time we'd spent together, so I assumed he spoke from experience. What secrets had I told him?

"Can I stay?" I asked.

He nodded. "I'll lift the 86. But no more drinking, and no more Pantages," he told me.

"Oh."

"You're back at Pantages?"

I shook my head. "No. But the bus bench was scary."

"Try another shelter. Go to the Way-In," he told me.

I shook my head. "I got kicked out of there after one night." The common phrase, The Way-In showed me "the way out," buzzed between us, unspoken.

He laughed. It was no secret that I was a misfit, or that shelters wouldn't keep someone like me for very long. "Fine. But just for a few nights."

"Thank you," I told him.

He nodded, and we parted ways. I never saw him again. Someone told me later that he traveled up north for break, but I never asked again after that.

Back at Pantages that night, I found Emma and Ava. They were in the middle of a photo shoot for some group of college students. Well, at least they told us they were college students. I watched as they mingled through the crowd of homeless teens and young adults, capturing some of the youths unaware. A few of them shielded their faces from the lens of the camera. Not everyone who was lost wanted to be found, I thought dryly.

"Sheri!" Emma called out. I ran to her and gave her a big hug. "We were worried about you!" she told me. I glanced around the foyer. Nora hadn't returned from New York.

"Hi!" I said. "How was traveling?"

Ava and Emma laughed and started to tell me about San Francisco. I noticed that Emma had on a new pair of steel-toed boots, and Ava had a whimsical smile on her face. They'd seen a different world, and it had changed them.

"I went traveling too," I told them. I quickly recanted my journey across the country with Nora and Sammie. I left off the part about my brother and Canada.

When nightfall came, I avoided the crowd in the corner with alcohol. Before, it had been easy to get a few drinks from them. But I'd made a promise. To Elijah. To Joker. To myself.

"Good night," I told my friends. I noticed that Ava was resting next to a boy I hadn't seen before. He was leaning against the wall, wearing a cap and watching people passing by on the sidewalk.

Emma smiled at me. "These photographers have been paying us to take pictures with them," she told me as we drifted off to sleep. I didn't say anything; I let the thought carry me through the night. Emma and Ava, they represented something I had lost. The world was beating down on them, but they were still young enough to believe people could be good.

The night passed too slowly, and the hard floor was unsettling to my back. I stared at my two young friends, wondering what the future would hold for each of them. For us. Before morning came, I knew I needed a better plan. I would try to get back into LAYN again and get my life on track. Maybe the girls would want to join me.

61
AVA AND EMMA

Several mornings later, we were awakened by the sound of the cleaning man. Such an ordinary thing, but it struck me as strange that a closed theater had a cleaning man. After we were up, we gathered our belongings and wandered back down to Gower.

We sat in our corner booth, at Burger Factory. Emma, Ava, and me. It'd been a long weekend, and the hunger pains in our bellies screamed for breakfast, but services were always closed on the weekends. We had run out of our emergency stash of chips and fresh fruit too soon this time. I pulled my last two dollar bills out of my wallet and set them on the table.

"Do you guys have any money left?"

Ava shook her head sadly. She was younger than Emma, just twelve. Her hair was growing out of its buzz cut, and the two long wisps of dark blonde bangs framing both sides of her face were tucked behind her ears. Her sweater was perfectly grungy and broken, and she wore steel toed army boots Emma had given her. A young runaway, from Santa Monica. She was a childhood friend of Emma's, now lost out here, just like us. I felt like I had to protect her from the mean streets around us, but I still had no idea how futile my attempts would prove to be.

Emma reached into her pockets, searching. She slowly placed the contents of her pockets onto the faded orange table top. A lighter, scratched and well worn. An almost empty pack of Marlboro's. Not the good kind, but the stale ones from Mexico the lady on Santa Monica Boulevard sold for two bus tokens. Three bobby pins, to keep her short, wavy hair in place. A folded piece of paper, which I knew contained the lyrics to Alanis Morrissette's song, "Perfect," a song we'd belted out at the top of our lungs together, when we'd been staying at the shelter. Three bus tokens, those little copper colored coins that could be exchanged for a ride, a dollar, or half a pack of smokes. A folded and torn services card, with phone numbers for all the drop-in shelters and other service agencies in the area. We all had several versions of that services card. A quarter and two dimes. A Narcotic's Anonymous chip. Damn, how was a thirteen-year-old already collecting NA chips, I wondered, not for the first time. I thought about my own AA book stashed in my backpack. We were all working some sort of program out here.

I sighed. I felt responsible for them, although I knew that wasn't really true. I just didn't want to let them taste the same fate as I had. Emma's mom had abandoned her, and I really didn't know Ava's story. I'd met her dad once, when he'd been passing out flyers in front of Teen Canteen. He had made missing posters with her face, pleading for answers. When he asked me if I knew her, I shook my head.

"We'll have to wait for the program to open, to eat," I said softly. My stomach growled from waiting two days to eat. "But I'll go buy us a cup of coffee, so they don't kick us out." There was only an hour and a half left, anyway. No use spending every last penny when free cereal was literally waiting around the corner.

I glanced up at the cashier. She had that look on her face. The one that said buy something, or leave. I really wanted to use their restroom and wash my face, so I had to buy something.

I walked over to her, forfeiting one of my last two dollars for a cup of coffee. A cup that we would share. One free refill. We knew the drill, we couldn't stay too long, and we couldn't have more than one refill.

"Thank you," I said to the cashier, collecting the twenty-nine cents in change. She eyed me with her usual disdain.

I tapped the sugar shaker and emptied ten seconds of sugar into the coffee, before pouring a large amount of creamer into the cup to fill the last inch of space. Once stirred, I strolled back to the table and handed Emma my change. "Keep it," I told her, as she gathered up all her belongings and the new change to add to her pocket. "I'll find more."

Ava smiled, swiping one of those strands of hair behind her ear again. She loved the taste of warm coffee in the mornings, and Emma always chased this moment with a cigarette. I studied them for a moment, grateful for a brief reprieve from whatever was out there, waiting.

I took a slow sip of the coffee and passed it to the girls. Too young to be out here. But I had learned something my peers had forgotten to share with me, when I was thirteen. Sometimes the best advice isn't "Go home, girl." Sometimes it's, "Stay alive."

I wish I would have told Ava those words. None of us knew what was coming for us. For her. Afterwards, we parted ways. I wanted to go down to LAYN, and the girls decided against going to a shelter. "See you later," I told them both. They smiled back at me.

62
SHELTER

After coffee, I hurried back down Gower to the big blue building that housed LAYN. So much had changed within me over the past few months, and I wasn't the same person who returned to Hollywood four months earlier. Sammie had been returned to her mom, and Hunter had disappeared. A part of me wanted to believe that he used his bus ticket, but the cynical part of me knew better. But we weren't really friends; I understood that now.

I hesitated for a moment before pressing the buzzer. "Maybe," I said softly to myself. Maybe. Maybe they would give me another chance.

The door hummed alive, and I pulled it open. How long ago had I slammed it, yelling at Guillermo? I cringed. I passed through the entryway and glanced at the front desk, noticing Jacob. Jacob was a friendly staff member who was always in a good mood. I regretted that I'd cursed him out when I'd seen him down the street a few months earlier, after I'd been kicked out.

"Hi," I said timidly.

"Sheri," he called out, stepping out of the office to face me. He was much taller than me, and when he stood so close, I felt small and unprepared. "Are you here to tell me to F off again?" he asked.

I paused. "Sorry about that," I said, shoving my hands into my pockets and staring at the wall. I couldn't meet his eyes.

"It's okay. Are you here for breakfast?" he asked.

I glanced back up. His eyes were still friendly. "Yeah," I told him. He stepped out of the way, and I proceeded to the dayroom. Michelle was camped out in front of the television, and I could hear kids out back. A cloud of cigarette smoke blew in through the window.

Guillermo came in a few minutes later and glanced in my direction. "Hey, they let you back in?" he asked.

I nodded nervously, taking another quick bite of cereal. My breakfast could be cut short, I realized. He went into the kitchen and started rummaging through cabinets.

When I stood to throw my bowl away, I saw that he was cooking something. I hovered in the doorway. "What are you making?" I asked. A part of me missed moments like this; cooking over a stove, preparing a meal for myself. I relied so much on others I'd forgotten so much of what I used to be capable of.

He turned to look at me. "Guillermo's famous chili pepper melts," he said with a smile. "Come on in, you can help," he told me.

"Really?" I asked quietly, but then I entered the kitchen and washed my hands.

"It's easy. I grilled the peppers already," he said, showing me an empty jar of green chilis that he'd used. They were waiting in a pan at the side of the stove. "Now, I warm a tortilla and melt a slice of cheese on it."

I watched as he put a row of tortillas on a long flat pan. He placed a slice of cheese on each one, then some peppers. After the cheese started to melt, he folded each of them in half. "LAYN quesadillas," he joked.

He removed them from the pan and told me to try. I placed six small tortillas on the pan and began placing the pieces of cheese on them. I tried to set the cheese perfectly in the center. Guillermo laughed. "They don't have to be perfect," he told me.

I stared at him. Yes, they did. I wanted to come back to LAYN. I couldn't mess up. I scooped fried green chilis onto each of them a minute later, and then folded them in half, making sure that both edges were toasted. When I placed my set of chili pepper melts on the waiting plate, I noticed that Guillermo was watching me.

"I heard you started AA," he told me, letting out a low whistle.

I nodded. "Yeah, it was time to stop drinking," I told him. I glanced back in his direction, not sure what else I should say.

"How's school?" he asked. I had started on the next set of tortillas.

As I spread the cheese slices, I answered him quietly, "I finished my first class, and I'm almost done with the next one."

"And work?"

"I got a job at the sandwich shop when I was staying at Pantages, but the manager was a creep," I told him.

"How so?"

"He trapped me in the walk-in freezer and kissed me, so I quit."

Guillermo paused, thinking. "And you're still not ready for reunification?"

I dropped my hands to my sides. My voice was hollow when I spoke, "I won't go back, Guillermo. I'd rather sleep outside than go back."

"You don't want to stay here, then?" he asked.

My face tilted up suddenly. "Yes," I said quickly.

Our eyes met. He, the man who currently controlled my fate. Me, the young, lost girl who would do anything to survive. "Okay," he said.

I smiled, perhaps the first smile I'd worn on my face the whole day.

"Go tell the others that food is ready," he told me. I nodded, hurrying out of the kitchen while he flipped the last batch of tortillas.

"Alright, everyone!" I heard Jacob's voice calling out from the bottom of the stairs. "We're leaving in fifteen minutes," he said.

I'd been back at LAYN for a week, and life was starting to feel normal again. I'd met the new group; a few newly immigrated kids had found the shelter over the summer. Amon was still there, and his English had improved. Itzel was a sweet, bubbly girl from Honduras who couldn't wait to start school in the fall and wanted to join the soccer team. Luis was a self-made boy from Mexico, who had been kicked out of his tribe for reasons that he wouldn't explain. He spoke an indigenous Mexican language, and he had a different name when he was with his tribe. He'd learned Spanish on his own and decided to call himself Leo, but when he'd come to the U.S., he decided his American name would be Luis. All of them were learning English, and that led to some interesting conversations.

Other familiar faces were there, too. Andrea, Leticia, and a big burly football playing kid named Cedric were staying at the shelter. Absent were Emma, who had been kicked out months ago, and Ava, who had never set foot in a shelter.

I checked myself in the mirror again. My bright green bathing suit was hideous, but it was the only one that was my size in the donation closet. I covered myself with pants and a t-shirt, and hurried downstairs.

We boarded into the LAYN van. It was a monstrous vehicle, donated by some celebrities several years earlier. I took a corner seat next to Luis and watched him design bracelets all the way to Raging Waters, a water park located east of Los Angeles. Guillermo and Jacob were in the front seats, and Pedro had squeezed in next to Itzel. They were having a long conversation in Spanish. I stared at them every few minutes, realizing how badly I wanted to learn the language.

The drive took over an hour, and by the time we'd arrived, Luis had made several bracelets. One of the art workshop leaders had bought him a steady supply of beads and string, and Luis consistently prepared traditional bracelets that looked like the kinds that street vendors could sell.

"We're here," Pedro called out as we drove into the parking lot. "Everyone needs to be on their best behavior," he reminded all of us. "Leave your stuff here in the van. We'll meet for lunch at noon, and we're leaving at four," he told us.

I sat up. Really? They weren't going to hover over us?

We entered the park as a group, and I quickly learned I had to remove my pants and t-shirt to get into the water. I hesitated for a moment, not comfortable with myself after everything that had happened. But Itzel walked up to me and smiled, and said, "It's okay. Let's have fun," in perfect, slowly spoken English.

I nodded and took of my outer layer before joining her and Luis on one of the water slides. Before long, I was laughing and enjoying myself like a regular kid. I'd forgotten what it felt like to just have a day off.

A day off from being a homeless, broken kid.

And it was amazing. We raced around the park and rode every ride at least twice. We sat down in the big circle boats that took us through a river and soaked us with icy water. We ate a picnic lunch as a group and left with smiles on our faces.

Afterwards, we all piled back into the van and Pedro started driving. He took us to a small restaurant called In-N-Out. I'd never been there before.

When we went inside, I glanced at the menu. "Pedro," I told him. "I can't eat anything here."

He shrugged and ordered burgers for everyone. I settled for a pack of French fries. "You should start eating meat," Pedro teased on the way out of the restaurant. "But until you do, that leaves more for the rest of us." He laughed, and so did a few of the others. I shrugged and stuffed a few more fries in my mouth. I was hungry, but I'd been hungry before. There was something about their playful banter that made the hunger more bearable.

63
AVA

A few days later, I walked back to the Boulevard to see what my friends had been doing. I didn't make it very far. Emma was standing on the corner of Hollywood and Gower, rambling about something. "What happened?" I asked.

"How could they fucking do this to her?"

"What? Who?" I asked.

Emma twirled around, seeing me. But not seeing me. Her pupils were smaller, and her face pale. A thin trail of sweat drenched her forehead. Her t-shirt was too thin, her pants loose and tucked neatly into her army boots. She was ready for combat.

"Why?" Emma asked me. Her eyes locked with mine for a moment.

"Emma, what happened?" Damnit, I thought as my eyes tracked her arms, the telltale needle marks betraying her prior sobriety.

"Ava," she said. "She's dead. Her boyfriend fucking murdered her."

"What?" I asked. "What are you talking about?"

"It's on the news." Emma's eyes swiveled around, and she peered at something that only she could see across the street. "She's gone. She's gone."

I reached for her arm, but she pulled away. "Come with me, to LAYN."

"No. Fuck that place." She sucked in a breath. "I'm going to Frisco. Do you wanna come?" she asked.

I shook my head. "No," I told her. No. No. No. Was Ava really gone? Or was Emma just high?

"Emma, where is Ava?" I asked.

She stared at me again, those pinpoint pupils out of place in the morning's bright sunlight. "They found her body. It was her boyfriend."

"Where?" I asked. But Emma didn't answer. She was not looking at me anymore. "Emma?" I asked again, trying to get her attention.

"I have to go," she told me after a while.

I watched as she walked away, her small frame carried down the Boulevard by heroin and pure rage. When her silhouette faded out of sight several blocks later, I ran back to LAYN.

"Guillermo," I called, running into his office. "Is it true?"

He looked up at me from his desk.

"Did a girl get murdered? Ava? She's twelve, from Santa Monica."

He stared at me as he spoke. "Yes. It's on the news."

"What?" I asked, my words suddenly feeling hollow and foreign in my mouth. Tears spilled out of my eyes. "How?"

"Come with me," he said, and he took me to the dayroom. All the others were already glued to the television, watching a reporter telling the world about Ava.

Her boyfriend had taken her to a warehouse, and he and his three friends had raped and murdered her. They were on the run, and police were looking for answers. Information.

"No," I whispered into a room full of sadness. While I'd been playing at the waterpark, my little friend was being murdered. I collapsed onto the sofa and sobbed for a long time.

Emma was gone after that. Perhaps she'd found her way to San Francisco, or perhaps she was just getting high. I couldn't go down that path with her. I couldn't be a statistic.

Most nights, I was haunted with my memory of Ava's dad, handing out fliers for her in front of Teen Canteen. He'd wanted her back. She'd had a family.

Why had she been out here? I'd never know.

Life was so unfair. I knew that. It was why I'd forced myself to move forward. Move on even as the news proclaimed a nationwide search, followed by an arrest of Ava's alleged murderers a week later.

She died, and they'd only been on the run for a week. Her death felt meaningless. I added her to my sad, growing list of people I'd loved and lost.

I eased myself into shelter life. What I needed was focus. Somehow, I had to convince Guillermo to let me stay until I turned eighteen.

A local karate class offered free lessons for the youth in our program. Timely, after the murder of such a young runaway. I thought about all the times someone had gotten the upper hand on me. Living on the streets was dangerous, and I hadn't survived without scars.

"I want to go," I told Evan. He assembled a small group of us, and we went to our first class. Itzel was there, and we practiced our punches and kicks in class and back at the shelter. She wanted to get in shape to try out for soccer, and I missed the feeling of freedom in my lungs that I'd found in cross country.

We started running together in the mornings. My demons were chasing me. I could've told Ava's dad where she was. I could've done something. She was twelve.

The school year started, and my new friends started to leave. Amon and Luis were placed in group homes. Itzel made the soccer team at high school, and a foster family was found for her shortly afterwards. Karate ended. Morning runs ended.

The kids I'd connected with were gone.

Then Rachel arrived. Loud and angry, a daughter of the streets. I hadn't found a job yet, and Rachel had the same plan as me. Find work, get an apartment, get the hell off the streets. I sensed a tide was turning.

But then, news came in that there had been another casualty of the streets. Zony. The sweet, quiet girl with spiky hair and a faraway look in her eyes. The kids who came in with the news said she'd been train hopping in Northern California and had missed the jump. She'd severed her arm and bled to death.

I wanted to vomit. "I can't do this anymore," I told Rachel. We'd both been looking for work, but neither of us had even been asked back to any interviews. The clock was ticking slowly towards our birthdays.

"Let's get out of here," she told me.

I couldn't think of a reason to stay. I shrugged. "Why not?" I filled a bag with my belongings and she walked with me to storage before we hurried back to the bus stop.

"Santa Monica?" she asked.

I nodded. I was getting tired of the Pantages scene anyway, and that foyer held too many memories of both Ava and Zony.

64
GRIEF

We stayed at one of the last unrepaired apartment complexes in Santa Monica. Construction was happening everywhere; the area was rapidly being gentrified.

I didn't talk much to the others. I was tired of growing attached to people, and then seeing them leave. Or worse.

Reggie. Ava. Zony. And I had no clue where Emma was.

Sparrow was sitting across from me by the dinosaurs. I hadn't seen her for several months, and she'd somehow managed to become even thinner. "Want to try speed?" she asked.

I shrugged. What the hell. Everything else was ruined. I'd walked away from my brother and his wife, when they had offered me a place to stay.

Too many memories flowed through me. And a few beers. I'd given up my hard-won sobriety after I left the shelter.

We walked down to the beach at dusk and sat on the sand. Me, Sparrow, and a girl I hadn't met.

"Are you sure?" Sparrow asked me. I shrugged. I didn't care anymore. My life had become a self-fulfilling prophecy. I wasn't expecting to make it to eighteen anyway. People were dying all around me. I honestly didn't expect to make it to eighteen, and I'd started to wonder how the end would happen.

Sparrow took out a spoon and a small rock, which she told me was meth. I watched as she prepared her drug kit. Lighter, needle. I glanced away, up at the sky, and thought, "Well, if you care one way or another, God, then don't let me do this."

She flicked the lighter on and began to melt the rock. I watched as it turned to liquid. She readied the needle. Just as she was about to collect the warm liquid into the needle, a strong wind blew across the beach and the liquid flew off the spoon. Nothing was left. Everything landed in the sand, unusable.

Sparrow cursed. The air around us stilled, and there was an eerie silence for a few moments. "I guess we'll do this another time," I said, staring at the horizon. I watched as the waves continued crashing against the beach. The girls stood.

"I think I'll sit here for a while," I told them. They marched away, angry. Twenty dollars, wasted. My anger was directed inward instead.

When they were gone, I was alone to collect my thoughts. "You've made your point," I whispered quietly as I stared up at the sky, before standing and walking back to the promenade.

Several nights had passed. I was drifting apart from Rachel and the street scene. I found myself sitting by the ocean a lot, sketching pictures of Zony and Ava. Landscapes of the ocean. Writing dark poetry.

One night after staring at the ocean waves, I went back to the squat a little later than usual. When I arrived, Rachel stood at the doorway and told me to go away.

"You're too late," she told me through the door.

"What the hell, Rachel?" I asked.

She didn't open the door. I couldn't make a scene, or the cops would find our squat.

It was late, perhaps past midnight. I had nowhere else to go.

I wanted, no, needed a drink. But there wasn't one I could find that night. Instead, it was me versus the world. I hadn't been to a meeting in months. I wasn't sure I really was an alcoholic, but the words of the guy from my first AA meeting echoed in my mind from time to time.

I made my way back to the beach. While therapeutic in daylight, nights drew out long shadows and memories of the old guy who sprayed me with my pepper spray.

The last tourists had left, and the lifeguard trucks were venturing back and forth across the dunes. I walked lazily towards a lifeguard tower to sit down; wrapping my arms around my chest for warmth. As I sat and felt a silent tear slide down my cheek, I heard a rattling noise behind me. When I turned to look, an elderly homeless man was sitting up from his hidden sleeping bag under the tower. "This is my tower, get out of here," he growled.

I nodded, standing on command. He had won; squatter's rights mattered. I continued strolling down the beach, watching the large sand mowers begin their nightly trek back and forth across the sand. Others had warned me never to sleep on the sand, as people had been flattened before. All to make sure that the sand looked inviting in the morning for the many tourists who visited the sandy beaches of Santa Monica.

My legs ached by the time I reached the next bathroom area. The night was passing too slowly. Everything was so silent, and I could feel the hairs on my arms stand up in complete, utter fear. Night was a scary time for homeless young women.

I stood, listening. Was anybody there? I had a strange feeling that someone had been following me. I decided not to stop at the bathroom. My senses had taught me very well; if I didn't listen to that inner voice, something bad always happened. The van. Hunter. Sammie and Hunter. Camila and States. The pepper spray guy. I needed to listen to that small voice.

I continued to walk, but this time not in the mountains of sand. The mowers were going back and forth, and I did not need to be stopped by a lifeguard or a police officer at two in the morning. I was still a minor, and minors could not be alone in this world. I felt the deep-seated fear that came whenever I remembered my tiny cell at Dillon. I would not be arrested again. I just could not bear the pain of imprisonment. I was seventeen already, less than a year shy of never having to be afraid to walk outside after curfew again. So, as I walked, this time, I walked in the long parking lot adjacent to the Pacific Coast Highway. I ducked behind trees when I thought I saw police cars. My feet carried me slowly at times and sometimes quickly, but I walked. I kept walking until my feet felt numb, long after I had passed the creepy campsite where that old man had tried to rape me. I kept walking, until I was passing signs declaring I was in Malibu. And then, I finally sat down to rest.

Daylight was approaching, and the night had finally broken. I could not do this anymore. I was tired of sleeping outside; tired of this life. I wanted something more, something better. I had not come to California to hide from the world. I had come here for opportunities, yet I had received very little. I felt the sting of tears rolling down my cheeks, and the weight of my meager belongings on my back.

I thought about my backpack for a long time as I walked. Inside of that small bag, I had a change of clothes, a notebook for my musings about the world, and my schoolwork. There was a folded piece of paper from when I'd gone to court for a bogus ticket for feeding the pigeons. I recalled the look on the officer's face as he'd questioned me. "How many times did I tell you not to feed the pigeons?" he'd asked. When I'd told him never, he'd written me a ticket. I went to court, and the judge laughed at the offense. We both knew the purpose of the ticket was to serve me with a bench warrant if I didn't show up in court or pay the fine, and I'd stubbornly stood up for myself in court anyway. Buried within my backpack were several completed school packets. I was just four classes away from my high school diploma, and I felt like it was past time to get back on track. The time had come to go back to Hollywood, I realized.

After walking another mile or so, I sat down on the edge of the sidewalk by a bus stop and waited for the morning bus service to begin. I still needed to go to the bathroom, but I had chosen safety over comfort. I fished in my pockets for my wallet, pulling out one of my remaining bus tokens and two quarters. Three buses to go back.

I watched as an older Hispanic woman approached the bus stop, looking tired from her long night at work. Several minutes later, she was joined by another woman, and they began chatting happily in Spanish. I caught a few words but reminded myself yet again that I needed to learn how to speak that beautiful language.

The familiar sound of an approaching MTA bus filled the air, and I stood up. Both ladies boarded first, and I followed them.

I found a window seat near the back of the bus and staggered into it. Sheer exhaustion had set in, and I knew my bus ride would be long. I rested my head against the window and watched as the miles I had trekked overnight became mere long city blocks for the bus to traverse. The world that had cost me so much was so simple for this bus to charge into; I felt the ache in my bones from so much stress and so many nights of walking without rest.

I must have drifted off to sleep; when I woke up the bus was full of teenagers, standing in the aisles, clinging to the overhead poles to keep themselves upright. It was a school day, and the rest of the world was back to business as usual.

The many, many miles I had traveled stretched out behind me and ahead of me. What was this life? Why was I stuck in such a trap? Backwards, forwards, all this traveling. To a destination of nowhere.

65
BOX OFFICE

I went back to Hollywood and begged my way back into the shelter. I'd come and gone too many times already, and I could see the exasperation in Guillermo's eyes when I told him I wanted to find a job. That argument had played out over and over, and I was still six months shy of eighteen.

"It's been a few weeks. You can come back now," he told me. Music to my ears.

Too easily, I settled back into the routine of being a shelter kid. My off again, on again relationship with the streets was easy enough to shed for a temporary place to sleep. But the only way I wanted permanency was on my own terms.

A few days passed before I ran into an old friend from the shelter. "Hey," Jose said to me when he walked into the dayroom. I was sitting at the table, sketching Ava's young face. Those soulful eyes haunted me. I still couldn't believe she was gone. Jose sat down at the table across from me. "My brother found a job in West L.A.," he told me. "He said they're still looking for a few more people."

I put down my pencil and glanced up at him. "Yeah?" I asked. "A job?" I hadn't put out any new applications since I'd returned. Never getting a return call was a bit depressing. It was as if they could smell the homelessness on my application. Or perhaps they read between the lines. Hollywood address. Pager number instead of landline. Independent studies high school classes.

"Yeah. Get dressed, I'll take you over there."

"Cool."

He was right. The movie theater was hiring, and they gave me a job on his brother Alberto's recommendation. I was suddenly employed again. The next day, I began my job selling movie tickets at a ritzy theater. They had an actual red carpet and big movie premieres every few weeks. And they paid minimum wage.

Jose's friend worked concessions. At first, I'd wanted that job. But that was before I found out what it meant to work in the box office. I was alone, in an air-conditioned office, selling tickets to a small crowd of movie goers. There was not much foot traffic, so I had a lot of free time.

I started to bring my schoolwork with me. I had to read another book to finish the second half of English. In between selling expensive tickets and listening to people rant about the steep parking price, I read through the *Story of My Life*, by Helen Keller. I'd heard of her briefly when I was younger, but I'd never really thought about what it meant to be blind and deaf.

"What are you reading?" someone asked me. It was my manager.

I closed the book quickly. "Sorry," I muttered.

He laughed. "It's okay. It's better to read than to just stare at nothing." He moved through the room behind me, grabbing a stack of credit card receipts from the week. "Keep up the good work," he told me.

I nodded and stared at the empty mall in front of me. This was a theater that wealthy people went to for privacy. They weren't worried about ticket sales, Alberto had told me. They were here for the big parties. The huge movie premieres with star studded carpets.

After another twenty minutes had passed with no customers, I picked back up my book. At this rate, I would be finished with my English course in a few more weeks, I realized. I spent the rest of my shift reading in between small spurts of customers, and during my break, I watched the third half hour of Independence Day again. With a smirk, I remembered I still needed to see the first part of the movie. But our breaks were not timed with movie beginnings. They were random thirty-minute breaks with free popcorn and unlimited soda.

66
GROUND ZERO

One night after work, I took the bus back to Hollywood with Rachel to a coffee shop she'd found called Ground Zero. It was a small spot on Sunset Boulevard that had just the right amount of darkness in the background. Every ten or fifteen feet, there was a small blacklight and a piece of fluorescent artwork. Usually, it was eerily quiet. Other times, there was a band set up in the front.

I scribbled a stanza of poetry onto the back of a postcard. They had a rack of postcard advertisements by the door. Free. We each grabbed a handful to write and draw on.

"This place is cool," I said quietly as I drew Zony's face. Was she really gone? Zony. Ava. Who else? What had happened to Hunter or Emma, I wondered.

"Yeah," Rachel answered me, taking a slow sip of coffee.

"Work was kind of boring today," I said as I drew.

Rachel had just started at the concessions stand the previous week. Alberto recommended her, too. Probably because Jose had a crush on her.

"For you, maybe," she said. She glanced out the window, something catching her eye. Her pager went off. She shuffled through the codes and put it back in her pocket. Those were the days of coded messages. It cost too much to return calls from payphones all the time. When she turned back to face me again, she said, "People are so demanding. They get mad about how much ice I put in their cups."

"Yeah." I thought about the lady who had yelled at me for her parking price. It wasn't my fault that she had parked without reading the sign.

Rachel glanced out the window again. "I met a guy. He's going to meet us here." I raised an eyebrow. "I don't like him. But I thought you might."

"Oh?" I asked.

"Yeah. He's a manager at a restaurant down by Sunset and Gower. Tall guy. Your type."

We each finished our large cups of coffee and requested a refill. Typical for Hollywood, there was one free refill at their establishment. I poured too much sugar into the cup and stirred vigorously. When I walked back to the table, I saw a tall man had joined our table. Was he the guy?

"Hey," he said. I flashed a smile. I was tired, wearing my work pants and a tank top. My movie theater shirt was buried deeply into my backpack. "I'm Damian," he told me.

"Sheri."

I sat down next to him and played twenty questions. We asked each other about work, favorite musicians, and other questions that could have determined right away that we were incompatible. But then, he smiled back at me and I felt something unfamiliar. "We'll go out sometime," he told me. He didn't ask. I nodded.

When we finished our coffee, he led us outside to where he'd parked his Volkswagen beetle. Rachel sat in the back, leaving me a spot in the front. "You're at that place on Gower, right?" he asked.

I glanced in the rearview mirror at Rachel. She'd told him we were homeless? She shrugged innocently. What was she planning?

"Yeah," I answered.

A few nights later, I rode the bus back to the shelter alone. There had been another well-attended movie premiere. It would've been fun, except they sent me to clean the men's bathroom. With men in it. Using the urinal right next to me while I cleaned.

I hated cleaning men's bathrooms.

The bus careened down Hollywood Boulevard. I stared out the window, wondering where the friends I'd met along the way had ended up. So many people had crossed my path in the past six months.

My new beeper went off, but I didn't want to get off the bus to answer it. I'd bought a pager earlier in the summer; a way for people to find me. If I wanted to be found. As the bus rolled onward, I stared at the number. It was local, but I didn't recognize it. Maybe it was a wrong number.

When the bus approached Gower, I pulled the signal for my stop. I shuffled my way up the aisle, tired from working a long shift. I'd decided to switch buses instead of passing by the studios on foot. I didn't like walking up Gower from Santa Monica Boulevard when it was this late. I was always on edge with all the long, dark shadows and hiding places.

As I walked down Gower, I felt my temples begin to throb. I should've had a cup of coffee or more soda before coming home, I thought. Home. It was a strange word.

When I arrived at LAYN, I pressed the button for the buzzer. No one answered.

Weird.

I pressed it again. A long pause. I was certain I'd heard the telltale sound of the doorbell through the thick door.

The door pushed open in front of me. "Sheri. What are you doing here?" Steven asked.

I stared at the staff member at the doorway. "What do you mean? I just got off work."

"Oh."

"What happened?" The pager. The weird feeling. The beginnings of a familiar headache forming across my temples.

"Well, Rachel and Sheela said you were leaving."

"No. I was at work," I told him. I was still wearing my uniform. My hair was frizzy from scrubbing urinals. I didn't even want to think about what moisture I'd been exposed to in there.

Steven stepped out of the way to let me in. He folded his hands across his chest, considering something. "They took your stuff with them."

"What?" I asked. "Why did you let them?"

"They said you were leaving."

Crap. The pager. "All my stuff?"

"Yeah." He looked flustered. Crap. "What do you need me to do?"

"I need to use the phone, I guess," I told him, pulling my turquoise pager out of my pocket. J&J Beepers. For nineteen dollars a month, people could contact me. "Someone paged me. It's probably Rachel."

I went into the office and quickly dialed the number. A hotel desk clerk answered. I asked if Rachel was there, and then asked for the address. "Steven, I don't want to go. But I have to. They have my stuff," I told him.

"I understand," he said.

"Damnit, I am so tired," I said softly.

"I'm sorry," he told me. I turned to face him before I left. He really was. It was past midnight, and I was heading out into the night. Sunset Boulevard. I said a silent prayer that no one would harass me on my quick walk to the hotel.

"What the hell?" I asked.

"We didn't have enough money, so we needed you to come too," Rachel explained.

"I can't afford a hotel. I'm saving up for an apartment."

Rachel shook her head. "Why? You can't rent one until you're eighteen anyways. Don't you ever get tired of playing by their rules?"

"No!" I told her.

The phone in our hotel room rang. We both paused, and Rachel reached over to answer it. "Okay, okay. We'll be quiet. Sorry, sir," Rachel mumbled.

"I'm only here because you took my stuff."

"Fine," Rachel said. Rachel and Sheela had already claimed the bed in the center of the room. I shrugged and marched over to the corner where our bags were at and began searching through them for something to wear.

Afterwards, I collected all my stuff into a pile, so I could carry it all up to my storage the next day. I wasn't going to take any more risks with these girls. Apparently, I couldn't even go to work.

When I set up a blanket on the floor and got ready to sleep, Rachel asked me, "You're off tomorrow, right?"

She did know my schedule, I thought with a touch of annoyance. "Yeah," I told her.

"Me too."

I rolled over and faced the wall. Whatever.

The next morning, I awoke to the smell of fresh breakfast. Rachel must have felt badly, because she'd gone to buy us something at the fast food restaurant on the corner. I accepted the egg and cheese sandwich from her as a peace offering.

After breakfast, I put my backpack on and started to pick up my bags. I'd accumulated too much stuff. Too many free donation shirts, too much stuff from the clothing closet. I didn't need all of it, I realized. I started to sort out what I could leave behind, to reduce the weight.

As I got ready to leave, it dawned on me.

I reached into my wallet and checked. "Damnit, Rachel. Give it back," I told her.

Rachel shrugged, then handed me my ATM card from her pocket.

"How much?"

"Forty bucks," she said. "I needed some cash. I spent everything on the room, so I figured you needed to pay your part."

She'd seen me put in my pin number enough times. She must've been watching more closely than I'd realized. "You had no right," I told her. "I didn't even want to come here."

"But you did."

"Because you had my stuff."

I gave her a piercing look before I walked out the door, ATM card securely back in my wallet. I'd forgiven her for the beach incident, but I wasn't sure I'd forgive her for this. I lifted the heavy trash bag in my hand and began my trek up to the storage unit.

67
DAMIAN

"Hey," he said. He hadn't been expecting me.

I stood in front of the man Rachel had introduced me to, trying to tell myself a million reasons why this was a bad idea. But he had a place, and I was temporarily kicked out from LAYN again. I'd tried to go back, but they said I was out. Apparently, the correct choice had not been to follow my stuff in the middle of the night.

I wished someone would've warned me. That trip had cost me my bed and forty bucks.

"Hi." Damian was getting off work, and I'd been waiting for him by his car. "Can I come over to your place tonight?" I asked.

"Sure, hop in," he said, making space for me in the passenger's seat of his beetle.

All I had with me was a small backpack. I had two days off before I needed to be back at work, and I'd gotten used to sleeping in a bed. I didn't want to go back to Pantages again. I didn't want to wander the beach. Something inside me was breaking, but I couldn't quite define it.

"I live kinda far," he told me casually as he merged onto the 101 South.

"How far?" I asked. Clearly, I hadn't asked the right questions when we were at Ground Zero.

He looked straight ahead, his eyes focusing on the freeway. "About an hour," he told me. "Riverside."

"Okay," I said. It was too late to back out; we were already soaring down the freeway towards downtown. "And when do you work again?"

"Day after tomorrow."

"Me too," I answered. Cool. He could get me back to Hollywood.

"Two nights, huh?" he asked.

I shrugged. Better than sleeping on the floor of a roach infested motel and having my ATM card swiped from my wallet while I slept. Better than having someone pretend to buy me breakfast, when it was really me who was paying.

"Yeah," I told him.

He smiled and turned the radio up. I watched as he maneuvered between cars on the freeway, sliding in between them with ease. At that moment, I realized I missed driving. I watched as his long fingers coiled around the clutch. "Is it hard to drive stick?" I asked.

"Nah, it takes practice," he told me. "You just have to figure out where to put your hands," he said, winking in my direction.

"Right," I said, laughing. I leaned back in my chair and watched as we passed through towns I didn't know. Places I hadn't been to. "Riverside, huh? Why?"

"It's cheaper, and I get to have a big place," he told me.

Reasonable, I thought. "Cool."

Damian's place was a two-bedroom apartment on the second floor of a well-manicured complex. I followed him up the stairs, feeling my heart begin to beat too fast. We walked in, and I shadowed beneath his tall frame. Standing beside him, I realized he was at least six inches taller than me.

"I'll show you around," he said, leading me on a tour of his place. He used his spare room as an office. Papers were stacked neatly all over his desk. "I do my other work from here," he said. He didn't explain, but I also didn't ask.

His bedroom had a large waterbed. I'd never actually seen one in person. "Is it actually comfortable?" I asked.

"You can tell me later," he said, laughing.

Right.

He showed me his bar next. I watched as he expertly poured shots, and then lit them on fire. He quickly blew out his flame. I stared at my shot glass, curious. "Blow it out," he said, laughing.

"Why?" I asked, still staring at the orange flame flickering over the alcohol.

"It gets more concentrated if you do that," he told me.

Oops. I blew it out as fast as I could. A memory of the gin and juice guy from so many months ago crossed my mind. A man who had poured higher and higher ratios of gin to juice in each drink, then tried to convince me to stay the night. I hadn't. That was the same night I'd almost been shot trying to cheat in spades, though. My love affair with alcohol had gotten me into trouble too many times.

"Drink it," I heard Damian say.

I took a small sip, cautious. It was warm and tasted like cinnamon. There were little gold flakes in the glass. "Goldschlager," he'd called it. Not bad, I thought, downing the drink. He poured me another.

I'm not sure how many drinks I had, but I woke up next to him the following morning. So it must've been enough to forget my abstinence from alcohol. I'd been sober since the beach, and one night with Damian had brought me back to that empty place again.

Something was soothing about how much I'd been able to forget, if only for a few hours. Damian was sitting next to me, laughing. "You liked the Goldschlager," he said.

"I quit drinking," I told him quietly, pulling the sheet up to cover myself. Everything was spinning. It felt like I was on a boat.

"Not last night, you didn't. What else do you want to try?" he asked.

"Huh?" I asked. Rachel must've told him a lot more than I'd realized.

He hopped out of bed and returned with a bag of weed. I watched as he expertly rolled a joint. "Ready for your first joint?" he asked.

"No thanks," I told him.

Damian watched me for a moment, curious. He placed the joint to his lips and pulled out his lighter. I watched as he lit it and took a deep breath. "You smoke cigarettes, though."

"Yeah."

"This is more natural," he said, releasing the hot smoke.

"No thanks," I repeated.

He turned to face me, blowing smoke in my direction. "Rachel said you were a square," he told me.

A square? Who the hell said stuff like that? "I just don't want it."

"Whatever," he said, rolling back towards his nightstand. I laid still for a moment, trying to figure out how to move on a waterbed. When I glanced back at him, he was facing me again. And he was holding a gun in my face.

"What the hell?" I asked.

"I can make you smoke it," he told me.

I didn't say anything. It wasn't the first time I'd had a gun in my face. His eyes twinkled. He'd mentioned to me that he was a veteran.

Was he one of those traumatized veterans?

We stared at each other for a long moment. Was he going to shoot me?

Did I care?

"Okay," I finally said. He laughed, the barrel of the gun still pointing at me. His free hand reached in my direction, and he handed me the joint.

Eyes on him, eyes on the gun, I held the joint up to my mouth. I took a deep breath, then inhaled. Blew smoke. Inhaled again. Blew smoke. "Fine," I said, staring at the gun.

His lips curled in a mischievous way. "Told you I could make you smoke it," he said.

I nodded. Yes, he had. And then I gave in and let him do all the other things he'd planned.

"Bye," I said when we got back to Hollywood. I couldn't wait to get away from him. I'd never been so afraid as I'd been for the past day or so. And I hadn't even been outside.

"Are you coming back next week?" he asked. He raised an eyebrow, waiting for my answer. I didn't say anything. "I can make you come back," he told me.

I nodded. Yes, he could. "Bye," I repeated. He had dropped me off at the bus stop on Santa Monica Boulevard. We were both running late, and I had to get to work.

When I arrived at work, Rachel was there. She glared at me. "Where have you been?" she asked. I didn't answer her.

"You were with him, weren't you?" she asked. "He's bad news. I was only kidding. I just wanted him to give us a few dollars. You weren't supposed to go out with him."

I adjusted the buttons on the top of my theater shirt. "I have to go clock in," I said, not answering her. I was ten minutes late.

The manager was on vacation, so the assistant manager was in charge. "You're late," he told me.

"Sorry," I said. "Bus trouble."

"Don't let it happen again," he told me.

I nodded. I hurried through my day, trying to avoid Rachel and stay out of trouble. Part of me was still a bit hungover, and I couldn't remember everything that had happened.

I went through the motions of my shift, then returned to Hollywood. It was too late to get into LAYN, so I went back to Pantages and found a spot in the corner. Everything about it felt wrong; Emma was gone, Ava was dead. I didn't know most of the kids anymore. Most of the travelers had left. The seasons were changing, and like birds flying south for the winter, street kids migrated too.

The following week, I fell back into the trap of going to Damian's again. He ran into me at Ground Zero and told me I should go with him to his house. It had been cold for the past few nights, so I agreed.

This time, I didn't refuse anything he offered me. We got drunk and watched a few movies on his large screen tv. When we awoke the following morning, I was grateful that I hadn't pissed him off too much.

"Do you ever see credit card lists at your job?" he asked.

"Why?" I wanted to know.

"Because I could use them." He explained a new concept to me; identity theft. It was in its early stages, and he wanted to make his millions. "I just need one list from those customers of yours."

I shrugged. "I'll look," I lied.

When I went back to work, I did see a list. It was a thick printout, next to all the receipts. There it was, just sitting unsecured in the office. I stared at it for a long time, remembering the bars closing behind me in juvenile hall. No good could come from doing anything for Damian, I thought. I shook my head and removed my nametag. Not worth it.

At the end of my shift, I told my manager that I couldn't come back anymore. He'd just gotten back from vacation, and he had been in a great mood all day. "I got kicked out," I told him. "I have to figure out where to live first. I'm sorry."

My manager told me he was sorry and told me he would cut me a paycheck right then. I waited while he prepared it. "Be safe," he told me. A lot of people had told me that, but it never made things right. I changed out of my uniform top and gave it back to him. Fortunately, I had my backpack with me, since I'd spent the past few nights at Damian's apartment again. I thanked him and walked back to the bus.

68
HALLOWEEN

A few weeks passed. I found my way back to Pantages and avoided going anywhere near Damian's work. By the end of the month, I'd grown accustomed to the streets again. In the mornings, I had breakfast at LAYN. I'd finally been allowed back into the building for drop-in services. Baby steps towards a goal.

I'd waited all month for my favorite holiday to arrive. Halloween.

I smiled as I looked at my reddish hair in the mirror. It was time to do something drastic. I'd quit my job, and I wasn't planning to see Damian anymore. I hadn't seen him for a few weeks by then. In my anger, I'd shoplifted a bottle of black hair dye that morning. Time for a change.

This was my night. I could be a freak and get away with it. Of course, I'd heard stories of many Halloweens past in the Los Angeles area. I smiled with pleasure; relishing the thought of finally being able to blend into a crowd.

I undressed and wrapped a towel around my body, remembering the potential for stains that can be caused during the process. Then, I hurriedly put on my plastic gloves and began mixing the contents of bottle one and bottle two. A thick, purplish color formed before my eyes. It seemed slightly different from the hair dyes of my past; those reds, browns, and blondes that I had reveled in since the first hair treatment when I was eleven, the first time I'd heard the words "dirty blonde." The many times I'd opted for a deep, dangerous red. The blue hair we'd all shared in Kansas.

The greasy mixture filled the palm of my gloved hand, and I ran it through my hair like shampoo. There wasn't time to be careful with it; I had an allotted shower time of thirty minutes, and the dye needed twenty-five minutes to set. I cast a quick glance at myself in the mirror after spreading the goo around my head. A few wispy strands of baby hair along my forehead lacked the dye, so I smoothed my forefinger carefully around the edges of my hairline. After another glance, I was satisfied with the look, and threw my gloves into the trash. The waiting game had begun.

I slid Emma's favorite CD into the music box the girls kept in the bathroom, and set it on repeat for my favorite, melancholy tune. "I'll love you, just the way you are, if you're perfect…" Alanis droned, her broken heart matching my own as I sang along with the melody. I hated my father, I thought. Why hadn't being me been good enough? I wished for the umpteenth time that I could've just been accepted for who I was, flaws and all.

After the fourth round of the song, a pounding sound got my attention. "Five more minutes!"

I sighed. So much for waiting for the entire twenty-five minutes, I thought. Well, it would really be temporary this time around. I stepped into the shower stall and began rinsing the hair dye out of my hair as I sang along to the words I knew by heart.

Tears fell down my cheeks. Where was Emma? The last time I'd seen her, she was strung out on heroin again and speaking a mile a minute. Ava's death had ripped apart her fragile sobriety. And mine, too. I'd heard that she was wandering back and forth between Los Angeles and San Francisco. Gone. Imperfect.

I stepped out of the shower, ready for whatever awaited me. I walked over to the mirror and swiped away the moisture. As I stared at my pale skin and dark hair, a key turned in the lock. Deanne was working that day, and she was a stickler for the rules. Rachel stood beside her.

"Are you ready?" she asked.

I was still mad at her, but I didn't want to spend my favorite holiday alone. We'd agreed to go down to the Promenade to trick-or-treat. My style. No one would be paying attention to two costumed girls shoplifting on Halloween.

I nodded; then placed the CD case into my backpack.

"What do you think? Will anyone recognize me?" My hair was still wet, hanging down past my shoulders.

She hesitated. "Maybe."

"I'll paint my face," I told her. I'd gotten face paint, too. I'd only managed to get a few colors, but I'd figure it out.

"Definitely. Let's go," Rachel said. I gathered my belongings and threw my towel into the hamper. I could fix my hair and face on the bus.

We hurried up to Hollywood Boulevard, where we caught the 217 bus. I flashed my bus pass to the driver, and then walked quickly to the back. Rachel fumbled around with her backpack in the front, pretending to look for her pass. I quickly handed mine to her, and she showed it to the driver. When she slipped it back to me at the back of the bus, I stared at her for a long moment.

As the bus carried us down Santa Monica Boulevard towards the ocean, I covered my face in black and white paint. One half was white, with a black heart. The other side was black, with a white heart. Half of the other patrons wore their own costumes. The night was coming alive.

"Not bad," Rachel said as we got closer to the promenade.

I smiled. It was nice to sort of have a friend again, I thought. If this was friendship.

The bus stopped at third street, and we got off. It would be a great night.

69
EXPECTING

The following morning, I woke up nauseous. I had spent the night in a squat with Rachel, and on awakening, I realized that I my face and hair were still a mess from the previous night. I wandered back to the parking garage next to the promenade, where I scrubbed the face paint off and tried to comb my hair. The strands were jet black, and my face was flushed from how harshly I'd washed it. I thought I'd beat the sudden wave of nausea, but instead found myself retching into the sink.

Afterwards, I brushed my teeth and tied my hair back into a ponytail. I paused, reflecting on all the other mornings that I'd awoken with pounding headaches and waves of nausea from the heavy drinking. But I hadn't been drinking. Maybe I'd eaten too much candy, I mused.

I forgot about getting sick, until the next morning when it happened again. Frozen, I started trying to recall my last period, and I couldn't remember the date. We were still in Santa Monica, so I wandered into a convenience store and stole a pregnancy test. I went down to one of the bathrooms by the beach, away from everyone. When the first line turned blue, I tossed it in the trash. Negative, I told myself, not looking closely at the package.

That day, I chain smoked a pack of cigarettes. The line had been blue. It had looked like a minus sign. I was fine, I had to be.

But the week progressed, and I kept vomiting every morning. My stomach rolled at the thought of begging people for their leftovers, and I'd been eating saltine crackers only. I'd caved in and bought a box from the store. Some things were just too big to shoplift.

Finally, I went back to the store for another test. I shoved it into the top of my pants and hurried out of the convenience store, avoiding detection. I jetted across the promenade to Johnny Rockets, a popular burger place with a fifties theme. I ordered a soda and rushed to the bathroom. Once the door was locked, I pulled the box from its hiding place and studied the package. The first line meant pregnant, the second line meant the test worked.

I couldn't remember which line had turned blue the other day, but I was pretty sure it was the first line. I hadn't waited to confirm. I hadn't wanted to know.

Worry filled me. I knew what was coming. I opened the box and peed on the stick, then set it on the counter. I squeezed my eyes shut, terrified. Crap. This was not good timing.

When I opened then, the cruel truth awaited me. Double bright blue lines.

I was pregnant.

I tossed the box and the test into the trash and covered them with crumpled paper towels. Wordlessly, I went back to the dining room and kept going, forgetting about the soda that I'd ordered.

"I have to talk to Damian," I told Rachel early the next morning. I had been sitting up all night perched at the top of a lifeguard tower, hearing the waves crashing rhythmically against the beach in total darkness. Rachel raised an eyebrow.

I boarded the bus back to Hollywood by myself. When I arrived, I went to Damian's work as the restaurant opened and told him we needed to talk. He told me to come back after his shift, so I wandered over to LAYN to kill time.

For the first time in my love-hate relationship with LAYN, I didn't want my cereal at breakfast time. I stared at the milk, feeling my stomach churn. I asked for a cup of ramen noodles instead and was surprised when Evan prepared it for me. Usually people were annoyed when I made special requests, especially since I was an obnoxious homeless vegetarian.

The day passed by slowly. I watched the other youth wandering around the shelter, carrying about their daily lives. Laticia was angry that she had run out of cigarettes. Michelle had broken up with her boyfriend, the man-with-the-truck, and was chatting with Andrea out back. Cedric was camped out on the sofa, opposite me.

"What have you been up to?" he asked from his half of the room.

I shrugged and looked away. Cedric had not given up and gone back to the streets. I was the one who couldn't get it together. He was awaiting a new placement, and he had a full scholarship to college waiting for him. If he could just finish senior year. I thought about the homework packets in my backpack that I hadn't started yet. It had been weeks since I'd worked on my courses. "Nothing," I finally said, glancing back at him.

Cedric shook his head. "You really need to get into placement," he told me.

"No," I said, our eyes connecting for a moment. "It's not for me. I won't go back into the system."

His face got serious for a moment. "Why not?"

I shrugged. "If I leave a placement, and they press charges. I'll be a 602."

He nodded, understanding filling his dark eyes as he spoke. "And you know that you'll probably leave."

I nodded back. "I always do," I told him. "I'm a flight risk."

Cedric smiled, then offered me a cigarette.

"Oh," I told him. "I quit."

He gave me an odd look before getting up to go join the crowd in the back. I dozed off and waited for the hours to pass so that I could talk to Damian.

"Hey," I said.

"Hi," he told me. I hadn't seen Damian in a few weeks, and we weren't as close as we should've been. Given the circumstances.

"I got a place down the road," he told me as his long legs carried him across the space between us faster than mine could. Interesting, I thought. I hadn't known that.

We both sat down in his beetle and I remained quiet as he drove the short distance to his new apartment. He was just up the road from LAYN, off Gower, in a small building. When had he moved here?

When had we last spoken?

Had it just been a few weeks?

How had he moved so suddenly?

I stared up at him, trying to decide if he was father material.

Was I mother material? I didn't want to think about the answer.

We got out of his car and I followed him up the stairs. He was on the second floor, in the middle. The door to his apartment was facing Gower, and he could almost see LAYN through the trees. If he wanted to.

"Hi," he said finally, once we were inside. His apartment was dimly lit, and he'd brought the familiar furniture with him from his place in Riverside. There were no pictures on the walls yet, and some stuff was still in boxes against the back wall.

"Hi," I answered back. We weren't really saying anything to each other.

"Where have you been?" he asked.

I shrugged. "I went back to Santa Monica with Rachel," I told him. I cringed when I'd accidentally said her name. She'd told me that he'd liked her first, and she'd turned him down. She'd sworn that he only liked me out of convenience. I was available.

And I had worked in the box office. Where the credit card receipts were kept.

Was she right?

Did I want to know?

He moved away from me, towards the kitchen. He started to prepare a drink. I knew where this was headed.

"Damian," I said, the words stuck in my throat.

He began mixing liquor and something else. I couldn't see.

"I can't drink."

He set the cup down. He was much taller than me, stronger. Powerful. A part of me had remained afraid of him since that first night, but the part of me that took risks was standing in his living room. Waiting.

"Why not?" he asked, folding his arms across his broad chest.

"Um," I said, not ready. "Your place is nice," I told him. I looked over at the living room, wondering if we could work.

Did I want us to? He stared at me, waiting.

"I'm pregnant," I told him.

He let out a sigh. "How can you be sure it's mine?"

Asshole, I thought. "Because I've only been with you," I told him. Now, standing in his living room of a place I hadn't known he wanted, nearer to his work but also nearer to me, I realized that weren't going to work out.

He stayed quiet. "I need time to think," he finally said.

I nodded. "Okay," I told him. Of course, it was shocking news. I'd only known for less than a day and my entire life had just been flipped upside down.

Something strange crossed over his face, but he walked towards me and opened the door.

As I walked through the doorway, I could feel the chasm growing. This wasn't a relationship. Neither of us had invested enough into it. And the power dynamic had just shifted. "Hey," I said before leaving. "Did you pack that box of my stuff?" I'd accidentally left behind a stack of photos and some personal items in my last visit.

"Yeah," he said, looming over me from the doorway. "I'll have to look for it."

"Okay. Maybe can I pick it up next week?"

"Okay," he said.

And then, I walked away. There was nothing left to say, really.

70
JERRY SPRINGER

On the bus back to Santa Monica, I leaned against the window and watched the familiar sights pass me by. How far along was I, I wondered. A month? Two?

I calculated that at least I'd finally be eighteen before the baby came. I could figure it out by then, I tried to tell myself. When a mother entered the bus with a small child in her arms, I tried to imagine what that life would be like for me.

I could do this, I decided suddenly. I really could do this.

When I arrived at the squat, Rachel wouldn't open the door. Again. "You're too late," she said. "Come back tomorrow."

Interesting, I thought to myself. I went back to my lifeguard tower and waited the night out, sleeping in small waves as the ocean howled next to me.

The next day, I went back to the promenade and tried to find Rachel. I didn't see her, but there was a small crowd of people by the dinosaurs.

I wandered over, curious. Who were the men that were talking to the other squatters? I approached, listening. One of them turned to look at me. "Are you homeless?" he asked.

Curiosity filled me. Who was this man?

Another kid saw my face and laughed. I would later learn that his name was Tannim. "They're recruiters. From the Jerry Springer show," he told me.

The man pulled a business card out of his pocket and handed it to me. I studied it. It did, in fact, say that he worked for Jerry Springer. I knew that some friends had just been flown out to New York for a taping of Sally Jesse, and I was intrigued by the idea of easy money. The man told us they paid at least two hundred dollars per person, and they were looking for volunteers.

Two hundred dollars. I could use any money that I could get my hands on. I was going to be a mother, and babies were expensive.

"I want to do it," I told the recruiter.

The recruiter took my info and told me he would have to call my parents for consent, since I was seventeen. I didn't care. Let them consent. A few other kids were selected, but most opted out. Nobody wanted to give up their parents' phone numbers.

The small group of us that planned to go on the show agreed to meet the film crew the following day to start taping.

When they arrived with large video cameras held over their shoulders, I was eager to tell my story. They prompted us to tell sensational stories. We eventually wandered to a squat where several of us had stayed.

There was writing on the wall. Poetry. Graffiti. Angrily written words, trying to express the hopelessness of our situation.

The cameraman asked for me to read my work.

I had apparently written something a few months earlier, and it looked foreign to me. But I recognized my familiar print on the wall. I had been drinking too much lately. I'd vowed to stop now that I knew I was pregnant. I read the foreign words and showed them some drawings I'd done. Apparently, I'd drawn a picture of my rat. The one that Ava had given me. I had failed her, and the rat had run away.

He continued through the squat, occasionally turning back to catch me or Tannim on camera. I said whatever came to mind, true or close enough. At the end, the cameramen thanked us each for our work, and we set our meeting place for a few days later. My dad had signed the consent, so I would be joining them in Chicago.

While I awaited the taping, Rachel and I got into an argument and she left to go back to Hollywood. She didn't have anyone to sign a consent for her, so she couldn't be a part of this group.

When I stood at the meeting spot a few mornings later, I met my fellow panelists. They'd selected a young couple with a baby. I had seen the mom holding a "need change for diapers" sign for many months. I wasn't sure where they stayed each night, but I suspected that they were renting a room. Tannim was there. I'd only met him a few nights ago, and he wore his telltale long black trench coat. He never talked much, but if the other night was indicative of our fifteen minutes in the spotlight, he would tell it all in front of the camera. I was also surprised to see people I'd never met. A young teen with her father. I'd never seen her around us; was she really homeless? He was a tall, lanky man. She was tiny, feisty, and had loud opinions.

The time for our meeting came and went. I started to get nervous. Were they going to move on; had they found a better group to interview? I glanced anxiously at the time on my pager.

Fifteen minutes later, a long, sleek limousine drove down the road. It pulled up in front of us and stopped. I stared at the couple, watching their reactions. They'd never been in a limo before. They were eager to board first, and Scrappy started chatting with the driver.

The driver opened the side door. Our recruiter exited and confirmed that everyone had arrived.

"Great, let's go to Chicago!" he told us, his boisterous voice corralling us towards our ride. The couple got in, followed by the dad and daughter, and then the quiet boy.

I paused, thinking back to the limo driver I'd met in Hollywood with Nora. He'd been trying to recruit me to go out on paid dates with some guys. Nora told me to give it a try, but the driver had been a creep and I had declined the offer after a dozen or so rides around town with Nora.

I was the last one to climb into the limo. I was not impressed.

On the ride to the airport Scrappy and his girlfriend started searching the refreshments. "They have alcohol!" he exclaimed, as he shoved several small bottles of liquor into his pocket. I watched as everyone loaded up on snacks, alcohol, and beer.

My stomach turned. I'd been vomiting every morning, and lately I'd had trouble holding down anything. I reached for a sprite.

"Not drinking today?" Scrappy asked, raising an eyebrow.

"Flying makes me nervous," I responded, glancing away.

We arrived at the airport without much fanfare. Flying in the nineties was easier; everyone was allowed through airport security, and our guide took us to the gate. Panhandlers with change jars attempted to win our sympathy, but they didn't realize we were poorer than them.

I sat down near the gate and stared at the scene. People rushing from place to place, families awaiting arrivals of loved ones. Our guide was still holding onto our tickets; his job was to make sure we got on the plane and arrived in Chicago. He was waiting impatiently a few seats away from me, tapping his foot on the floor while he watched the clock.

My only plane flights had been one-way trips to North Carolina. I'd always arrived to the airport in handcuffs, been deposited on the plane first, and flown with free hands on one-way flights back to Charlotte. And then I was always picked up by at least two police officers, and they never made any attempts to hide their annoyance with me. I closed my eyes and thought about the officer with curly hair and blue eyeshadow. She had yelled at me when I'd boldly stated, "Maybe I'd be better off dead." She'd confided that her dad had committed suicide, and she'd spent her whole life believing he'd made the wrong choice. I wondered about her for a moment, but then refocused my attention on the group. This group of unsavory characters, waiting to bear their souls on national television for two hundred dollars.

When it was finally time to board the plane, I walked onto the large jet without a police escort for the first time. The other passengers were largely ignoring me, and I wasn't regarded with a series of accusatory stares. I gratefully slumped into my seat by a window near the back of the plane, grateful for anonymity.

After we landed in Chicago, they took us to our hotels and told us where to meet up the following day. Apparently, the "better" hotels were sold out that week, and they left us in a nearby hotel behind the studio. We had a stack of food vouchers for the diner next door, and once the morning sickness had subsided, I went out for a meal.

The next morning, we were picked up and driven to the studio. There was a long line of people waiting outside; the audience. We were shuffled in through a back door and taken to "the green room."

Tannim and I laughed out loud when we saw the green paint on the walls. "It's actually green," I said. A few members of the group murmured in acknowledgement.

There was a clothing rack of solid colored shirts to choose from, if we wanted to change our clothes. A stylist appeared and showed us an adjacent room where they would do our makeup and hair. There were two separate doors, but we were all escorted through the one on the right. Everyone who was waiting could sit on the sofa against the wall or pace the room. Gina sat down on the sofa and played quietly with her baby. None of us knew what to expect, and the air in the room was heavy with nervousness. What would they ask us?

I wandered to the clothing rack and picked through the clothes, finally selecting a black t-shirt to match my jet-black hair. I stared at my reflection in the large wall mirror across the room, and every few minutes, I turned back to look at Gina's baby. Was I ready for motherhood?

Scrappy was always so damned perceptive, so I kept reminding myself never to get sick around the group or touch my stomach. Never to indicate that I was going to be a mother. I excused myself to go to the restroom, where I changed out of my musty top into a fresh clean shirt. It'd been too long since I'd made it back to Hollywood to wash my clothes. Everything had a strange scent of ocean breeze mixed with cigarettes and that heavy odor that can only be described as homelessness. There were no pants to choose from, so I kept my own dark pants and black army boots that Emma had given me. We each had a pair of those sturdy boots, with steel toes to defend ourselves against sudden attack. Like when she'd escaped the two guys with the brown van.

The stylist called me into the hair room soon afterwards, and she decided to braid my hair. I let her style my weathered hair and cover my face with makeup. It'd been a long time since I'd made so much effort to clean myself up, and for a moment, I wished I could be anywhere else. With pretty hair and nice makeup. Instead, I was waiting in the green room stylist chair for our impending episode. Whatever it took for those two hundred dollars. The baby would cost so much more than that, but at least it would be a start.

Afterwards, I went back to the green room and sat next to Gina. She looked as nervous as I felt. The false bravado that we'd all worn on the plane had begun to slip away, and we were about to face an angry studio audience full of people who would never be able to understand who we were or why we were there. Why we were homeless. Why we'd chosen the route that made us feel safer than whatever awaited back home.

We heard someone in the hallway, outside of the green room. We all looked up simultaneously as Jerry Springer entered the room quickly and rushed into the room to get his own makeup and hair styled. "Hey Jerry!" Tannim called. There was no response. He didn't even look at us.

I had a sinking feeling that we were going to have a very bad day.

Scrappy pulled Gina to the corner and they started whispering to each other. I could only make out a few words, but he was obviously upset. Gina clutched the baby over her own new black t-shirt. Her hair had also been styled, and her makeup made her look less pale. For homeless kids living in Los Angeles, several of the other youth in our group had not seen much sun, I thought to myself. My own skin had wavered between tanned and sunburnt throughout the summer.

When the door to Jerry's makeup room opened, he paused for a moment. I wondered if he was planning to speak to us at all. He might have been considering it but chose to stride towards the exit without commenting.

Angry, I called out to him. "Hey, Jerry," I said in a snide tone. He glanced over at me, perhaps recognizing that we were actual people, but still not saying anything. I noticed a faint trace of powder above his lips. Probably makeup, but it could've been anything. I laughed. "Spare a line?" I asked him.

He scowled at me and grabbed the doorknob, pulling the door open quickly. He exited and slammed the door shut behind him. I shrugged, and the rest of the group chuckled nervously. "What an asshole," Scrappy said from the corner where he stood.

A middle-aged woman came in and collected Gina and Scrappy's baby. She was supposed to babysit him during the show, so he wouldn't have to come out on stage until the ending credits. Several minutes later, Steve came to get us. We all recognized Steve before he even introduced himself, as he had become a television sensation breaking up several recent fights on the show.

"Sheryl and Tannim, you two go on first," our handler told us. He was standing beside Steve and summoned both of us out into the hallway. Microphones were affixed to each of our shirts before he escorted us to the stage. The audience was already seated, waiting like an angry beast. The energy of the crowd was already robust by the time we each sat down in the seats waiting for us. Butterflies, or perhaps the baby, scrambled around in my belly. Queasiness set in.

Tannim sat in the first seat, so I sat beside him, closer to the center of the stage. I really didn't know Tannim very well; we'd run into each other a few times around the Promenade before the show. But none of us were friends and we'd probably go our separate ways as soon as the taping stopped. He had shoulder length hair, which was growing out from a long-ago hair dye. Like me, he'd dyed his hair black. But the blonde roots were showing, and encompassed half of his head. He wore glasses and a long black trench coat, with dark clothes underneath. I smiled nervously.

"Good luck," I whispered. He nodded and repeated my words back to me.

"Five, four, three, two, one," I heard someone from behind stage counting down.

Suddenly, we were live. Jerry spoke into the microphone, his voice condescendingly concerned. "Imagine being eleven years old and not knowing where your next meal is coming from," he said. "Today we'll find out why these kids are on the streets, and what life is really like for them." As he spoke, a brief video played overhead for the audience to see excerpts of what was coming. Some of the film that was prepared before we'd flown here. Immediately, the audience broke into cheers and applause. "Jerry, Jerry, Jerry!" they chanted.

I cringed and sat back in my seat. This wasn't going to go well. Maybe I should've kept my mouth shut in the green room. Jerry was already giving me a dirty look. I tuned him out for a moment, wondering what questions he would ask me. No one had asked us for much history before the show, so he was entering our lives blindly.

"Please welcome Tannim and Sheryl to the show," I heard him say. He held the microphone in his hand and kept referring to a little blue cheat sheet that someone had prepped for him. The audience started clapping, so Tannim and I awkwardly clapped too.

"Tannim, first, can you tell us what a squat is?" Jerry asked. Tannim sat up straight in his chair. That was an easy question.

"A squat is basically an abandoned building or an earthquake damaged building that no one lives in anymore; no one cares about it, no one does anything with it. Basically, it's a place to keep ourselves warm at night and stay out of the rain," he said. It had started to rain over the past few weeks, and the others had warned me that Los Angeles indeed had a rainy season. "Basically, it's somewhere to

268

live, somewhere to store your possessions without having to worry about having them stolen," he said.

"When you say we, it's a whole bunch of people?" Jerry asked for clarification.

"Usually, there's more than one person staying in a place," Tannim stated. He was starting to look annoyed. How much did he need to define a squat, I wondered? Hadn't we taken videos in one of the abandoned squats that no one was staying in anymore?

As if Jerry was reading my mind, he told the audience that he had footage from our squat. A place I'd stayed at once, when I was drunk, several weeks earlier. Before I knew about the baby. I sat up straight and glanced at the monitor, wondering which clips they'd choose.

"Here is how they 'squat' in L.A.," Jerry said, as the screen above us changed to reveal the video.

I was first. There was a close-up of my face, with my long black hair hanging around my face. "I'm seventeen, and I've been on the streets on and off since I was eleven," the video version of me said. The video continued, showing pictures of homeless people in the background, wrapped in blankets or sitting off to the side, just at the periphery of the Santa Monica Promenade. "The first time I came out here, I was thirteen," I told the audience. "I was raped my first night in California," I said in a matter-of-fact voice. A voice that dared anyone to question what right I had to sit in front of them, selling my story for two hundred dollars. "Then I went to a shelter, because I didn't know what else to do."

They cut to a video of a guy grilling Rachel and I about whether we were actually homeless. He said we had trendier clothes than him. Rachel shrugged him off, and I defiantly told him I'd stolen them. I wasn't sure; I'd probably gotten them from the shelter. But clothes weren't something we paid attention to anymore. We mostly just wanted to eat and survive. And drink. For not the first time that day, I thought about how much better I felt when I was numb.

The video continued, with Tannim walking the cameraman through the Promenade, and I followed behind with Rachel. She'd wanted to be on the show, but no one knew how to contact her mother, so no one could sign for her to come to Chicago for the taping. She'd been the one who had stayed at this squat more than me; I remembered the night when she'd locked me out and I'd wandered from Santa Monica to Malibu. Always moving, always trying to stay warm and stay safe.

Tannim elaborated on the discreet pathway over a gate, through a hole in the fence, and through a small opening to get back inside the building. We followed him in and passed through several dirty rooms. Trash and cigarette butts lined the rooms. It hadn't looked this bad when we'd been here before. Something had changed.

The walls of the room that we'd stayed in were lined with drawings and words. I recognized my own handwriting and drawings but didn't recall writing anything. Tannim pointed out some of his artwork from when he was "tripping on acid." I waited my turn, then read a gruesome poem that I must have painted onto the wall when I was drunk. I still couldn't remember writing it.

The segment continued, and they brought the younger girl out on stage with her dad. She was wearing a hat that covered her face, although the pre-taped segments showed her entire face. She started to talk about how she idolized living on the streets. I shook my head. "You don't want this," I told her.

Jerry noticed the interaction. Me and Tannim shaking our heads, muttering under our breaths about how ridiculous this kid and her dad sounded. A kid who had apparently spent one night on the streets, and now wanted to join us. Her dad kept going on and on about his childhood, when finally, Jerry interjected.

"Sheryl, you look like you have something you want to say," he told me.

I turned to face Rebecca. We'd never met before the show because she wasn't homeless. She wasn't one of us. She had a dad, she had a home. "You don't want this life," I told her. Tannim jumped in, and we both started sharing stories of the worst that had happened to us. She shook her head defiantly. "I know what I want," she declared. Her dad rambled on, and I couldn't understand why he was sharing such random details.

I watched as the couple came out next and shared their story, and then got berated by the audience. I couldn't hear everything they were saying over the shouting from the audience. I crossed my legs and tried to think of the reasons that had brought me here. Two hundred dollars. I needed this money.

Later, a man we'd never met was brought on stage. "A lot of youngsters run away because they're being abused," said the guest psychologist. He then commented on Tannim's hair, telling him to "get a job." Then, he shifted his talk to announce to the audience that we were probably all on drugs.

I glared at him. The psychologist hadn't talked with us at all prior to the show. He didn't know our individual stories on why we'd ended up on the streets. How could he presume to know our motivations? And why was everyone fixated on Tannim's hair?

A lady in the audience stood up and Jerry passed her the microphone. She started yelling at each of us, and the audience's roaring laughter and applause blocked out her actual words. I asked Tannim if he'd heard her. He shrugged.

I shook my head. These people didn't understand. This wasn't real. At least, not for them. They didn't care. I stared at Jerry, wondering if he would intercede.

He didn't.

The show ended abruptly, and we were rushed back to the green room. Steve stood at our doorway, keeping us trapped inside while we awaited our payment. Scrappy was pacing, and he kept muttering that Jerry was full of it.

It was my fault. I'd pissed him off before the show. My one joking comment had shifted the tone of the entire episode. Rebecca's dad had been bizarre and had made so many off the wall comments, but none of that mattered. The real story had never even been addressed. Did we use drugs? Well, sure, eventually everyone turned to something to forget. It's impossible to live completely in the moment all the time. It beats at your soul and exacerbates memories of things endured.

Our guide arrived at the door and handed each of us a thick envelope. "Let me talk to Jerry," Scrappy demanded as he took his envelope.

I grabbed mine and began counting. All of us had thick envelopes, full of one-dollar bills. "What the hell?" I muttered as I rapidly counted. The security guard, Steve, was still guarding our door, keeping us separate from all the audience members and the crew.

"It's one hundred dollars," I said first. I'd worked long enough on the cash register and could speedily count stacks of money. "He promised us more."

"Where's our money?" yelled Scrappy.

I sat down and cradled my head in my hands. We'd been tricked. Exploited. For one hundred dollars.

I shouldn't have come here, I thought to myself. Not even the sensationalist Jerry Springer had given a damn enough to hear the real story. Nobody wanted to know why people like us were on the streets, lost, wandering through life. Instead, they wanted to imagine us sitting in alleyways, drunk and dazed on whatever drugs we could find.

We were kept in the room for another twenty minutes, before Steve finally opened the door. Our guide reappeared next to him. "The limo is waiting," he said.

"You lied to us," Scrappy shouted.

"The flight leaves soon," he said, pointing towards the exit. Steve stood with his muscular arms folded over his chest.

I slumped my shoulders. Of course. I recognized the futility in the situation. "I think I'll skip the flight," I said quietly.

Everyone turned to face me. The guide shook his head and Steve was suddenly standing dangerously close. "Go to the limo," he commanded.

"I should just hitchhike back to North Carolina. I need to make amends with my family," I said.

"That wasn't the deal," the guide said.

"Who the hell cares about the deal?" I asked. "The deal was two hundred dollars and you gave us this," I said, holding up my stack of ones.

"If you don't want it, I'll take it back," the guide threatened.

I shoved the bills into my pocket.

"Let's go," they repeated, and I fell into step with the others as they ushered us out of the building.

"When does the show air?" I heard Tannim asking.

"In December," the guide said.

We exited the building and an old, miserable looking limo awaited us. We climbed in and a quick search revealed that this limo had none of the amenities of our previous rides. "They tricked us," Tannim said.

I stared out the window, feeling nauseous. It was mid-afternoon, and I felt a fresh wave of bitterness in my throat. The tattered limo weaved expertly through city streets and deposited us at the airport. As soon as it stopped, I proceeded to vomit all over the sidewalk.

Rebecca's dad raised an eyebrow. "Are you expecting?" he asked.

I shrugged. It was nobody's business anyway. Everyone knew that Gina was pregnant, and they'd brought her to tears on the show. There was no way I was sharing my news with anyone after what had happened on that stage.

We walked into the terminal, the guide watching us from all angles. When we got to the gate, he handed us our tickets and stood with his arms crossed over his chest. "Another car will pick you up in Los Angeles," he told us.

"You aren't coming with us?" Scrappy asked, his voice accusatory. We were all livid, but Scrappy and Gina had the most to lose by coming on national television.

They were now at risk of falling under the radar of CPS. And for what? Two hundred dollars total? An hour of utter humiliation?

Our handler shook his head. They called for us to board and we stood in unison. "Have a safe flight," he said, an odd intonation to his voice.

I begrudgingly sat in my assigned seat, next to the older man and his daughter Rebecca. I placed my head against the window and pretended to sleep. In a few short hours, I'd be stuck trying to figure it out again. Eventually, I did drift off to sleep.

71
PREGNANT HITCHHIKER

The plane touched down in Los Angeles that afternoon, and as expected, another beat-up old limo picked us up. We rode without much fanfare back to Santa Monica. As soon as we arrived, I walked straight to the freeway. The 10 freeway began there and crisscrossed the country. I planned to hitchhike back to North Carolina, with wild hopes of making things right with my family.

I managed to get a few short rides, which I'd come to expect. Most people were driving locally. Usually the long-distance rides were found after traveling to the outskirts of large cities. When I got close to downtown, a silver Cadillac with four Hispanic men pulled over to pick me up. They were chatting rapidly in Spanish, and I could only understand short phrases.

The driver edged back onto the freeway, but quickly diverted the car to the 5 north. I was seated between two men in the backseat. My exhaustion from the flights and disappointment from the talk show had allowed me to let my guard down.

"This isn't the right way," I said, but they kept talking in Spanish. I knew they understood me, because they'd spoken to me in English when I'd gotten into the car. I cursed myself for not studying harder when I was in Spanish class.

Night had fallen. I studied the car; it was immaculately clean, and its only decoration was a pair of faded dice hanging from the rearview mirror. The driver noticed my eyes looking up at him, and locked eyes with me for a moment in the mirror. He had a menacing look in his dark brown eyes. I looked away, unable to hold his gaze.

Instead, I focused on the backpack on my lap. I felt the gentle movement of my pet, hiding expertly in my coat pocket. I'd picked up a new rat in Santa Monica right after we had landed, haunted by memories of Ava. It made me feel closer to her, somehow. Even though I'd lost the pet rat that she'd given me. Now, he sat in my pocket, munching on scraps of bread I'd fed him earlier. At least I had one friend, I thought sadly as I stared at the well-worn straps of my backpack.

Suddenly, the car stopped. I glanced up, surprised. I had been ignoring my surroundings until I had heard the engine die down. I looked up, suddenly aware that we were in the mountains.

"Get out," the driver said. I looked at him again, noticing the coldness in his words. He meant to harm me.

I followed the guy on my right out of the car, and then stood by the edge of the Cadillac. Where was I? I breathed in the cool mountain air. There were no nearby lights; the only lights illuminating the darkness were the headlights of the car. The driver had purposely left them on.

I backed up against the car, feeling my way towards the trunk. I held the edge and tried to identify my surroundings. Trees, mountains. I didn't know where the land stopped; I could fall to my death if I wasn't careful.

These men could kill me, if I wasn't careful.

I gasped for breath, unable to distinguish my surroundings. I let my hand trace the edge of the car, not letting go of my one point of contact. How had I let myself get into another bad situation? I was always rushing towards somewhere but ending in disaster.

Shrill laughter filled my ears. Shit, they were going to kill me! I began to tremble. I would not die like this; I would not be a body that a hiker stumbled upon next spring. I would not let them kill me.

One of them approached me. "Hey, baby," he told me. I forced a smile that he would not see in the shadows. He would save me. I would not die tonight.

"Hey," I replied. "I'm cold. Can we sit inside of the car?" My hand found his arm, and I clung to him, pulling him closer. His warm breath was blowing on my face.

"Hmm." He smiled. "*Ya me voy*," he called to his friends, who cackled in reply. "Let's sit down, sweetheart."

We sat in the backseat of the car. I feigned sleepiness, laying my head against his shoulder. He caressed my arm, causing my body to jump into high alert. But I allowed him to touch me; it was better to befriend one of them than to have all of them attack me. I recognized that mischievous glint in their eyes. They were capable of it.

He kissed me, and I forced myself to permit the contact. I curled into his arms, sure of my plan. No, I would not die tonight. I would just lose another thread of my soul, but it could be sewn together again.

After long minutes that seemed to stretch for hours, his friends returned to the car. They all gave him that knowing look, and then started talking in rapid-fire Spanish. I only caught bits and pieces of their conversation but understood that he was "the man" and he would be "lucky" tonight. So what? It was better than being buried in the Angeles National Forest.

The atmosphere of the car had changed. I mentally thanked myself for choosing the right guy. The others might have tried to "share" me. I wouldn't have been able to stomach that. Already I felt the uneasiness and wariness of what was happening, and what was about to happen. I hated myself, but hid it well, as I burrowed my head against the guy's shoulder. At least it was dark; they would not be able to recognize the deadpan fear in my eyes until I had escaped.

"*Que pasa?*" he was asking me. I looked up, aware that only he was looking at me. There was something innocent in his eyes, and I felt a little safer. He was much more harmless than the driver.

I tried to smile but failed miserably. I squeezed my eyes shut, afraid that tears might escape. "Just tired."

"Hmm." The car sped down the mountainside, approaching the freeway.

"Where are we going?" I asked, not for the first time that evening. The last detour had unwillingly taken me twenty or so miles off course, to the north.

The man conversed in Spanish with the driver for a few minutes, before staring back at me. "To my house. Inglewood."

"Alone?" I whispered. "I only want to be with you," I told him. Minimize the risk, I warned myself.

More Spanish. Angry voices, and then abrupt laughter. All of the men talked to each other for a few minutes. Then, he whispered to me again, "Yes, alone."

Out of the corner of my eye, I saw the frustration on the driver's face. I was sure I had seen a bulge in his pocket. Perhaps a weapon? Who cares, I told myself. I would be safe now, but at a cost. A cost that I had convinced myself I could pay.

I pretended to fall asleep in the arms of my chosen captor. I listened to the animated conversation among the friends yet understood little. I would have to learn Spanish, I vowed to myself. This was not the first time my lack of understanding had put me in harm's way.

What seemed like an hour had passed, with the Cadillac speeding rapidly down the freeway. Drops of rain began to fall, but they quickly receded. Finally, the car exited the freeway, and I peeked up to see where we were.

Lights shone brightly and the car turned onto a wide street. I kept a wary eye on my surroundings, unsure of what they were planning to do next. "Where are we?"

"Inglewood." A ray of light from the streetlights above flashed across our faces. He must have sensed my nervousness, because he stroked a stray hair behind my ear. Another time, another place; perhaps he would've been a decent guy to know. Perhaps in another life. But circumstances as they were, he was my means of escape from what I was sure would've been my end. "We're stopping to eat."

I sighed. The car pulled into a small, 24-hour taco stand. I eyed the after-hours crowd, and realized I still felt safer with the man I didn't know. Several of the patrons were obviously high, or drunk, or both. Many were *cholos*, and I wasn't about to take another chance. No sense running. I was miles from the freeway, anyhow.

He ordered two tacos for me, but I didn't eat them. "I'm not hungry," I whispered to him. He shrugged and ate them for me. My stomach hurt, but I already knew why. It wasn't from hunger; the baby was not taking kindly to any of this evening's events. I sighed, sipping on soda while I waited for his friends to finish their meals.

Survival sex, I thought. That should've been the topic on the Jerry Springer show. Talk about what it's really like to live on the streets and have to put out or die. Being young and alone was definitely not as glamorous as it was made out to be in the media. Too bad it was my life.

"*Vamanos*," the driver said, tossing the remainders of his food in the trash. A police car had just rolled by, and it was nearly 2 a.m. Surely, he didn't think I wanted to talk to the police? He really didn't have a clue who he'd picked up.

We got back into the car, and I was grateful to hear that we were getting dropped off first. I ignored the compliments and catcalls, and the way that all the guys gave the man that I was with high fives. I was just grateful to arrive in one piece.

I grabbed my backpack from the floorboard and slung it across my shoulder. I felt the warmth of his jacket around me and shrugged. At least he had been kind with me. That was what really mattered.

I followed behind him, glad to finally be away from his friends. We entered his small, one-bedroom house, and he whispered to me to be as quiet as possible. His mother was sleeping.

He removed his jacket from my shoulders and looked at me. "Why did you come with us?"

I shrugged. "I didn't have anywhere else to be."

"How old are you?" he asked, suddenly aware of how young I looked.

"Seventeen," I told him. Normally, I lied about my age. But I hoped that maybe he would have been kinder with me if he knew the truth. Well, at least the truth that could be shared with total strangers.

He pulled me towards him. So much for nobility. "Let's go to bed."

I woke up in the morning to the sound of a woman, speaking in Spanish. "Stay under the covers," the man commanded me. I nodded, trying to fight back my nausea. As long I stayed perfectly still, I could delay the onslaught of morning sickness.

He sat up, tossing several comforters in my direction. I felt trapped, and very sick. The bed felt like it was swaying.

After several minutes of talking back and forth to each other in words I didn't understand, his mother left. He checked under the covers to see if I was all right.

"Where's the bathroom?" I asked, and when directed, I practically ran to the room. I fell to my knees in front of the toilet and began to vomit, much more violently than I had in the previous weeks.

Concerned eyes watched me from the doorway. "You're not feeling well?"

"It's okay. I'm used to it," I told him when I was finished, and had rinsed my mouth. I held a hand over my abdomen, gesturing my problem to him.

"Oh," he said. "*Estás embarazada.*"

I nodded sheepishly, walking out of the bathroom. I let my eyes focus on the room that had been just shadows the night before. His bed occupied a corner of the small living room, and there was a small kitchen. He and his mom coexisted in a very tiny space. "Yeah. I think I understood you that time."

"Do you want me to drive you home?"

I shook my head. "I don't have one." The tears that normally stung at my eyes were well hidden. "I just need to get back to the 10 freeway, please. It goes all the way across the country."

"Still going to North Carolina?"

"Sure. Just in time for Thanksgiving."

It was raining outside. That meant that it would be a long day. Hitchhiking was too difficult in the rain. But I knew I couldn't turn back. I was too timid to admit defeat, and too proud to beg for readmission to the shelter. Forget it. I might as well get it over with; I needed to make amends with my family before I would be able to bring a child into this world.

The man I had spent the night with looked at me awkwardly. "Are you sure you're alright? I mean, that the baby is alright?"

I shrugged. "Yeah, I'll survive." I'd made it through worse, I thought to myself.

The car stopped next to the freeway entrance, and his friend, who had driven us again, told me, "That bus stop over there will take you all of the way to Pomona. Right next to the freeway."

"Are you sure?" I asked. He nodded, so I thanked him. I thanked them both, grateful to have slept in a warm bed, at whatever the cost, especially since it had begun raining. I got out of the car, waved goodbye, and watched another small piece of myself drive away.

I mentally screamed at myself for having taken such a risk, and then shrugged it off. I had survived, and I would make it through my next task. Following the driver's advice, I walked over to the bus stop and sat down. If the bus veered away from the freeway, I would just get off at the next stop and walk back.

The bus did take me several long miles down the road, sloshing through rain puddles. It eventually ended at a bus terminal in Pomona, the end of the line. I was well over thirty miles outside of Los Angeles, yet it had taken over twenty-four hours. Nightfall would come soon, and I was in an unfamiliar city, under a torrential downpour. I had to get back to the freeway again, and fast.

I went into a convenience store and bought some pretzels and a soda. That would get me through the day. It was the only food that I could afford – I had already spent too much of my Jerry Springer money. I only had eighty dollars left, and I wanted to use that to buy a bus ticket back from North Carolina. Hopefully, I could spange some money on the way back east, so that I would have enough for one-way bus fare to return to my beloved California.

When I arrived at the freeway, I went straight to the on-ramp. I was grateful that it had a wide shoulder, which provided an opportunity for a passing car to pull over and give me a ride. I knew better than to walk up to the freeway; the cars moved too fast here, and there were far too many highway patrol officers. I would not be arrested for trying to hitchhike.

After about twenty minutes, and numerous catcalls and horns honking, a car pulled over. The driver offered to take me past Riverside, where there would be a truck stop. It was a hitchhiker's dream come true.

I made polite conversation and followed my prepared storyline. "Yes, sir. I understand. Hitchhiking is dangerous. But I just want to make it home for Thanksgiving. I've been away from home for too long."

When asked my age, I always said nineteen. Eighteen was too obvious, and I couldn't pass for anything over twenty. I was quick with the birthdate calculation, for those moments when a savvy adult would ask too many questions. But of course, unless the adult was far too preachy about what teens should be doing nowadays, they tended to follow the, "don't ask, don't tell," vise.

I thanked the driver when I arrived at the truck stop and rushed inside. It was chilly, and I wouldn't dare lurk around in the parking lot. I would not be mistaken for a "lot lizard," one of those truck-stop prostitutes out to make a living. Neither would I get arrested for trespassing with the intent to hitchhike. That had landed me in juvie back in Atlanta when I was thirteen. I wasn't going down that road again.

My quick thinking led me inside to the cafeteria. The aroma smelled so wonderful, yet somehow my stomach was still angry. I remembered I had barely eaten all day, and decided I had to eat something. I knew from experience that the longer I waited to eat, the harder it would be to eat something when I was tried.

I sat down in the café, instantly frustrated that I would have to spend some of my remaining money on a tip. If I didn't leave at least a dollar, they'd become suspicious of me. I sighed, and then resigned myself to look for a cost-effective dinner.

I eventually ordered a baked potato and a small vegetable soup. I filled myself with crackers and water, both of which came free with the meal. I even managed to stuff a few extra crackers into my pocket for the morning. I had quickly learned that a few saltine crackers could help curb morning sickness.

Afterwards, I strolled to the bathroom, where I was able to quickly clean myself up. I brushed my hair, changed my shirt, and applied a hint of fresh makeup. I refused to put anything more than the standard lip gloss, eye shadow, and mascara, since I did not want to be mistaken for a lizard. Anything to look less pale, less sick.

When I was finally ready, I went outside discreetly, and walked to the road. As soon as I was off the truck stop property, I felt safe enough to begin searching for a ride. I waited next to the eastbound on-ramp, I didn't have to wait too long this time. I was picked up by a semi, and once again, I was on my way.

I woke up in the early morning hours to find the truck driver trying to unbutton my pants. My eyes flew open, and my knee kicked him hard in the groin. My rat was standing up on top of me, staring at him.

He mumbled those unforgettable words; "I was going to rape you, but then I saw your rat." I grabbed my backpack, quickly let the pet rat hop back into my pocket where it lived and rushed towards the passenger's door.

"Asshole," I shouted as I leapt from the truck.

Instantly, my eyes took in my surroundings. I had traveled far; I was already in the desert. It looked like Arizona or New Mexico, but I couldn't be sure. Such a stark contrast to the downpour from the previous day. I ran as fast as my legs could carry me, and then I kneeled over to vomit. The truck revved up and drove away, and I was grateful. My would-be attacker was gone. But that didn't mean he wouldn't call the cops and try to report me for hitchhiking.

Against my better judgment, I rushed back to the interstate. I threw my thumb out dramatically and inwardly pleaded for a safe ride. I had already been through two hellish ordeals in less than as many days, and I was still licking my wounds from the previous day. I felt like such a fool.

A small RV pulled over, with an elderly man at the wheel. The window rolled down, and the man asked where I was headed. I told him the shortened version of my story, grateful for the quick escape. I felt myself clinging to the edge of the seat, waiting for the next attack, watching for the next missed turn. It's true that women who have been attacked before are more likely than others to be attacked again in the future. I mean, look at me; I was living, breathing proof of that atrocity. How many times had I fallen victim? How many more were waiting?

"I have a daughter who is a few years older than you," he was telling me. "I would hate to see her in your situation, but if she was, I would want her to be picked up by good people."

I looked up at him, seeing crinkly skin around his eyes and a kindness emanating from them that I hadn't seen for a while. I allowed myself to relax. "Thank you, Sir."

"Are you hungry?"

I shook my head. I didn't want to stop. I had already lost too much time when I spent the night in Inglewood. "I'll be alright."

The man motioned to his snacks. "At least help yourself to some chips, or a soda," he told me. I accepted, thinking of my father. He always kept snacks in his car when he traveled. Perhaps it was something about men from that generation; perhaps they travelled with everything they might ever need, so they wouldn't ever need anyone else.

I lazily ate my chips and drank from the soda bottle as the miles rolled underneath our tires. I passed a few chips to the rat in my pocket, the precious beast who had saved me from getting raped by standing up and staring down my would-be attacker. We finished the long stretch from the edge of Arizona through New Mexico. Small talk filled the RV, with both of us purposefully avoiding the obvious topics that weren't up for discussion. When he dropped me off near the Texas border, almost two states later, I felt refreshed. The following driver took me into Texas, and then deposited me by the side of the roadway again.

No wonder I hated Texas, I thought as I kicked up a mixture of dust and pebbles into the stale air. Every time I traveled across the country, it seemed I got stuck in Texas for endless days. I walked alongside of the freeway, frustrated it was so cold in the desert, and equally irritated that whatever scorpion or snake or whatever lived alongside the freeway might bite me while I waited.

The freeway looped into several different directions; I followed the path that led back to the 10. I supposed that I ought to be grateful to my last driver; he had been kind and hadn't tried to hurt me. But being left in awkward places put me at risk, so I was nervous.

The ground was covered in little white rocks. My shoes felt too thin as my feet travelled over the manicured surface. I could feel the beginnings of a callous on the arches as I trudged ahead. At least I'd grown up a little, and socks finally protected my feet inside the worn shoes.

No one was stopping. I couldn't just stand still. That would make me a target for the police. They were much more likely to pull over and arrest me if I was facing traffic and they could see my youthful face.

Businesses began to crop up every now and then. It was obvious that I had come close to the Mexican side of El Paso. The signs were mostly in Spanish, and I noticed a few restaurants and stores that catered to the Mexican residents.

A white Cadillac pulled up next to me. Great, I thought. Another winner. What was it with me and Cadillacs?

The driver rolled down his window. "*Adonde vas?*" he asked. I shook my head. "Where are you going?" he asked very slowly. He was probably Mexican and he wore a large cowboy hat.

I hesitated. "North Carolina."

"I'll take you there," he said, smiling. I shrugged. What a weird guy. How could he possibly drop everything to take me to North Carolina? It was at least a two-day ride. Whatever, I thought. I was tired and had been wandering next to the freeway for well over an hour.

The interior of the car was bright red, and he had pictures and prayer cards affixed to the dashboard. Rosary beads hung from the rearview mirror. "Are you hungry?" he asked. I shook my head no. The man tried to chat with me, but I was too exhausted to fake my way through another conversation with someone who really didn't give a damn about my situation.

I didn't want to pull off the freeway. I was petrified of being taken to a remote mountain again. More than anything, I wanted to continue eastward. It was only five days until Thanksgiving, and I was beginning to wonder if I would still make it there on time. I should've just snuck away from the group when I was in Chicago the previous week, I thought, for probably the fortieth time. They wouldn't have even noticed, and I wouldn't have had to waste so much money on food.

The car veered to the right, quickly snapping me out of my thoughts. "What are you doing?" I asked the driver. We had exited the freeway.

He glanced at me nervously. "I'm taking you to North Carolina Street."

My eyes opened wide. Was he kidding? No wonder he'd said he could take me. "No, I want to go to the state. North Carolina. Um, *el estado*?"

The man looked thoughtful, then shook his head. "I'm sorry," he said. Yeah, me too, I thought. He pulled over the car, and I quickly got out. "Goodbye," he said, and I gave him a frustrated half-wave.

I sat down next to the side of the road on one of the thick metal guardrails. This was ridiculous, I thought. If only I hadn't let my bus ticket expire. I could've used it. A part of me was still riddled with guilt for the elderly couple that had purchased them for us so many months ago.

Tears streamed down my face while I watched headlights flash quickly past me. Why was I going back, when I knew it would only cause me more pain? I knew better than to visit my family; the last time I had passed through my hometown, I had managed to break my ties with my brother David and his wife. Was it worth the risk?

I smeared the tears away with the back of my hand. So be it. I had to give it one last try, if only for the baby. After all, it would only be a short visit. It wasn't like I was dumb enough to get tricked into staying again.

Resigned to my fate, I stood up and approached the side of the road. I would make it home for Thanksgiving, at whatever the cost. I stretched my thumb outwards again and waited for the first car that would offer me a ride.

As I approached the Eastern states, the days grew colder. I felt the chill of the wintry air as I waited for my next ride. I had traveled hundreds of miles since the previous day, and my body was growing tired. Weary and hungry, I was too exhausted to be scared. I accepted my fate, handed down to me along with each new ride and each new milepost that I passed. Grateful for a brief interlude away from the cold, I wandered inside of one of the traveler's rest stops that dotted the roadside from time to time across the nation.

My too-thin California jacket was no match for the cold weather. I hovered in the rest stop foyer, somewhere off the 40 freeway in Tennessee, trying to warm my body. I feigned interest in the maps along the walls, pretending to be a traveler who was waiting for her family or friends. All the while, I allowed my body temperature to return closer to normal and thought back to the last time I had ventured alone into a roadside rest stop.

I shivered, remembering how cold the juvenile hall in Wilkes-Barre, Pennsylvania, had felt. I could still feel the chill in my bones from the lack of heating. I could've stopped then, could've accepted my fate. My hometown was sick of me, sick of purchasing plane tickets to extradite me back from one place or another. I could've accepted their decision that I must have been crazy and let myself seek help in the Cumberland Psychiatric Hospital that I was shipped to next. But I wouldn't let myself be that crazy person everyone expected me to be. I escaped from yet another unwanted label, another unwelcome place to call home. I had kept trying to reach my beloved California yet hadn't quite made it. It had felt like grasping for straws, and always pulling out the shortest one. I could still hear my probation officer taunting me, "Try to escape from there," after I'd been sentenced to Dillon four years earlier.

I glanced around myself, trying to get my bearings. This was different. I was seventeen, almost eighteen. I was passing dangerously close to Asheville, which was probably why my memories were on hyperdrive. And I wasn't running away from anything anymore; I was running towards something. I wanted; no, I needed to make amends with my family before beginning one of my own. I was running towards a last chance. And I had been away from my childhood home for far too long.

I swallowed my fears, pride, and fought back the ever-present nausea. It was time to go "home."

72
MAKING AMENDS

The last few miles seemed the longest. I watched for familiar landmarks, glimmers of my past along the way. Signs and buildings from memories long forgotten rose before me. I watched as we passed the North Carolina Welcome Center. The water tower loomed above, proudly displaying the name of my hometown. Familiar exits appeared, and I signaled to the driver that we were approaching my exit. My last ride had been the easiest – I was riding with a two-man truck driving team that was able to cover more ground at a faster rate. They were also older and seemed genuinely kind.

The truck exited at New Hope Road, and I climbed down. "Thanks," I told them, and they both wished me luck. I had made it, only two days before Thanksgiving.

I stretched my legs, feeling slightly dizzy from the movement of the truck. After a moment's hesitation, I began walking the last few blocks to my father's house.

When I arrived, I discovered that my brother Nick was home. He wasn't exactly happy to see me, but let me inside nonetheless. My new stepmother, Kathleen, called my father at work. I knew instantly that I had made a mistake to visit them. My father had scheduled a road trip to New Jersey for the holidays, and I was unwelcome if he wasn't there.

Finally, a compromise was made. Since Nick was staying behind, I could be home only when he was there. If he left, I needed to leave. I wasn't allowed to have keys, and the security code for the home alarm had been changed. Additionally, I would have Thanksgiving dinner with David's in-laws. And they were still mad at me for leaving several months earlier.

I decided to try to make the short visit work, despite the stipulations I had encountered. It was for the baby, I reminded myself. For the little, innocent child that was growing inside of me, I would do almost anything. I had to get along with my family, no matter what they decided to throw my way.

I visited the church I had formerly been a member of. My peers regarded me as an oddity, and I quickly recognized their resistance to speak with me. After all, I had left, hadn't I? I had abandoned my faith and returned to the only place where I had ever felt safe – California. Who cared about the details of why I had left, when the result was so astonishingly clear? I didn't fit in anymore. I had chosen to take a different path with my life.

The youth pastor approached me. He glanced around his office, eying a calendar. "What's it been, six months or so? I guess we'll see you again in spring, right?"

I glared at him. No, they would not see me again. This would be the last visit I would make for quite a while, I predicted.

A few days later, I went to Denise's parents' house for Thanksgiving. Since my father was gone, my visit had apparently been planned out by my family. They picked me up and drove me over to the family's small house in the outskirts of town, where I quickly began to feel like an unwelcome guest at a family dinner. I tried to make small talk, but my sister-in-law's words from so many months ago seemed to linger in the air between us. "You abandoned all of us," she had told me over the summer.

I served myself a small plate of vegetables and bread. Being a vegetarian in the South was as difficult as being a homeless vegetarian. Almost every dish included some sort of meat. Even worse, I felt incredibly sick. The morning sickness had persisted, and I was struggling to make it through the meal.

My older brother Kevin sat down next to me. "When are you going back?" he asked me. He seemed to be the only one that understood what I needed to do. He knew what it was like to not fit in and to have someplace else he'd rather be.

"Tomorrow," I told him. "I shouldn't have come," I added.

He offered to drive me to the Greyhound station. I sighed, knowing I would have to buy a ticket as far west as possible, since I didn't have nearly enough money for a ticket to California. They were still at least one hundred and twenty dollars, and I had a little over seventy left.

What surprised me was that when we arrived at the bus station, Kevin bought the ticket for me. "Remember a few years ago when I needed gas money to go home?" I thought for a moment then realized that I had paid his for him to get back home once, so he could visit us for the holidays.

"Take care, Sis," he told me, and we hugged goodbye.

73
BACK AGAIN

I took the familiar path westward. Predictable stops, every six to eight hours. I had memorized the route over the years. I watched as the familiar greens melded into hot desert reds and browns. The path became long and treacherous, with mountains and distant train tracks running adjacent to the straight line of freeway that stretched out in front of me. Deciduous trees had been left behind, making way for cacti and tumbleweeds. My heart soared; this was home. There was no place like this foreign world that I belonged to, this land of opposites that had called to me for long before I even knew of a place called California.

The bus arrived in Los Angeles without much fanfare. I'd made it across the country on cheap snacks and free cups of water. I was back to my usual forty or so dollars in my wallet, but I knew that would never be enough for what was coming next.

I boarded a city bus and headed back towards Hollywood. Home, for now. It felt weird, thinking of a place as home, when I knew I didn't actually have a place to truly call home.

I exited on Sunset and Gower, walking the short half block back to LAYN. The bright blue paint on the side of the building had formed some small cracks, and the blueness had begun to fade. Home.

But I walked past it, up the road, and to the right. I needed to see Damian first. I needed to talk to him about what we would do next. We were going to be parents, ready or not.

I hadn't disillusioned myself with a dream of a perfect life, or even a happy family. But I certainly didn't expect what I found when I arrived at Damian's apartment complex. I saw a stack of trash on the ground, near the dumpster. Torn photographs. My photographs. My memories. I'd forgotten a bag of my stuff at his apartment in Riverside, and he'd brought it all the way to Hollywood just to throw it away.

I raced up the stairs to his apartment, banging on the door. I expected answers.

The landlord heard me and stepped outside. "He isn't there," he told me from the ground floor. "He moved out."

"Where did he go?" I asked frantically, hurrying back down the stairs to talk with him. "That's my stuff," I said, pointing to the littered trash. My clothes, my memories. Everything ruined. I hadn't left much at his place, but I'd left enough to already feel the stab of pain that such a violation brings.

"He disappeared without paying the rent," the landlord was saying.

I felt the hot tears stinging against my cheeks. "He ran," I said softly. "He really didn't want this baby."

My hand had absently slipped back to my abdomen, where my future awaited. A future that now included being a single mother. The landlord looked regretful, but firm. "Sorry, Miss," he told me, his eyes conveying to me that he couldn't help me.

I nodded in acknowledgement, then wandered over to the pile of trash. I sifted through my belongings, recovering a few pieces of photographs. Shreds of my history.

I sat down on a concrete wall on Gower Street, half a block from LAYN. I was worried they wouldn't take me back again. I had left too many times. "This is not a hotel," Guillermo had told me so many times. "You can't just check in and check out whenever you want." Where would I go? What would I do? I was seventeen, pregnant, and I had nowhere to live. I had envisioned some sort of solution to end all the trouble I'd gotten myself into; some relief to the problem in sight. An end to nights on the streets; those cold, shivering nights in lifeguard towers in Santa Monica, or restless nights of walking around Hollywood hours past midnight. I wanted something better out of life, but so far, it had stayed just beyond my reach.

It was time to go home, I told myself with a long sigh. Only this time, I fully understood that the place that I considered home was a temporary homeless shelter in the middle of Hollywood.

I rang the doorbell, stared up at the camera. Curtis's voice boomed over the intercom. "Come in," he called out, as the door buzzed me in.

The door opened, and I walked the short distance to the dayroom. A short Hispanic boy that I didn't know was standing in front of me when I entered the room. "Hey, that's my coat!" he called out as he saw me. Curtis approached us.

"No, it's mine," I said loudly. I'd chosen this jacket from the donations closet a few weeks ago, before my trip to the east. "I've had it for weeks."

"My mom bought that for me," he argued. "Curtis, you can call her," he commanded.

Curtis took me into the office to talk with me, and then called the other kid's mom. Apparently, it was his jacket. I turned away, reluctantly removed it while letting the rat slip into my backpack. I zipped the small compartment almost closed, just enough to keep him out of sight, before turning back around. I handed the jacket back to the kid, shivering in my sudden absence of warmth.

He put on the jacket, stretching his hands into the pockets. He felt the hole that my rat had chewed through the pocket. "Hey, you ruined it!" he yelled at me. "You have to buy me a new one!" He took it off and draped it over his arm.

I shook my head. Nope. "You got it back," I told him.

"Stupid squatter," he retorted, walking away with the jacket in his arms.

Curtis watched me curiously, waiting for my response. Nothing came. I'd never been so defeated. I shrugged. "Curtis, I need to look for a new jacket," I told him, and he let me search the donations closet for new clothes. I found a suitable replacement, and quickly put it on. Afterwards, I wandered back into the dayroom. I sat down on the sofa, where I quickly fell back asleep.

"Wake up, Sheri," I heard Guillermo's voice telling me. My eyes fluttered open, and I glanced around the dayroom. It was lunchtime, and all the other clients were sitting at the table. "We need to talk."

I sat upright, waiting. "Can I come back?"

"I don't know yet. Let's go to my office."

I looked longingly at the food, wondering if I would have a chance to eat something for lunch. Guillermo noticed, and asked Pedro to set aside a plate for me. I smiled, remembering just how much of a father-figure that Guillermo had become for me.

"So, Sheri, what's it going to be this time? A week, two weeks?" he asked me after I was already sitting down in his office.

I suddenly felt very tired. "I won't leave again."

"Yes, but what are you going to do about the baby? You know that you can't stay here for very long. Maybe you should go to Children of the Night."

I felt my eyes widen. Rachel must've told them I was pregnant. I shook my head. "Please don't make me go there."

We settled on a trial period of a week, but Guillermo expected me to transfer to Children of the Night soon. I couldn't be there and be pregnant.

"Fine," I agreed. "I guess I'll go to school now," I added, not willing to continue talking with him. He handed me a packet of bus tokens, and I deposited them in my backpack. I needed to go buy a new bus pass for the month, and I really wanted to stop by Damian's work. But school was always my go-to answer when I talked to Guillermo.

I walked the short distance of three blocks to buy my new bus pass sticker. Twenty dollars. I had ten bus tokens in my pocket, and just over twenty dollars cash remaining. I needed to pay for my storage locker.

I stopped at Teen Canteen and requested more bus tokens. I needed to be able to get to school, I pleaded. They handed me four tokens and asked for me to meet with a case manager the following week. I thanked them and rushed away.

Next stop, Damian's work. I looked in the parking lot on both sides of the fast food restaurant, and in the lot behind the business. His Volkswagen bug wasn't there. I took a deep breath and entered the familiar restaurant.

I walked up to the counter and smiled at the cashier. "Hi. Do you know when Damian will be back?" I asked.

She looked annoyed. She'd never been kind to me, and that day would not be an exception. "He quit," she told me.

I looked from her to her nearby coworker. "He changed his number, too," said the other girl.

He'd skipped town while I'd been away. This was really happening. He'd really given up on me, on us.

I was alone.

I wandered the few blocks back to the shelter and found my way back to the sofa. At least I had a week of safety ahead of me.

Morning came. A new day. My first full day back, and I needed to figure it all out. Instead, I gave in to the morning urge to vomit and then eased myself down the stairs for breakfast. Dry cereal and milk were waiting for me in the kitchen. I smiled, grateful for the coziness that the shelter offered to me. I prepared a bowl of cereal and then sat down at the table.

After I had taken a few bites of my breakfast, Pedro approached me. "Come on, when are you going to admit that you're having a squatter's baby? Do you know how mean it is for you to ruin that guy's life? And do you even know how they take a paternity test? They use a big, long needle, and they do it as soon as the baby is born."

I closed my eyes. So much for being home again, I thought. I begged the tears to subside, but they fell down my cheeks again. How many times could a girl cry in one morning? The pregnancy hormones were making me crazy; I was crying for almost everything.

When I opened my eyes, Pedro was still staring at me. I stood up and threw the bowl of cereal into the trash. I wasn't hungry anymore.

"What the hell do you know, anyway?" I told him. "If it wasn't his baby, then why did he leave? Why did he go to the trouble of quitting his job and moving away?"

"Maybe he's smart," Pedro muttered, and returned to his work.

My hands were shaking, and I felt ill. It took everything in me to maintain my resolve. I fought the urge to smoke a cigarette, knowing that I had given them up for this baby. Instead, I raced down the hallway to the restroom, where I threw up the breakfast that I had so carefully eaten.

Defeated, I settled into my place on the sofa. Ignoring the voices of the other teens around me and silencing the deafening noise of the television and radio playing simultaneously, I closed my eyes and drifted into sleep again.

"Time for group," I heard Dr. Gregory calling for all of us. I sat up groggily. I was tired, I felt queasy, and I still hadn't stopped by school yet. I sat up from my corner of the sofa, ready to sit through another round of self-loathing and promises to get my life together.

The other youth were corralled into the dayroom, mostly from the smoking area behind the building. The smell of cigarette smoke now bothered me, and I didn't want anyone else to sit too closely to me. I physically and emotionally separated myself from my peers, as I curled into my corner of the black fake leather chair.

"Scoot over," Cedric commanded. I groaned in annoyance, allowing him to sit next to me. Cedric was big, built like a linebacker. I wondered once again if he really wanted that scholarship. He'd turned down a placement while I'd been gone, and he looked high. I stared at him, wondering if he was like me. Was he unsure of himself too; the way I had felt when I had not applied for NCSSM?

A week passed, then another one. I'd found a squatter to give my rat away to, realizing that I needed to take care of myself for now. Winter was fast approaching, and the programs were starting to throw holiday parties for the youth. LAYN had been invited to a jazz club in West Hollywood, where we would get a Christmas meal, presents, and Stevie Wonder would perform.

I wanted to stay. I begged Guillermo to let me stay through Christmas, before making me go to Children of the Night. "Please," I told him. "I'm not that pregnant yet."

"But you haven't even seen a doctor yet," he told me.

"Yeah," I said. I knew that. I'd tried to sign up for the state's Medicaid program, known as Medi-Cal. I'd been turned down, since I was not an adult. No prenatal care for me, unless I had a parent's signature and agreed to live with them.

I would have to find another solution.

"You can see a doctor at Children of the Night," he told me.

I shook my head. "They'll all be full until after the holidays anyway," I said. It was a week until Christmas. This was becoming my home. My awkward shelter family. I didn't want to spend the holidays in a new place.

"Okay," he said finally, after conferring with the director.

A few nights later, the staff announced that we were staying up late to watch a television show. I groaned, realizing the date. "Oh, no," I said.

Pedro laughed. "Yup. It's Sheri's Jerry Springer episode."

They popped popcorn and bought soda for us, and the dayroom was transformed into a dark viewing room. Everyone had a bowl of popcorn and a red plastic cup full of soda. I cringed as I took my seat. The opening credits rolled across the screen.

An hour later, and amid numerous cheers and laughs from the group, the lights came back on. "Damnit," I said.

"What?" one of the staff members asked, a serious look on their face.

"They removed a lot of what we said and tried to make us look stupid." I glanced at my fellow shelter-mates. "That dad, he's crazy," I told them. "They removed all the scenes where he ranted about nonsense and tried to make us look like a bunch of spoiled brats."

"It's okay," Cedric said.

I shook my head. "No, it's not. They lied about the money. They lied about everything," I told them, then burst into tears.

"It's okay," one of the others said. I wasn't sure who was talking to me anymore. There was a jumble of voices and suddenly I was being pulled into an awkward group hug. "It's okay."

The next day, I walked down Hollywood Boulevard. A police car pulled up a small alleyway and stopped in front of me, the officers looking right at me. I froze. They rolled down their window, ready to tell me something.

Crap.

"You looked good on TV," one of them said.

My eyes grew wide and my heart thudded in my chest. Oh My God. They watched the show. They knew I was seventeen. They watched the show.

I wasn't safe here anymore.

I waited for them to drive away before rushing to the bus stop. No more walking. I would use the bus to get around, to avoid any more police officers who enjoyed late night talk shows.

The jazz club was off Sunset Boulevard. I'd passed it dozens of times when riding on public buses. A line was wrapped around the edge, and kids I recognized had been bussed from shelters and teen programs all over the city. Some street kids waited in line, too. My pregnant nose took it all in, and the stench was overwhelming. I made a beeline for the bathroom, to throw up again.

When we finally got inside, each of us received a Walkman radio and a pack of batteries. We were seated at long tables and food was brought out to us by cheerful waiters. The piano strummed along in the background, and I could see the silhouette of Stevie Wonder, tapping the keys marvelously by the bar.

Afterwards, we went back to the shelter in the van. The mood was subdued. There was something odd about spending holidays in such a setting. Fake cheer, kindness that was extended to us for just one day. One of the kids got mad and threw his Walkman on the ground, stomping on it with his foot. "Why did they give us this shit?" he asked. I kept quiet, knowing that he was mad his mom hadn't shown up. None of us knew how to handle moments that went right. Moments when people were kind. A part of me wanted to throw mine, too, but the sound of music from the local radio stations was able to perfectly drown out the echoes of fear growing within me.

A few days later, and after receiving a handful of presents at the local programs, I packed my belongings and stepped into an awaiting taxi cab. Windbreakers, Nike shoes, brand new jeans, a backpack, and a handful of toiletries and small items. I'd already sorted through them and dumped half of the stuff in storage. I'd even picked up a few extra packets of school work for the trek into the San Fernando Valley. Guillermo and I had agreed I would leave after Christmas, and sure enough, Children of the Night was waiting. After my incident with the local cops after the Jerry Springer show had aired, I was ready to get away for a while.

74
CHILDREN OF THE NIGHT

The drive lasted less than I'd expected. I'd grown used to long travel times, since much of my time was spent on public buses. When the taxi cab stopped at an unmarked building a block from a local courthouse, I shivered. This place was too close to law enforcement. I'd seen dozens of police cars within the last few blocks, and the courtyard was too close for comfort.

A woman came outside to greet me, her eyes darting quickly around the block. "Sheri?" she asked, confirming my name.

I nodded cautiously. I passed the taxi vouchers to the driver and he backed away. I wished I could too, I realized.

The woman led me inside the front door. There were a series of doors that we needed to get through before we got to the actual shelter. I followed her into an office.

Guillermo sent me here? I wondered. But he'd said they were the only local shelter who dealt with pregnant minors and had access to health care. Apparently, they worked with some local doctors.

I went through the motions of another intake. Same questions, until we got to a series of prostitution questions. "Do you have a pimp?" the woman asked.

"No, of course not," I told her.

She grimaced at my quick remark. Nonetheless, she continued.

"And I heard you're pregnant?" she finally asked, after finishing a long series of explicit questions.

I nodded.

"And the father?" she asked.

"He's gone. It's just me."

She looked at me curiously. "Who is he?"

"A guy," I said. "Look, I'd rather not talk about it."

She finished her set of questions, then showed me around the program. It was an all-girls program, and I'd always known their primary focus was working with ex-prostitutes. Girls trying to get off the streets. But as I went through the building, I felt uneasy.

"And when do I go to the doctor?" I asked.

"You have an appointment on Wednesday," she said. In two days. I could make it through two days, I thought to myself.

I was taken to a small room with two beds in it. "I'll send your roommate in," she told me. Wordlessly, I moved across the room to the bed that would obviously be mine. My roommate's bed held a grungy stuffed animal on it and there was a decorative blanket over her sterile white sheets.

"Hi," a girl said from the doorway.

I glanced up. I'd been sitting in the room, staring at the white wall. The walls, the cabinet, the dresser, the sheets. Everything was sterile. Like a hospital room. I shivered slightly from the memory.

"Hi," I replied.

The girl studied me for a moment, then came into the room and sat on her bed. Across from me. "I'm Marla," she said.

"Sheri," I answered back.

"Are you from Hollywood?" she asked.

I nodded.

"Do you work the Boulevard?" she continued.

I shook my head. "No. I'm pregnant. LAYN sent me here."

Her face was a mask for a moment. "Pregnant," she repeated. I wasn't showing. Just vomiting every single morning for over two months.

"So, what are you going to do?" she asked.

I shrugged. "I'll figure it out."

She continued asking me questions until she seemed satisfied with my answers. "Alright," she said. She left me alone so I could put my stuff away.

I stepped over to the cabinet. The drawers were heavy, and as I pulled out the first one, the latch didn't catch it. It thundered down to the ground and landed on my right foot. "Ow!" I screamed.

Marla and a few other girls ran back into the room. "What happened?" one of the staff members said. I struggled to pull the heavy drawer off my foot. It had to weigh at least fifty pounds. I let out a string of expletives as I hopped to the bed to check my foot.

When I took off my sock, I saw that my entire big toe was turning purple. The staff member put the drawer away and I chose not to unpack. I already hated this place.

Afterwards, I skipped dinner and chose to go to sleep early, clinging to my unpacked backpack.

The next day, I went through the motions of breakfast, group, lunch, group, dinner, and more group. So much therapy. "My doctor's visit is tomorrow," I told Marla that night, relieved. I was trying to figure out how I was going to make it through the next several months here. Group sessions weren't therapeutic for me. They triggered bad memories and made me feel more tense than usual. I'd sat upright and absently rubbed my right foot during group. I hadn't put my shoes back on yet because my big toe was too swollen for the tennis shoes.

Nightfall came slowly, and the night dragged along at a snail's pace. I tossed and turned, and eventually settled for lying awake and trying to figure things out. I stretched my hands behind my head and tried to make sense out of the past year.

Damian was gone. I was all the way in Van Nuys, in a shelter program I didn't fit into. I still had my bus pass until end of the month, but I didn't even know which bus I would have to take to get back to Hollywood.

And I didn't know where I would stay.

So many complications.

I must've finally drifted off to sleep, because the next time I opened my eyes to stare at the ceiling tile, the room was bright, and a wave of nausea overtook me.

I rushed to the bathroom and collapsed onto the floor in front of the toilet, where I proceeded to retch.

In the afternoon, a bunch of girls piled into a van and we were told that it was time to go to clinic. There was a doctor who agreed to see girls from the program in their clinic a few times per month. We drove in a nondescript white van to a small clinic in a brick building. A short ride up the elevator later, and we were waiting in an otherwise empty waiting room.

"We're their last patients for the day," one of the staff members told me when she saw my confusion. "For safety reasons," she added.

I nodded slowly. Safety. Right. Most of these girls had people looking for them.

That was where we were different. No one was looking for me.

I waited my turn, and finally I was called back to meet with the doctor in a small exam room. A woman stood in front of me in regular clothes and introduced herself as my doctor. She shook my hand and then sat down on a stool across from me. I took the seat angled towards her. A staff member had accompanied me to the room.

"So, I hear you're pregnant?" the doctor asked. They'd already made me pee on a stick to confirm it.

I nodded. She asked my last menstrual period, and I told her.

"That would make you about twelve weeks," she said. "We should be able to hear the heartbeat," she told me. She indicated for me to climb onto the exam table, so I did.

She brought a small handheld device into the room and she explained to me how would use it to hear the baby's heartbeat. I laid down and pulled up my shirt, eager to hear her. Somehow, I'd suddenly decided that it was a girl. It became she in my mind.

"Will I get an ultrasound?" I asked.

"Maybe," the doctor said, plopping a large amount of cold gel onto my belly. I jumped. "That's so we can hear," she told me.

I nodded and tried to stay still while she pushed the device over my belly. Back and forth. All I heard was static. "Is that the baby?" I finally asked.

"Hmm," she said. "When was your first pregnancy test?" she asked me.

"November."

"Alright. Let's do that ultrasound," she said. She covered me with a sheet and left the room again. When she returned, she wheeled in a small cart with a monitor on it. Wordlessly, she began moving a thin probe over my belly, watching the screen. Concern filled her eyes, and she started pressing some buttons. Small squares of black and white paper began to print.

"Is that my baby?" I asked.

Finally, she spoke. "No, sweetie. The baby didn't make it," she said.

I froze. What?

"What?" I demanded.

The staff member's hand pressed down on my shoulder. An unwelcome but needed boost of strength. "Wait here," the doctor told me, handing me a towel to clean the gel off my belly.

I sat up slowly, dazed. I absently wiped the gel off my flat belly.

When the doctor returned, she tried to explain to me, but I didn't understand. "But I throw up every morning," I said.

"You need a procedure, to remove it," she finally said.

"Oh," I told her.

I looked over at the staff member. "I'm going back to Hollywood," I told her.

She nodded. There was a fullness to the air around me, and my lungs felt heavy. "Alright," the doctor said. "I'll print everything, but you need to go to the Free Clinic as fast as possible," she told me.

I nodded. I would go, the following morning, carrying that thin envelope with very bad news in it. They would get on the phone with a local hospital and arrange everything. I checked back into LAYN without too many questions. They'd already called Guillermo and filled him in. After I went to the procedure the following day, which they called a D&C, I went back to LAYN and laid down onto my bed.

.

75
ROCK BOTTOM

Hours later, I awoke. Pain stabbed at my belly. I held my hands together, clasping one beneath the other, the fingertips turning dangerously white from the pressure. "Breathe," I told myself, but then collapsed into tears. I released my death grip and stared down at my hands. What could be done? How could I fix this mess?

Seventeen years old was far too young to have to ponder such life and death issues. I squeezed my eyes shut, trying to block out the images... The sounds. A large part of me remained in disbelief. Had I been lied to? Had the staff members at Children of the Night tricked me into aborting my child? But a sadder, darker part of me recalled the sadness in the doctor's eyes when she could not find a heartbeat. The hushed whispers between the staff member and the doctor. The quiet words from the staff at the Free Clinic. The lonely bus ride to the hospital to have the fake fetus or ball of cells removed from me with a vacuum device. The even lonelier bus ride back to the shelter where I was temporarily living.

Of course I couldn't even make a baby right. I couldn't do anything right, actually. No home, no family, no job. Struggling to finish high school. A case worker at the shelter who kept pushing for me to go back to a place where I didn't belong. What did I really have to hold onto?

I cried silently at first, and then wailed for the loss of the imagined future I had with my baby.

A baby that wasn't even a baby. A "hydatidiform mole." A warped, twisted version of reality. A nonsensical fetus that would never form, but instead grew into a globulous ball of useless, dangerous cells. Nobody came upstairs to the girl's sleep room to check on me. Nobody really knew what to say, or how to soothe my brokenness. I felt like I'd finally hit the rock bottom I'd been running so hard to get away from. There was nothing left.

I reached into my backpack and pulled out a few bottles of pills. I'd tried to kill myself before, but that time I had taken the wrong combo of pills. Not this time, I told myself, confident in my selection. I quickly downed both bottles and laid back down on the bed, tears streaming down my cheeks like waterfalls. Memories replayed in my mind. My shitty childhood. The ten months I'd been locked up at Dillon. The way that un-baby's father had packed up and fled while I was away, tossing all my stuff outside like it was garbage. The futility of becoming clean and sober, for a non-existent baby. If ever I'd needed a drink, it was right at that moment.

I eventually drifted off to sleep, ready to die. But instead, I was awakened by a frantic staff member and paramedics. In a haze, I felt them bringing me downstairs and loading me into an ambulance. I closed my eyes and woke up in an ER bed, and suddenly a doctor was yelling at me and a tube was being shoved down my throat. Black, gross charcoal was poured down that tube, and I was suddenly vomiting everywhere as the tube was withdrawn. I cried so much, fought them terribly. Why couldn't I escape this nightmare? Why were they keeping me here? My eyes flitted open and closed, and I could see a scurrying of medical personnel moving beyond the half-opened triage curtain.

I expected them to lock me away. I was seventeen and I truly wanted to die. I had nothing left. I couldn't imagine a tomorrow followed by another tomorrow. I couldn't keep fighting for an existence that wasn't meant to be. I laid there, waiting, wondering what would become of me. *Of course I couldn't even kill myself right.* Someone was surely on their way to interview me, to send me somewhere else. I had just killed my chance to stay in California. It would be juvenile hall, or foster care, or worse – the psych ward.

My nurse stood in front of me suddenly, a stack of papers in her hand. "Why are you wasting our time?" she fumed at me. "Don't do this again. We don't have time to save your ass," she muttered as she pulled the IV out of my arm.

My head was spinning. Why was she yelling at me?

Why was I still alive?

My eyes focused on the papers that she'd handed to me. Discharge papers. I blinked, astonished. No 72-hour hold? No loss of my freedom?

I shoved the papers into my pocket and stood up but felt wobbly. Some of the pills had gotten through; I had that hazy feeling still. Not quite drunk; no, there was no forgetting. This was worse than a drunken stupor. I walked groggily towards the exit sign, and then stepped into the bright sunlight of the tomorrow that I wasn't ready for. Everything hurt, from my throat to my heart to my vacuumed uterus. I walked slowly down the street, not sure what would come next. Was I really still here? I pinched myself to be sure that I hadn't succeeded and actually gone to hell. Which would have been right back where I was.

I sighed, then trudged forward the dozen or so city blocks until I was back at the shelter. I supposed that if I was alive still, I might as well go back "home."

Of course, no one tells you that a failed suicide attempt will turn your life upside down. When I arrived at the shelter, my bags had been searched and there were no more pills. The staff allowed me to lay down for a while but informed me we would have to "talk." I curled into the familiar black sofa in the dayroom, its worn material used to the feel of my broken body. I sensed that all eyes were on me. My heart was aching, and I felt lost. I somehow knew there would be no escape from this misery. I squeezed my eyes shut. Enough!

When I awoke, they did talk to me. Janine was standing over me, her perfectly layered hair framing her face and bouncing as she spoke. She was the program director; I'd spent many afternoons wandering past her office and trying to make her like me. Trying to get her to offer me a piece of candy from the glass candy dish, the way she always offered it to Rachel and Michelle. Sometimes, she felt sorry for me and shared a piece with me. Other times, I grabbed one and took it anyways, pretending that it had been offered.

She stood over my reckless spot on the sofa, where I'd crashed and waited for whatever was coming next. "You have to go back to Children of the Night," she told me.

I sat up abruptly, my head spinning from the sudden movement. "No," I said firmly.

"You can't stay here," she said, her words equally strong. Cutting like knives.

"We could get shut down for what you did. Our liability doesn't cover us for suicide."

I nodded, slowly. Understanding. I was too high risk for them. I was beyond their reach. I wasn't pregnant anymore, but they still wanted me to go back to that place for pregnant girls and prostitutes.

"I won't go back there," I said firmly. I couldn't go back to that place. They were the ones that had told me it was my fault I had lost the baby. They blamed it on drugs. As if they'd believe a chronically homeless girl like me had only ever smoked a few joints. As if they would believe my story about my ex-boyfriend and the way he'd forced me to try marijuana by gunpoint, "to teach me". The non-father of the non-baby. I'd blamed it on an uncooperative egg that had never become a fetus, but became a "mole," or whatever the hell that was. I wouldn't go back and be told again how I was a screw up.

I sighed heavily, feeling suddenly like the air around me was too thick. I reached for my backpack, which had been positioned safely underneath my feet while I'd slept. I knew this routine. My time was up. It's not a hotel, can't check in and check out. I needed to go someplace else for a while, until my staying here was "more palatable" for the board members who had to approve long stays.

"Where are you going?" Janine asked, her brown eyes widening as she spoke. Her voice sterner than I was used to. A little less soft. But concerned.

"I don't know. I guess I'll figure it out," I said. I was staring at my hand, at the small scar that had formed over the burnt skin. How many times had I burned myself, just trying to feel anything?

I still felt nothing. I started to stand, feigning strength that my body didn't feel.

"Wait," she said.

I looked up. Those eyes, usually perfectly devoid of emotion, were piercing into me. Janine had walls around herself, much like my own.

"Why don't you stay, at least for a few more days?" she offered. "We can talk more about this in my office, next week."

A peace offering. "Thank you," I said softly, aware she'd just given me my last chance. Somehow, she must have sensed how little hope I truly had left. I, who had gone through dozens of last chances, had one more opportunity to not screw up my life.

"Time to go to group with the other youth," she answered. That was the most maternal thing she'd ever said to me.

76
DIPLOMA

I supposed everyone knew what I had done. I was the ex-pregnant, homeless, little-bit-crazy, useless, throwaway girl who wasn't quite an adult and was stranded in a Hollywood shelter. I sat through our regular group session and remained skeptical, quiet. When a former client stopped by with her two babies, I went behind the building and chain-smoked a pack of cigarettes to keep myself from crying in public.

I began fighting my way back into a routine; wake up, pretend to give a damn, stop by school and pick up a few assignments, hang out with Michelle and Rachel, usually over coffee and more cigarettes at Ground Zero. Since that was how I had met the not-quite-a-baby's father, I was somewhat lost at first. I wrote depressing poetry during our coffee breaks, then headed back to the shelter and stayed up late to finish my assignments.

If I never had to lay back down and think about it, about the little baby that wasn't, about how the man who didn't want her had abused me and left, about the million and one other things that had gone wrong in my life; I was fine.

"Sheryl," called out Evan, one of the staff members, drawing me out from my thoughts. At some point after I'd lost the baby, I started demanding that people call me my given name. Sheryl. I wasn't a kid anymore. I'd lost one.

I looked up from my stack of homework. I had two classes left before I would graduate from high school. It was an adult school, but that didn't matter to me. Classes were held at night, and I would typically pick up all my homework before heading over to smoke and drink coffee with my friends. But now, I was staying up after the other youth went to bed, forcing my way through the thick packets of school work. Questions from chapters that my eyes expertly skimmed for "good enough" answers. Quickly scrawled answers to meet the bare minimum requirements for passing. I turned in completed packets, took required tests, and finished each contract. That was what each course entailed. I'd always known what needed to be done, but suddenly, I felt a longing to finish. I had to get through those last classes. Melancholy had focused me in a way that nothing else had been able to.

I watched as the staff member took a seat across from me, trying to be friendly. "How are you doing?" he asked. He had a carefully weighted smile on his face; not too happy, but kind. A practiced smile; built upon years of working with broken teens.

All the other youth were in bed. I had devised a perfect system in which I could get away with staying up late after goofing off with my friends, and then do the homework I should've done at school. It shouldn't have been so easy, but it was. I shrugged.

"I'm glad to see how hard you're working. How much more do you have to do?" he asked.

Small talk. I should've known somebody would eventually expect me to open up a little more, and I realized I couldn't get away with not answering him. "U.S.

History, A and B."

He glanced at the history assignments in front of me. They were chapter excerpts; someone had cut up a history book and bound each chapter into a thick brown folder. I was supposed to answer the questions at the end of each section on clean notebook paper. The paper had been labeled with my name, date, and assignment number. Soon, it would be filled with answers to each of the questions. Regurgitated words to pretend I gave a damn about what happened in the U.S. one hundred years ago, or at any other time point. Hard to fake, when I didn't even care about what was happening right that moment.

"Then what will you do?" he asked, his voice dangerously paternal.

I shrugged again, trying to sound optimistic. The opposite of how I really felt. "I guess I'll go to the community college for a while. I'm not really sure." I broke away from our eye contact and stared at the wall. The poster on the wall of the celebrity softball game seemed awfully important all of a sudden.

He ignored my discomfort and continued, telling me, "That's great. We're all so proud of you."

I nodded again, then turned back to my school work. I pretended not to notice when Evan stood up and went to the kitchen, to organize the pantry. He stayed close, as all the staff had, since my suicide attempt.

My fake family, my shelter staff, were proud of me. My own father kept saying I was getting a GED, which wasn't true. He was definitely not proud of me. I could hear his voice in my head, on repeat, "I have three kids," now that he'd excluded both Kevin and me from his family. Or, "What will you do with a GED?" I was working towards an actual high school diploma, but of course, he kept calling it a GED. I sighed and completed the rest of the work I had brought back to the shelter. "Home" work. An oxymoron, for a kid without a home.

The next day, I asked for double assignments. I did the same for the rest of the week, then increased my workload even more. By the end of the following week, I had completed both classes. Finished. I turned in the last assignment and took the last quiz. I was done with high school. I walked the short distance from my evening high school class to Ground Zero, where my friends were waiting for me.

Michelle was drawing something onto the back of another postcard, an unlit cigarette resting between her index and middle finger of her free hand. Rachel was sipping coffee from one of the large ceramic mugs, her eyes fixated on something across the room. The air was thick with smoke and laughter. I'd always treasured the darkness of this room; the way the room was painted black and small purple lights around the room illuminated the glow in the dark paint.

I sat down with my friends, the air already heavy with the weight of what was coming. "Well, it's been fun," I told them as I positioned my backpack on the floor between my legs. Rachel put down her coffee. Michelle stared at me as she tapped the base of her cigarette across the table, packing the tobacco firmly into the cigarette.

They were both there with permission from their shelter, The Covenant House. Since they were adults now, they stayed at a different shelter. I was still a kid, for a few more months. Rachel passed me her pack of cigarettes. I accepted one, pulling it to my lips. I'd missed this. They'd been attending class minimally, and occasionally turning in packets. They hadn't expected me to finish so suddenly, but we'd never discussed a timeline.

I sat back in the wicker chair and inhaled deeply from my clove cigarette. I could feel my lungs screaming from the harshness of the smoke. "But I won't have any more work to pick up. I guess I'll get a job," I said, my eyes not focusing on anything. The neon colors that dotted the angry paintings on the walls stared back at me. I hadn't noticed the contrast before.

Michelle was the first to speak. "Wow, you finished," she said. "I need to do that."

Rachel stared at me, her cigarette caught between her lips. The end grew with a stem of ash before she swept it away onto the ashtray at our table. "But we won't be able to hang out anymore," she said, her words floating in the distance between us.

I laughed. "Of course, we will," I said. But I wasn't too sure. What would my plan be now, if I was done with high school? Would my case manager continue to harass me about returning to North Carolina?

We agreed to hang out at other times, since I wouldn't have permission for late curfew anymore now that school was finished. I sighed, then rode the bus down Sunset Boulevard, heading 'home' to my shelter once again.

Evan was working again. He opened the door and walked with me to the dayroom, where he allowed me to enter the kitchen to prepare a meal. During the daytime, the kitchen was generally off limits. But at night, when the other youth were sleeping and I was completing my night classes, I'd been granted a few small permissions.

"Are you staying up late again?" he asked.

I shook my head sadly. "I'm done," I told him as I sat down at the dayroom table, food in hand.

"What do you mean, done?" he inquired. Kind, but concerned. Was he wondering if I was giving up again? They'd been on edge since my suicide attempt.

I shrugged. "I graduated tonight. They're going to grade everything and print my diploma."

"That's great," he was telling me, but I didn't feel great. I had nothing left to do, and once again, the sadness was weighing me down, like a heavy cloud over my life. The grief that came from not being a mother, from not having anything real to look forward to. And now, I was losing one more part of myself. I would not be a student anymore. I was supposed to know things. I was a high school graduate.

Evan sat down next to me at the table. I was twirling my plastic fork in my cup of Styrofoam noodles. Ramen for dinner, since I'd missed another meal. The noodles were almost soft enough, but not quite. The peas were too green, and the diced carrots were too orange. Artificial. Rehydrating into their true forms.

"You did it," he said proudly. I looked up at him, my eyes glistening with unshed tears. I was not much of a talker, and he had certainly learned that about me over the past year. Most of what I said was reactionary; I was quick to curse and storm off in anger. It was rare for me to say how I really felt.

He handed me the remote control. "It's okay, you can stay up tonight. It's your night."

I smiled sadly. It didn't feel like my night. But I finished my ramen and curled up on the sofa, backpack snug against my lap in much the same way that people hug their throw pillows. I flipped from channel to channel, watching television shows that I wasn't really seeing.

I pondered the cruel twist of fate. Done. I'd rushed through my schoolwork over the past few months, to finish before the baby arrived. And I'd finished everything, but there was no baby. Now what? I eventually became sleepy, and the lure of sitting alone in the dayroom was replaced with the desire to close my eyes and forget everything. I wandered upstairs for bed.

When I laid down that night, I wondered what would come next. The tears that had been waiting for me since I'd been discharged from the ER finally poured out, and I cried myself to sleep. Definitely not the way I had pictured my culmination of thirteen years of schooling. I couldn't shake off the feeling I was falling back into the darkness that had prompted me to attempt suicide just a few weeks earlier.

77
CITYWALK

"You need to get out," Rachel was telling me as we sat behind the building the next day, smoking again. I'd stopped buying cigarettes, but she always had a few to share with me. She had come to LAYN to pick me up. "I need to apply for jobs at CityWalk, and you're going with me."

I sighed heavily, not quite able to come up with an excuse to stay at the shelter. Begrudgingly, I followed her to the bus stop and we began a journey to Universal Studios. Or at least, to the outdoor mall just outside of the studios. I hadn't ever been up to CityWalk before, and it was surprising to see so many tourists crammed into one location.

We walked around first, staring at the different shops and watching the tourists wander by with their perfect families. Rachel went to several stores to apply. I was waiting for her, feeling both bored and overwhelmed. While waiting, I wandered into a strange store filled with neon lights and signs, touristic gadgets, and numerous toys. A young woman was standing at the doorway with a toy pistol that shot out a string of bubbles.

I walked through the aisles, struck with a weird sensation. I needed a purpose. In a moment of extreme courageousness, I approached the cash register and smiled. "Are you hiring?" I asked politely. I hadn't even been thinking about getting a job.

A cheerful middle-aged woman with perfect hair and shiny teeth smiled back at me. "Are you from California?" she asked. A younger girl with long hair stood beside her.

I shrugged. "North Carolina, actually," I confessed.

"Are you still in school?"

I smiled. "I graduated from high school early. I'm just waiting for my diploma to arrive."

She looked me over from head to toe. Innocent looking country girl, she must have presumed. Probably thought I'd come to California for 'my big break.' But there were no stars in my eyes.

"Yes, we're hiring," she told me. She handed me an application, which I went outside to complete.

After filling in yet another standard application form, I went back into the store and handed it to her.

"Great," she told me. "Can you start tomorrow?"

I couldn't believe my dumb luck. I wasn't even the one looking for a job, and here I was, accidentally getting hired. "Absolutely," I told her. I discussed the details with her, then walked outside with a strange sense of newfound hope.

"A job," I thought aloud to myself.

I sat in the food court and waited for my friend, who was inside the park applying for a job at one of the rides. She came back out and told me her good news; she would work on the Back to the Future ride starting the following week.

I smiled nervously. "I start tomorrow at my new job." Her eyes widened, and

I filled her in on the strange interview that I'd had at DAPY. I had a job.

If we hadn't both been broke homeless girls living in shelters, we probably would have celebrated with and ice cream or something. But instead, we cheerfully strolled back to the bus stop and made our way back to our shelters in Hollywood.

"I got a job," I said proudly to Guillermo when I returned to LAYN.

He glared at me. "You are on the reunification plan."

I shook my head. "No, I am on independent living," I told him, anger filling the space between us. I was almost eighteen. He really needed to let go of his plan for me.

It was our usual argument. He saw a naïve girl from North Carolina, but when I looked in the mirror, I saw a broken girl who had no place to call home. I wasn't going back. I'd been there for ten months by that time, so it was surprising he still assumed I would leave the one place I'd fought so hard to return to. I wished, not for the first time, that I had a different case manager. Michelle's case manager was Curtis, and he had never tried to send her home.

He shook his head. I shook mine. I crossed my arms over my chest and glared at him defiantly. Finally, I told him, "I start tomorrow. I will need to have a later curfew so that I can go to my shift."

We negotiated that I would start my job as scheduled, since I had finished my high school courses already. But of course, he had to have the final word. "You're still on the reunification plan."

I shrugged, and perhaps even rolled my eyes.

Right. Reunification plan. Not a chance.

The next morning, I arose with a strange feeling of excitement. A sense of purpose. My body still ached from the recent events, and my heart was weary, but I was ready to try something new. I walked as quickly downstairs as my body allowed. I searched the clothing closet for something suitable for work, hoping that someone had donated a pair of black pants that would look new enough. I rummaged through the bags of secondhand clothes, finally finding a pair that were moderately worn. A few bags later, I found a blouse that would work. There were a few snags in the fabric, and a stain on the bottom edge, but I could tuck it in and pretend it was new.

Unfortunately, there were no size ten shoes for girls like me with wide feet. I considered my options, and ultimately returned to the girls' dorm where I dug my black Nikes from the big Christmas event out from under my bed. They were fairly worn by then, but redeemable. I grabbed a black Sharpie and colored over the scuff marks on both shoes. I changed into my outfit, which was not quite the right size, but passable as a worker's uniform. Dark blue blouse, black pants, black shoes. At least I had opted not to wear a black top.

I returned to the office again, like a child on the first day of school. My backpack was ready, on my shoulders, and I needed to leave. Breathlessly, I told Guillermo, "I need bus tokens." That was a lie, but tokens still sold for a dollar apiece, and I wanted to have lunch. He obliged, handing me a pack of bus tokens. I pocketed them next to my wallet, where I kept my student bus pass.

Over the months, I had devised the perfect system. I went to three different programs for bus tokens and collected as many as I could get. I then walked up and down the Boulevard and sold those tokens for a dollar each. In turn, I paid my monthly storage fees and bus pass. Everything else got tucked away. Sometimes I spoiled myself with a small snack, but mostly the money was for cheap coffee.

I finally headed out the door, full of nervous anticipation, on my way to the bus stop. A new job, another opportunity. But this time, the stakes were higher. My entire life depended on me finding a reason to go through the motions of existing.

When the bus left me at the bottom of the hill, down the road from Universal Studios, I paused and took in my surroundings. I always needed an exit strategy, and it didn't take too long to figure out where I would catch the bus after work. The southbound bus stop was at the edge of a small parking lot, where there was a Subway, a Fatburger, and a small donut shop. The stop had its own covered bench. I knew from the schedule I'd picked up on the bus that there were hourly bus rides after ten pm.

I chuckled, thinking back to my first ride to the food bank with Pedro from the shelter. It had been me, him, and another kid. Leaving the food bank with a van load full of supplies for the shelter, he'd been lost. The other kid and I gave him flawless directions back, from a place where we'd never been before. He asked us how we knew our way around, and I'd grinned proudly and said, "It's a survival skill."

Exactly what I needed to do. Survive. One day at a time.

78
DAPY GIRL

Work was easy. It was the moments when I wasn't busy that became hard. I stood in front of my new job, grateful for a reprieve to silence my thoughts. I waved the bubble gun around with a huge smile plastered on my face. I had a job. I could do this. I could pretend that I was happy, until maybe I could be.

My coworkers were kind with me. Most of them were a few years older than me, in college, and working for spending money. They treated me like I was a regular teen. Like I came from a normal home, finished high school the traditional way. Like college was just a summer away.

A group of small children was running around in front of me, chasing bubbles and laughing as they played. I squeezed the trigger on the bubble gun slowly, then fast, to alternate the speed and size of the bubbles for them. They squealed with delight as they raced to catch them. I wore my smile, striving to focus on just this moment. On just these kids, these customers.

Daisy, one of the other sales girls, came and stood next to me, handing me a folded paper towel. Sometimes the cup that we dipped the gun into became saturated with soap. She handed me the towel and I replaced it around the bottom of the cup.

"You live in Hollywood, right?" she asked, surveying the kids.

I nodded, glancing over at her. She was shorter than me, a few years older. Long dark hair tied back in a ponytail. Small gold hoop earrings. She looked normal.

"Interesting," she said. "Where?"

"Oh, off of Gower," I replied, wondering where this conversation was headed.

She nodded slowly. "Is it the big blue building with Dorothy on it?"

My smile faded, and my eyes betrayed me for a moment. "How do you know?" I asked softly. I'd been discovered.

"It's okay. I used to live there too," she told me, noticing the fear that had crept across my face. "I recognized the address from your application." I thought back to the day I'd been hired. Daisy had been standing next to Margaret, our manager.

"Did you tell Margaret?" I asked. Margaret was the one who had thought I was young and innocent. A transplant from another time and place. She had no clue I was anything but who she imagined me to be.

Daisy shook her head. "Of course not," she told me. "Your secret is safe with me." She glanced back at the register, with the growing line of customers. "Hey, let me know if you ever need anything," she offered before she went back inside to tackle the line of eager tourists.

Work became my place of solace. I was available to work any shift because the work restrictions disappeared for minors who held high school diplomas. I usually worked as late as I could, if only to avoid going back to the shelter until midnight.

One evening, as I stood outside again with the bubble gun, I watched as the security guards began their 10 p.m. stroll down City Walk. Usually I was ignored, because I was working. For some reason, one of them separated from the group and came to stand next to me.

"What do you think about the security sweeps?" he asked me. I read his nametag – Juan Carlos. I had watched the security officers parading down the sidewalk for months, always grateful they had no reason to question me. The last thing I needed was another ticket.

I shrugged. "I guess it's needed," I answered, not meeting his gaze. The guards were checking ID cards from a group of teenagers nearby.

"How old are you?" he asked me suddenly.

"What?" I replied, spilling some of the bubble soap over the edge of my cup. "I'm working," I answered.

"I know," he told me. I glanced over at him then, noticing the serious expression in his eyes. "But after you get off from work, you need to leave."

I nodded slowly, fully understanding his warning. How had he known I wasn't an adult? As he walked away, I glanced back into the store, but I didn't see anything different. A few Japanese tourists were picking through the magnet stands, selecting stacks of rectangular magnets bearing the images of I Love Lucy and Marilyn Monroe. A couple stood by the lava lamps, enjoying the gentle ebbing and flowing of the melted wax against the fluorescent oils. Daisy and another one of the managers, Jayson, stood at the register, cashing out customers. Another coworker, Oliver, was cleaning a broken stress reliever from the floor, where its thick gooey insides had been squished by a customer.

I looked back at the security guard, and he flashed a smile at me. "Have a nice night," he told me. I watched as he rejoined his group of fellow officers, and they continued their stroll away from my workplace. I wondered, what had provoked that? I hadn't stayed more than a few minutes after my shift each night, since I had to get back to the shelter.

A month had passed. Despite relentless harassment from the security guards, who often "carded" me while I was on break to double check my age, I was beginning to feel more comfortable at work. Daisy and I had become friends. It was easy to talk to her, since she understood me better than my other coworkers could.

Each night after we closed the store, a group of us would make the trek down the hill, to the bus stops. I always went south, to Hollywood. Daisy and my other coworkers went north, to Panorama City.

The northbound bus usually left first. True to form, it hurled around the corner and enveloped my coworkers. Alone, I strolled into the Fatburger restaurant on my corner, grateful for a warm place to wait for a few minutes. A few of the workers from Universal Studios were already in there, laughing and sharing stories about their shift. I wondered what it would be like, to sit down after work like a regular teen, enjoying a meal with friends.

I approached the counter, reading the menu options. I was still avoiding meat, mostly out of a desire to have control over just one thing in my life.

I knew the menu already, but it was comfortable to stand there and read over my choices. There had been another Fatburger in Santa Monica, and the workers had often recognized me from the promenade. Here, no one knew me as the kid who sat on the corner, asking for spare change. Or begging for their leftover containers, hoping to have something to eat. No, I'd been transformed into the DAPY girl. My beige t-shirt with bold black letters, shouting the store's name much like a college logo on a shirt, signified that I had a job. I had a purpose. I was allowed out after ten in the evening.

I looked back at the bus stop. Everyone was seated. The bus wasn't due for another ten minutes. I smiled at the cashier and ordered a side of fat fries.

When I wandered outside to the bus stop a few minutes later, I carried a small brown bag with fries and condiments. I didn't have to wait long for the bus and when it arrived, I was ready for my trek home.

The bus was waiting beside us, door open. But the workers standing in front of me were hesitating. What was holding up the line? I tried to stand on my tiptoes to get a better view, but the back of the bus was empty. After we finally boarded the bus, I found myself jammed in between dozens of people. Standing room only.

That was odd. Hadn't the back of the bus been empty?

I glanced up at the black rectangle above the driver, the space where street names would appear in yellow letters. Instead of announcing the next stop, it read CALL 911. And the words kept darting against the screen. Cell phones weren't common yet, and my pager sat uselessly in my pocket. How could any of us call? Why had he let us on the bus?

There were several people between me and the driver. I couldn't ask. The back of the bus had appeared empty. I craned my neck to try to see what was going on.

I couldn't see anything.

And then I heard him. An angry, possibly crazy, definitely drunk or high man was shouting from behind all the people. His voice carried through the crowd.

Each stop, people shoved their way off, hoping to be free from whatever was about to happen.

I had two options for my route home. Sometimes, I would get off on Hollywood Boulevard and wander down the street to Gower. Other times, I would let the bus steer me a little further, down Highland, turn left on Santa Monica Boulevard, and then I would get off on Gower and trek back up to the program. Either walk was around the same distance, and I usually just picked based on how I felt each night.

Hollywood and Highland couldn't get to me fast enough. When the bus peeled down the hill, past the Hollywood Bowl, past the hotels, and approached my stop, I saw it. A dozen police cars with bright blue lights. Officers with guns drawn.

I imagined that they would storm the bus, guns at the ready. I pushed my way out the front door, following a sea of passengers. Almost everyone exited, flooding onto the sidewalk. I dodged the sidewalk, darting in front of the bus and rushed around it to make it to the crosswalk. Instinctively, I knew that I didn't want to be caught between that man and a bullet. I rushed into the street, crossing towards home.

"Stop!" I heard someone yell.

I froze. Turned my head slightly. The man from the bus had followed me into the intersection and was standing right behind me. The guns were all pointed in my direction. Damnit, I thought. I should've looked. I stared squarely at one of the officers, whose gun was pointed directly at my chest. Sure, there was a crazy homeless man in between us, but that didn't mean anything to me.

Cars were stopped. People were frozen. It was like a moment in time had completely been memorialized, for all to see. I flashed back to the last time I'd had a gun in my face. Damian. I hadn't thought of him in weeks. To the detention center when I was fourteen, and the officers stormed the building. Then to that other time, when I'd been drunk and reckless. I was immobilized.

The man was a few feet behind me. He was an older, grotesquely dirty white man with long wiry hair and mean eyes. Loose facial features, a combination of liquor and craziness. Sunburnt skin covered his face and exposed chest. He was wrapped in one of the shelter blankets; those thick gray blankets that they pass out during the winter. He carried a large plastic bag of his belongings in a barely exposed hand.

I watched in horror as the police descended on the man, and as soon as he was tackled to the ground, I ran.

I ran as fast as I could. Faster than when I'd been racing in cross country meets. Faster than that time when I jumped from the white van, faster than after that old homeless guy sprayed me with my own pepper spray while I was sleeping. Even faster than when the pimp tried to lure me off of Sunset Boulevard into his friend's car.

Down Hollywood Boulevard, past the Guinness' Book of World Records Museum, past the McDonald's, past the Scientology recruitment center. I finally stopped to catch my breath in front of one of the many lingerie shops lining the boulevard. I paused, gasping for air. I glanced back, and no one was within my line of sight. I looked up at the mannequins wearing stripper clothes and laughed at the absurdity of where I was.

And then I felt the emptiness in my hands. I'd lost my fries.

My shoulders sunk, and I walked the rest of the way to the shelter with a scowl on my face. I buried my empty hands in my pockets, wrapping my fingers around my wallet so that at least I wouldn't lose that, too. I'd wasted almost three dollars and I had nothing to show for it.

When I got to the shelter, I skipped the kitchen and went straight to bed. I didn't want a measly cup of noodles now, not if I'd had a chance for something different. Something regular seventeen-year-olds got to buy themselves after work. I was angry, and as I fell asleep, I realized that it didn't have anything to do with the forgotten fries.

79
BURGER FACTORY

It was too early to go to the bus stop, I realized. I decided to stop for coffee at Burger Factory before taking the bus to work. I felt antsy from the previous night and hadn't gotten enough sleep after the incident. I kept flashing back to the sight of the guns pointing in my direction.

When I went into the familiar restaurant, I noticed that the young lady wasn't behind the register. One of the cooks was standing there, a smile on his face. He wore a blue apron and a hat over the trademark Burger Factory shirt.

"Hi," I told him. I had been going to that restaurant for almost a year, and I'd never paid much attention to this guy before. He'd always been in the background, preparing meals I couldn't afford. "Can I get a large coffee?"

He glanced at the clock. It was lunchtime. Obviously, not a normal time for coffee. "I'll brew you a fresh pot," he told me as I handed him exact change for my coffee. I'd rarely ordered anything except coffee.

All the booths were full, so I stood by the counter, waiting.

When the coffee was ready, the cook handed it to me. He was still smiling. He seemed much happier than I felt.

"You have pretty eyes," he told me.

I instantly closed my eyes. "Right. What color are they?"

He hesitated. "Brown?"

I opened my eyes. Light blue. I accepted my coffee and laughed. "You weren't looking at my eyes," I told him.

I poured sugar and creamer into my cup and left for the bus stop, still chuckling. What a funny guy.

The next day, I felt a sudden urge to try something else on the menu. I went back to Burger Factory, wondering if that guy would be working again. He'd seemed nice, and I was tired of the typical guys that weren't kind.

I walked into the restaurant, expecting to see the cook with the blue apron and matching hat. He was usually there, day or night, working the grill. But that day, he wasn't there. I tried to hide my disappointment as I studied the menu. I'd never actually ordered anything besides coffee, and it was nighttime. I really didn't want pancakes. There weren't many vegetarian options, so I finally settled for a side of beans and rice. To go.

I carried my warm sack of food back to the shelter with disdain. I'd wasted two dollars. And he hadn't even been there.

When I sat down in the dayroom with my food, Evan was in the kitchen preparing dinner. He glanced at the bag in front of me. "What did you get?" he asked me.

I shrugged. "Just beans and rice. Trying to get more protein," I lied.

He smiled. "They have great breakfast burritos, too."

I nodded. Right. Like I was going back there again. I'd felt humiliated when I had ordered my food. Did they know why I was there? Because some guy who worked there had given me a compliment?

I was so used to being treated badly that I jumped at the chance to meet someone nice. And honest. And funny. And maybe he wasn't even any of those things.

I took a few bites and threw the food in the trash. I didn't want it anyway, and I was angry. I didn't know what I wanted.

I had gotten into an easy rhythm at work. Surprisingly, I was very good at arranging the merchandise in the store, and I'd redesigned the lava lamp section without breaking any lamps. Everything looked clean and inviting. I had started to add small touches each week, as the new stock arrived from the company.

In between blowing bubbles and working the register, I tidied the magnet displays and reorganized them to display popular and less noticed magnets. I would wander by the kiosks during my shifts and move a few magnets up to fill the empty slots as the day progressed.

I found myself whisking around the store, memorizing SKUs and making everything look trendy. It was soothing for me to spend a little time on a display, instead of having to engage the customers in small talk every few minutes.

My manager had noticed my work. "Sheryl," I heard Jayson calling my name one day. I glanced up from the magnet tower, where I had subconsciously moved a handful of magnets. The I Love Lucy magnets belonged at the top, especially the one where she was standing in grapes trying to make wine. Her quirky nature made me smile, and always reminded me of those brief moments in my early childhood when I used to sit next to my mom on the sofa, watching Lucy's escapades. Never too close; not physically touching, but next to her. Those were easier times.

"Hey," I replied, placing the last magnet where it belonged. "What's up?"

"Do you know what our number one selling item is?" he asked.

I nodded. Of course, I did. Everyone knew that. "Bubble guns."

"Right," he said. "That gets everyone in the door. But do you know what our number two selling item is?"

I glanced around the small store, then back at the register, where we had a huge display of disposable cameras and batteries. "Film?" I asked, raising an eyebrow.

"Close," he replied. "We do sell a lot of film and cameras. But this week, it was magnets."

They were flying off the kiosks, literally. I'd started paying closer attention to the little items, not because I was trying to be a great employee, but because I needed to keep my hands busy. Busy hands to keep them from craving a cigarette, since I'd been trying to quit again. Full hands to keep them from running them through my hair and stretching those wounded arms up towards the sky. Busy, to forget. But I hadn't actually been paying attention to why the kiosk always needed to be replenished.

"Keep it up," he told me. I beamed.

I wandered back into the restaurant on the corner a few more times, like I was being summoned there by an internal force. Burger Factory was a special place for me. I'd spent much of the previous summer staked out in their window, waiting for time to pass by. My vigil towards adulthood.

I ordered my coffee, and that was it. I didn't try the burrito, because they cost five dollars. I liked my seventy-one-cent cup of coffee, and that was my limit.

And that guy was usually there. Always smiling.

"Going to work?" he asked me as I prepared my coffee. Too much sugar, an inch of creamer.

I nodded. Of course, I was. I was wearing my work shirt.

"Where's DAPY?" he asked.

I shrugged. "Up at Citywalk," I offered, watching his expression.

"How late do you work tonight?" he asked as I placed the coffee cup to my lips.

I swallowed the coffee in my mouth, too fast. I paused, trying not to choke or cough up my coffee. That wouldn't be very attractive. "I don't know, sometime after ten-thirty. It takes a while to clean the store."

"Okay," he said in response. It was obvious that we were both very bad at flirting.

"Bye," I told him as I rushed away with my coffee. I didn't want to miss my bus, and I hadn't calculated a conversation into my coffee purchase time.

I rushed to the bus stop across the street and pulled out my bus pass, anticipating that the bus I saw driving towards me from Bronson. I always needed to have my pass ready, yet concealed, in case any of the shelter employees saw it. I didn't want to give up my bus token racket just yet; that's how I kept my storage fees paid. As I boarded the bus, I dared to look back at the shop. He was still looking in my direction as the bus carried me away.

80
BYRON

After work, my manager Eunice had offered to drive me home. The four of us were walking together towards the main entrance; Eunice, Oliver, Daisy, and me. Oliver had his own car, Daisy took the bus in the other direction, and Eunice lived near me and wanted to give me a ride. I wanted to decline, because I didn't want her to know where I lived. I kept glancing at Daisy, trying to figure out how to get out of this.

We rounded the corner where the giant Universal Studios globe twirls slowly alongside a large water fountain. I had seen the globe a dozen times, but I hadn't looked closely at it before. The intricate metalwork was spinning away from me.

I glanced back towards the walkway when I saw him. The guy from Burger Factory. Standing between the globe and the path to employee parking.

Crap. I didn't even know his name.

My dismay was quickly replaced with relief. At least I wouldn't have to show Eunice where I lived.

I hesitated for a moment, then said, "Eunice, I think my friend came to pick me up." I pointed in his direction, and three sets of eyes glanced in his direction.

Eunice nodded in approval. Daisy raised an eyebrow, but the group allowed me to gracefully exit. "See you tomorrow," Daisy called.

I wandered slowly in his direction, suddenly nervous. I'd been visiting him at work for a few weeks by then, but neither of us had initiated a next step.

He was wearing a brown leather jacket. And he'd changed his shirt. I stood a few feet away from him, uncertain.

"Hi," I said shyly.

"Hi," he responded back. "I figured you might want a ride home."

I smiled at him. Yes, I would. He certainly knew where I was staying. He had seen me on the mornings when I'd been kicked out of the Pantages lobby and I was waiting for the drop-in programs to open before I could shower. He'd watched me scrape by on nothing. He knew who I was, and it didn't seem to bother him.

"I'm Sheryl," I told him. It still felt weird calling myself that, but it was a grown-up name. I was in the middle of an identity crisis, and the formal name was helping me find myself.

"Byron," he replied.

I shivered a little from the cold. He quickly removed his jacket and placed it over my shoulders. Wow, I thought. I'd always seen that in movies, but I'd never had anyone do it for me. Well, except for that jerk from Inglewood, I thought. A frown might've momentarily crossed my face, but I shrugged away the memory.

He led me to his car, a small blue two door car parked in the circle by the entrance. The employee drop-off area. He'd been waiting for me for a while, I thought to myself.

He opened the door, and I sat down. His car was clean, and there were no strange knick-knacks in it. Just one of those little air freshener trees. Yellow. I breathed in its scent, recognizing that it was new.

"Byron," I repeated, trying out his name on my tongue after he'd sat down. "How late did you work tonight?"

"We closed at ten," he told me. They usually did. Whenever I passed by the restaurant at night, it was always dark, and the parking lot was empty.

He turned on the radio, and it was playing a song in Spanish. I smiled. For the thousandth time, I told myself I really needed to learn Spanish. "What are they saying?" I asked, as Byron began to drive down the hill.

"The guy is singing about a lost love. He can't get over her, no matter how many years pass." I smiled, thinking it was a sweet song.

He was driving down predictable streets. Not missing turns. Not taking me to unsafe places. He was really driving me home. I felt completely relaxed for a change.

When he turned onto Gower Street, I glanced over at him. He was really nice. And he seemed genuine. "I don't have to be there for another thirty minutes," I told him. "They're expecting me to take the bus."

He nodded in understanding. "Are you hungry?" he asked.

"No," I told him.

He looked at me again, then turned down the street before the shelter and parked the car. "What did you want to do?" he asked.

I hesitated for a moment, then leaned over towards him and boldly kissed him. He kissed me back.

When he dropped me off at the shelter that evening, I was dizzy with nervous excitement. It felt so different to be treated kindly. And of course, I'd blown it all to pieces by kissing him first. But I didn't care. He was nicer than most of the guys I'd met over the past few years.

I removed his jacket and placed it back on the passenger's seat. "Thanks," I told him, before hurrying up to the entrance, hoping they wouldn't notice the car that had dropped me off. I buzzed for the staff to let me in, and after several minutes, they did. Good. That meant they weren't watching the surveillance camera.

I could feel Byron's eyes watching me as I went inside, making sure I arrived home safely.

I continued to busy myself around the store, continued to smile at the customers. Days became weeks, weeks became months, and I had finally started to shed the pain from my loss. A few times a week I would get picked up by Byron, but not too often. We hung out, kissed, laughed. He kept translating great Spanish hits to me. I was enjoying his company.

But something was wrong. I couldn't figure it out. I didn't want to be in a relationship. I was too messed up after what had happened with Damian. I was filled with emptiness, and I had an overwhelming sense that everything was about to fall apart.

He came to pick me up one night, and I walked past him. Pretended I didn't see him. But I did, standing across from my store. Waiting for me.

I stopped going to get coffee.

I told myself I was doing the right thing. Deep down, I knew I wasn't ready. I couldn't be in a serious relationship. The Depo-provera shot they'd given me after the D&C would wear off soon, and I was too afraid of my own pain. Desire to have a baby was buried underneath the layers I was building of the new me.

I started to walk the long way to work instead, passing behind the Bally's gym, down the side street, right on Argyle, and then to a bus stop near Pantages. It was the path that avoided Burger Factory completely.

March was almost over, and my birthday was around the corner. Playtime was over. Adulthood would mean adult responsibilities; I was planning to find a second job and dreaming of getting my own apartment.

81
LAST NIGHT AS A KID

April 10. My final night of existing as a crime. An unaccompanied minor. The security guards had been checking in every few days, and Juan Carlos had made a habit of telling me I was out past curfew whenever he saw me. I couldn't wait until I'd be able to proudly show them my ID as an adult.

I rushed through the motions of work, nervously anticipating what tomorrow would bring. I'd been told I had to spend the night on the downstairs sofa at the shelter, because adults couldn't be in the same room with minors. And I would become an adult while I slept. At least they weren't kicking me out until the next day.

My manager Eunice called me over to the register to count the deposit with her. I had been trained on the cash register and was becoming increasingly comfortable ringing up customers. I filled out the check deposit slip while she prepared the thick stack of bills; tourists tended to pay with cash. She handed me the money when it was ready, and watched as I moved expertly through the hundreds, twenties, and smaller bills. I paused at the end and told Eunice the number I'd counted. It matched hers. She accepted it from me, placed it in the plastic envelope, and sealed it shut. We both signed the outer edge of the bag, which was now ready for deposit. She locked it into the safe, and I watched as the safe door sealed shut.

After we finished cleaning, Eunice, Rita, and I went to the back to get our bags. Eunice reached into her purse to get her keys, but her expression changed. She suddenly opened the bag widely, searching for something. Rita and I watched in horror as she didn't find whatever she was looking for.

"My wallet!" she exclaimed.

"What?" I asked.

"Someone stole my wallet," she told us. She looked at both of us, her eyes suddenly accusatory. "Show me your bags."

I glanced at Rita, suddenly nervous. Would she think I'd done it, if she knew that I was homeless? I picked up my backpack from the floor and began to open it. I opened the large pocket, then the middle one. When I opened the last pocket, my mouth gaped open. "No!" I cried out.

"What is it?" Rita asked, her hand hovering over the zipper of her small handbag.

"My wallet is gone, too," I said, now frantically dropping to my knees and dumping the contents of my backpack over the floor. No wallet.

Rita nervously opened her purse, only to discover that her wallet had also been removed.

"Eunice, do we have cameras?" I asked. My eyes immediately started surveying the ceiling of the small office, then turned to look at her.

Rita and I stared up at her, intently. We needed to find the thief.

Eunice shook her head, anger building in her eyes. No, there were no cameras. "Who would do this?" We watched as she checked the back door, ensuring that it was locked. She opened the door from the stockroom to the store, and we all heard the chiming sound that always triggered when the door was opened. "I had my wallet when I went on break. At eight," she said.

"I didn't hear the door at all, except when Vanessa left," I said.

We had been the only three closers, and the last person to leave was Vanessa. At nine. She had left a few hours earlier.

"When Vanessa left, didn't she have a large purse with her?" Rita asked. She had begun searching the trash cans in the room, making sure the remainder of her wallet wasn't tossed out.

"That's a great idea," I said. "We should check the trash cans nearby, just in case." I started shoving all my belongings back into my backpack before anyone noticed what else I had been carrying with me. Notebook. Emergency cup of noodles, in case I was starving. Services card, which I quickly buried inside of a well-worn book that I'd been reading for the past few weeks. No giant keychain. Homeless kids didn't have keys.

"Wait," Eunice said, her managerial voice suddenly returning to her. The panic had been replaced by her typical strength. "We need to file a police report."

We walked together to the register, and I set down my backpack. There were two cash registers, one on each side, and a glass counter bridging between them. A display case sat beneath the glass, offering last minute film and other touristic items. Eunice settled in at the cupboard behind both registers, picking up the phone and placing it to her ear.

I reached over and absently adjusted an I Love Lucy magnet on the kiosk. "There's been a robbery at DAPY," she said to whoever was listening on the other end. "Yes, we'll wait here."

She put the phone back on its receiver and placed her hands on her hips. She was angry. Someone had robbed not just her, but all three of us. And we were all suspecting the young mom who had just started working at the store a few weeks earlier.

I sighed and picked up the key for the magnet kiosk from next to the first cash register. If we were still on the clock, I might as well work. I would need the money to replace what was lost. I began organizing the magnets; some had fancy shapes as they had been cut out to silhouette Marilyn Monroe's body, or small caricatures from Universal films. Most of them were rectangular, and those were assorted by the orientation of the magnet. I had arranged them in alternating rows of tall and wide magnets. I busied my hands, replacing the Three Stooges and Jurassic Park, then moving on to the Hollywood sign and another set of pink stars from the sidewalk. I didn't want to think. I needed to keep myself busy, and soon, Rita and Eunice were straightening up shelves as well.

The keychains were glistening from their tower, more organized than they had been recently. The stack of Kermit the Frog t-shirts by the door were perfectly stacked, with flexible Kermit stuffed animals hanging off the metal racks in stretchy positions.

Fifteen minutes passed before the sheriffs arrived. A gentle tap on the door told us they were there. We all froze for a moment, tense from the robbery. Eunice unlocked the glass doors to let them in.

"What happened?" the taller one of the two sheriffs said, his eyes surveying the room.

"Someone stole our wallets from the office," she told him. "We believe it might've been an employee." She filled him in on all the details, while Rita and I watched.

Afterwards, the shorter officer started to take our information. What was missing? How much money did we have in our wallets? The officers thanked us and said they'd be on the lookout.

My shoulders sunk a little as we stepped outside. Eunice locked the door, and we double checked it. The full weight of my missing wallet was starting to hit me. No ID. I couldn't prove that I would be an adult.

And no bus pass.

"I don't know how I'll get home," I said softly, to no one in particular. "My bus pass was in my wallet."

"And tomorrow's your birthday," Rita added, her voice heavy.

We checked a few nearby trash cans for our wallets. Nothing. I stood under the upside-down car from the Haagen Daas display over the doorway of our neighboring ice cream shop, lost in thought.

"I'll give you a ride home," Eunice told me. "You live in Hollywood, right?"

I nodded. I didn't have a choice, really. I'd avoided free rides before, so that no one would know where I lived. But my bus pass was gone, along with all the money I'd collected from selling tokens. I was done with school now, so there was no way to get a new student pass. My monthly pass would now more than double, from twenty-dollar stickers that were added to my formal student bus pass, to the generic forty-two dollar passes that everyone else bought each month. This theft would cost me.

I walked alongside both women to the car. It was already eleven. One more hour of childhood. When I sat down in Eunice's sedan, I sunk into the seat. My backpack found its way into my lap, and we began the drive down the hill and onto the 101 freeway. "Which exit do you take?" she asked.

"Gower," I said, watching the trees give way to tall buildings. We coasted past the other cars, past the Capitol Records building and over the Hollywood Bowl Self Storage. When she exited on Gower, I let out a breath. I hadn't realized I'd been holding my breath until then.

"You go to the right," I said, an uneasy feeling building in my stomach. She turned right, and we headed south on Gower. Across Hollywood Boulevard. Past Burger Factory. Past Bally's. "And you stop there, at the blue building," I told her quietly.

Eunice pulled the car to the side of the road. "What is this place?" she asked, suddenly seeing me. She turned to face me, those eyes filled with concern and possibly fear.

I looked up at the familiar building, with its well-worn Wizard of Oz mural. There's no place like home. I'd never picked up on the irony before that moment. "It's a teen shelter," I told her. "But it's my last night here, since it's my birthday tomorrow."

She glanced back over at the building. Dorothy looked sleepy, like she was high or broken. I'd heard rumors that the actress who played her so many years ago wandered these streets too. *There's no place like home.* "But then where do you go after tonight?" Eunice wanted to know.

I shrugged. Nobody ever promised that it would be easy. My mom used to keep a book on her shelf, *I Never Promised You a Rose Garden.* My mind flashed to the book cover for a moment. No, never easy. "I go to an adult shelter for a few months, until I get my own apartment," I told her.

"But, why?" she asked. I shook my head. I'd already revealed more than I could bear.

"Thank you for the ride," I said to her, and reached for the doorknob.

Eunice paused, wavering between asking more and letting me go. I chose for her and opened the passenger door. "Happy birthday," she said, her voice hollow as I thanked her again and walked away. She sat in her car, watching, waiting for me to go inside. After I rang the bell and was buzzed in, she drove away.

I entered the lobby. Jonah was working. "We shouldn't even let you in, since you just went out partying after work," he told me from behind the glass. I walked around to the office where he sat, his tall body stretched out over a too-small chair.

"I didn't go out partying. Someone at my work stole all our wallets," I said, shoving the sheriff's business card in his face. "My boss made us file a police report."

I shook my head, frustrated. This man couldn't wait for me to turn eighteen. In twenty minutes, I would, I thought sourly as I glanced at the clock on the wall.

"You're sleeping in the dayroom tonight," he told me, and I walked away.

"Happy birthday to me," I muttered to myself as I laid down on the well-worn sofa. No wallet, no bus pass, no money, no bank card. No home. And now my manager knew I was a street kid. I closed my eyes and let sleep come, closing out the final chapter of my childhood.

82
EIGHTEEN

Morning came too fast. I awoke to the sound of the night staff setting out cereal canisters and stacking the Styrofoam bowls on the counter. I sat up, my head spinning. I should go buy a cup of coffee, I thought.

Shit. My wallet was gone.

"Hey, happy birthday!" Wanda said. She was a slender, middle-aged woman with brown hair that she always wore in a ponytail. She moved around effortlessly in her tracksuit, setting out milk and juice. Refilling the cups.

My backpack was nestled against my chest while I slept, its solid mass connected to me. If there really was no place like home, I supposed home was my little pack of belongings. "Thanks," I said quietly. Eighteen. It had finally happened.

"How do you feel?" she asked.

I hadn't really talked to Wanda very much. She usually arrived for her shift as I was going to bed, whenever I had finished work or back when I was still working on high school packets. In the mornings, I tended to get up at the last minute on the mornings after my late shifts, and I usually didn't get downstairs until the day shift staff had arrived. She'd always smiled at me and seemed friendly. But I was particularly wary of nice people. They usually had ulterior motives.

"I don't know," I said. "Tired?"

She smiled. That unnerving, toothy smile that told me she hadn't known the kind of pain that people like me muddled through. "Welcome to adulthood," she told me before busying herself into another room.

I had been asked to move my belongings to the office the previous day. I ate a quick breakfast and then went to retrieve them.

Dr. Gregory was sitting at one of the desks, looking at a folder. "Happy birthday," he told me. I nodded in acknowledgement. "Any big plans?"

I reached down to grab my black trash bag full of clothes. "Sure. I have to go to the DMV to get a new ID, since my wallet was stolen at work last night," I said dramatically.

"Hmm?" he asked. "That's terrible."

I wondered if he might be psychoanalyzing me, but realized I was too old to care anymore. While I stood there, waiting for just the right smart-aleck comment, Guillermo arrived.

"Hey, hey, would you look at that? You're an adult," Guillermo told me, patting me hard on my shoulder.

"Independent living, finally," I said halfheartedly. It was my second birthday that I would spend at LAYN, and it was already starting off worse.

"Happy birthday," Guillermo told me. He sat down at his desk, and I hovered awkwardly in the center of the room. The words fell past me like litter in the breeze. Eighteen wasn't as great as I'd hoped. "Are you going to Covenant House tonight?"

I shook my head. I'd planned a fun weekend for my entrance into adulthood; my sister was coming to town and I'd rented a hotel room on Sunset Boulevard for two nights. She was driving in with my nephew Matt, and we would spend the next day at Magic Mountain, a nearby amusement park.

"I had a problem last night at work," I told him nervously. "My wallet got stolen. My boss and another girl lost their wallets, too."

He raised an eyebrow. "What do you need?"

"Um…" I paused, uncertain. "I need more bus tokens to get to work."

"I gave tokens to you yesterday, though," he said. A full bag. I'd sold them on the way to work and was hoping to buy myself a small slice of birthday cake somewhere. With coffee. And I'd bought nothing, because the wallet went missing before my break.

"Maybe two?" I asked. I would actually have to use them, now that my bus pass was missing. I wouldn't be able to hop on and off the bus as freely anymore.

Guillermo reached into his desk for the metal lock box where he kept bus tokens and taxi vouchers. When he opened it, he glanced back up at me. Suddenly an adult. Red hair, slightly frizzy from sleeping on the sofa. Tired eyes. My guard was down and the weight of everything that had happened was staring back at him.

"You have to get to Covenant House early when you check in," he told me, handing me two tokens. "They don't always have beds."

I nodded and thanked him for the tokens. Hopefully they would have space for me after my sister's visit. There were several options for minors; LAYN, Children of the Night, the Way-In, and other shelters that were farther away. The Covenant House was the only local shelter for teens over eighteen, and the alternative was Skid Row.

It was time to live independently, I realized. I reached down to grab my black trash bag full of clothes and exited the shelter on my way to my nearby storage unit.

83
MELINDA

My sister arrived later that day, and I was waiting at the hotel I'd paid for a few days earlier. I'd been there once before, when I'd split the cost for a few nights with Rachel. I laughed when I'd checked in, remembering the horrible moment when Rachel had lit her acrylic fingernail on fire when smoking a cigarette. Yup. We were classy.

I was dressed in my purple windbreaker from Christmas. Everyone had gotten a matching set of windbreaker and pants, and for some reason I'd chosen purple. Perhaps, I'd thought it was maternal. I grimaced at the thought. Let it go, a voice inside me screamed as I stood in front of the room, watching for my sister's car. She had started driving over from Phoenix early that morning. It was at least a six-hour drive, but perhaps eight hours if you brought a five-year-old.

Melinda finally pulled into the parking space in front of the hotel, and I ran downstairs to greet her and my nephew Matt. "Hi!" I called, eager to see her. We hugged quickly and then I helped them carry their bags to the room. We had planned for a trip to an amusement park, Magic Mountain, the following day.

We went out for dinner, and I tried to see my world through my sister's eyes. I told her I was working up at Universal Citywalk, and she wanted to see it. So I directed her to the employee parking lot and we took a long walk up and down City Walk. The place was filled with tourists, and fortunately no one told my sister how I'd been living. I'd learned long ago that in my family, certain topics were off limits.

We toured DAPY, and I bought a bubble gun for Matt after I'd quickly borrowed some cash from a coworker. "Did Vanessa come back?" I whispered to one of the girls behind the counter.

"No. She called and quit over the phone."

I nodded. We all knew she'd robbed us. "Thanks for the loan," I told them, and then paid for the gun with my employee discount. I would just have to not spend any more money until payday.

And I would need a new ID card, I thought to myself. My new bank card was already on its way and would arrive in the mail after my sister left.

We toured through shops I'd never been in, and I let my sister use my employee discount to buy some souvenirs. Matt shot bubbles into the sky and I pretended I still enjoyed playing with bubbles.

The next day, we went to Magic Mountain as planned. Matt was too little for any of the fast rides, but I was okay with it. I didn't really feel like going on anything too fast or upside down. I'd been caught upside down on a roller coaster once when I was much younger, and it had made me forever uncomfortable on scary rides.

When the two days were up the following morning, my sister dropped me off at an apartment building across from LAYN, and I waved goodbye to her. I pretended to walk inside, and when she left, I quickly darted back across the road. I wasn't ready to confess how hard the past few years had been to her.

The day shelter had moved back to Cahuenga Boulevard, the building I'd encountered during my first visit to Hollywood at thirteen years old. I had already had breakfast at the hotel, which consisted of old English muffins, jelly, and bad coffee. Grateful for a familiar bowl of cereal, I sat down and ate my breakfast.

"Going to the Cov?" someone asked. I glanced up. Guillermo was hovering over me, that same old look in his eyes. The Independent Living debate was forever overruled. I was now an adult, for whatever that was worth.

"Yes," I said. "I'll go after breakfast."

He handed me a few more bus tokens, which I gratefully shoved into my pocket. I hung out until the mail arrived. After I'd received the envelope from my bank with the new bank card, I hurriedly shoved it in my pocket and rushed out of LAYN. It was time to go figure out what Covenant House could do to help me get my life in order.

84
COVENANT HOUSE

"Hi," I said to the guard at the front desk. I'd never been inside this building before. The outside was a beautiful desert red, with some areas painted bright yellow. I hesitated as they picked up the phone to confer with a case manager.

"Yeah, there's space," he said. "Simone will be with you in a few minutes."

I sat down in one of the awaiting plastic chairs, placing my backpack between my legs. I was off work for the day but had to go back the following day. I'd managed to rearrange my schedule for a few days off so that I could figure out my new housing situation.

An older African American woman came out and stared at me for a moment. I was wearing the same purple windbreaker, jeans, and my hair was tied back. I didn't look like a homeless kid anymore. Work had been good for me.

"I'm Simone," she announced.

I plastered a friendly smile on my face, the kind that never quite reached my eyes. "Hi, I'm Sheryl."

I followed her into her office, where she sat down at a large desk and stared at me. "So, you just turned eighteen?" she finally asked after confirming with LAYN. I didn't have ID, so I was in a unique situation. I explained to her what had happened at my work a few days earlier.

"So you have a job already?"

"Yes, ma'am," I told her. "I'm hoping to save up to get an apartment, now that I'm old enough to sign a lease."

"Hmm," she said, folding her hands together and staring at me.

I waited.

"We take eighty percent of your check every week and keep it in the bank until you leave."

I nodded. "Okay," I told her. I would agree to any terms she demanded of me, as long as I had a place to stay. I wanted to keep my job, and I knew I couldn't do it from the streets. I got back to Hollywood after midnight most nights. Where else could I sleep?

"Alright. We'll need your boss to fill out-"

"No," I said suddenly. "I don't want anyone to know that I'm homeless."

Simone stared at me for a long time before speaking again. "We require that you get these filled out."

I chewed down hard on my lower lip. This wasn't going well. "Does it have to be my boss? There's one girl there who knows that I'm in a shelter." Daisy.

She pondered my suggestion. "What's her position?"

"She's in training to be a supervisor."

"I see." She continued staring at me, her hands absently straightening the paperwork in front of her. "Tell me what your schedule usually looks like."

"Oh. Um, I usually work afternoons to close, although I'm hoping they'll let me try mornings when summer comes," I told her. I paused. "I work 4 until 11 or

322

11:30, depending on how fast we can get the store organized. Usually we get finished faster on weeknights." I stared at her hands as they held a stack of papers in their grips.

"And you take the bus?"

"Yes. The 420 usually passes by every hour at night, so we try hard to make it down the hill on time. It gets cold waiting for the bus." The wind at that intersection was incredible late at night. I shivered, thinking of the times that I'd sat for almost an hour waiting for a bus after mine had been missed.

Simone nodded. "Alright, then. Let's bring you in and let you meet your roommates." She stood, so I mimicked her and followed her through another set of doors, leading to a U-shaped dayroom with large glass windows. There were numerous teens relaxing around both sides of the room, some playing cards, others doing hair, and still others just watching tv. This would be my new home. I trained my eyes on each face, figuring out who I knew and sizing up the ones that I didn't.

"This is Jasmine," Simone said, introducing me to a dark-skinned girl who was braiding another girl's hair. "She'll be one of your roommates."

Jasmine looked up at me. "Christina's not coming back?" she asked Simone.

Simone shook her head. "Bed's been reassigned."

I feigned a smile. This was already starting off wrong. I was taking someone's spot. I'd heard for the past year that people would lose their spots and have to wait for another person to leave. There just wasn't enough space when there were less beds available. Shelter space for minors was more plentiful. Everyone wanted to help broken teens. Until they became adults.

"Hi," I offered.

"Hey, mon," Jasmine said. Interesting, I thought. Her accent reminded me of something I'd heard on tv. Later, I would learn that she was from Jamaica, and that she had a propensity to curse in the mornings. She was not a morning person.

Rachel came up to us. "Sheryl!" she said excitedly. "You're here!" A few other heads popped up. People who I recognized from LAYN.

Simone stood quietly, watching. "Are you working tonight?" Rachel asked me.

"No, I took a few days off. I go back tomorrow."

"How was your sister?" Rachel knew that Melinda had come to visit.

"Great. It was good to see her."

Simone nodded and walked away, the sound of a large cache of keys clicking together as she made her way back to her office.

I followed Rachel to the other side of the dayroom, and we sat down near Michelle. Michelle looked exhausted and was dozing against one of the chairs. "What are you up to today?" Rachel asked.

I shrugged. "Getting settled in, then I guess same old routine."

Rachel smiled. "I have to work in a few hours, but we can go get coffee," she offered.

"Oh," I said. "They don't let you leave the first day that you come here," I reminded her.

Rachel nodded. Right. That's why I'd asked off from work. "Alright. I'll get coffee and bring you one?" she asked.

I smiled back. "Sure," I told her. I perched myself in a smaller chair meant for one and waited for her to return, or at least, for Michelle to wake up.

Life at the Covenant House was simple enough. I woke up in the morning to Jasmine's angry groaning that morning had arrived, then waited my turn for the shower. There were four girls per dorm room, and we shared one bathroom. Bedrooms were small and housed two side-by-side bunk beds. I'd won top bunk because I was new.

Breakfast was in an actual cafeteria. A serving line reminiscent of grade school had been set up, and we asked for each item they placed on our trays. The women behind the counter wore hairnets and fake smiled as much as I did.

We sat down in a small dining area, mingling with the rest of the youth. There were at least thirty kids here, and there was a separate building around back for kids who rented tiny apartments from the program. The Covenant House and the Way-In were the only two programs in Hollywood that offered transitional housing back then, and there was always a waiting list comprised of kids who were desperate for something better.

Lunch and dinner were also held in the same location. Since I was leaving for work early each day, they prepared a sack lunch for me and the other kids with jobs to take to work. I took my sack each day and felt at ease. Life was finally steady.

Each week, I begrudgingly gave them most of my paycheck and pocketed my remaining twenty to forty dollars. It was reassuring to know it was being saved, but I didn't like it. In fact, there were a lot of things I didn't like about the program.

One afternoon, shortly after my birthday, I sat down in the dayroom and stared at my W-2s from the previous year. They'd all been mailed to LAYN's drop in shelter, the place where I'd been receiving my mail for the past year. I was confused, trying to figure out how to complete them. I knew my dad always did his own taxes, and I didn't want to pay someone to do them for me. I was an adult now, so I needed to learn.

I struggled through the math and couldn't figure out what I was doing wrong. Frustrated, I called my dad.

"Hi," I said quietly. We hadn't spoken for a while.

"What do you want?" he asked. He'd made it clear that he expected me to have a reason for every call. I'd called sometimes just to hear his voice, other times to ask for addresses and phone numbers of family members. Just to check in. To pretend that we were normal.

"Oh. I'm trying to do my taxes, and I have a question."

Quiet for a moment, then, "Okay. Sign the bottom of the form and mail them to me with your W-2."

"Wait, why?" I asked.

"I need the deduction," he explained.

"But I haven't been living with you," I told him. I'd left in February of the previous year.

"I'll get a bigger refund than you."

I bit my lip. This wasn't helping. "But then I'll be an out of state college student in the fall," I said, my tone growing angry. "Are you going to use your bigger refund to pay for my fees?" I'd started to imagine a future for myself, including enrolling in community college in the fall.

"No," he told me.

I hung up the phone, not willing to talk to him anymore. If I ever needed a reminder of why I'd left, I just needed to pick up the phone and call him for a few minutes. As I stared at the phone, I wondered if my dad was still paying premiums on the life insurance policy he'd taken out on me when I'd left for California. He'd made an offhand comment once about "recouping his investment" in me, in case something happened to me.

85
FIRST APARTMENT

When Rachel offered to split the cost of an apartment with me, I jumped at the chance. The staff gave me a hard time every night when I returned, asking if I was really at work. I wasn't allowed to sleep in, and I had to wake up at the same time as everyone else, even if I returned late from work. It didn't take long for me to feel like I was running on empty, for a prize I wasn't sure I would obtain.

But Rachel found a place. She hadn't told the shelter that she got a monthly benefit check from her deceased father, so she had money available while all our work money was tied up in the Covenant House bank accounts.

We were both eighteen, and I had just finished high school. We found a small single furnished apartment in Van Nuys, across from the local community college, Los Angeles Valley College. We eagerly packed up our stuff and checked our money out of the Covenant House bank, hastily signing our first lease.

I walked out of Covenant House less than a month after I'd first moved in, and I vowed to never return.

We both worked five days a week at Universal. Sometimes we left together, and sometimes one of us had an early shift when the other had a late shift. The apartment had one of those fold-up queen size beds that you can push up against the wall and close a small closet around it. There was also a sofa and a small table with four chairs. Our one room had a small living space but contained a functional kitchen. The closet was large, and the bathroom was perfect. It had a bathtub and shower combo, something both of us had missed desperately. All in all, it was a perfect first apartment for two girls escaping the streets.

We went to My Friend's Place in Hollywood to ask for independent living supplies. We'd heard that they offered stuff for people who got their first apartment, and we were thrilled to find out that they had blankets, sheets, towels, kitchen supplies, and even canned foods for us. I hadn't calculated how much it really cost to be on our own, and each bill that got mailed to us reminded me that we needed more than we had.

I finally emptied my storage, and all the belongings that I'd collected over the past year filled my closet. I had stockpiled clothes, shoes, blankets, and a cheap coffee pot.

A calendar went up on the fridge, and we labeled our pay days and each bill that was owed. Rent was four hundred sixty dollars. We only had to pay electricity and gas, since water and sewage were included in the rent. Groceries and an occasional taxi ride back from the grocery store cut into our budget.

I went to work early one morning and began filling out applications for a second job. Later that week, I started working at the smoothie shop in the middle of Citywalk, Surf City Squeeze. Between two jobs, I figured I'd have enough money to start breaking even.

The same security guards that had harassed me earlier about being a minor started to be nicer to me once I was an adult. I wandered between both jobs, wondering what I would do next. It was summer, and most of my coworkers at both jobs were college students.

Would I study for a security position? The security guards told me it paid well. Would I study for management? I could try to move up at DAPY. Would I do something else, and study business? I wasn't sure.

Once I had a second job, DAPY offered me the early hours, as one of their stock people. I shifted my schedule with the smoothie shop and started working as a stock girl, counting and organizing shipments with the stock manager. The two of us would sit behind the store, facing the fence for the Waterworld show at Universal while we worked. We listened to the show in English, Spanish, Japanese, Mandarin, and any other language that it was projected in while we worked.

I realized quickly I was still good with numbers. I memorized most of the important SKU numbers and organized the merchandise inside the store. My manager Jayson kept complimenting me, and I was hoping that I could get a promotion like Daisy had.

What I didn't realize was that Rachel was dating a guy. I was working so much I hadn't paid attention. One night, when I was exhausted and sweaty from working stock all day, I returned home to find her hanging out with her boyfriend in our apartment. "He needs to go home," I told her. We had one room. There was no space for an overnight guest.

We hadn't planned ahead.

A big fight broke out, and at the beginning of the next month, I learned that Rachel had arranged to move into the apartment next door. She took all her things and left.

I was stuck paying the whole rent on my own. I'd expected to pay half, and now I was due for the whole amount.

"Damnit," I muttered to myself as I surveyed the half empty place.

Rachel stopped by. "My boyfriend moved in with me," she told me. "Don't worry, you can afford it. You have two jobs."

I rolled my eyes. Right. She didn't have to worry, she got over five hundred a month from her dad's veteran benefits. She'd always had more, and she only worked one job. I hated the unfairness of it all.

After I recalculated the math, I decided I would have to cut corners to be able to afford college in the fall. I'd been trying to save enough for tuition and books. I wouldn't be able to buy any textbooks at this rate.

86
COLLEGE

Summer screeched to a halt, and it was time for me to figure it out, on my own.

I enrolled in business classes, deciding to take a chance on getting promoted at my job. I was nervous, since this would be my first time setting foot in a real classroom in over a year and a half.

My boss allowed me to change my work schedule, since summer was ending and tourism died down in the fall. The smoothie shop didn't need help during the slow season, so I had to let go of that job. I was suddenly down to one job, with no roommate. I decided I would just have to make it work.

When I was off, I was alone. The little part of me that had started to trust people again had been shut down after Rachel had moved out. One night, I was hungry and tired of being alone, so I took the bus back to Hollywood. I hadn't been buying much food, since I had to save up for textbooks. My staple meal had become ramen mixed with either canned vegetables or a slice of cheese.

I stopped by My Friend's Place to pick up bus tokens, and they gave me a pack. Too easy, I thought. I wandered down the Boulevard, selling each one for a dollar. My new work bus pass was forty-two per month, so I figured if I started coming back to Hollywood every week, I could fund my bus pass on token money.

What I hadn't expected was that I would end up at Burger Factory. A familiar place, with my familiar corner table. I wandered in and asked for a cup of coffee.

Byron was at the counter. He looked me over carefully and didn't charge me.

When I sat down, I faced him instead of the Boulevard. I watched him for a while, wondering why I'd broken things off with him. He had always been nicer to me than I'd deserved.

Business was slow, so he came to sit across from me. "How have you been?" he asked.

I shrugged. "Tired. I'm working a lot."

"Still at DAPY?" he asked.

I nodded. He smiled at me, an easy smile.

"I'm starting college next week," I told him. I'd enrolled in an Introduction to Business class, an Introduction to Marketing, and a few other courses. Anything that sounded good and was listed on the Business pathway. My boss was impressed, but still hadn't offered a promotion.

"That's really good," Byron said.

I ended up sitting at the corner table until he finished his shift, and then he drove me home. I took him up to see my apartment, and he liked it. He told me that he was happy for me. I was fragile, and he knew me well. I invited him to stay.

We started dating, but only once every week or so. We both worked too much, and school was starting. I fumbled through my first week of classes with no books, calculating how much each used book would cost and trying to figure out when I could buy each one.

I didn't qualify for financial aid as an independent student, because I'd never gone back to foster care. Homelessness didn't count as being in the system, so apparently, I had sabotaged my choices. It cost thirteen dollars per unit, and I was enrolled in twelve units. I wouldn't be able to buy my books for a few more paychecks.

I was a month into my semester when I woke up feeling sick. I tried to remember what I'd eaten the previous day, but I couldn't recall anything unusual. Maybe I was drinking too much coffee, I told myself.

I stumbled through my morning classes, skipping the coffee. My marketing group was doing a simulation to see which group would win. "We should advertise," I whispered to them as we huddled our desks together. "People are more likely to buy our product if they know about it." My stomach lurched, but I ignored it.

"No, we should invest in research," said one of my partners.

"Let's spend all our money on both," I told them. "Look at it this way, you have to spend money to make money."

We calculated a percentage of money to put into both research and design as well as advertising. The class was simulating different companies, trying to compete to sell fictitious shoes. The winning group would get extra credit and would surely get easy As in the class.

One of our group members carried our expenses sheet to the professor and folded it before handing it in. Our spending was secret. We wanted to win.

I smiled, but then felt my stomach lurch again. I needed to check the expiration date on everything in my fridge, I thought to myself. I had always gotten sick easily, and I wouldn't have been surprised if my milk had spoiled.

When we stood up to leave class for the day, it hit me. A wave of extreme nausea. I excused myself from my group and darted through the bungalows to the nearest bathroom, where I lost my breakfast.

Mornings became predictable. I started waking up nauseous every day, and I knew. I just knew. I finally took the bus up to Van Nuys Boulevard one morning when I had a few hours to spare. I went to one of the clinics that advertised free pregnancy tests.

I walked in nervously, then filled out the paperwork. When they called me back to tell me my results, I bit my lip with nervous anticipation. Pregnant.

They explained to me how to apply for Medi-Cal, and I listened while my head began to spin. I couldn't do this again. I couldn't lose another baby. I wasn't strong enough.

I hadn't started birth control after the Depo had worn off. I hadn't thought ahead.

The words of Roger, my high school teacher in Hollywood, rang through my memory. "If you're having sex without a condom, especially during your fertile time," he'd said, pointing to a calendar that he'd marked and was using to teach a co-ed group of us about avoiding teen pregnancy, "then you're asking to get pregnant. So don't come in here and tell us you're surprised that you got pregnant."

Pregnant. Damn.

I would need insurance to see a doctor.

I would want to see a doctor.

"When is my due date?" I asked nervously.

"June 15."

I thanked them and hurried back to the bus, my mind spinning.

87
PREGNANT, AGAIN

Byron was sitting in the driver's seat, taking me to eat somewhere. I waited for the right moment. He'd always been kind to me. I'd never met someone who was this nice, this decent.

"I have to tell you something," I said.

"Me too," he told me.

He pulled over the car.

"You first," I offered. I was still trying to figure out how to tell him.

"My dad was in an accident," he told me, facing me. "I have to go back to Guatemala to help him." I nodded slowly. He was leaving.

"I won't be able to come back. I don't have papers."

Bile rose in my throat. It was happening again. I would be alone.

"Oh," I said.

"What did you have to tell me?"

I chewed down on my lip. I could tell him, and he would stay. But his father needed him. I could not tell him, and he would go. And that felt worse. "Nothing," I said quietly. "It was nothing. I'm sorry about your dad."

He dropped me off afterwards, and I didn't invite him inside. I needed a clean break. If he was leaving, then he needed to leave.

I watched from my window as his car backed out of the parking lot. The tears were already flowing. I was destined to be a single mom, I thought bitterly.

The month passed slowly. I awoke each morning, feeling nauseous. I went to work and confided in my boss, and they pulled me off stock duty.

I calculated what I owed and realized I wouldn't be able to keep the apartment. We'd signed a six-month lease back in May. I went downstairs and talked to the landlord, explaining I would be moving out on December first.

I scraped through the month, spending as little as possible on food and other expenses. I had finally bought my last textbook in October, for my marketing class. When the professor commented on how shiny and clean my book was, I confessed I'd just bought it because I'd been saving all semester.

He looked at me sadly and shook his head. "Sheryl, you should have come to me. I have two extra copies in my office." I'd been reading the reserve copies in the library all semester. If only I'd known. I agreed with him that I would speak up if it happened again.

I started a routine of waking up each morning, vomiting, then going to class. After class, I usually went to work. On days that I wasn't scheduled to work, I went to Hollywood and got a free meal. I would be back at Covenant House the following month, I thought bitterly. I might as well get used to going to services again.

88
BACK IN THE SHELTER

At the end of November, I re-rented a storage unit in Hollywood. I asked a classmate to help me move my belongings after class one day. I was planning to skip classes the following morning to get back into the shelter.

I hadn't accumulated too much, since I'd been in a furnished apartment. I had dishes and sheets, and all the other items I'd kept after Rachel had moved out. A cheap coffee pot, my television. Stuff that could be replaced, but other things that couldn't. A heavy feeling settled over me as I slept for my last night in my empty apartment.

"I need the money," I told myself.

When I gave the manager the keys, I glanced up at the second floor. Rachel was standing there, staring at me. She had a strange look on her face. We hadn't spoken since we'd had an argument after she had moved out. I shrugged and got into the front seat of a coworker's car. They had stopped by to give me a ride back to Covenant House.

Rachel and I hadn't ever really been friends anyway, I told myself as I drove away. We'd just been two lost teens, holding on until there was nothing left to tie us together.

The Covenant House hadn't changed much. Most of the same kids were staying there. I was back in Jasmine's room, with a new girl from Vietnam. Her name was Diana.

We sat up late at night, sharing stories. Diana's journey to the U.S. had been tragic. Her father had invited her to come join him here, and she'd agreed. She'd always wanted to know more about her father, and she'd been living in poverty with her mom. Eager for family, she'd come to Los Angeles.

Her father was religious, after all. He had to be peaceful, kind.

When she arrived, he took her to dinner at a friend's house. And promptly sold her to that family.

She told her story of how she'd escaped, and how she'd arrived at the shelter. I sat up, staring at her with wide eyes and panic soaring through me. "I'd never let that happen to my child," I said quietly.

Jasmine caught my mistake. "What child?"

Oops. Jasmine had a big mouth. By the end of the next day, everyone knew I was pregnant. My case worker called me into the office and tried to convince me to go to a maternity home.

"I can't," I told her. "I have a job."

"But for how long?" she asked.

"I have to finish my semester. Can I at least finish my classes?"

My case worker reluctantly agreed. I was granted at least another month to figure out a plan. I was in four classes, and working full time, so at least she could see I was trying to do something with my life.

The security officer at the front desk for the Covenant House kept track of what time I arrived every night. Sometimes the bus didn't bring me back until after one in the morning. Exhausted, I accepted rides home from coworkers whenever I could.

One night, I boarded the late bus in front of Universal Studios. I had been getting rides from coworkers lately, and it was the first night I'd needed to take the bus all week. I walked slowly to the back of the bus and sat down.

Immediately, the person from a few rows behind me stood up and moved to my seat. "Where have you been all week?" he asked quietly.

I glanced sideways over at him. I'd never noticed this man before, but he had clearly noticed me. "Do I know you?" I asked, jogging my memory. So much had happened since I'd come back to California.

He smiled. "I'm your stalker."

"What?" I asked, my voice incredulous.

"Yeah. You get off on Western, and I follow you home every night. You live in the red building."

I stared at him for a moment. "No," I told him. "You don't get to be my stalker," I said defiantly. "I'm pregnant, and it's late at night when I get off the bus." I extended my hand to shake his hand. "I'm Sheryl. What is your name?"

"Mauricio."

"Okay, Mauricio," I said as he put his clammy hand into mine. He was bigger than me, stronger. "You will walk me home every night. No more following me in the shadows."

He stared back at me, his mouth open in surprise. "Okay."

And from that night on, Mauricio accompanied me from the bus stop to Covenant House.

My plan did not involve going to a maternity home. I kept stalling, trying to figure out how to stay at the Covenant House for as long as possible. I was working and trying to save up as much money as I could. But soon, I was drowning. I needed to find another job. I just wasn't making enough, and I couldn't get ahead of the numbers. We were required to deposit eighty percent of our paychecks to our future housing funds.

But I'd screwed up. I'd gotten desperate and taken out a payday loan one day when I was hungry and wanted to buy a meal at work. I couldn't pay it off. I had to pay twenty dollars each week to postpone my payment. That was all I got back from my check. Maybe if I found another job, I could use the first week's paycheck to pay off the debt.

I went to the computer lab to work on a new resume. I was tired. But I could squeeze more hours into the day. Thinking back to the previous summer, I remembered I'd been able to work two jobs. I could find a second job, since I'd finished my semester at college finally. I'd even managed to get three As and 1 B.

"Good morning," I heard the instructor saying. They offered classes on resume writing, but I didn't have time for one of those classes.

"Hi," I said, rushing past her to sit at a free computer.

She tsked loudly. "No, you have to go to a workshop first."

I looked up. "But I just need five minutes to make a resume," I pleaded. I glanced up at the clock. I needed to catch the next bus to get up to CityWalk early. I wanted to apply for a nearby job before my afternoon shift.

She groaned loudly. "Everyone does a workshop first."

"But I have to go to work," I told her forcefully.

I saw heads starting to turn. We were making a scene.

"It doesn't matter," she said.

"Damn it," I muttered, standing up quickly. I shoved the chair back into place, tucked neatly in front of the computer screen.

I heard her pick up the phone off the receiver on the wall as I slammed the door behind me.

The computer lab was on the opposite side of Western Avenue from the shelter. I looked both ways, then rushed across the busy road. I was furious. How was I supposed to look for another job now?

My case manager was waiting for me at the security desk. "We need to talk," she told me.

My senses were on high alert. It's never a good sign when someone says we-need-to-talk.

I followed her into her office and sat down. She shook her head, anger radiating from her as she watched me from behind her desk.

"You can't stay here anymore," she said.

My mouth twisted in anger. "What?" I demanded. "For what reason?"

"You need to go to a maternity shelter."

I shook my head. No, I needed to go to work. I listened as she reviewed my options. Well, her options for me, but the options that I was willing to accept.

"Fine. I want my money," I said.

"Do you want me to call the shelter for you?"

Our eyes met. I was trying my hardest to stay strong, to not cry. I bit down hard on my lower lip. "No," I told her. "I need to go to work."

The security officer accompanied me upstairs to collect my belongings. A trash bag full of clothes, a handful of toiletries, a well-worn backpack. It was far too easy to throw my life into a bag and move on. I accepted a taxi voucher to drop off all my stuff at storage, but I had no money. The check would be ready next week, I had been told.

89
NOWHERE TO GO

My spirit was crushed that day. I had managed to throw all my junk back into the storage locker and make it on time to work. The journey from storage to work was too short; I didn't have enough time to come up with an answer to the question that plagued me: Where would I stay that night?

The world had shifted. I was eighteen now, and I'd been kicked out of yet another shelter. And I was four months pregnant. I'd been working at my job now for almost a year, and I'd come so close to independence.

"Hi, Sheryl," Daisy called to me when I walked up to the store. She was working the entrance, holding that damned bubble gun.

"Hey," I replied quickly. I didn't feel like working tonight. I needed a plan. I rushed to the back and threw my backpack onto the floor, by the lockers.

When I emerged out of the break room, I saw that the room was crowded with tourists. I didn't have the strength to muster a fake smile for them. I wouldn't be able to do this.

I clocked in and looked at the schedule. I was on the register for most of the shift. That wouldn't work.

My manager Farah passed by. She was young, hot-headed, and trying to prove herself to everyone. She didn't let us pick our schedules.

"I need to work the door tonight," I told her.

No one ever volunteered for bubble duty.

Farah paused, perhaps seeing my tear stained eyes and the frailty I had tried to hide with my false bravado. I watched as she glanced at the schedule and maneuvered it so that I could demo the bubble guns.

I relieved Daisy, who was thrilled to get away from the entryway. I took the cup of bubble soap and began blowing the best damned bubbles that I'd ever blown. I wouldn't have even cared if another batch of drunk tourists decided to comment on my blowing skills that night.

A few hours into my shift of mindless bubble blowing, the tears started to fall. The sky was getting darker. My world was unsteady. I didn't like unsteady.

And then, it happened.

A moment that reminded me that I was not alone.

The girl from the coffee cart saw me. She'd been working across the sidewalk from me for months. We'd never spoken. We had sometimes waved casually. But I didn't even know her name. She saw my tears and left her coffee cart.

She crossed the short distance to where I stood, and wrapped a gentle arm around my shoulder.

"What's wrong?" she whispered. I read her name tag. Martha.

I didn't dare wipe my eyes; I'd made that mistake earlier. My hands were drenched in soap suds and I was still waving the bubble gun at the sky with my free arm.

"I don't know where I'm going to stay tonight," I told her honestly.

She didn't ask for details. She squeezed hard and promised that she'd come back.

"Bubbles!" little kids screeched, and I watched helplessly as they followed my trail of tear stained spheres that blew into the wind. Past the ice cream shop, past the art gallery. Almost to the little boutique down the way.

Martha came back, and she had two guys with her. The coffee shop guys.

"I'm Mario," the tall, skinny one said. He had always been kind to me when I had bought coffee. Although, I hadn't bought any for the past few months.

"Hey, I'm Jose," the other one said. He was shorter, pudgier. Always smiling.

Mario stepped forward. "You can stay with me," he offered. "I have an apartment."

I looked at each of their faces, trying to figure out if this was real. If this was safe. If I really didn't have to sleep on a city bus tonight.

"What?" I asked. My voice was hollow. Broken. "Why?"

Mario shrugged, his skinny frame pulling upwards with the sudden motion. "Because you need a place to stay," he said. As if that was all it took. As if it was that easy to save somebody.

I found myself nodding. What did I have to lose? I wondered.

90
MARIO

When I got out of work, I sat down on the bench near the coffee shop. The outdoor coffee bar had been cleaned and shut down much earlier. I could see the employees tidying up inside of the expansive bookstore, and Mario was working quickly to clean up the café.

I watched in hopeful silence as the lights turned off, and the employees came outside. They were ready to go home.

Home. It was a word that ached in my mind.

Mario walked directly towards me. "Are you ready?"

I nodded, trying hard not to shatter into a million pieces. Was this safe? And more importantly, did I care? I was out of options.

We walked as a group down to the tram, which took us down the hill. The bus stop was around the corner. I followed their lead, and we walked towards the northbound bus.

This was different. I usually took the southward bus. I wondered where he lived.

We rode along the familiar bus line. We passed the college, passed the road I used to walk down towards my old apartment. Passed the familiar spaces I had come to know when I'd briefly lived in the Valley. His friends had gotten off already.

We turned onto Van Nuys Boulevard. I watched for clues about where we were going.

He pulled the cord to signal for a stop. Sherman Way.

He stood, and so did I.

We exited the bus. I was too nervous to speak.

He smiled, a big goofy smile. "It's okay," he told me.

I smiled back. Tentatively. "Okay."

We walked down the block to a large white building. Three stories tall, filled with apartments. This would be my shelter for the night.

We took the rickety elevator up to the third floor. "Ay, don't look so scared," he told me. "I'm a nice guy. All I do is work and sleep." He paused. "Well, and smoke weed."

I nodded. Honesty. It was refreshing. He seemed safe enough.

I'd resigned myself into whatever fate awaited me.

"I have a roommate," he was telling me, as he unlocked the door to his apartment.

I nodded. Interesting. I hoped his roommate wouldn't be upset that he was bringing a random chronically homeless girl home with him.

When we entered the apartment, I felt relief wash over me. It was such a normal place. Kitchen, off to the side. Clean. Living room, with sofa and entertainment center. Hallway to the right, leading to a bedroom and bathroom.

"I usually sleep in the living room," he told me as I toured the place. "But I can stay in Sergio's room tonight if it makes you feel safer."

I nodded. "Okay," I told him.

He brought me a stack of sheets and a pillow and prepared the sofa for me.

"Okay, well, good night," he told me. He disappeared to the small bedroom.

"Mario," I said sheepishly. He turned and looked at me. It was a rare gift to have a safe, warm bed. No strings attached. "Thank you."

Morning came, and I could smell eggs cooking. The familiar wave of nausea hit me all at once. I sat up abruptly and glanced towards the kitchen. There was a guy there, wearing a beanie. Also Hispanic. He locked eyes with me for a moment.

My stomach lurched. Nope. No time for a conversation.

"Excuse me," I said, and rushed to the bathroom.

I retched until I was liberated from all my stomach acids. Crap. I hadn't mentioned the baby. I looked at my face in the mirror. Pasty cheeks. Tears trickling from the sides of my eyes. I couldn't help it; every time I vomited, I involuntarily cried. It was like I was losing yet another piece of me each time that I hugged the toilet.

I rinsed my mouth, ran water over my face. Pushed my fingers through my hair. I could do this.

I smoothed the wrinkles from my shirt and opened the door. I saw both Mario and the other guy standing in the kitchen, chatting in Spanish. Waiting for me.

"We made you breakfast," Mario was saying.

I nodded. Eggs. "Thanks," I said automatically. I could probably handle eggs, now that I'd already vomited my morning bile.

"I'm Sergio," the guy with the beanie said. He was a little older, had a chiseled face and broad smile.

"Sheryl," I told him.

I looked around for a moment, not sure what to do next. I noticed they didn't have a dining room table, but they did have a large glass coffee table. Right. They ate at the sofa.

Quickly, I made my way back to the sofa and folded the sheets. I tucked them into a nice pile near my backpack.

The boys brought plates to the table; eggs, tortillas, salsa. I smelled coffee brewing in the kitchen.

"Are you feeling okay?" Mario asked once we'd all sat down.

I faked a smile. "Yeah. I just get sick in the mornings."

Sergio glanced at me closely. "How far along are you?"

"Four months," I confided.

The boys both stared at me for a moment, and something silent passed between us. Not only was I homeless, alone, and kicked out of the only shelter where I could stay; I was also pregnant. And I had to be back at work in a few hours.

"What are you planning to do?" Sergio asked.

I shrugged. "I don't know. I was thinking about buying a cheap car to live in."

"No, that's not what I meant," Sergio shook his head. "What are you going to do about the baby?"

I sighed heavily, still staring at the offending eggs on my plate. "I guess I'll work as long as I can. I'll figure it out."

Mario reached for a bottle of hot sauce that had been sitting on the table and began dousing his eggs in bright red liquid. I watched, trying to imagine a time when I could eat spicy food. He took a few bites before speaking again.

"You can stay here," he told me. "We'll rent our sofa to you. One hundred dollars a month."

I looked at both of their faces. One hundred dollars? Were they serious?

That little buried part of me that wanted to be hopeful rose up. I could save money for the baby. The money that was waiting for me at the Covenant House was already at least eight hundred dollars.

I smiled timidly. "Yes. Thank you."

We finished our breakfast, like a newly formed family. And then, Mario and I got ready to go to work.

Riding the bus with a new friend was like seeing the world differently. Mario was funny; always making jokes and his sarcastic humor resonated with me. It was like finding a new brother in my darkest hour. Somebody who was willing to stand up and fight alongside me.

On days we both worked, I would wait for him to get off work and ride the bus with him. It was nice to not have to ride the southbound bus with my "stalker" anymore.

One night, we stopped with a few of his coworkers at the taco shop near our apartment. We had started going there a few nights a week for a late-night snack. As it turned out, that was the time of day when I was able to eat without throwing up. I'd become fond of tacos and big cups of horchata.

We sat down with our tacos, and I watched as the boys tossed countless salsas and hot sauces on their food. I couldn't eat like them; my stomach was far too sensitive.

Mario had a habit of shouting out funny phrases. We were all laughing when he called out, "*La Migra!*" It was a feared phrase in our parts; immigration raids were not uncommon.

I stared at him as he continued to eat. "That's not nice," I told him.

Everyone stopped eating and stared at me.

"Why?" he asked. He had that goofy teenager look on his face, ready to be scolded.

I pointed to the nearby tables. Food was scattered; tacos left uneaten. "Everyone left when you said that."

"What did I say?" he asked.

"When you said *La Migra*."

The boys roared in laughter. "Oops," he said, but he kept chuckling. I shook my head, knowing by then that if *la migra* came, they would take him, too. I'd been learning from him what it meant to be undocumented, living in the United States. He had shared many stories with me, and he was burdened by his lack of papers. I was beginning to understand the choice Byron had been forced to make.

We walked home and every few minutes, he repeated softly, "*La Migra!*" and we both laughed. I guess I couldn't stay mad at my goofy roommate.

Months passed. I was growing more pregnant, but I had not been able to get insurance due to my income. I sat down with my boss and tried to figure out a way to cut my hours to fit the national poverty guidelines. I needed to make half of what I was making. Half of full-time work at minimum wage. It was either that, or no maternity coverage.

I needed health insurance.

I'd gone a few times, sporadically, to the doctor. The first visit, I'd qualified for presumptive Medi-cal. That's the one they give you when you test positive for pregnancy, and then you are supposed to turn in all your paperwork to the welfare office to get approved. When I'd gone, they'd told me the horrible truth. I was poor, but not poor enough. I'd gotten a second visit, when they'd done an ultrasound and proven to me that this baby had a heartbeat.

I had started going to the Los Angeles Free Clinic for my maternity visits a few months later. I'd messed up. I'd started prenatal care late in the game. I was at least five months pregnant when they'd agreed to see me. They gave me another month of presumptive Medi-cal. But I had to change my income amount, and fast.

How would I feed the baby, if I didn't have a job?

But how could I go to the doctor, if I didn't have insurance?

I wrestled between two opposing problems. Which would I choose? Doctor visits, or work? I'd been throwing up daily and felt unwell most of the time. But I was young and capable of work. Something had to give.

My boss sighed heavily as we crunched the numbers. I watched as he tried to maneuver the schedule to accommodate me as a part time employee. It didn't work. We were about to start the main tourist season.

"I'll have to quit," I told him, seeing that this wouldn't work. I couldn't come up with any other options.

We negotiated my last day, and I finished out my last two weeks at a job I'd grown to love. One year of service. "Maybe I'll come back after the baby," I told him.

"We'd love that," he lied.

I still had so much to learn about the world.

I quit my job without much fanfare, and then went to the welfare office to apply for my Medi-cal. Sure, now I wasn't working. But I still didn't qualify for insurance. I needed 30 days to pass before I could have benefits.

Sergio's cousin had moved in, and word had come to them that his cousin's wife would be crossing the border soon. No one knew whether she would bring their two kids with her. The one-bedroom apartment had filled up quickly, not leaving enough room for me.

When I told Mario and Sergio what I had done, they were upset. They offered no solutions. "If you aren't going to work, you have to look for another place," Sergio commanded. Mario said nothing.

91
MATERNITY HOME

Nothing good ever lasted, I thought bitterly. I gave Mario my apartment key and said goodbye.

I packed up my belongings again and used a taxi voucher to take them back to storage. As it turned out, that storage locker was the only constant in my life. It remained steady, through all the life-altering twists and turns.

In my small backpack were my most important items. Essential clothes. Identification. My copy of What to Expect in the First Year, which I'd been reading voraciously for the past several months. I could learn to be the best mother ever. The baby's ultrasound photo. What a beautiful little boy. I'd stared at that picture through many rain showers of tears. It would be worth it. I could find a way through any minefield because of that little guy.

I took the bus back to the Covenant House. "I'm ready," I told the case manager. "I'll go to the maternity home."

By then, I was six months pregnant. My belly had grown, and June was approaching fast. I needed a plan.

I knew I wanted to work and go to school. I had big dreams, and big dreams required hard work. I had been told young women could work while in maternity homes. I hoped that I could do both.

The home that they found for me was in Long Beach. The program was expecting me. I boarded the train and began the two-and-a-half-hour journey to a place I'd never been to before. A place that would help me figure it out.

I arrived at a modest two-story house. Well-manicured grass. No children's toys on the lawn. I peeked into the backyard. Not much back there, either.

I rang the bell. Waited.

A woman answered the door. She was older, and had a stern look on her face. "Are you Sheryl?" she asked.

I nodded. Uncertainty washed over me. This was a mistake.

"Did you get lost?"

I shook my head. It had been a long ride.

"You're late," she told me in an accusatory tone.

Unease filled me. I had taken two buses and a long train ride. I was exhausted, and starving. "I came straight here," I defended myself.

"Come, we're having dinner."

I followed her to a dining room, replete with several young pregnant women and girls with their babies. There were high chairs seated alongside the young moms, and the babies were in various stages of their meals.

"Everyone, this is Sheryl," the woman announced.

"Hi," I said to the group. A chorus of hellos followed.

I sat down at the only empty seat. They really had been waiting for me, it seemed. Food bowls were passed in my direction, and I gratefully filled my plate with homemade macaroni and cheese, mashed potatoes, and veggies. A full meal.

I ate everything. I could feel the baby awaken and start fluttering around. I'd forgotten what it had felt like to be full.

Most of my money from the past few months had been divided on food, rent, and my monthly bus pass. I hadn't been able to save much, because eating out was expensive. I'd spent too much money on meals during and after work. But I never ate enough. I never had a full meal. I snacked on dollar items and pretended that it was enough.

A brunette sat next to me, her belly full with child. She introduced herself as Charlotte. "Each girl has to cook the meal once a week. This was my night," she told me.

"Everyone does chores here," she continued. "The dishes need to be washed after each meal, trash needs to be taken out. We clean our rooms. We clean the bathrooms. Everyone does their part."

I nodded. I had expected that.

The matron, who I'd discovered was named Beverly, spoke up. "We have Bible study every evening, and we pray before every meal."

I bit my lip. I'd been very far from God. For a long time. I was not ready for Bible study.

"No one will force you to pray, but you have to attend," she said, answering my unspoken question.

We cleaned the table, and I was assigned dish duty. I helped clean the dishes, and then we all went upstairs for Bible study.

I sat in the back, not really listening. My mind was spinning. I wasn't sure this would work.

Afterwards, Beverly sat down to explain the rest of the program to me. "Some of the girls work, and some go to school."

"I want to do both," I told her. I'd gotten mostly As in my first semester of college, while working full time. I knew I could handle the work.

"That would be very hard," she told me. "You can't leave before 8am, and you have to return by 5pm every day."

I stared at her. "Why?" I asked.

"You can't work more than part time here. Everyone gets their WIC check and contributes to the food supply. Everyone contributes part of their welfare check to their cost of rent."

I shook my head. Something didn't add up.

"But then, how can I ever leave?" I asked. I would have no way to save money. No way to get ahead. No way to get my education.

The woman chuckled softly. I must've been a foolish child in her eyes. "Some of the girls graduate to our apartment program next door, and then they have more flexibility for their schedules."

I glanced out the window at the adjacent apartment. I couldn't stay here. Sure, it offered full meals and a roof over my head. But if I left once the baby was here, they would call CPS in a heartbeat. I couldn't stay. I needed to find another way.

I couldn't not go to school. I couldn't not work. I needed to move forward. This was a step in the wrong direction.

"I can't accept that," I told her.

"Then why did you come here?"

"I didn't know that you wouldn't let me work and go to school. How can anyone ever leave, if those are your rules?"

She sighed heavily. "We want you to stay."

Yes, she did, I thought to myself. She wanted my WIC check and my welfare check. She wanted me to be stuck; no other option except her program.

I was excused to go to my room. I sat down on my bed and felt a heaviness in my heart. What else could I do? What would be best for the baby?

I shouldn't have quit my job.

I shouldn't have left Mario's apartment.

I should've saved my money.

I shouldn't be six months pregnant with a fatherless child.

Another girl came and sat down next to me. She was meant to be my roommate. Veronica. "You should stay, Sheryl," she told me.

Great, they'd sent someone to tell me to stay. I shook my head.

"They've been very good to us," she said. "It's a good program, and they help us with our babies."

She handed me a bag of baby clothes. I hadn't even noticed that she'd been holding it. "They have presents for you, for your baby."

I opened the bag. Beautiful blue onesies. Socks. Hats. Blankets. Things I didn't have. Things I would need.

I closed the bag. This gift would have to be for the next pregnant girl.

"I'd like to go to sleep now," I told her. I yawned sadly. I needed my rest; who knew where I would sleep the next night?

I set the bag down on the floor and laid down on my bed. I did not unpack my backpack. I was not planning to stay.

When I awoke the next morning, my roommate had already gone downstairs. I stood up slowly, taking in my surroundings. She had stacks of baby items on her side of the room. She was ready for motherhood.

But this place was not for me. I needed something more. I couldn't quite define it, but this was not where I would have my child.

I changed and repacked my backpack. I glanced at the bag of baby clothes, thinking how much I wanted them. Instead, I left the overflowing bag beside the bed.

I walked downstairs, my backpack heavy on my shoulders. My life, in one bag.

They were all sitting down for breakfast. The girls were talking about their plans for the day. A baby next to my empty chair was blowing bubbles.

"I'm going to go," I told them, my voice high pitched.

The matron shook her head dramatically. "Not yet," she said. "Sit down, eat some breakfast. Nobody's kicking you out, so you really need to sit down and eat."

I stared at the table. Happy girls, cute babies. Trapped girls. Girls who were willing to accept years of waiting for an imagined future.

Eggs. Bacon. Toast.

My stomach rolled. "I can't eat in the mornings," I told her. I hadn't thrown up yet. The longest days were always the ones when I didn't vomit as soon as I rolled out of bed. This would be a long, queasy day.

I headed towards the door, but Veronica told me to wait. She went upstairs quickly and came back with the bag of clothes.

Beverly stood behind her. They both smiled sweetly. "These are a present. You can take them, even if you don't stay," Beverly said.

"We love you and your baby," Veronica told me.

I accepted the bag, discomfort washing over me. "Thank you," I told them, and then I walked out the door. And left.

92
MY FRIEND'S PLACE

No matter what, I would get through the next few months. I would wait out the thirty days until I was eligible for welfare. I would find a way. This baby deserved a future I could only guarantee if I was able to work and go to school.

I took the train and two buses back to Hollywood. It was lunchtime by the time I got back to My Friend's Place.

Peanut butter and jelly sandwiches.

I accepted my sandwich, chips, and cup of water. The sandwich tasted heavenly. Something about it screamed of freedom; escape from an impossible situation.

My case manager, Suzie, came to sit down with me.

"How have you been?" she asked.

I'd never been much of a talker. I hadn't been there in months, and I had showed up with a large, pregnant belly. "Okay," I told her. Liar.

"Are you still working up at Citywalk?"

I shifted nervously in my chair. The heavy backpack and sack of baby clothes sat beside me. My plight was obvious. "I had to quit," I told her. "I couldn't get Medi-Cal because I was working."

"What are you planning to do?" she asked me, the expression on her face serious.

"I'm not sure," I told her. "I'll figure it out."

What I liked about Suzie; and all the staff, for that matter, was that she heard me. They heard me. They didn't interject when I was obviously wrong. They let me speak and didn't judge the words that I shared.

"How can I help you?" she asked.

I knew what she meant. Did she want me to go to a maternity home? Probably. Did she want me to apologize for losing the apartment? The stuff they'd given me? I hoped not. The dishes and stuff were in storage anyway.

"I'm not sure," I confessed.

She smiled. "It'll be okay."

I nodded. Yes. It would be okay.

She offered me bus tokens, this time with no goal. I'd finished high school. I'd skipped this semester of college because my life was falling apart. Again. I'd quit my job. But still, ten tokens. I accepted them. She knew I had some big decisions to make.

After I ate, I walked back to storage and put away the baby clothes. I wouldn't need them for a few months but felt an overwhelming sense of relief that I finally had something for my baby. Before I left, I opened the bag and unfolded each of them, holding each piece against my pregnant belly. "This will fit you so perfectly," I spoke softly to my unborn baby as I held a gorgeous blue outfit against my skin. Little socks, with soccer balls and dinosaurs. Beanies. A long gown. Onesies. I liked the soft feel of the fabric.

When I closed everything into my storage locker, my resolve was strengthened. I could do this. I would find a way.

I wandered back down to the boulevard and made my way to Hollywood and Highland. I stopped at the big cement block that was resting there while the metro construction took place. I leaned against it, letting myself pause. In less than forty-eight hours, I'd gone from having a job, living on Mario's sofa, to living in a maternity program, then back to homeless again. I was not adulting well. And it was almost my nineteenth birthday.

I watched as people passed me by. Numerous tourists, mostly with their eyes on the ground to read the stars on the sidewalk. Locals, passing by on their walk to and from work. Had it really been almost two years since I'd returned to Hollywood? Was I really back out on the streets again?

More importantly, where would I sleep that night?

Concern propelled me into action. I stood and walked over the bus stop in front of McDonald's. "Would you like to buy a token for a dollar?" I asked a woman who was standing near me, waiting for the bus. She had a dollar bill in her hand, and the bus was coming. The bus cost a dollar and thirty-five cents, so this was a discount. She glanced at me, and then at the token.

"Is it real?" she asked.

"Of course," I told her. We exchanged the token and dollar bill, and I moved through the crowd.

Thirty minutes later, I'd sold the whole pack of tokens and was up ten dollars. Easy, I thought to myself. As I exchanged my last token, I caught the next bus down to the Way-In.

Dinner time. I rode the bus to Hollywood and Gower. The crossroads of three programs. I walked the half block to the Way In, a program run by the Salvation Army. They offered an evening drop-in program, complete with a home cooked meal and shower time. I hadn't been there for quite a while. I stood in a winding line around the building; some kids recognized me and asked me how I'd been. I smiled nervously, my hand over my growing belly.

"I thought you had an apartment?" one of the kids in line asked.

There were no words to describe the loss of a stable home. The disappointment of screwing it all up again. I shrugged and patted my belly. "Couldn't afford it anymore."

Another girl glanced at me. "When's the baby due?"

"June," I answered, watching the girl's face as she calculated how far along I was.

Over the years, I'd excelled at passing time. I'd spent most of my teenage years passing time, waiting for whatever was coming next. I began going back to the Way-In every night to pass time until they closed, and afterwards I would head back down to McDonald's and sit at a back table for most of the night. It was the era of eight cent hamburgers, and my doctor at the free clinic had told me to start eating meat again. Apparently, I was a very unhealthy vegetarian, and vegetables were rarely on the menu. Probably because the shelters only offered high carb snacks and sandwiches. Whatever the reason, I was back to nibbling slowly on hamburgers.

McDonald's was open all night, and most of the tables filled with the homeless crowd during the longest hours of the night. I sat at my table in the corner, picking relentlessly at the flat hamburger that I'd bought for eight cents. A gimmick, or a promotion, or whatever. I could eat for a week on one or two bus tokens, depending on whether I occasionally splurged on a pack of fries.

93
MICHELLE

My belly was growing, and by the time that I ran into Michelle a few weeks later, I'd finally qualified for welfare. I was suddenly eligible for medical care and a small monthly check. Since then, I had set up weekly appointments at the Free Clinic, and they were trying to catch me up after so many months with no care.

"Hey," I said to her when we saw each other on a bus. We were both riding back from a picnic at a local park, which had hosted an annual event for homeless youth. I was sitting near the back of the bus, across from her.

"Hi," she said. "What've you been up to?"

"Well, I'm pregnant," I said. She laughed. Obviously. I was past seven months by then. My birthday had just passed, and for tradition, I'd spent it at LAYN's drop-in shelter. Three years in a row, I thought morbidly. I really needed to come up with a better plan for my twentieth birthday.

"Where are you staying at?" she asked me.

I shrugged. "McDonald's."

She was staring at me, and I couldn't read her expression. "Come stay with me," she finally said.

"What?"

"I got married to this guy," she said. "And I'm staying with him and his brothers in Burbank."

"Really?" I asked. We hadn't seen each other in a long time.

She didn't really know me that well.

I could think of a million reasons why she shouldn't offer to help me.

"Yeah," she said, still staring at my belly.

Michelle's apartment was a small one bedroom off the main road. The neighborhood was loud, overcrowded, and her husband only spoke Spanish. "You really married him?" I asked.

She shrugged. "Yeah. He's supposed to pay me."

"Oh."

"Who *es theees?*" a heavy-set guy stood in the doorway, glaring at us.

"Hi," I said. "I mean, *Hola.*" To Michelle, "Is that your husband?"

Michelle shook her head. "That's just Charlie, his brother," she said. "Don't be nice to him. He's an asshole."

"Oh," I repeated.

"What the hell, Michelle?" a smaller guy said from the living room. He was shorter than both of us, and he had curly black hair and tan skin. Raul.

Michelle stared at the man that I would later learn was her husband. "This is Sheryl. And she's going to stay with us."

"No," he said.

"You haven't paid me yet," Michelle reminded him. He said something to his brother in Spanish, and the two of them grabbed their keys and walked out.

"Whoa," I said. "I can go. I don't want to cause trouble."

Michelle shook her head. "Don't worry about them."

I sat down on the sofa, exhausted. I'd been walking around for so long, trying to find a place to rest. Drifting off to sleep for a few minutes at a time in McDonald's or at drop-in shelters wasn't enough.

Michelle went to her room to change, so I closed my eyes. Too many thoughts were racing through my mind. I had just gotten my first welfare check, and I was trying to figure out the math. The two hundred and eighty dollars they'd given me wouldn't cover rent anywhere. How was I supposed to find a place with less than two months to go?

The heavy sound of the front door slamming woke me up. "Great, they're back," Michelle said.

Startled, I opened my eyes and looked around. It took me a moment to remember that I'd gone to Michelle's house. Charlie and Raul were standing a few feet away from us, and they looked angry. Another tall guy had joined them. He was wearing a soccer jersey and had an indifferent look on his face. I couldn't tell if he was angry too, or just didn't care.

Raul and Michelle argued for a few minutes. I watched from my seat on the sofa. Eventually, Raul threw his arms up in defeat. "Fine, fine. But not for too long."

"Fine," Michelle said.

Charlie and Raul passed us to go into the bedroom, and the third brother stood next to Michelle for a moment. He looked at her, then me, but didn't say anything. When I asked her about it later, she said he didn't speak English.

"Are you sure I can stay here?" I asked her later that night. She had set up the sofa for me, and she was camping out next to me on the floor. She'd given me her spot.

"Yeah," she told me. "He's an asshole. I don't care what he says."

We alternated between hanging out in Hollywood during the day and relaxing at her place. I went to my weekly prenatal visits, and I found out that Suzie at My Friend's Place had planned a baby shower for me.

The clinic sent me to a car seat safety class, where I was awarded a coupon for a free car seat after sitting through the lesson. I went to my doctor for an ultrasound, just a few days before the baby shower.

Marvel filled my eyes as the fuzzy image of my baby filled the screen. "How big is he?" I asked the doctor. She frowned.

I watched as she ran the probe over my abdomen again, then she turned to look at me. Dread filled me, remembering the concern etched on another doctor's face as she performed my ultrasound when I was seventeen. Finally, she asked me, "Who said you were having a boy?"

Both relieved and startled, I told her about my first ultrasound.

"Have you had your baby shower yet?" she asked me.

I shook my head. "It's next week."

"Good. Because this is not a boy. You are having a baby girl."

A girl.

A girl?

What would I name her?

My sister and brother both had boys. My sister was pregnant with her second boy. There were no girls in the family yet.

A girl.

"Thanks," I told her, watching as she printed out a new ultrasound picture for me. She'd written "It's a girl!" on the picture.

I walked out of clinic and hurried down the street to My Friend's Place.

Suzie was sitting at the desk. "What happened?" she asked. I was never good at hiding my emotions, and I wore the shock of my news across my face.

"It isn't a boy. It's a girl."

"That's great," she told me, watching my face. "Are you okay?"

"Yes. I wanted a girl, I did. But I got a bunch of stuff for a baby boy from the maternity home."

Suzie nodded, understanding my fear. I didn't have anything for a baby girl.

"It's okay. I'll call the ladies and let them know. There's still time," she told me.

94
BABY SHOWER

Michelle was my invited guest, and a group of volunteers from a local church arrived at the drop-in program with presents one morning the following week. We quietly ate cake and played a few baby shower games, and then they gave me several bags of girl clothes and some baby bottles.

There was an unspoken tension in the room, though. I couldn't figure it out. The ladies hurried out of the shelter as soon as the presents were opened.

"Thank you," I told them. Afterwards, I waited to talk to Suzie. She was cleaning up the leftover cake and rearranging the tables for afternoon services.

"Suzie," I said quietly. "Can I ask you something?"

Michelle was organizing the presents and packing them into the empty backpacks that we'd each carried with us. Suzie paused and looked up at me.

"Why were they acting so weird?"

A strange look crossed her face.

"It's nothing," she told me.

I shook my head. "That wasn't nothing. It was spooky. They weren't even really talking to me."

"I shouldn't say," she told me.

"What was it? Was it because I found out I'm having a girl?"

Suzie shook her head slowly. I watched as she carefully chose her words. "They were worried," she told me.

"Why?" I asked. Michelle was listening now, from across the room. I could see her from my peripheral vision, watching.

"Well," Suzie said quietly. "This was their second baby shower. We had one before yours." I stared at her, waiting. "And they were so excited for the baby. They visited the girl in the hospital."

Silence filled the room. No one was cleaning anymore. Everyone except Michelle and I knew the way this story ended. I glanced around, watching the frozen faces of the staff members, hanging on every word that Suzie was telling me.

"And then she killed her baby."

My mouth gaped open in horror. I pointed towards the doorway. "Those women think I'm going to kill my baby?" I asked, my voice high pitched.

"No, it's not that," Suzie said.

"But it is," I said, my hand instinctively connecting with my belly. "This was a mistake. I shouldn't accept any of this."

Michelle put down the backpack, understanding.

"I can't," I said. "They think I'm going to hurt my baby." Tears were forming, and my eyes grew heavy. "I would never."

"We know," Suzie told me. "But you have to understand, this was hard for them."

"It's hard for me, too," I told her. The first tear made its way down my cheek. I swiped it away with the back of my hand defiantly.

"Sheryl, take the stuff. Your baby needs it. Forget what I told you," Suzie said.

I glanced back at the pile of baby clothes, blankets, and our two backpacks. Michelle had started removing everything from the bags, and a lopsided pile was forming on the table.

"You need it," a voice from behind us said. It was one of the other workers. "For the baby. For your baby."

"I don't know," I said, my voice shaky with the threat of more tears.

"Michelle, tell her to take it," I heard the man say from behind me.

Michelle waited until I turned to face her. She had a bewildered look on her face. We were both thinking the same things; I could read it on her hardened features. "Yeah, take it," she told me. "You know you won't hurt your baby."

I nodded slowly. "Okay," I said. "But Suzie," I added, "they really shouldn't come back to help another girl unless they believe we can do this."

Suzie nodded. "You're right. I'm sorry."

"Thanks," I told her, my voice heavy. "We should go."

The bus ride back to Michelle's apartment was initially quiet. I didn't know what to think or say. No one thought I could do this, I presumed. Why else would they have brought in a church group that thought I would murder my baby?

"So the whole time they were talking to you," Michelle said, "they were thinking about that other girl."

"Yeah."

"That was so weird," she continued.

"Yeah," I told her, snapping out of my thoughts. "Who was that girl?"

Michelle shrugged. "I have no idea."

"I can't believe they thought I could hurt her," I said softly. "I'd do anything for this baby."

Michelle nodded. I stared at the tattoo on her chest, the one that said Fuck the World. We'd been at this for so long. She'd grown up in foster care. I'd been in and out of hospitals, juvenile hall, foster care, and shelters since I was eleven years old. Were we too damaged?

"I can do this, right?" I asked.

"Of course, you can," she told me. "Don't let those ladies scare you."

"Okay," I told her, but my confidence had been shaken.

We got off the bus a few blocks from her apartment and walked slowly with the heavy bags of gifts.

"Hey, what are they doing?" I asked as we approached her place.

Michelle looked up and saw her pseudo-husband and his brother, coming down the stairs carrying their furniture.

"What the hell?" she asked.

She hurried over to where they were and began arguing with them.

"Be out by the end of the month," her husband told her.

"Where are you going? You never paid me," she told him.

He shrugged. "We're moving out. Goodbye."

Michelle and I hurried up to the empty apartment. That had been their last trip. The sofa frame had been left behind, but they'd taken all the cushions. The bed, the dresser, the dining room table. Nothing was left. Just a small corner with our stuff and a sofa frame.

"Assholes," Michelle said.

We looked in every kitchen cabinet and searched through the house. Almost nothing had been left behind.

"We can do this," I told Michelle, my words braver than I felt.

"How?"

"It's the beginning of May. We have a few weeks left," I told her. "I have food stamps for the month, we'll be able to eat. And WIC."

She nodded. "Alright. I guess I'm getting a divorce."

"He's a jerk anyway," I told her.

In the end, we fashioned pillows out of the foam edge from the sofa and t-shirts as pillowcases. We prepared a table with a leftover piece of wood and the box from my car seat. We found one fork, one spoon, one knife. One cup. One plate. The dirty dishes that they'd left behind in the sink. Yes, we could do this. We still had a few weeks.

95
SURPRISE

We went back to Hollywood with plans to stop at Teen Canteen, but I wanted a taco. "Can we stop at Burger Factory?" I asked. I hadn't been there for a long time.

"I love their tacos," Michelle said.

Maybe I just missed Byron, or maybe I wanted to hear news about him. I wasn't sure. He must still have been taking care of his dad in Guatemala, I thought sadly. I wished I could have told him about the baby.

Our little girl.

We walked in, Michelle a little ahead of me, and I wobbled behind her. My belly was growing, and I couldn't see my feet anymore.

The cashier behind the register stared at us with disdain. She'd barely tolerated me when I was a Pantages girl, sipping cheap coffee and waiting for programs to open. "Two tacos please," Michelle said.

I pulled out a few dollars to pay, just as I saw him.

Byron was there. Walking from the back office to the grill. "You're back from Guatemala?" I asked, stunned.

He looked at me strangely, his eyes hovering over my belly. "I never left."

"What?" I asked. The cashier was staring at me with her mouth hanging open.

Michelle paused, glancing from him to me. "Wait, is he-?"

I stepped back, away from the counter. "I'm not hungry anymore," I told her, leaving the dollars on the counter.

I shook my head and walked back outside, where I stood in front of the restaurant for a few minutes. I sucked in a deep breath of warm air.

Byron stepped outside and looked at me strangely. "What are you going to do?" he asked.

I glared at him.

"I mean, what are we going to do?" he asked.

I was furious. "You never left?"

"Where have you been?" he asked. "Are you still working?"

We both had a million questions for each other, but I wasn't ready. "Can we get our food to go?" I asked him.

"We need to talk," he told me.

I shook my head. "No."

"Do you still have the same pager number?" he asked.

"Yeah," I told him. "To go, okay?"

Byron retreated inside to make our order, and Michelle eventually joined me outside. "Can we go back to your place now?" I asked her.

We walked back to the bus stop in silence and waited for a ride to our temporary home.

96
ACCIDENT

At the end of the month, Michelle chose to move in with another friend and I opted to try out a different maternity home. Neither of us had planned for her husband to leave, but I clearly wouldn't be having the baby there.

I waited impatiently for the baby to arrive. Meanwhile, I rationed off my welfare check and bought my monthly bus pass and a crib.

I went down to the community college and registered for summer classes and bought the required books. I would go back to school and raise this baby. My sister had finished college with a baby. I could do this too, I told myself.

Meanwhile, a heat wave settled in Los Angeles. I took the bus to visit Michelle at LAYN, and as I stepped out of the 7-11 down the street from the drop-in shelter, I fainted.

I landed flat on my enormous belly. A car pulled up with an elderly driver. They'd seen me go down. "Are you okay?" his wife asked, slowly stepping out of the car.

When I pushed myself up and started to stand, they saw my belly. "When are you due?" the husband asked.

"Tomorrow," I said nervously. My big cup of soda had broken underneath me when I fell, and my shirt was covered in soda.

"You need to go to a hospital," the man told me.

I nodded. "Can you take me up the street? I'll go with my friend."

They drove me to LAYN's entrance, and when Michelle saw me, she ran to get Guillermo.

"Guillermo, I need a taxi voucher," I told him. "Can you call them?"

I explained what had happened, and they sat me down to wait for the taxi. I had an emergency one in my wallet, for when I went into labor. I was trying to save that one, just in case.

Guillermo called a taxi, and Michelle and I rode across town to Cedars-Sinai Medical Center.

"We'll put you on the monitor and run some tests," the nurse told me in the triage room. They moved me to a regular patient room and told me I was being admitted.

I laid down on the bed in my new room, my heart beating fast as I described blacking out. They drew blood from my arm and started me on IV fluids. Soon, I was connected to the fetal monitor and a doctor came in to study the strip.

"Good. Baby looks good so far," she told me. Next, she examined me. "You're not in labor, but we need to keep you for twenty-four hours to make sure the baby is okay," she explained.

"Okay," I told her. When she left, I told Michelle, "I'm so scared. What if she's hurt?"

"It'll be okay," she told me. "Do you want me to go get anything for you?"

I thought for a moment. Finally, I asked for her to get me a snack from the mall across the street. "I'll be back," she said.

When she returned, she had sub sandwiches and cookies for each of us. She camped out on the reclining father's chair, and I fell asleep on the bed.

They discharged me the next day with a clean bill of health. On my official due date.

"It could be any day now," the nurse told me. "Try not to go out in the heat again."

I agreed. I told Michelle I would stay at the program except for doctor's visits. "I'll see you soon, when the baby comes?" I asked her.

She agreed. "That's a good idea."

This had been scary for both of us.

97
INDUCED

A week and a half later, after a series of doctor's visits, I watched as another physician prepared to check my baby. The ultrasound probe was pressed against my overly pregnant abdomen. I stared at the doctor expectantly. I was already nine days past the due date. Nothing had worked. Not the "pregnant salad," with a special balsamic vinaigrette dressing or walking until my legs felt like they would fall off. This baby was stubborn. Just like me.

I watched as the ultrasound glided across my belly, measuring little black areas, which the doctor explained were pockets of fluid. Finally, the doctor sighed. "Do you want to have this baby today?"

I nodded. I felt enormous, overwhelmed, and wanted to just see her. Alive. In my arms. The waiting had been more than I could bear.

"Well, then today's the day," he told me, unemphatically. "You don't have enough amniotic fluid anymore, so we'll induce." He wiped the gel away with a washcloth, then tossed it into an overflowing bin behind him.

I smiled. "Really?" This was the first doctor's appointment that I had attended in the past month without my car seat and baby supplies. I'd gotten tired of carrying them everywhere, and as it turned out, the one time I needed them, I didn't have them. Every triage visit, every chance I had, I'd carried the blue and white car seat and my diaper bag. For a baby that would remain in hiding for much longer than I'd expected.

The doctor told me to wait for his nurse. I sat up and rearranged my flowing shirt to cover my belly. It had grown so much in the past month. I held my hand nervously over my lower abdomen, soothing against the pressure of another round of kicks. "Soon," I whispered to her.

The nurse walked with me from the clinic to the hospital across the street. We boarded the elevator that would take us to Labor and Delivery. "Do you need to call anyone?" she asked.

I paused. Not Byron. He hadn't asked me to call him.

Michelle.

"Yes," I told her. She took me to the nurse's station, where they allowed me to send a page to Michelle. They promised to forward her call to me when she called back.

Then, they took me to a private room. It was the same set up as the previous week; blue sheet on the bed, baby monitor to the side, a reclining chair for the "dad." I sighed. I could do this.

My nurse was an older woman with short hair and glasses. She handed me my gown and told me I would need to undress. I complied, and when she returned to the room, I was waiting on the edge of the bed.

"Lay down," she commanded. I laid down and waited patiently while she applied thick ultrasound gel on my large abdomen and attached the two monitors. One for me, one for baby. Then, she quietly inserted my IV line.

"Will it hurt?" I asked. I was getting nervous about what was coming. Frantic thoughts were filling my mind, and I could only imagine the worst pain of my life. Multiplied by one thousand.

She scoffed at me. "I feel like I'm babysitting," she muttered. She didn't answer my question.

I stared at the monitor, feeling suddenly unprepared. How could I do this, alone? How long would it take for Michelle to arrive?

I watched the numbers on the monitor, keeping an eye on the baby's heart rate dial. They'd taught me that the goal was anywhere between 110 and 160. Perfect.

And the contraction line. Nothing. I sighed and reached for the remote control.

My doctor had ordered a medicine called oxytocin to make the baby come, which was dripping into my veins while I stared at the television. Jerry Springer came on. How ironic.

I watched as the panel of characters came alive. Angry, broken. With Steve standing between them, to block any potential fights. And Jerry Springer standing just far enough away, insulated by the audience. He'd really hated me, I recalled with a chuckle. Oh well, my fault. I had a habit of saying whatever I wanted to say.

Next came Sally Jesse. That show was less interesting, so I transitioned to a crime drama.

The nurse came to check on me just as Michelle arrived. I looked up at the nurse nervously. "I think I had an accident right now," I said quietly, embarrassment flooding my cheeks.

Michelle sat down in the reclining chair and took in the scene. Me, finally preparing to have the baby. A nurse who was less than interested in "babysitting" me. A television. She sat back to relax, waiting for the nurse to leave.

The nurse pulled back my covers. "Your water broke," she told me confidently, then left to get the doctor.

My eyes widened. "That felt so weird," I told Michelle. "I felt like I was going to the bathroom, but I couldn't control it."

Michelle laughed. "How are you?" she asked.

"Scared. The nurse is a bitch."

Michelle nodded. "I can tell."

A very pregnant woman in scrubs entered the room, her badge proudly proclaiming that she was my physician. She smiled briefly, then stared at the strip of paper printing out from the monitor. I would learn, many years later, that she was looking through the fetal heart tracing to check my progress. She was also looking for contractions, but there were none yet. But more importantly, she was looking for little blips called decelerations, which would show if my baby's heart was not responding well to the induction. She put on a pair of sterile gloves and checked to see if my cervix had changed. "We're moving along," she said, not really defining what that meant before stepping back out of the room into the busy hospital.

I watched the clock. I'd started the oxytocin drip at nine in the morning.

Several hours had passed, and nothing obvious had changed. The day staggered onward, with numerous visits from the nurses and the doctor. Minimal changes had occurred; the baby was hovering at plus 1 station and not moving. I'd read about plus 1, and I knew that it was a pivotal station. It meant that we were close. Meanwhile, I'd been gradually dilating.

Michelle was seated at the far end of the room, near the television. She'd made the mistake of glancing in my direction while I was being examined, and since then had not been looking at me. Not even when I was fully covered with the sheet. "It's time for Montel," she said, eager to watch another talk show. Not for the first time, I was grateful that my episode of Jerry Springer had not come onto the screen. That would have caused an awkward moment between me and my delivery team.

The next time that the doctor entered the room, she had a serious look on her face. She checked my cervix again. "Ten centimeters. We're going to start pushing," she told me. It was eleven at night already.

I listened to her determined commands. "Breathe. Now push," she told me. She counted to ten for each push, then had me breathe for a moment. I pushed as hard as I could. Nothing.

"Still plus 1," I heard her say after a long time. The nurse began checking my vital signs. I was drenched in sweat, and I felt like I'd been pushing for hours. I glanced up at the clock. One in the morning.

"She has a fever," I heard the nurse say to the doctor.

The doctor looked at me, her steely dark eyes staring squarely into my own frightened eyes. "What do you want to do?" she asked. I'd been pushing for two hours, and the baby hadn't moved. I froze for a moment, letting her review my options with me. "You can keep pushing, or we can move on to a c-section."

I squeezed my eyes shut for a moment, muttering my first prayer of the evening. Please let this baby live. I'd had a recurring dream over the past few weeks; I would deliver a beautiful baby, but she was still. Cold. Lifeless. Like the stillbirths that my mother had delivered into the world. The graveyard and her tombstone flashed through my memory. "Cut her out. Now," I commanded.

Everything moved fast after I'd spoken those words. A team of nurses transferred me to a gurney, since I'd had anesthesia and my legs were uselessly numb. Michelle quickly packed our stuff and chased behind us but was escorted in a different direction so that she could change. I was wheeled into the operating room, where my gown was pushed up above my abdomen. A nurse quickly shaved me, and I watched as the doctor, now dressed in a blue gown complete with a mask and surgical cap, began painting an orange liquid over my abdomen. A curtain was pulled up over me, and Michelle was brought into the room. She was wearing a white paper onesie, covering her whole body. She wore her own mask and cap and was instructed to stand by my side.

Another doctor entered the room and stood by the baby warmer. I began praying again, my eyes glued to the doctor. She would save my baby.

The nurse handed her a scalpel, and she made a sharp cut. I sucked in a breath and began to vomit. The pain was unbearable. I threw up into a basin that a nurse handed to Michelle. Green bile.

I started to scream at the top of my lungs. Michelle would later tell me that my mouth was open, but no audible sound was coming out. The pain was sharp, and I could feel every cut. Tears flowed from my eyes; first tears of fear and anguish, followed by tears of joy as I saw the doctor lift a baby above my abdomen. A healthy scream soared out of her lungs, and I felt myself finally begin to relax. She was alive. I was a mom. Me became we, with one scream.

"Time of delivery, 1:06 a.m.," the doctor said. She passed her to the waiting pediatrician, who quickly began examining her at the baby warmer. "It's a girl," the doctor confirmed, returning to my abdomen to begin putting me back together. I stared at the doctor, waiting for that first cry.

As my newborn's soft cry filled the room, I let the tears fall. She was here. She was alive. "Ten fingers and ten toes?" I whispered to Michelle. She didn't hear me, so I repeated myself, louder.

She glanced over, counting the fingers and toes. She looked back. "Yes," she said, a smile on her face.

I nodded and bit down hard on my lip while the physician sewed me back together. Every stitch, every movement caused searing pain. I wouldn't realize until years later that I didn't respond well to anesthesia, and I hadn't been completely numb for the emergency cesarean.

One of the nurses brought the baby over to me. She was wrapped in a white receiving blanket, with a stripe of pink and blue along the side. The nurse wouldn't let me hold her, since I'd had anesthesia, but she held her close enough for me to see her face.

"She's perfect," I whispered.

The nurse nodded, and asked Michelle if she would be following them to the nursery. Michelle looked at me for confirmation.

"Go with her," I pleaded. Michelle nodded and was whisked away with my baby girl.

The physician finished her handiwork, and the drape was removed. My belly was smaller, like a deflated balloon. Still covered in a mixture of orange cleanser and blood from the delivery. A nurse began cleaning me up, as the physician pulled off her blue gown. "Good job, Mama," she said.

"Thank you," I told her.

She hurried away, and soon it was just me and the nurse. She silently finished her task and prepared me to be transferred to a recovery room.

Everything had happened so differently from how I'd planned, and suddenly I felt an emptiness. My baby was somewhere else, and I wanted to hold her more than anything.

"When will I get to see my baby?" I asked.

"You need time for the anesthesia to wear off," the nurse told me. "Usually several hours."

98
ROXANA

Six hours had elapsed since she was born. Six hours before I could hold her, see her, smell her. Six hours from the moment they cut her out of me, before she finally was returned to my arms. Michelle had gone to the nurse's station numerous times for updates, as we were both weary of a system that very well may have been trying to take my baby. We both knew about the baby from my clinic; the one that the other girl had murdered and left in a dumpster. The nurse had kept repeating, "Enjoy your rest, she'll keep you up for the next eighteen years."

By the time they finally brought my newborn daughter back to me, I was impatient and anxious to have her next to me. The nurse obliged and brought her to the room, pushing her bassinet slowly into the private space that would house us for the next three days. I waited as my nurse raised the head of my bed, lifting me up so that I could memorize her little face.

"Roxana," I whispered, as the nurse placed the bundled newborn into my arms. I stared at her small features, suddenly understanding the force of a mother's love. Perfect little round face. Tiny button nose. Rosy lips. Ten fingers, ten toes. I cradled her in my arms, grateful for this one thing that I had done right.

The nurse helped coach me with my first attempt at breastfeeding. While she helped Roxana latch on, she tsked and said, "You're too young to have a baby." I was stunned, ashamed, and said nothing. Soon after, she left the room. I was finally alone with my baby.

I pulled back the cap and whisked my fingertips over her bald head. There were the faintest strands of brown hair covering her round head. She opened her eyes briefly, and I saw they were grayish blue. "I wonder if they'll be blue, like mine," I said.

Michelle sat in the reclining chair next to me, her eyes out of focus. She was strangely quiet.

I touched a finger into Roxana's hand, and her tiny fingers wrapped around my index finger. She already knew me. I smiled, finally at peace. She was here. She was safe. I didn't want to think about what the next day would bring, or the next day after that. For now, for that moment, I basked in the scent of newness.

A few hours passed, and a different nurse came back to check on us. Michelle had fallen asleep, and I was still cuddling Roxana against my chest. "How is your pain?" she asked, hurrying through her assessment.

"It hurts, especially when I'm breastfeeding," I told her. My lower abdomen felt like it was on fire. I had never known such sacrificial pain; the pain a mother feels when a child is carved out of her.

The nurse scowled at me. "Would you like pain meds?" she asked. I recognized that look; it was the same as the nurse who had cared for me the previous day. The nurse who had chided me for asking questions. The one who said that she felt like she was babysitting me.

"I'll try to wait," I said softly, placing a protective hand on Roxana's back as she rested on my chest. A hand between my baby and this nurse, the one who clearly disliked me.

The nurse raised an eyebrow. "You should try to rest," she told me. "We can take the baby to the nursery for a while."

I shook my head. "No, I prefer to keep her here."

The nurse held my gaze. I would not budge. This was my baby. "Fine," she said. "Do you need anything else?"

"No," I told her. She left.

Hours passed. I bit my lower lip as I bent forward to change Roxana's diaper. The pain stabbed, but I had to be strong. Finally, the nurse came back to check on me again. This time, when she asked if I needed pain meds, I had to fight back tears before shaking my head yes.

When the nurse returned with pain medication, I gladly accepted the pill that she offered me. Afterwards, she brought in my lunch tray. Michelle opened her eyes as the nurse was leaving.

"Hey," Michelle said, rubbing at her eyes. "How's little Roxana?"

I smiled. "Great. She's sleeping," I told her.

Michelle stood up and walked over to the bed, eying the lunch tray. I'd ordered double portions of everything that I could, so that we could both eat. I pointed to the tray, and Michelle smiled.

"I love their cookies," she said.

"Yeah, me too," I told her. We'd had several cookies during my last admission. They reminded me of the gooey chocolate chip cookies they used to serve in my elementary school, for fifteen cents each. I would always debate if it was worth the fifteen cents, since my allowance was so small, and I could probably afford one or two cookies per month. Until I found my dad's coin jar, and then started treating myself more often.

We divided the meal and ate quietly; me with a baby cradled in my arm. I was learning a valuable maternal skill, eating with one arm.

"I liked the chicken and rice," I commented after we'd both finished our meal. "Should I order that again tomorrow?" I'd been slowly circling menu items throughout the day to prepare for day two of life. What meals would we eat before we had to go back to our lives?

"And more cookies," Michelle said. I nodded. Absolutely more cookies.

Afterwards, Michelle asked if she could hold Roxana. She carefully accepted her from my arms and sat back down in the reclining chair. She was staring at her with the same love and hope in her eyes I knew I had in mine.

"Roxana Michelle," I said. Michelle smiled. She held her for a long time before excusing herself to buy more cookies. I gladly accepted her back into my arms and whispered to her, "Auntie Michelle loves you, little Roxana."

After another attempt at breastfeeding, Roxana fell asleep in my arms. She was resting comfortably when Dr. Broudy came into the room. He encapsulated everything that I'd ever expected in a young, eager physician. Smiling, but timid. He stood next to another doctor at my doorway.

"Hi," he said. "I'm Dr. Broudy, and I'm a pediatric resident." He was a tall, thin man with curly dark hair and a crisp long white coat, atop a dress shirt and tie. He wore nice slacks and shoes. Most importantly, he kept that smile spread evenly across his face. In all my visits, and since being admitted the previous day, nobody had consistently smiled at me. Nobody had been happy to see me or take care of me.

I sat still, regarding him carefully. His smile seemed genuine. Very unlike all the other healthcare professionals who had been taking care of me. "Hi," I returned. "This is Roxana," I said, motioning to my ten-hour old baby.

"Today is my first day, and she's my very first patient," Dr. Broudy confided. "That makes her special."

I smiled broadly, grateful that Roxana would have a doctor who was eager to see her. He approached the bed and looked at her as he spoke. "Have you chosen a pediatrician?"

"Not yet," I admitted softly. "I wasn't sure how any of that stuff works."

"I can see her in our clinic," he offered, as he donned gloves and gestured for me to pass her to him. I carefully wrapped her in her receiving blanket and allowed him to take her into his skilled hands. It may have been his first day, but he clearly had held babies before. I sat up a little, curious. His attending physician stood nearby, watching. I could see his title listed on his badge, indicating that he was an attending, whereas Dr. Broudy was a first year-resident. On his first day.

He placed her back onto the bassinet and began to examine her. I watched intently as he listened to her with his stethoscope, and then checked her soft spot on the top of her head. She opened her eyes lazily, staring up at the strange man who was studying her perfect body. He checked her eyes with a fancy light, and then looked in her ears, her mouth, and undressed her to check her skin from head to toe. He even maneuvered her hips strangely and moved her into a frog-leg position. "What does that check for?" I asked curiously, fascinated by his expert movements.

Dr. Broudy paused, suddenly aware that I was eager for knowledge. "This shows that her hips are strong." He repeated the motion, and I watched in awe.

He started to tell me each part of the exam as he went through his internal checklist. He ran a finger next to her mouth and she turned slightly towards him. "This is a reflex that guides babies towards their moms," he explained. And as he donned a clean glove and put a finger into her mouth, "This reflex shows us that she has a good sucking ability," he told me. He reached up to the roof of her mouth. "And her palate is closed." I nodded, understanding. I recalled children I had seen on a church trip so many years earlier, with deformed cleft lips and palates.

When he finished her exam, his attending repeated the exam and confirmed that Roxana was healthy. He stepped aside and let Dr. Broudy put her outfit back onto her. He fumbled a little with the buttons on the onesie but was able to wrap her in her blanket decently. He handed her back to me gently. "She's beautiful."

"I want you to be her doctor," I told him. He beamed, and I noticed his attending smiling from behind him.

"I'll be back tomorrow," he said, and handed me one of his newly printed business cards. I accepted it from him, feeling hopeful. Everyone else had handed me their cards too, but none of them had been as kind as this young doctor. An idea had started to spark in my mind, but I couldn't put it to words just yet.

"Thank you," I told him as he left. His supervising doctor exited with him, quietly observing his interaction.

After they left, I glanced at the card. Resident Physician, Pediatrics. Roxana had a doctor now. I tried to think back to my first doctor, and I could only recall one visit to a physician's office. I remembered being seen at a small clinic the day that I fell from the monkey bars when I was five years old and broke my arm. The doctor had said I probably needed surgery, but that it was expensive. I'd ended up with a cast instead. I kissed Roxana's forehead again, mentally vowing to do whatever I had to for her to be healthy and safe.

Michelle hadn't come back yet. I'd made all the right phone calls; my mom, my dad, each of my siblings. The staff at My Friend's Place. I'd changed the message on my pager to tell everyone that Roxana was here, and I had waited all day for a page from her father. He didn't call. I stared at the receiver, debating dialing his work number. As I stared at the phone, I realized he'd never given me his home number. I hadn't asked.

I thought back over our last conversation. He knew I was overdue, but he hadn't asked me to call when the baby was born. I held her closer and kissed her sweet forehead. She had that perfect baby scent. I finally whispered to her, "It's just me and you, sweetie."

At regular intervals, I placed Roxana back on my breast. I was nervous about breastfeeding, but I remembered that Melinda had been able to juggle breastfeeding with school. If she could do it, I had to try. In between feedings, I flipped through my copy of What to Expect in the First Year, a book that was beginning to have rumpled corners over the first several chapters. I'd read and re-read the chapters covering the first few months of life.

The night nurse came in and introduced herself. She borrowed my handwritten list of feedings and diaper changes and recorded the data on her own set of notes. When she finished, she placed the paper back on my bedside table and paused. Roxana was in the bassinet, swaddled in her blanket. "We can watch her in the nursery for a while, so that you can rest," she offered.

I shook my head. "No, I'd prefer for her to stay here," I told her, trying to remain calm.

"Really, I insist."

I tried to sit up straight but felt a strong tug of pain in my lower abdomen. I bit my lip, trying to fight back against the stabbing pain. "I want her to stay here," I told the nurse, but she was already pulling the bassinet in her direction. I hadn't stood up yet since the surgery, and I was alone.

"You need to rest. She'll be fine," the nurse added as she left the room, pulling Roxana out of the room with her.

"No, leave her here!" I called out as the nurse was leaving, but she maintained her course. The door swung closed, and suddenly, I was alone again. Just me, my book, and an envelope of emptiness.

I stared at the door, waiting for the nurse to return. I wanted to keep Roxana close to me. What if they mixed up the babies? What if they gave me back someone else's baby?

What if they didn't give me back my baby at all?

I needed a plan. I stared at the phone again, wondering what to do. I couldn't go back to the maternity program. I'd never have permission to leave if I went there. I was already enrolled in summer classes, and had read the required books, but my gut told me that I wouldn't be ready to leave Roxana so soon. Where would I go?

I didn't want to call Byron. Michelle had lost her place because of me.

Before I could talk myself out of it, I started to dial. I only had one friend who would take me in, no matter what. One friend who had offered me a safe place to stay, no strings attached.

The phone rang three times before he answered. "Hello?" I asked. "Mario?"

"Hey, Sheryl," I heard his response.

"I had the baby," I told him. "She's beautiful. I named her Roxana, after that girl that I worked with at DAPY."

"That's great!" he told me. I believed him. His voice was enthusiastic. I'd missed our late-night bus rides back to his apartment. I'd missed hearing Mana and the Cranberries interchangeably. He was the closest thing to a brother that I'd had in California. I grew quiet, reminiscent. "Where are you staying now?" he asked.

"I don't know," I told him. "I was staying somewhere, but I don't think it's a good place." I let my words hang in the air. He waited.

"Hold on, okay?" he said. I stared at the clock, lost in the silence of the moment. How long had it been since they'd wheeled Roxana out of my room? Was she crying? Did she miss me?

Several long minutes passed before Mario came back to the phone. "You can come back to our apartment," he said.

"Really?" I was elated. I'd dared to dream, dared to ask. And he'd said yes.

"Sure," he said, his voice soft for a moment. "When are you getting out of the hospital?"

"On Sunday," I told him. It was Thursday. Three days to figure out my life. Three days to prove that I was worthy of having my baby in the room with me. We chatted for a few more minutes, and then I hung up. For the first time in weeks, I felt at peace. I relaxed against the bed and allowed myself to sleep.

"Where's Roxana?" I heard Michelle's voice as she entered the room. I tried to sit up but felt that jab of pain again.

"The nurse took her," I told her. "I told her not to, but she took her anyway."

Michelle crossed into the room, standing over my bed. "What do you mean?

"She took her to the nursery. I told her to let me keep her here."

Michelle looked like she'd been on a long walk. She wore a layer of sweat, from the heat wave that had been plaguing Los Angeles. The tattoo on her upper chest screamed out at me, and again, I understood the anger that had led her to carve those words on her skin. She set down a bag on the reclining chair, then turned back to me. "I'll go talk to her," she told me.

Michelle passed by my bed and walked back out of the room, as quickly as she'd come. When she returned a few minutes later, she was accompanied by the nurse, who did not have my baby with her.

"Where's Roxana?" I asked.

The nurse shook her head. "You need to rest."

"I want my baby," I told her, my voice growing stronger. But the nurse would not budge. She walked back out, and left me sitting in the room, seething in anger. I looked at Michelle. "I'm not a kid. I'm nineteen. She's my baby."

I started to buzz the nurse call light every ten or so minutes. "I want my baby," I replied every time that they asked what I wanted. After another hour passed, the nurse wheeled her back in. I could hear her before she crossed the threshold into my room; she was screaming at the top of her baby lungs.

After the nurse passed her to me, Roxana laid her head down on my chest and stopped crying. I glanced up at her, awaiting an explanation.

"She wouldn't stop crying," the nurse admitted. "She was keeping all of the other babies up."

"That's because she belongs in here." My hand covered most of her tiny back, shielding her. "She wanted to be with me."

The nurse nodded slightly and walked away. The door closed behind her. I stared at the space where she'd been before turning back to Michelle.

Michelle shook her head. "That isn't right," she told me.

"I know," I told her. "She's my baby, and they can't just take her like that." Roxana's cap had come loose, and half of her head was exposed. I recalled reading that babies lose most of their heat from their heads and their feet. I carefully re-positioned the cap to cover her head, humming softly to her. She sighed heavily in her sleep.

"She taught them a lesson," Michelle commented as she sat back down in the reclining chair.

"Yeah." I stared at her, memorizing every detail of her face. She had the softest eyelashes, and they curled just slightly at the tips. Her head was so perfectly round. "I called Mario," I said. "He said I can move back in with him."

Michelle nodded. "That's much better," she told me. We both knew I needed to go someplace safe, where there was no risk of someone taking this baby from me. The threat of the Child Protective Services loomed over me all the time, and I was not about to allow this child to go through even a fraction of what I'd experienced. Every ounce of me was filled with a fierce maternal love that I'd never realized existed.

Michelle turned the television on, and both of us distracted ourselves with the latest talk shows. It was easier to watch other people's drama instead of focusing on our own.

Suzie came to visit, along with another staff member. She brought me Roxana's car seat. I couldn't believe that she'd driven all the way out to the maternity program to pick it up for me. I thanked her profusely and let her hold Roxana for as long as she wanted to. Suzie had become an important part of my life, and by default, that meant that she was also important for Roxana.

They took pictures with her and left us with a few presents. I smiled at them as they left and had thanked them profusely. Motherhood had brought on a new vulnerability I hadn't expected. I'd run from help for so long. It felt weird asking for someone to help me. To help us. But it also felt necessary.

I spent the next few days recovering and practicing walking despite the throbbing pain over my cesarean scar. It hurt to laugh, or cough, or stand. I wasn't sure how I would make it home with the level of pain I had, but I would do anything for this new chance.

Even when the doctor arrived and told me I needed to get a Depo-provera shot, I managed to remain calm. "I'd prefer the pill," I said. I'd never been on any birth control before, and I'd hated the Depo shot I'd had the previous year.

The doctor had stared me down, her expression serious. "If you don't agree to get the Depo shot, I'll have to send the social worker to talk to you."

Red flag. I immediately agreed to the shot. Whatever it took was what I had decided. I would leave this hospital with my baby. So, I let them inject me with the Depo-provera shot, even though I knew it was coercion. I accepted the continuous string of authority figures, telling me what hoops I needed to hop through, since I was a free clinic patient.

When day three finally arrived, I was elated to go to my new home. I was still angry about the Depo shot, and I had just finished signing my name to Roxana's birth certificate. One parent. The rules had been explained to me: if no father presents himself, and the woman is unmarried, she cannot list a father without his signature. Roxana would be mine alone. The nurses had continued to remind me of my age throughout the three days since she was born, and by the time the last one reminded me I was a teenager, I was frustrated.

"You're too young," she told me. A phrase I'd heard too often.

"Too young to have a baby?" I asked. She glanced at me, her face stern. "Doesn't matter. Either way, I'm taking this baby home with me. It would be nice if you encouraged me instead of telling me I can't do it," I told her boldly. I held her gaze. I'd had enough.

The nurse nodded and helped me pack. I was trying to gather all my belongings and consolidate them into my backpack and the complimentary diaper bag that had come with a canister of baby formula. A sample, just in case breastfeeding didn't work out. The nurses had given me a few small baby bottles with formula also, since my milk hadn't come in yet. Mostly Roxana had been drinking colostrum, which I'd read about in my book. Three days of antibodies, to keep her body strong.

She brought a wheelchair to the room and helped me load myself onto the chair. After my bags were packed beside me, she handed me the car seat. Roxana was sound asleep in the car seat, her tiny body enveloped by a too large seat. I covered the seat with a large receiving blanket.

The nurse pushed me in the wheelchair to the elevator, where we traveled together to the first floor. I didn't have a car to pick me up, so I'd chosen to go home by city bus. She led me to the bus stop in between the two large hospital towers. I'd waited until fifteen minutes before the next bus for my discharge time, and when we arrived at the bus stop, there was a bus waiting at its first stop. This bus would take me from Cedars-Sinai through the canyon and into the San Fernando Valley. I'd memorized the route from all the triage visits.

"Thank you," I told the nurse, even though she'd made me angry. Even though she'd repeated the same line as the nurses before her. Yes, I was too young. But nineteen years old used to be the normal age for childbirth. I waited defiantly, expecting her to repeat her unkind words.

"Good luck," she said.

I boarded the bus slowly, weighted down by the car seat, diaper bag, and my backpack. I grimaced with sharp pain from my incision as I climbed the two stairs onto the bus. When I was finally aboard, I sat gratefully in the first row of seats. Roxana and her car seat sat in the chair next to me, against the window. Protected. I was beginning my new life as Roxana's mom.

When the bus finally came alive, I rested against the chair. I was safe. They were not taking my baby. They would not be able to take her against my wishes again. I would be a better mom than my parents had been for me.

Three buses later, and I was two hours early. I watched through the window of the bus as the scenery passed me by. The bus was forging its way down Van Nuys Boulevard, getting closer and closer to Mario's house. Past the car dealerships. Past the clinics offering "free pregnancy tests." Even past the one where I'd done my initial pregnancy test.

I knew he wouldn't be home yet. Frustrated, hungry, and hot from being on the bus in the middle of the day during the unending heat wave, I pulled the signal two stops early. Roxana was crying softly, and I needed a break.

I lugged my belongings and the car seat off the bus and crossed the road slowly. Everything hurt, but mostly, my incision. My shoulders burned from pain also, but I could bear that pain. I walked the short distance to the Arby's, which I'd calculated would be one of the few restaurants open in this area on a weekend. I would wait in their air-conditioned restaurant for an hour or so, until Mario got off from work.

I entered the restaurant and paused just within the doorway. The trademark cowbell loomed overhead, waiting for a tug from a pleased customer. Not too many people were there, since it was a little early for a Sunday lunch crowd. I walked to the counter, where I ordered a roast beef sandwich from the dollar menu and a cup of ice water. It was already the end of the month, and I'd almost run out of money. I would still have to figure out how to get all my stuff from the maternity home.

After I'd ordered, I found a seat by the window. I pulled back the blanket and saw Roxana's whimpering face. Her skin was pink, and she let out a wail once she saw me. "Aw, Roxana," I whispered, removing her carefully from the car seat. She was sweaty, so I removed her blanket and let her curl against my skin. She continued to cry, softly at first. Her cry was soon replaced with loud, angry cries. Rocking was not soothing her. I rubbed my thumb against her cheek, and she rooted towards it, just as the pediatrician had shown me. She was hungry.

I glanced around the restaurant, deciding. I wasn't ready to breastfeed in public. My sister was the only woman I'd ever seen breastfeed before, and it was so common to see everyone pop baby bottles into their crying babies' mouths. Besides, my milk hadn't come in yet. I cradled her against my chest while I used my spare hand to remove one of the two-ounce formula bottles from my diaper bag.

Pink cheeks and wailing immediately stopped when the nipple touched her lips. Roxana opened her eyes wide, and I saw that they glistened with unshed tears. She let the nipple rest solidly on her tongue for a moment, before wrapping her lips around it and testing her strength. When she figured out the movement and began to drink the formula, I sighed gratefully. I had been terrified for her; afraid I'd already damaged her.

"Here's your sandwich," I heard a voice say from above me. I looked up, noticing the Arby's employee. She had brought a tray to me, with my sandwich and water cup. The employee was roughly my age, and had shiny black hair pulled into a bun. Her eyes danced with excitement as she stared at Roxana. "How old is she?"

I glanced from Roxana to the worker. "Three days," I said, my voice heavy. I'd never felt such strong emotions as I was suddenly feeling. Three days, and everything in my life was turned upside down. Three days with no page from Burger Factory. Three days with a baby staring up at me, depending on me.

"She's beautiful," the girl said. I thanked her, grateful for positivity. She hurried away, back to her work behind the counter.

I ate slowly, marveling in the way that Roxana's eyelids hung heavy with sleep after she finished the first half of her bottle. I gently rolled her over and rubbed her back, letting her burp out the extra gas with ease.

After almost two hours had passed, I began to pack up. It was time to find my way home, back to Mario's.

99
SECOND CHANCE

When I arrived at the familiar apartment complex, I felt a twinge of guilt. Had it really been necessary to leave three months ago? Could I have found a way to stay? I waited for a tenant to come out, so that I could get past the locked entry way. I'd given back my keys when I had left.

I trudged past the foyer, which was filled with mailboxes. My back ached, my arms were sore, and my abdomen was on fire. I pressed the button to call the elevator, waiting impatiently.

The door opened, and the elevator took me to the third floor. I walked down the long corridor. This was such a large apartment complex. I remembered the first time I'd seen it, and I'd chuckled because I had looked at several apartments down the block over a year earlier when I'd considered renting a place with Michelle, Andrea, and Rachel. That would have been a disaster.

Number 333. I stood in front of the door, hesitating. The familiar sound of the Mexican band Mana floated into the hallway, and I forced myself to knock three times against the wooden door. Nervousness tingled through my hand as I released my clenched hand.

Mario answered the door less than a minute later. He had a goofy grin on his face, the one that I would expect an uncle to have when he was meeting his niece for the first time. I smiled. I didn't know why I'd been so afraid. I was home.

He grabbed my diaper bag and directed me to the living room. They'd cleared out an area for me in the corner of the room, for when I brought all my belongings. Everything else looked the same. Same sofa, same coffee table, same entertainment system with a large television. Same small kitchen, off to the side.

"How have you been?" he asked as I set down the car seat on the sofa. Bending was still incredibly hard, and my belly hurt more than I'd expected.

"Okay," I answered. I didn't want to tell him too much. I'd gone through so much, and I couldn't figure out why it had all been necessary now that I was standing back in Mario's apartment. "Is Sergio here?"

Mario shook his head. "He'll be back later. He says congratulations."

I was detaching the car seat straps and began removing Roxana from her chair. She was asleep, but I wanted to hold her. I needed to keep her close to me. "I think she has my eyes," I told him. Mario had told me before that he hoped my baby would have my eyes. Many people had told me that. It was the one feature that everyone noticed. My ocean blue eyes, the one window that sometimes even I forgot to close. I had never been good at concealing my emotions, and people could often figure out if I was angry or upset with one glimpse at those two pale pools of blue.

"Can I hold her?" he asked. He sat down on the sofa and held out his arms, so I placed her in them. I knew that Mario had younger siblings in Mexico, and he held her with experienced hands. "She's so little."

Roxana yawned and opened her eyes briefly. Those two little pools of blue-gray. While she rested, I placed her car seat beside the sofa and sat down.

"Where's all your stuff?" Mario asked. I explained to him where I'd been most recently, and he told me he would drive over to get everything with his neighbor. All I had to do was rest.

Mario gently placed Roxana back into my arms, then left to go get my things.

Mario and his friend Ruben had delivered all my belongings from the maternity home, and they'd lined them in the corner of the living room. I stared at the wooden crib pieces that stacked against the wall. The perfectly measured wooden slats met the criteria that I'd read about in my What to Expect book, so that Roxana wouldn't injure herself. But I couldn't imagine trying to put that crib together, with the stabbing pain in my belly. I thought back to when my nephew Matt was little.

"Can I borrow a dresser drawer?" I asked Mario. He shrugged and brought me an empty drawer from his roommate's room. I set it on the floor next to the sofa and lined the bottom with a thick but firm blanket. Afterwards, I set Roxana down on the makeshift crib, facing up, her tiny body wrapped snugly a soft receiving blanket. "Back to sleep," had been drilled into me by my continued reading of the first few chapters of my book.

Once Roxana was nestled in her drawer, I sat back against the sofa. I'd done it. I'd had a baby and managed to find a safe place to live. Our future seemed brighter, even if it was just for the moment.

I fell asleep sitting up, and when I awoke Roxana was crying. When I placed her to my breast, she screamed louder, until her face was red, and she shed a few angry tears down her cheeks. I finally gave in and brought her one of the other sample formulas. She guzzled it down, then pooped, then cried again. I lulled myself into the rhythm of feed, change diaper, sleep and went through my third night of motherhood with fresh eyes. She was mine, and only mine. Byron still hadn't called.

When I awoke to her cries in the morning, I reached for her through my haze of sleeplessness. I was slowly becoming exhausted. Her little pink face would bunch up when she wailed. I found myself marveling at the way that her lower lip trembled while she cried. As quickly as I could, I prepared her bottle and offered it to her. She settled down immediately, and her grey-blue eyes stared up at me with curiosity. I was her milk source. And that was enough for both of us.

After I finished feeding her, I noticed white spots on the top of her tongue. "Oh no," I mumbled. I went through the motions of changing her and laying her back down to rest before grabbing my parenting book. I re-read everything and decided it could be thrush, which I'd read was a fungal infection that newborns sometimes grew on their tongues. The book suggested that she needed treatment. I set down the book and sifted through the stack of discharge paperwork that I'd received the previous day and dialed the pediatrician's office.

"Hello?" I asked nervously.

"Cedars Sinai Pediatrics," an operator answered.

"Hi. My daughter is four days old, and I need to talk to her doctor," I explained. My voice wavered slightly. The operator on the other end took our information and promised a call back.

I rocked Roxana back and forth in my arms as I paced the room for the next twenty minutes. When Mario's landline rang, I answered on the first ring.

"This is Dr. Broudy," I heard a familiar voice on the other line.

"Hi. This is Roxana's mom," I said. A line that would become familiar to me over the next several years. My identity was shifting. I was becoming someone else. I was becoming the protector of a little one. The replacement of "me" for "we."

"Roxana has white dots on her tongue."

Dr. Broudy asked a series of questions. Any fevers? Changes in eating? I regretfully informed him that breastfeeding had failed. He didn't tell me I'd failed, although I felt like I had. Any change in wet diapers? Finally, "I suspect that she has thrush," he told me.

I agreed with him. "That's what I was thinking too, after reading about it in my book." He'd seen the book while I was in the hospital and acknowledged that it was a good book.

He told me that he would send a prescription to the pharmacy for her. After I hung up the phone, I stared at the receiver for a while. Medicine was surprisingly interesting; who knew that there was order in all the chaos? I'd thought about studying medicine before, during that calm year and a half after Terri had left and I'd felt a sense of order in my life. But I'd dismissed all my thoughts of hope and future for the past several years. Who was I, to imagine something better? But now, with Roxana, I knew I needed something better. Something more. And I already knew that I would do anything for my beautiful new baby.

I set Roxana back down in her makeshift crib and picked back up my new favorite book. I decided that I would read for a while and then walk to the pharmacy once the medicine was ready.

Mario returned to the apartment carrying a big shopping bag, filled to the brim. I was lazily holding Roxana in one arm and feeding her a bottle of formula. We had progressed to the sample jar of formula, and she was drinking almost an ounce per meal. She stared up at me when I shifted to look in Mario's direction. He was smiling, a big goofy teenager smile.

"I told the ladies at work about Roxana, and they all want to meet her," he told me. I watched with incredulous eyes as he placed the large bag next to me. "The owner packed up a bag of presents for Roxana."

"Really?" I asked. People were excited for me? I'd never grown up with a sense of community, and in fact, I barely knew people within my family outside of my parents and siblings. I'd rarely met my cousins, and all members of the family lived far apart from each other. My mom's mom had been crazy like her, and my dad's mom didn't like me. It felt so strange shifting into a makeshift family. I stared at Mario with the beginnings of hope in my eyes. People cared. That was something.

He began to take items out of the bag and show them to me. Almost everything was in the classic Winnie the Pooh design, a pattern they sold a lot of at the bookstore. In fact, I'd bought an Eeyore watch there when I had first started working at DAPY. Eeyore was the character I understood the most; the one who was heavy with sadness, yet willing to try to fit in with the group. "Wow!" I exclaimed when he pulled out a large thick blue blanket showing Winnie the Pooh and his friends. The edges had frilled threads, like a carpet, and it had a hand-stitched quality to it. I spread it out on the floor and placed Roxana on top of it. This would be her special blanket. I began pulling out onesies and outfits and dresses, followed by hats and socks and books. Everything Roxana would need for her first few months was in this bag. "Mario, thank you," I told him. "Tell them thank you."

He grinned. "They had one condition," he said. "They will want to meet her, when she's a little bigger."

I laughed. "Of course, they can," I promised as I put a brand-new pair of Pooh socks onto Roxy's tiny feet.

At six days of life, I decided that we needed to take pictures. I wanted to send something tangible to my family, and it was before the age of social media. I placed Roxana carefully into her car seat, which I carried with me when I took her on the bus. I was petrified that I might drop her on a city bus and had decided to stick to the car seat for the first few weeks. At least until she was big enough to ride in the baby pouch that I had bought for her several months earlier.

We rode the bus down Van Nuys Boulevard, reaching our destination within fifteen minutes. I kept the car seat covered with the Winnie the Pooh blanket, so that Roxana would not be exposed to the other passengers.

When I got off the bus at the Panorama City Mall, I walked slowly towards the entrance with Roxana. My lower abdomen was still hurting, but not as much as the first few days. I still had to walk carefully, not taking too many steps at a time. My body felt like I'd been in a train wreck, but with a glorious prize at the end.

I walked through the small side entrance and went directly to the small portrait store that I'd passed by so many times. There were several teenagers snapping pictures together, the ones with the sepia or gray undertones and the angry yet beautiful faces.

I stared at the different background choices while I waited, and finally settled for a bright blue background. It would contrast nicely with my green dress and brightly dyed red hair. When our turn arrived, I carefully removed Roxana from her car seat and held her in my lap while the photographer took our picture. I posed her according to the photographer's instructions, and then selected the picture that I would pay for. Thirty minutes later, he handed me an envelope of our first pictures. She looked so small, and I looked so young and innocent. My smile encompassed all the hope and fear of young single motherhood. Could I do this? Could I be enough for her?

100
NEW BEGINNINGS

My pager went off that afternoon. I glanced down at the number, and my heart thudded faster in my chest. Byron. He'd heard my voicemail message. He knew that Roxana was here. I stared at the number I had memorized several months ago. What could I do?

I crossed Mario's living room and stood next to the telephone receiver. What would he say? Would he be mad that I hadn't called him? But he hadn't called me. I paused, chewing on my lower lip. It was a bad habit, one that would persist throughout my life at times of stress.

Momentarily courageous, I dialed his number. He answered with his typical cheerful voice. "Burger Factory," Byron announced.

"Hi," I said.

"Hi," he replied. I realized I missed his voice.

"I had the baby," I told him. There was a moment of silence. I glanced over at my sleeping newborn, her little eyelashes casting shadows against her sweet cheeks. "She's beautiful." My baby. I wasn't sure that I wanted to share her.

"I want to see her," he told me. He wanted to meet her. She could have a father, if I allowed it.

A series of emotions passed through me. Fear. Joy. "Okay," I said softly. "I can bring her tomorrow afternoon, after her doctor's appointment."

We ended the conversation quickly. There were too many unspoken words. Why hadn't he called? Why was he calling now? I didn't know what I wanted. My sister was doing an excellent job as a single mother, although she was living with a guy now. And they were having their own baby at the end of summer.

I could do this on my own, my heart echoed. I could be strong enough. I could be enough for her. For us. But did I want to?

I crossed the room and stared out the window, watching the cars passing by on the busy street. There was a church on the corner, directly in sight of the window. I'd seen it many times, but never felt drawn to it until that moment. Was I supposed to do this alone? Or was I meant to share my child with her father? I thought back to my earlier faith and decided that I would take Roxana to church that Sunday.

Alone or not, I needed to be better. For her.

I arose before dawn the next morning. I had an early appointment with my doctor, the one week follow up appointment for each of us. Thankfully I'd managed to schedule both on the same day. We would have to take three buses to get to the hospital, and then two more to get to Hollywood afterwards. It would be a long day.

I packed several changes of clothes and diapers in the bag. Next, I filled several small bottles with two ounces of water each and packed her formula. She really liked the Good Start sample that we'd been given, but it was almost finished.

We had a WIC appointment scheduled for the next day, and the welfare appointment would be a few days later. I had already disenrolled from my summer school classes and would return the books in a few days so that I could get a refund. I would need to enroll for fall classes during that school trip. I mentally calculated all my upcoming tasks, trying not to feel overwhelmed.

We rode on the first bus, following the route down Van Nuys Boulevard to its last stop at the intersection with Ventura Boulevard. I followed the last stream of passengers off the bus and joined several of them at the bus bench, awaiting the southbound bus.

We crowded on together, and I was offered a seat once I boarded the second bus. Morning commuters and schoolchildren climbed on, so I placed the car seat firmly on my lap and hugged the bulk of my tiny child against my healing body. I watched as we passed the familiar places I had enjoyed during the previous summer. The summer when I'd been eighteen and testing my adulthood. The coffee shop where I'd studied during my first semester of college. The juice bar where I'd learned I like vegetable juice. The Aaahs store, which had been DAPY's only direct competitor. I'd enjoyed their merchandise almost as much as DAPY's, but I refused to buy from them.

I pulled the signal to stop at Laurel Canyon, where I stepped gingerly off the bus and hurried to my next stop. When I sat, I stared across the street at the coffee shop where I'd stood behind the lady with the dragon tattoo. That was when I'd become mesmerized with dragons. I paused, thinking about the dragon I'd had tattooed on my own shoulder that same summer. My second tattoo, a rite of passage for an adult working two jobs and planning some sort of a future.

The ride through the canyon was slow, since many commuters used the canyon as a bypass between the San Fernando Valley and West Los Angeles. The bus curved along the mountain roads, winding its way up and then back down again, spilling out into West Los Angeles. I had found a seat towards the back, where I could put Roxana and her car seat next to me, and I could relax. I was lost in thought; my mind retracing all the pathways I'd traveled since arriving in Los Angeles three years earlier. So much had been lost, but so much had been gained.

When the bus pulled up at its last stop, Cedars Sinai Medical Center, I proudly stood and carried my child off the bus with me. I held my shoulders high as I carried her into the obstetrics clinic with me, where my scar was checked. A female obstetrician entered the small exam room to see me, and after smiling at Roxana in her car seat, she turned to me. She went through a series of terse questions before examining me. She told me, "There is some redness around the edges, but your incision is healing well. You can follow up with your regular clinic in five weeks."

I nodded. She reviewed my birth control method. The Depo shot that I'd been forced to get before my hospital discharge. I stifled a frown, instead plastering the cheerful maternal smile to my face. "Thank you," I told her politely, then headed out of the office. I could wear my false new courage in public, if that was what was necessary. I had already been avoiding calls from one of the hospital's home health nurses, a woman who kept trying to set up a time to come check on Roxana at home. I figured that had everything to do with the clinic where I'd gone for my prenatal care, and that other youth who had killed her baby. She'd even called from the outside of LAYN, asking me what kind of building it was, and whether I lived there or somewhere else. No one had my actual address, so that no one could steal my kid away into foster care.

There were still several hours to wait for Roxana's appointment, which was scheduled for the afternoon. I didn't want to wait in the hospital cafeteria, so I carried the car seat across the street, to the large mall that occupied several city blocks. The Beverly Center. I had spent many days applying to every store in this mall when I was seventeen, but without luck. A few interviews, and an awkward attempt at meeting up with a store manager in what turned out to be a date. That had not been pleasant, I recalled.

I could not afford to shop, so I wandered up to the food court. Perhaps I would buy a drink and sit for a few hours. That was a tactic I'd learned long ago. Arms sore from life without a matching stroller, I finally set Roxana's car seat onto a chair. I silently wished, not for the first time, that I could have nice things. There was a bulky stroller among my belongings; used, gifted to me at the baby shower. But it was not compatible with her seat and would have to wait until she was a little bigger. She would slide out of the bottom if I tried to use it now.

I stretched my arms, then relaxed them against my side. Roxana was asleep. There were several hours until one o'clock, and a quiet part of me wanted to be a normal person for just a moment. That's when I glanced over at the adjacent movie theater and read the movie titles.

Mulan. And it was still early, so I could get in for less than five dollars. If I skipped food and watched a movie, it would be almost time for her appointment. I remembered from my box office days that Roxana should be free.

I scooped up the car seat and walked briskly to the ticket window. I was in luck! The movie was starting in fifteen minutes. Grateful for the reprieve, I pulled out several one-dollar bills and flattened them before handing them to the ticket seller. I'd adopted the habit of always turning them the same way when I'd worked at DAPY. "One matinee ticket, please," I said.

The seller smiled and handed me a ticket. At that moment, I was a young mother in a mall, buying a normal movie ticket, with my beautiful new baby. Anything was possible. I could rise above these past few years, and I could be the mother I had needed. The part of me that was still homeless, still struggling to find my place in the world, was temporarily masked. Another mother passed by me with her small child, and we shared a knowing maternal smile. One that meant, we can do this. She'd been where I was, and she'd survived. Babies grew, nights eventually would be for sleeping, and little ones would one day sit alongside their mothers and cheer as movies unfolded before their eyes. I'd been invited into motherhood.

As I sat down to watch the movie, I heard the movie's message loud and clear. A tear slid down my face as the father told his daughter, "The flower that blooms in adversity is the most rare and beautiful of all." Roxana was lying in my arms, dressed in her softest new outfit. She'd received so many beautiful gifts from the ladies at the bookstore. I leaned down to kiss her sweet baby forehead; she smelled of milk and that glorious scent of new beginnings. Something better was coming.

My future was undefined, but I had every reason to fight. To push on. We could do this.

EPILOGUE

Writing this book has proven to be one of the hardest yet most rewarding things I've ever done. I've had a chance to reflect on the journey that helped me become the person who I am now. Reflecting back, in hindsight, I realize that a lot of my reactions to the world around me were trauma-based reactions. I didn't know it then; I couldn't understand why I was so angry and why I couldn't form healthy, trusting relationships with adults. But looking back through the lens of a mother and physician, I now understand my actions much better.

When I started to prepare this book, I reached out to people who knew me then; Michelle, Byron, and the staff at My Friend's Place. The impression of people who knew be back then rang true for me; I was the kid who didn't care about anything, until I found out that I was pregnant and I knew I had to get my life together.

Getting off the streets was hard. Pushing forward, day after day, with the constant weight of "what if?" and "am I good enough?" I found strength in my schooling, and I was grateful for normative experiences like being a college student, taking my kids to school, and finding work as a high school biology teacher. As the years stretched by, my confidence grew. We survived; my husband and I were making our way in the world, raising our three adorable kids.

But then, the dream took hold, and I couldn't let it go. The call to medicine pulled me back into the hospital. I fell in love with medicine and the hospital when Roxy was born, even though my experience was less than ideal. I was able to see the joy of practicing medicine through the kindness and informal mentoring by my daughter's first pediatrician. Each visit, he checked in with me to see how my schooling was progressing. Was I still interested in medicine? Did I still want to learn more details on how to apply to medical school? From my very first volunteer shift at a small community hospital in Van Nuys, I knew that I had to fight for my dream. Medicine was calling me, and I focused all of my spare time on the application.

This book is a culmination of many years of hard work and healing. My family walked alongside me in the completion of the book and its cover design. The cover itself began as a conversation between my kids, Michelle, and me. My youngest daughter, Carmen, had read through my entire first draft and felt that she could portray a younger version of me. Michelle, Carmen, and I ventured down to Hollywood to take a series of photos that we could choose from for the cover. I knew that I wanted the Hollywood sign incorporated into the cover; so much of my story and experiences took place in Hollywood. I graduated from Hollywood High Adult School.

The cover came together from those photos. Carmen's arm wasn't held high enough; not quite sure of herself as she posed as a teen hitchhiker. And I realized how beautiful the moment was as we sifted through the photos. She captured everything in that one pose; fear, hope, redemption. Michelle and I each looked through the photos independently, and we had the same favorite picture from our photo shoot.

Roxy, my oldest child, the daughter that saved me twenty years ago, designed the cover. She's now majoring in art, working towards a degree in animation. She listened patiently to what I wanted, and developed dozens of covers before we found The One. The cover that represented my journey. Open space to signify the feeling of being lost; searching. The mountain with my title as the Hollywood sign, showing the overriding theme of my life. The girl, lost, searching for safety. Bright red hair to symbolize the pain in the journey; the overwhelming desire to hide in a sea of lost youth, yet to stand apart somehow. Red, for the times that I viciously changed my hair color to reinvent myself, from a dirty blonde to something cleaner, brighter, more full of life.

Twenty years have passed, and my life has flourished. Byron and I married, and I returned to college after Roxy was born. Two years later, I was accepted into UCLA as a transfer student, where a whole new world of opportunity was available. Afterwards, I found a career in teaching high school science for eight years before a close friend and colleague convinced me to follow my dreams. I started medical school in 2010, and after graduation four years later, I completed my residency training in Family Medicine.

It's been a whirlwind looking back at where it all began, but it's also been amazing to realize that because of what I went through, I became a better mother and human than I could've ever imagined. My kids are compassionate, decent people who care about others. As I've seen them grow up, their normal experiences have reinforced for me why I had to survive such difficult times. I am grateful for the journey, and I will continue paying it forward.

This year, I was able to start a scholarship fund for youth at one of my favorite youth programs, My Friend's Place. I've always wanted to reach back and uplift as many youths as possible towards safer, more secure futures. The world is changing, for the better.

Thank you for taking this journey with me.

ACKNOWLEDGEMENTS

Thank you, to all of the people who have encouraged me during this writing process. The journey to completing Hindsight has taken me back through some of my darkest memories, and I am eternally grateful for the love and support of my husband, Byron, and my wonderful kids, Roxy, Isaac, and Carmen. Thank you for letting me be me, and helping me become the best possible version of myself.

Michelle, who walked much of this journey with me, thank you. Thank you for laughing and crying with me, thank you for rehashing old memories as we chatted about what that life was like. You are amazing and you inspire me daily!

Mom, who taught me to love with my whole heart, even when it hurts. Even when there is no reciprocity or rational thought. Thank you for hearing me when I needed to be heard. I will forever miss you.

David, I am so grateful for all the times that you reached out to try to help me. I wasn't ready, and that's okay. I am forever thankful that you cared enough to open up your home to me and loved me in spite of my many flaws. I just wish I could've saved you, the way you tried to save me. I miss you daily.

Denise, I've known you since I was a pesky kid and you've been a beautiful sister to me throughout the years. Thank you for every kind word, every time I bugged you guys for coffee and attempted to influence your kid. You're the best.

Kevin, I'm sorry that your journey has been equally hard. It's been a long road and I'm so grateful to have you in my life. Thank you for that time when you bought me that ticket and sent me back to CA. I know no one understood my need to leave better than you.

Melinda, I have always looked up to you. I admired you when I was an annoying kid, and I've always considered you to be one of the strongest women I've ever met. You've inspired me to be better than I thought I could be. Thank you.

Nick, we went through some tough times together and you always managed to power through. I am amazed by that internal fortitude that you've had since childhood. Thank you for teaching me how to be brave.

Lisa, you are such an important part of my life. I adore you and your girls, and I am so grateful that you married my brother. Thank you for becoming a friend and sister for me.

Dad, it's hard to say what I really need to say. I needed something different, I needed more. It's too late for that. I struggle with knowing what to let go of and what I need to hold onto. Because those years and that pain shaped me into the woman who I am today. I wish things could've been different. I hope that underneath everything that happened back then, you loved me even when I was flawed.

For the people who I lost along the way; Reggie, Ava, Zony. I will always carry your beautiful memories with me. You are not forgotten.

For the programs and people that saved my life, WOW. I don't have adequate words to describe how grateful I am for this second chance at life. Thank you to My Friend's Place, especially to Suzie, my first case manager. You saw something in me before I could even see it in myself. Thanks for trying to bring me sandwiches at my job, you always thought of everything. Thank you for loving Roxy and helping me believe that I could do this. To Heather, you are the kindest, most amazing human being that I have ever met. You love all of the young people who walk through those doors, and you seek to give them a place where they can express themselves freely and safely. Thank you for that. Thank you to LAYN, for giving me shelter. I know that things were harder back then, when federal rules wouldn't let you keep me for more than three weeks at a time. I am grateful that you kept me anyway for those last two months until I turned 18, when I was rediscovering myself and finding my resilience. Thank you for helping me survive. For Covenant House, The Way-In, and Children of the Night, thank you for giving me a temporary place to stay. I am grateful that each of your programs provides such amazing hope and a safe space for youth.

I am especially grateful that many of the programs in Hollywood have championed trauma based care, and I look forward to seeing the beautiful results over the next several years; kids like me who are heard and loved. I can't wait to see more success stories. Thank you for each survivor that I have met. I hear you and I see you. You are beautiful. Together, we can change the world.

For my AEWC teachers, Valerie and Roger. Wow. You could've never known how far I would go after you let me into your school. I was just a broken homeless kid trying to finish high school, and you bent the rules and let me in. You gave me a safe space to learn and to finish what I'd started. I did it! I studied a lot more after high school. Thank you for telling me that I could be more than who I was back then.

Carmen and Alex, I will always appreciate how you taught me to be a better mom. Thank you for taking the time to show me what really matters as a parent. I miss you both. Your children are beautiful, wonderful people. I see your strength in them.

Dr. Broudy, the first example that I ever saw of a true physician. Thank you for taking the time to answer all of my questions about medical school and residency, and especially thank you for telling me that I could do it. I did! Thanks!!

Erin, my childhood friend, thank you for staying true to yourself and being an amazing mother and friend.

Jerri-Anne, the BFF that I found in college bio class. You knew me when I was recovering; when I was fighting to be better than my past. Thank you for supporting me over the years and listening to my crazy stories. I miss our UCLA days; we need to take another campus stroll for the memories.

Ruby, the friend that I found when Roxy and Isaac were little; thank you for being such a great person to chat with and swap stories with.

For the many people who helped me with my writing; thank you. A special thanks to the healthcare professionals writing workshop at Harvard, to my classmates and professors in the Creative Writing program at UCLA Extension, and to my fellow mom docs in our Facebook writing group – you have been my inspiration. Thank you for everyone who read pieces of this book along the way and offered feedback; I am eternally grateful.

For the teachers who reminded me to chase my dreams when I was a high school teacher dreaming of becoming a physician, thank you. Thank you Sylvia,

Debbie, Alicia, Christine. A special thanks to Dr. Green, for always believing in me.

For my fellow volunteers at the Clinical Care Extenders program and at LAC-USC; all of those long shifts and crazy schedules were worth it. I'm amazed to see where we've all ended up. You've all been such an inspiration; thank you!

For my classmates at Ross University School of Medicine, thank you for accepting me; medical school was the time when I started to realize the impact that my early years had on my life, and you guys were my strength as I began to piece it all together. Class of 2014!

For the people of Dominica and the beloved staff at Princess Margaret Hospital, who gave me a place to begin my studies in medicine, and welcomed me back after Hurricane Maria.

For my co-residents at Riverside University Health Systems Family Medicine Residency, thank you for helping me become a great physician. A special thanks to my mentor, Dr. Hamade, I appreciate all of your kind words and advice. Thank you to Dr. Aguilera and Dr. Farhadian for choosing me as your resident. Thank you to Treva, for being my rock during those thirty-six months. Thanks to everyone for being so supportive along the way. Class of 2017!

For the UC Irvine undergraduate students that go to Mexico with me for the Flying Samaritans trips; I can't wait to see where all of you end up as you complete your own training to be our future physicians, pharmacists, and dentists. Study hard, and remember to always be kind.

For my Horizon family, especially my work wife Kayla, thank you for listening to all of my crazy stories as I pieced this book together. Thank you Dr. Panoussi, Dr. Mousa, and Dr. Wan for giving me a beautiful work family. And thanks to all the lovely people at AVH! Thank you for continuously showing me that we can make this world a better place!

For every single patient I have ever and will ever see, thank you for trusting me to help you on your journey.

For Hala and the Physician Mom's Group, for creating an amazing shared space for us to journey together as physician moms.

Thanks to my amazing editor, Kate Padilla. I'll try not to use the word "that" ever again!

Thanks, everyone! Let's share this story with the world!

HINDSIGHT PICTURES

David, Kevin, Melinda,
Nick, and me

At 3yo, Christmas

11yo, "dirty blonde"

15yo, cross
country team

16yo, Nora, Sammie, me
(Kansas)

17yo, LAYN, on New
Year's Eve

Ava and Emma, at Pantages

18yo, with nephew Matt

18yo, "DAPY girl,"
with coworker

LIFE AFTER HINDSIGHT

20yo, Byron, me, and Roxy

Roxy and my mom, duck pond

32yo, me, Byron, Dominica

20yo, scholarship night

Celebrating with Mexico clinic team and family

35yo, MD graduation

Byron, Carmen, Roxy, me, and Isaac; MFP Alumni Award

Michelle, Heather (MFP DIrector), me

ABOUT THE AUTHOR

Sheryl Recinos is a mother of 3, wife, and family medicine physician living in Los Angeles, California. She holds a BA in Sociology from UCLA, a BS in Cell and Molecular Biology, a Master's in Education from California State University, Northridge, and obtained her medical degree from Ross University School of Medicine. She currently works as a hospitalist.

She is happily married to Byron Recinos, and his mother inspired her to finally learn Spanish.

When she isn't writing or taking care of patients, she can be found hanging out with her family or volunteering. She regularly travels to Mexico with the UC Irvine branch of Flying Samaritans to volunteer in their free clinic in Testerazo. She has also travelled to the Caribbean for hurricane relief and community building.

She also works closely with My Friend's Place in Hollywood, and recently started the Impact Scholarship at their program to help youths who are transitioning off of the streets and enroll in college.

Her website can be found at: www.sherylrecinosmd.com.

Made in the USA
Las Vegas, NV
27 May 2023

72596182R00229